FORM AND MEANING IN FICTION

NORMAN FRIEDMAN

FORM AND
MEANING
IN FICTION

THE UNIVERSITY OF GEORGIA PRESS
ATHENS

Library of Congress Catalog Card Number: 73–90843
International Standard Book Number: 0–8203–0357–7

The University of Georgia Press, Athens 30602

Set in 10 on 13 pt. Electra type
Printed in the United States of America

For Michael
my son, my friend

Contents

Preface

This book began as a collection of some ten essays on fiction I have published in the journals over the past fifteen or twenty years. Many have been and are being reprinted, a few more than once, in various textbooks and anthologies, both here and abroad, and hence it seems a fair assumption that they are playing a role—however small—in the recent and current flowering of interest in fiction theory and criticism. To gather them between a single set of covers would appear to be therefore justified.

But as I worked on it, this book became much more, I hope, than simply a collection. To begin with, a lot has been done in the field since I first began formulating my ideas, and one of my main tasks has been to bring myself up to date. This catching up has meant, at the very least, that I have had to fill in my references and bibliography, and in some cases that I have had to reconsider and redevelop some of my own principles and interpretations.

Secondly, since these very principles and interpretations have naturally undergone some inner development, I have had to modify and extend many of them in terms of my own growth. In fact, since they were written over a period of time, these essays reveal distinct changes in theory and approach among themselves. What might otherwise seem to be a disadvantage, however, I hope I have turned into the main value of the book.

The point is that I have organized, revised, expanded, and added to these essays in relation to an overall argument in support of a unifying thesis. That thesis concerns my conception of pluralistic criticism, which I shall explain further in the first chapter, but which can be defined briefly here as the examination of how different methods and approaches may be used to solve different critical problems. Thus, even though my interests have varied over the years, this very variety will help to unify the book. My own development, it seems to me, reflects many of the crosscurrents in literary theory and criticism during the past three decades, and I hope that my present mood of integration again reflects the general mood.

I am not sure, however, that the logical spirit with which I pursue this integration is a mere reflection of the current mood in the field, and it is this which I trust shall be my main contribution. It is common and easy enough these days to find agreement on all sides that criticism should be flexible and tolerant and many-faceted, but it is not so common and easy to find clear formulations of what these agreeable virtues actually mean in theory, and of how they actually operate in practice. Many times protestations of pluralism are at best vague and at worst represent pious lip-service concealing some form of almost instinctive monism.

Thus, although I examine dozens of particular novels and stories in what follows, many of them in great detail, I am concerned not simply with the cogency of each particular section of "practical" criticism, but also with the structure of its argument and how this relates to the cogency of the thesis of the book as a whole. I am basically concerned, that is, with how various approaches to fiction can be constructed, how they may be related, and what they may be expected to reveal. That I am also concerned with the cogency of my particular interpretations, and that they affect, as well as are affected by, my theories, goes almost without saying.

These essays are related, then, not just because they are about fiction, or merely reflect an underlying point of view, as is so often the case with such collections, but more because they are organized to bring out a set of related critical questions. The fact that I have not started from scratch and rewritten the whole from beginning to end serves further, I would hope, to underline my main point of diversity unified, as well as to preserve some of the urgency and intensity of the original essays.

Many portions of this book *have* been written from scratch, however: I have done afresh as much again as I have reprinted. Most particularly, the introductory chapter, the chapters on the problem of meaning and on vision, and the two essays on Camus and Hemingway are significant in being among the last to have been written. Some time ago my main interest was in formal criticism, and I developed a certain impatience, because of obvious confusions in the field, with the interpretation of meaning. Now, however, I have found that a proper concentration on formal analysis does, when mediated by a constant study of the problems of theory, lead on back to the interpretation of meaning with renewed clarity. Formal criticism, in other words, need not be the mechanical and arid thing it is often taken to be, nor need one put it aside when coming to the question of theme. That there is a necessary and organic connection between these two critical approaches, it is the intention of this book to show.

For typing the manuscript, grateful thanks are due to Thelma Daub,

Wendy De Fortuna, Elizabeth R. Gasser, Catherine T. O'Looney, and Florence Waldhetter, all of the office of Dr. Sidney Axelrad, Dean of Graduate Studies at Queens College. I would also like to thank the staff of the Paul Klapper Library of Queens College, and especially Samuel Pinzur, for providing me with a study; Wendell B. Daniel, Olive C. James, and Edith Y. Dressler, of Acquisitions; Mimi B. Penchansky and Ruth Hollander, of the Inter-Library Loan Office; and Martha Nemeth for xeroxing.

PART ONE
PLURALISM

Chapter 1

Introduction: Pluralistic Criticism

It is a commonplace of modern criticism that fiction theory and analysis have begun catching up with poetic theory and analysis only lately, and that they have done so largely in terms of the same definitions and principles. This similarity is not strange, since most modern critics have been concerned with a unitary or monistic notion of literature, and to apply the same methods to fiction as to poetry is quite consistent with the nature of their characteristic theory.[1] However this may be, beginning with Henry James and then Percy Lubbock, and continuing with E. M. Forster, Edwin Muir, and Joseph Warren Beach, and coming to the present with Mark Schorer, Northrop Frye, R. S. Crane, Wayne C. Booth, Robert Scholes, and Robert Kellogg (a more detailed history will be found in chapter 8), fiction theory and analysis have become a fully flourishing branch of modern criticism; and they now are also becoming more and more conscious of themselves, partly through the influence of Crane and Booth, as a separate branch of criticism, and consequently as requiring additional or distinctive definitions and principles.

The main purpose of this book, therefore, is not only to examine some of the ways in which certain more general critical questions may be distinguished and explored, but also some of the ways in which a special "poetics" may be constructed for fiction.[2] This is not to say, however, that fiction bears no relation to other literary types, or that various critical questions, in being differentiated, cannot or should not be seen in relation to one another. The case is exactly otherwise: logically speaking, it is only *because* certain things are related that meaningful distinctions can be made among them. And it is only when meaningful distinctions are made that the exact nature of the similarities becomes clear.

There are various other clichés of modern criticism which, although they are by definition commonplaces, appear to me to call for closer thinking. We all agree by now, for example, that the best criticism should be "flexible" and use a variety of "approaches," but just what this flexibility and variety entail is not always self-evident—certainly not from merely placing examples of different approaches side by side in an anthology or textbook. It is also generally agreed that formal analysis is properly the central focus of criticism, and that meaning is a function of form, but again it is not easy, on the basis of modern criticism, to determine just what form is, or precisely how it is related to meaning—certainly not, as I hope to show, by *equating* them, as is usually the case.

If there is an air, then, of familiarity about the questions I raise in this chapter, we need not be surprised. But what we must ask ourselves is whether we have, in fact, thought them through, or whether we have rather accepted them routinely for the commonplaces they seem to be. Not everyone who claims to be a pluralist is in fact pluralistic. The value of this book, therefore, such as it is, is not to be found in a dazzling display of new questions and angles, but instead in a thoroughgoing search for ways of actually understanding and exploring the old ones.

I

What are the marks, then, of a genuine pluralism in literary criticism? My answers, and much more throughout this book, it should be noted here at the outset, owe much to my reading of the Chicago critics or neo-Aristotelians.[3]

To begin with, in relation to criticism itself, pluralism emphasizes methods of inquiry rather than doctrines, answers, and results merely. It is concerned with theories of theories, or the criticism of criticism, and is therefore abstract—or, if you will, philosophical. It examines the statements of critics in the context of their arguments; it is aware that the meaning of such statements depends upon how they are made; and it is consequently alert to the shifting meanings any given term or concept may have in different contexts.

I realize, of course, that this description sounds very much like what the New Critics have taught us about reading a literary work, and I think it would be marvelous if we could learn to do the same thing in relation to criticism as well. In fact, I think it would be marvelous if we could do it in relation to *works*, for everything depends, as we shall see, upon what we mean by *context*. The New Critics, it seems to me, in seeing it generally as the reconciliation of opposites and all the rest, see the context of each work in pretty much the same terms as every other work, depending for their distinctions among them upon a rather vague notion of "particularization" or something of the sort.

This problem, indeed, illustrates very well the kind of thing the pluralist is interested in. If we all agree, for example, that meaning is contextual, we may disagree as to what we mean by *context*—or even what we mean by *meaning*. The concept of pluralism itself, as I have been suggesting, varies as its users vary.[4] No one term necessarily has a single meaning, and nothing is more common than for the key terms of criticism—*form, structure, theme, meaning, content, technique, style, symbol*—all but the most mechanical terms—to mean slightly or greatly different things for different critics (see chapter 3). I do not think that this diversity is a bad thing in itself, and if we should not pass an act of uniformity against poets, neither should we legislate a dictionary for critics. I think merely that we should be aware of these differences, and that we should take it upon ourselves to define our terms as we use them. We should not assume, that is, that there is a "correct" meaning, or that the one we happen to use is the correct one. The unexamined term is not worth using. That is why it has seemed to me worthwhile to attempt a reconsideration of these old questions.

Context for the pluralist, then, in relation to analyzing criticism, will mean something like the following: what aspect of the literary work the critic is talking about, what question he is asking about it, what method of reasoning he is using in seeking the answer, and what underlying assumptions are affecting the outcome. The famous comment in chapter 9 of Aristotle's *Poetics*, for example, that poetry is more philosophical than history, is usually interpreted to mean—as it is by Sidney, for instance, and most modern critics—that poetry is in some way more *true* than factual knowledge. But since "truth" is not what Aristotle is talking about in this context, it would seem best to the pluralist to interpret the statement in terms of what Aristotle *is* talking about. And that is the problem of the unity of an action: its incidents form a sequence having a beginning, middle, and end; and they are bound by what is humanly probable or necessary. Thus poetry is more philosophical than history in the sense that a plot has causal unity, whereas history is limited, as it should be, by the facts (see chapter 10). The writer, as the *Poetics* insists time and again, is concerned, *as* artist, primarily with artistic wholeness, and Aristotle says that his distinguishing characteristic is his ability to form unified plots.

Of course, Aristotle does discuss, in chapter 25, the relation between poetry and factual truth, and he does conclude that poetry has its own standards of judgment, but he does not argue the question on the basis of "truth." His basis is, as before, the problem of achieving a unified artistic effect, and his principle is simply that, if the effect can be better achieved by violating factual truth, then the poet should do so. To extrapolate from this principle the further notion that the poet deals with a "higher kind of truth" is to exceed, if not violate, the context.

Nothing is more common, alas, than for critics to quote other critics out of context. It may be that a poet can invade his predecessors like a monarch, but if a critic does it, he should go about it in a slightly more rational way. Or it may be that one critic can take fire from another, and then go rocketing off in his own direction, but he should neither praise nor blame the other for an interpretation which owes more to his own ingenuity than to his predecessor's argument. I do not think that Sidney or modern critics are at fault for developing Aristotle's idea in their own way, but it is a fault to say that their idea is Aristotle's. This distortion is especially damaging if we are interested in properly understanding Aristotle to begin with—not to say the nature of critical discourse itself. The pluralist does not say, however, that any extrapolation is wrong out of hand. As I hope to show, he often needs to do some extrapolating of his own, but he prefers to do it within the terms of the text he is interpreting.

II

If pluralism interprets critical statements in context, and if one of the factors which make up that context is the writer's choice of some aspect of literature to examine, then it follows that pluralism is further defined by its awareness that literature offers different aspects for inquiry, and consequently that each calls for its own approach. Indeed, one of the causes of not reading in context, of minimizing the study of method, of assuming that there is a correct definition for each term, and of the obsessive sense that there is one legitimate form of criticism, is the notion that literature has an essential nature which the critic must discover, define, and adjust his ideas to. This notion results in the further idea that the order the critic discerns inheres objectively in the material, and thus is logically prior to the approach which discerns it.[5] It might be useful to call this form of nonpluralism "monism," because it regards literature as a single thing and derives its critical approach from this determining model—whatever it may happen to be.[6]

Pluralism, on the contrary, believes that literature presents many facets for our inspection, that each may be regarded from different angles, and that no single facet or combination of facets is in and of itself naturally or logically or necessarily prior to any of the others. If one wishes to say that this or that aspect is more basic or fundamental or essential, one can only do so within the context of a given inquiry. Plato's concern in Book 10 of *The Republic*, for example, is with the just state, and so it follows that his focus is on the relation of literature to society, while Aristotle, in being concerned with the formal unity of a certain kind of play, focuses on the relations between the parts and the whole. Each focus is appropriate to each inquiry. I have often thought, if it would not seem pompous to do so, of coining yet another critical "fallacy," the fallacy of overassumption: we do not have to say, as Sainte-Beuve and Taine do, for example, that literature *is* basically historical in order to study it historically.[7] We can study it historically, that is, even if we acknowledge that it can be legitimately studied in other ways as well. Nor do we have to assume, as has been common in twentieth-century criticism, that literature *is* basically nonhistorical or ahistorical in order to study it formally. There is no such thing, in this sense, as "intrinsic" vs. "extrinsic" criticism, except in terms of some particular interest.

The pluralist finds it convenient to regard literary study as a matter of causes and effects, and he can discuss effects in terms of their causes and infer causes from their effects. He can also distinguish between causes and effects in his material—and causes and effects in his interpretation of that material. And he can see that a given aspect can be a cause when regarded from one angle, and an effect when regarded from another. Thus, from certain points of view, one might say that formal analysis is logically prior to the study of the historical context of a work, and from other points of view, one might say that it is subordinate. Accordingly it can be said that you cannot reasonably place a work historically before you have analyzed it formally; on the other hand, it can just as reasonably be said that you cannot properly understand a work formally before you have placed it historically.

This interdependence need not lead us either to skepticism or chasing our own tails: in the first case, formal analysis is in the forefront of our attention, but we can keep checking our results against our historical knowledge, while in the second, historical relations are in the forefront, but we should check our results against formal analysis. Neither is right or wrong in itself: it all depends on the situation—upon what is known and what needs to be known. No amount of formal analysis can give us the answers to historical questions, although it can serve as a basis for answering them. The fact that they are interdependent does not alter the fact that they are separate, and it is only after they are separated that they can be fruitfully related.

III

If pluralism is contextual, and if the other factors in that context are the methods of reasoning and the assumptions used in answering questions, then pluralism is also defined by its concern with logic and the procedures of argumentation, and hence with distinctions between deduction and induction, with the means of validation and verification, with the canons of hypothetical reasoning, and with the difference between a priori and a posteriori assumptions.

But there is a bias in modern criticism against logic and method, the assumption being that reasoning abstracts from the concrete experience of the work itself, and hence that it violates the very nature of literature.[8] We must submit humbly to the work, and proceed inductively, without preconceptions, letting *it* tell us what it is, how it is organized, and what it means.[9]

No one can deny that it is the experience of the work itself which really matters, but the answer to the evils of abstraction is not to discard logic and method, but rather to use them properly. And this means keeping them always subordinate to the experience—not in the sense that they are determined by the object, for there is no such thing, but rather in the sense of keeping the ultimate purpose of criticism in view—to know that we are using logic and method willy nilly, and to be aware of when they are aiding and when they are hindering the critical process.[10]

The case is exactly contrary to what is generally supposed: it is when you assume that you are *not* using theories and methods that you divorce criticism from the experience of the work. Thus the New Criticism finds itself in the anomalous position of opting for total meaning, while at the same time being accused of arid formalism and of separating the work from experience.[11] It is precisely when you assume in advance that you know the nature of your object, and hence do not need to worry about theories and methods, that you are being deductive rather than inductive, a priori rather than a posteriori.

For there is no such thing as "induction" as it is usually imagined. What is by now a commonplace of science is still misunderstood in the humanities: induction is as much a form of reasoning as deduction, and no interpretation of the work—not even any experience of the work—is possible without some form of reasoning taking place, whether explicitly or implicitly.[12] We can neither respond to a work nor come to any conclusion about it, that is, without bringing something which is already in our heads to bear upon the concrete particulars before us. When we do this, we are making inferences, and making inferences is the basis of reasoning. The concrete particulars before us tell us nothing in and of themselves until they are combined with assumptions; our responses and interpretations, however much they may be based on observation, are not in themselves observable in the work.[13]

In Donne's "A Valediction Forbidding Mourning," for example, although we are not told who is speaking to whom, we may conclude that the speaker is a man and that the person he speaks to is a woman, on the basis of what he says and how he says it; and we may conclude this because we bring to bear upon the words in the poem a series of generalizations derived from prior knowledge and experience—both of life as well as of other poems—about what is usual and probable in man-woman love relations. Our conclusion is an inference rather than a fact. The problem is that we make such inferences so rapidly and habitually that we are often not even aware that we are doing so, thereby confusing fact and inference frequently.

The question then becomes one of checking and safeguarding the mind's process in making inferences, and to do this we must know what it is and how to test it. If we know that reasoning is either deductive or inductive, however, it is not clear just what this distinction means. Usually we are told that the one moves from the general to the particular, while the other moves from the particular to the general; or that the one makes assumptions, while the other lets the facts speak for themselves. But these distinctions are only rough rules of thumb, representing merely partial or approximate truth in a vague sort of way. Both deal with the particular and the general, and both relate facts to assumptions. Wherein do the actual differences lie?

Take our inferences regarding the Donne poem again. We see that the speaker is trying to console the listener over their impending separation, and that (if the speaker is to be credited) the listener is close to tears. We conclude that the former is a man and that the latter is a woman, not on the basis of anything observable but rather on the basis of combining what we observe with a generalization which says something like "it is usually the man who leaves the woman and who must be strong, and it is usually the woman who expresses her feelings more openly and who must be consoled." (The fact that the new feminism may be overturning such generalizations, both in literature and in life, may be salutary, but it does not alter the point.) Now, not only is this conclusion not an observable fact, it is not even an induction. It is in reality a deduction, moving—à la Sherlock Holmes—from an assumption about certain things in the world (major premise: the generalization), to the observable facts in question (minor premise), and on to the conclusion.

On the other hand, the generalization itself represents the conclusion to a prior (again often implicit) induction, which has moved from an assumption—not about something in the world, but this time about method—to certain observable facts, and on to the conclusion. To make a generalization, we must assume something like "what is true regarding some lovers when they part is probably true of all." Then we rely on what we have ostensibly observed: "those lovers whose parting I have knowledge of reveal that the man consoles and the woman is consoled." And the conclusion is: "upon parting, men are usually the consolers and women the consoled."

It will be noticed, further, that the *form* of this induction is, in fact, deductive. And it is subject to the same rules of validation: there must be three terms rather than two or four, the middle term must be distributed, and so on. The differences, however, are three: the major premise of the induction is analytical rather than empirical, as I have pointed out; there are additional tests for verifying that the observed sample mentioned in the minor premise is an adequate one (whether it is sufficiently large in proportion to the whole, sufficiently representative, and whether exceptions can be sufficiently explained); and the conclusion, in being based upon a calculated leap from observed sample to unobserved whole, is only probable rather than necessary.

In order to clarify this matter of validation and verification a bit further, let us contrast pluralism not only with monism but also with relativism. As opposed to monism, pluralism believes that our conclusions are relative to our questions, our assumptions, and our logical procedures. Relativism also believes that there are many approaches, but it believes that each is as good—or as bad—as any other, and that it all depends on opinion anyway. As opposed to relativism, pluralism says that, if criticism is relative to the context of the inquiry, it is nevertheless also true that, once we have framed that context, we can distinguish among better and worse answers to any given question. How can this be done?

An answer must be the best in relation to the other possible choices, and this is a problem of efficacy. The solution is empirical, in depending on consequences, and relative, in depending upon the context of the inquiry. That answer is best which brings us to the goal of the inquiry most adequately—which gives us, that is, the most complete, the most coherent, and the most economical explanation of the facts and their relations, in comparison with the alternative explanations (see chapter 3).

Why, for example, does Donne's speaker in "A Valediction" use the stiff twin compasses image the way he does? Two answers might match the facts equally well, but only one will satisfy the rules of hypothetical reasoning. One critic might say that the compasses provide the required paradoxical tension between the precisely scientific and the passionately emotional, while another might say they comprise a rhetorical device, in line with the speaker's effort as a whole, for assuaging his lady's grief. They are precise and scientific, to be sure, but they function not so much to set up a general tension as to resolve a particular one. The second explanation is more specific—that is, economical—and more consistent with the actual artistic whole in question. If both explanations are supported by the facts, only one explains more.

To be inductive, therefore, is not simply a matter of merely deriving one's ideas from a long experience with literature, or of sticking to the text without making assumptions,[14] or of citing many passages—it is more a matter of whether one actually tests one's ideas against the facts. The fourth and final problem, then, since we must use assumptions whether we are aware of them or not, is to use those which will give us the most help in reaching our answers while at the same time being the least determinative in prescribing in advance what those answers must be, and this is a difference between a priori and a posteriori reasoning.

Where the monist frames his questions so that they contain their answers—what is the reconciliation of opposites which organizes *this* poem? for example—the pluralist frames his so that a variety of answers remains possible—simply, what is the *form* of this poem? for example. The former begins with a definition of what he is looking for, while the latter is merely defining the nature of the question. Each conceives of form, in other words, on a different level of generality. The monist tells us what form is, but the pluralist tells us only what it involves.

We begin, not with a definition of literature, but rather with a concept of form and then proceed to apply a set of multiple differentiae for setting off one form or kind of form from another (see chapters 3 and 9). And, according to the process of induction, this concept is more analytic, as we shall see, than empirical. The inquiry then becomes a study of forms and of the different kinds of forms rather than an attempt to base definitions on the supposed differences between science and art. The pluralist believes it is futile to try to define the "nature" or "essence" of literature, or even of poetry, drama, and fiction, or even of the novel. We can do so only in terms of one literary work or type of work at a time. If it is possible to work up the ladder from the particular to the general, and arrive at definitions of groups of works, and then to use these generalizations as an aid in examining particular works, it is nevertheless doubtful whether literature itself, since it involves so many disparate items and so many independent variables, is any one thing and not some other thing.[15]

It would be foolish to claim that the pluralist has no advance idea of what he is looking for: it is logically and humanly impossible, as I have argued, to find something without any prior idea of what one is looking for. Some limits are implied in asking any question simply by virtue of asking it. But if we can conceive of the question-answering process as a spectrum, progressing from the more undifferentiated stages on the left toward the more differentiated stages on the right—and by progression I mean moving from many possible answers to only a few—then it can be said that the pluralist starts further to the left, while the monist starts closer to the right.

Thus we must distinguish between theories of *criticism* and those of *literature*; we must realize that the latter are determined by the former; and hence must be wary of confusing the two things.[16] In the *Poetics*, for example, there is the *way* in which Aristotle approaches the problem of formal analysis, which is a matter of critical theory, and there are the *results* of this approach when it is applied to literature, which is a matter of literary theory. Neglecting this distinction between method and conclusions is what causes some to say that the *Poetics* is no longer applicable to modern literature, for example, or that Aristotle was answering Plato, or that he believes plot to be more important than character in literature, and so on.

Thus as I have suggested, the frequent complaint that an overconcern for theory and method tends inevitably to lead to a closed system applies more to the monist than the pluralist. The idea of system in itself is neither closed nor open.[17] If a system is one of answers and definitions of literary types, it will be closed; if it is one of questions and principles, it will be open. If one assumes that there is a definition or order of literature to which criticism must conform, and neglects the fact that what he sees only looks that way if regarded from a certain point of view, his assumptions become not working hypotheses but rather self-evident truths, and so it will seem that he is not assuming much at all. In the name of induction and flexibility and pluralism, therefore, he will turn out to be deductive, dogmatic, and the fashioner of closed systems.

IV

Let me come now to the ultimate purpose of my introduction, which is to explain the particular system which organizes this book—a system which I hope will illustrate what pluralism may look like in practice. What I want to do is to schematize various approaches to literature according to the variety of facets it presents for inquiry, and then I want to show how these approaches may be related.

Many such schemes are possible, and, so long as they confine themselves heuristically to describing various orders of criticism rather than pretending to be based on the supposed order of literature, each will serve its own particular uses in different situations, and each is to be judged according to how well it performs its designated task.[18] The aim, for example, of my own scheme is twofold: generally to suggest the possibilities of criticism, and particularly to raise certain questions about the criticism of fiction which the present essays attempt to solve—both in themselves and in their relationship to one another. My development of this scheme, then, is governed by this twofold aim, and is to be understood and interpreted in that light.

Over the years of teaching, writing, and thinking, I have found it useful to describe the variety of facets which literature presents for inquiry in terms of a diamond-shaped diagram containing five points of reference:

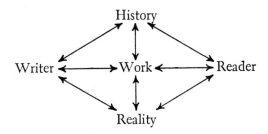

It can be seen, of course, that this diagram is based on the intersection formed by two axes at right angles to each other and that various triangles emerge as a result. The point of the diagram is simply to bring into view as large a variety of relationships as possible. Thus one can frame an inquiry into the relation between the work and reality, or between the work and reality and the author, and so on; and additionally one can see each relation as flowing in either direction, as when one asks either what the work explains about the history, for example, or what history explains about the work.

Further, although one may properly argue that a formal analysis of the work itself is at the center of all inquiry, as indeed my diagram indicates, and hence that it ought to limit and control other approaches, one nevertheless should not argue, as I hope I have already shown, that it is better or more legitimate than the others: it all depends upon what one wants to find out or accomplish, and this in turn depends upon the situation giving rise to the inquiry in the first place. The teaching situation, for instance, may very well call for a different approach from the situation of the scholar writing a learned article for his peers, just as various teaching situations themselves may call for different approaches—depending upon whether one is teaching high school, college, or graduate students, for example, or whether they are native to the literature in question or foreign. Not that each situation calls for an approach which is hermetically sealed off from the others, or that one waters down his ideas to suit the audience, but rather that one naturally shifts his emphasis and angle of approach as the situation shifts, and yet can keep various approaches in perspective at the same time.

It would be appropriate at this juncture, however, to develop the implications of each facet or point of reference a bit further. At the center of the diagram is, as we have seen, the work itself, and the primary questions are how to read and understand it as such, and how to analyze its artistic form. This is a matter of part-whole relationships, and it is resolvable largely in terms of internal evidence—although, as I hope to show in due course, it is not possible even for formal analysis to treat the work literally as an autonomous or self-contained object, for the writer must produce responses in the reader based of necessity on values and attitudes and ideas which exist in the reader's mind before the poem comes into being.

The other points of reference can indeed be seen as arranging themselves around the periphery of the diagram, but this is not to imply that they are peripheral in any absolute sense, but only in the sense, as I have said, that they should be limited and controlled by formal analysis. Whether a given approach is primary or subordinate in any other sense will depend, as we know by now, on the situation. The way that I have arranged them around the center does not represent any intrinsic order but rather simply the way I have become used to seeing them, although there does seem to be some flow of causality from writer to work to reader implied by the horizontal axis, and some implication of other causes operating on the work by the vertical axis. I will develop these implications shortly, when I come to discuss relationships among various critical approaches, but for the moment let us regard the order in which I take up these other facets as being more arbitrary than logical.

The relation between the work and the writer involves such questions as those of the author's biography, his psychology, his temperament, his outlook, his values and attitudes, and his vision of life; and here, as with all these peripheral points of reference, external as well as internal evidence will be appropriate. Also, as with the others, this relationship, as I have indicated, can be seen as flowing in either direction. If we regard the relationship between writer and work as one of cause and effect, then clearly we can infer causes from effects and can explain effects in terms of causes. Thus the work (or works) may be used as evidence for determining something about the author, or information about the author may be used for determining something about the work(s).

The relationship between the work and reality involves such questions as whether art imitates life or life imitates art; whether art copies or transforms or ignores reality; what the artistic imagination is, what it does, and how it functions; and the like. Such metaphysical terms as *nature* and *truth*, such psychological terms as *imagination* and *creativity*, and such aesthetic terms as *imitation* and *form*—and such questions as the relations between literature and knowledge, art and science—dominate inquiries focused on this aspect. Here too we can ask either about how reality affects art or how art reveals reality. Also when we talk about imagination we are clearly verging upon one of the previous questions concerning the writer's vision of life, except that the present question is more general, while that one was specific. Of course, *reality* may refer to such things as man, men, and society; or to nature, the world, the universe, and the cosmos; or to "inner" and "outer" reality; or to "higher" and "lower" reality; or to "evident" and "hidden" reality.

The relation between the work and history involves such questions as the backgrounds of the work (social, political, cultural, economic, and so on); its sources, traditions, models, schools, influences; its conventions, genres, commonplaces, and occasions. In other words this aspect concerns itself with the work as an occurrence in a given moment of time, and the student of history may legitimately go to literature for evidence about the age, while the student of literature may legitimately go to the age for evidence about literature.

The relation between the work and the reader involves such questions as those of popularity, of censorship and morality and religion, of education, of politics, and so on. Here we may study either the way the audience affects the writer, or his work the audience.

These points of reference do not exhaust the range of critical questions we may ask: they merely suggest the kinds of things we may ask questions *about*, and even here I do not pretend to have exhausted the range of critical subject matters. Nor have I indicated all the possible approaches to literature: if there is such a thing as the psychological approach, then there will also be such a thing as the Freudian approach, for example, or Jungian approach. Only one of the variables of critical discourse lies in the choice of a subject matter—the kinds of questions asked, the assumptions used, and the modes of argument employed all constitute further governing factors. But I have said enough here, I hope, to indicate the nature of the possibilities.

We turn, finally, to a consideration of the orders of criticism, of the question of relating various approaches to one another. I have been insisting all along, however, that each critical discourse should be understood in terms of its own context and that each critical approach is as potentially important as any other. This emphasis would seem to leave us not simply with a pluralistic view of criticism, but with a fragmented and atomistic view as well. I think this emphasis is correct, though, so long as we think of a synthesizing approach, as we too often do, in terms of pulling various pieces out of different systems and combining them into a system of our own.[19] On the other hand, so long as we think of simply using different approaches one after the other without any sense of how they may be logically related, we need a different emphasis.

How, then, can the pluralist conceive of relating them? Generally speaking the correct way is already implied in the description of the wrong way: first, to use ideas from any given approach strictly in terms of what they mean in their own context; and second, to hook them up with ideas from any other approach in terms of their logical relations. Not to dismantle and then to digest, in other words, but rather to preserve and connect. Or, as I have suggested, in order to relate things in terms of their similarities, it is necessary to understand their differences.

One scheme of relationships I have found useful, drawing upon my previous diagram, is that formed by combining an analysis of the work itself with a study of the writer's vision and the background of his age. The rationale of this scheme is that we become involved in progressively broader areas of causality as we move from the work to vision, and then to history, Thus I picture the combination as forming a series of concentric circles:

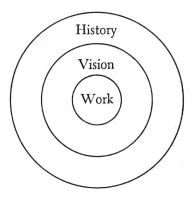

A novel, like many other things, is the result of many different, and different kinds of, causes. If criticism is, as Elder Olson says, the study of causes,[20] then it follows that there is no one best or right way to analyze a work. What the critic must do, then, is to understand what these different causes are and what their relationship is, and then to design a way of applying these principles in practice.

To view the work as a unique artistic form, unlike any other, is to ask what shaping principles are functioning within the work itself to make it what it is and not some other thing. But nothing is really entirely unique, and so there are also things about that work—even aspects of its artistic form—which it shares with other works, particularly other works by the same author. It follows therefore that not all the causes operating on the work are strictly formal ones and that some of them come rather from the author's vision. It is formally appropriate in *Great Expectations*, for example, as we shall see in the next chapter, that Pip be an orphan, but that additional necessities are at work is revealed by the fact that many of Dickens's other novels also contain orphans.

Further it can easily be seen that not all the causes are either formal or temperamental, for a work may share certain traits not only with others by the same author, but also with others written at the same time by different authors. Thus, for example, while it may be shown that the stanzaic pattern of one of Shakespeare's sonnets functions organically in the form of the poem as a whole and also that his sonnets resemble each other in certain ways, it is nevertheless true that many other poets of his day wrote sonnets as well. It must be logically the case then that the reasons why any Shakespeare sonnet has this particular stanzaic pattern are not simply formal or temperamental but are also historical.

My view of these causes rests on the standard textbook distinction between necessary and sufficient conditions, or, more simply, upon the commonsense distinction between immediate, intermediate, and remote conditions—or, if you will, between specific and general causes.[21] And my way of making these distinctions, as should be evident, rests upon the standard rules for establishing the constant conjunctions basic to causal analysis: a supposed cause cannot be a true cause unless it is present whenever the effect in question is present, nor unless its presence is always accompanied by the presence of the effect (rule of agreement); nor unless its removal results in the disappearance of the effect, and vice versa (rule of difference); nor unless a variation in the one results in a corresponding variation in the other (rule of correlation).

Thus, if a work has certain effects in common with other works, the cause of these effects cannot be located merely within that work itself: the presence of those effects in other works calls for the same cause there as here, and if it is a cause here, it must also be a cause there. We cannot give it to the one and not to the others. So I view the traits of a work which it does not share with other works as the product of immediate causes, those traits which it shares with other works by the same author as the products of intermediate causes and those which it shares with other works of the same period as the product of remoter causes. My concentric-circles scheme, then, reveals my conception of the work as being framed by more and more general causes.

As before, of course, the flow of the inquiry may be reversed, and instead of explaining effects in terms of causes, we may explain causes in terms of effects. In other words, instead of saying that the presence of orphans in many of Dickens' novels is caused by his early experiences and his consequent outlook on things, we may ask what the presence of orphans reveals about his vision of life. And the same is true of the diagram as a whole. It all depends, as I have said, upon what is known and what needs to be known.

I am sure that I have not covered all the factors needed for completely understanding a work (if there is such a thing), nor has my second diagram even exhausted the possibilities outlined in my first, but I *have* tried to show how different approaches may be related, even while retaining their distinctive characters. And I have attempted this by showing that, although a work has different causes, they can be related in terms of whether they operate in that work alone or in others as well. Thus, while a formal cause is still a formal cause, a temperamental cause still a temperamental cause, and a historical cause still a historical cause, they may nevertheless, when seen as bearing upon the same work at different levels, be related to one another.

Finally, for convenience and to help make the organization of this book clearer, I have collapsed the threefold distinction between form, vision, and history into one between form and meaning, stuffing into the term *meaning* such a variety of topics as vision, historical commonplaces, cultural implications, psychology, literature and reality, literature and society, and archetypal symbols. I have done this because I feel that the problem of form and meaning is one of the main critical problems of our time, and that handling it in this way will enable me to set up my own scheme while at the same time addressing myself to the common concern of others. The fact remains, however, that my original two diagrams will continue to operate implicitly and explicitly throughout the book.

I hope to explain at the appropriate time more fully what I mean by *meaning*, but a few words will be useful here. I do not refer to what Crane calls explication of grammatical meaning: the interpretation of the meanings of words, phrases, sentences, and so on, in the work. This level of criticism is, as he says, a necessary precondition of formal analysis.[22] What I have in mind is what follows—or should be preceded by—formal analysis. Formal analysis, properly speaking, deals with meanings only in terms of the role they play in the artistic whole, and so they are regarded simply as parts and materials of that whole. The finished product, when formally considered, is just that—a product, like a clock or a tree—and as such, it does not "mean" or "say" anything: it simply functions; it merely *is*.[23] It functions, in terms of its parts and their relationships, to produce an effect. It is, as current criticism has been saying, an object.

The trouble, however, is that current criticism sees that object as a structure of—and not simply as containing—meanings, thereby confusing the issue immensely. My point is, on the other hand, that if a work may be seen as the result of immediate and remoter causes, it may by the same token be seen as the cause of immediate and remoter effects. To produce an artistic effect is its formal or immediate result, but there is no reason in the world why its intermediate and remoter effects may not be seen as results stemming from this cause as well. Thus a chair, for instance, while designed structurally to serve a certain specific purpose, may be seen as having effects in such larger contexts as its users' lives and their society. So too with a literary work: although as an artistic object it has no meaning, it nevertheless implies meaning when seen in such larger contexts as the author's vision, the background of his age, and so on. It is these larger implications that I refer to when I speak of meaning.

In order that these matters be made clearer, let us begin with an example of pluralism in practice.

Chapter 2

Pluralism Exemplified:
Great Expectations and
The Great Gatsby

'Tis a very old strife between those who elect to see identity, and
those who elect to see discrepancies.   —Emerson

I place this essay here at the beginning of the book because, in approaching actual works on four different levels in sequence, it exemplifies in
little the pluralistic method of the whole and so prepares concretely for
what is to come. The approaches are substantially those outlined in the
introduction—form, vision, and history—with the addition of archetypes,
which seems appropriate to this particular purpose. My scheme is based
on the concentric circles idea, whereby we see the work as a product of
causes which move in from the more remote and general toward the more
immediate and specific. Thus archetypal causes, in being the most remote
and general, because they are common not only to the works of a given
author or period but also (supposedly) to all mankind, are pictured as
forming the largest outer circle, enclosing history, which encloses vision,
which encloses form, which is the smallest and innermost circle.

The causal sequence then is seen as flowing from the outer to the
inner circles, and the introductory section of the essay is an argument
purporting to show that, if one wants to explain the form of a novel, one
cannot rest content either with the archetypal or historical or biographical
approach, because each unearths causes which are not unique to that
particular work but are rather commonly found on various levels in other
works as well. That is to say, each of them is reductive in that it necessarily
deals with similarities among works rather than differences. Only the
formal approach is designed to deal with unique causes, and the use of
two novels having many things in common provides an effective way, I
hope, of illustrating such similarities and differences.

Of course, the issue of similarities and differences is a relative one: the

works of any one author, although forming an obvious group of their
own, are normally distinct in many ways from those of another author;
the works of any one period, although sharing many things in common
with each other, must be different from those of another period or else
the period concept itself would be meaningless; and works seen archetypally, as Northrop Frye has shown, can also be seen in terms of different
modes and genres. We are not confined to the formal appproach only,
that is to say, if we would look for differences: it all depends upon whether
we are looking for them from work to work or from group to group. The
biographical approach, in other words, is adequate for distinguishing a
Dickens novel from a Fitzgerald one; the historical approach is adequate
for distinguishing pre- from postrenaissance works; and the archetypal
approach is adequate for distinguishing certain kinds of phases and
modes. But it is only the formal approach which is adequate for distinguishing one individual work from another as an artistic object.

In thus describing the nonformal approaches as reductive, however, I
do not want to be misunderstood as conducting one more attack on extrinsic criticism and consequently to be seen as attempting one more
defence of formal analysis as the only path to truth and beauty. Obviously
these other approaches are reductive only if one limits himself to them—
or if one confuses them with the formal approach. Otherwise, when seen
for what they are, each is perfectly legitimate, and each, as I have been
insisting, has its own importance. And each is better when seen in relation to the others instead of exclusively and competitively; the best is
the relational composite which results from using them all in some sort
of logical order.

The order of the inquiry here proceeds from formal outward to archetypal analysis, the argument being simply that formal analysis, in dealing
with the most specific causes, will give us a clue, first, to those elements
of the work which appear to be unaccounted for in those terms—which
are left over, so to speak—and second, to how these elements may best
be interpreted. The same thing is true of vision, history, and archetypes,
respectively. This order then is that of coming to know or understand the
work: clearly, all other things being equal, one must interpret more general causes in the light of more particular ones, for it is primarily in terms
of the particular causes that the general ones are embodied, shaped, and
revealed. It is only in this sense that formal analysis is prior to the other

approaches and more important than they. For the order of the inquiry could have gone just as well the other way, by beginning with similarities, then going on to differences not accounted for by the larger circle, and then proceeding inward to the smaller circles. This sequence would have had the advantage of following the direction of causation, and of eliminating similarities rather than differences, but it would have lost the advantage of beginning with a controlling and limiting formal reading.

In other senses, therefore, formal analysis may be subordinate and less important. If one is concerned with the influence of the author's life and historical background on his very choice of formal principles, for example, or with the way in which the work reveals to us information about history that enables us to interpret the work more fully, or with how the pressure of universals helps shape the work, then the order of the inquiry would have to be reversed, and formal analysis, although still ultimately a limiting factor, would become secondary to the other approaches. It is not within the scope of the present essay, however, to explore all these other avenues—they will be treated or touched upon in the second part of this book.

I have made very few changes in this essay, except to bring the footnotes up to date. The only modification I might have made is in my varying use of the term *form* in the introductory section. I begin by accepting it as a term to cover the different things which modern critics use it for, and then go on to distinguish among these uses, while at the same time trying to confine the term to the specifically artistic aspect of a work. Perhaps I have not sufficiently clarified this shift, but I do not think it would have been worth the trouble to clutter up the argument by trying to revise.

Furthermore, when I do discuss formal analysis, I take up briefly both the New Critical and Chicago approaches, and this might be taken as repetitive of similar things in the first and third chapters; but it does fit here, and since it takes up very little space, I have let it stand. *Some* repetition, when one is trying to explore an intricately-related series of points, is inevitable and even useful, resulting in a view of similar questions in differing contexts rather than in mere repetition.

Finally, in outlining the neo-Aristotelian approach to form, I find I collapse the distinction between *structure* and *end*, speaking of them as if they were the same. This blurring is not particularly harmful in the introductory section, and I do bring in, however implicitly, a proper sense of end effect or "working power," as distinguished from structure, in the second section. This problem will be more fully worked out in subsequent chapters.

I

What are the factors governing the author's choice and organization of his materials? This, I take it, is the basic question to which statements about the particular form of any given literary work are answers. When we have discovered, that is, the principle or principles which account for these two things—selection and arrangement—we have defined the form of that work. The trouble is, however, with all the critical diversity surrounding us today, that no single version of the kinds of causes which may be seen to govern such artistic choices has received uncontested currency, nor does the confusion show signs of being resolved.

We are told by the symbologists, for example, of the existence of universal patterns in myths, rituals, dreams, and folktales which, when their presence is detected in literary works, explains their organization and their moving power. The structure of these patterns, which derives from the felt parallels between the curve of human life and the natural cycle of the seasons, is largely subconscious and compulsive, being common to mankind at large; works which are archetypally organized, therefore, touch the deepest springs of human emotion, and raise thereby the artist's vision into the sphere of the universal (see chapter 16). Thus one may account for the form and force of *Moby-Dick* by finding analogues in such various works as *Pinocchio* and the Book of Jonah, where the theme of death and rebirth seeks its image in the sea journey involving incarceration in a whale's belly and the subsequent escape therefrom. The reason why Melville's novel took the shape it did (Ishmael's initial melancholy, the journey-hunt, the evolution in his attitudes, and the death of all but Ishmael, who survives by using a coffin as a lifebuoy) is explained by reference to the hypothesis that such a theme frequently finds its embodiment in such an image because of a primordial necessity of the human mind to search for psychic equilibrium through a ritualistic projection of its basic conflicts through natural symbols.

It may be objected, however, that such an approach in itself, while extremely useful in its own way, tends to reduce literary works to a common denominator, with the result that any number of poems, plays, and novels are seen as having the same form. If we want, then, a sounder view of the unique particularity of any work, we will be well advised to narrow down the range of determining factors a bit further; for, if the archetype is by definition ubiquitous, it will also by definition be found everywhere.

That kind of inquiry which traces the rise and fall of literary modes and themes in relation to the surrounding cultural and intellectual milieu offers another kind of answer. An author, we are told here, writes in such and such a way, and uses such and such materials, because these are the subjects, techniques, and forms made available to him by his age. Thus Shakespeare wrote sonnets and verse plays because these were the dominant forms used by his contemporaries; the theme of revenge in *Hamlet* is seen in relation to the other revenge plays of the period; the development of dramatic blank verse is studied as a phase of the growth of the English language during the sixteenth century; and the ideas and attitudes embodied in Elizabethan drama are analyzed in relation to the religious, military, economic, and intellectual commonplaces of the period (see chapter 11).

But this endeavor is open to a similar objection, in that its notion of literary form is only a little less reductive than that of the archetypalists. Assuredly Elizabethan can be distinguished from Restoration drama by such a procedure, but how are we to distinguish *Hamlet* from *The Spanish Tragedy*, *The Way of the World* from *Love's Last Shift?*

A third step in limiting the range is found in those efforts to locate the causes of a writer's productions in himself. Here we may be merely biographical, and look for as much evidence relative to our author's life and habits as we can assemble—his letters, the testimonies of his friends, his reading, his travels, and so on—or we may be psychological, and look for evidence relative to his temperament, his attitudes toward his parents, the quantity and quality of his sexual experiences, his repressions, anxieties, fantasies, traumatic experiences, and so on. Thus we will explain, for example, the imagery of *Kubla Khan* by reference to Coleridge's reading, the ambivalent structure of *Sons and Lovers* by reference to D. H. Lawrence's unresolved attempts to free himself from his emotional bondage to his mother, the prudery and orthodoxy of Wordsworth's later poetry by reference to the guilt which haunted him as a result of the Annette Vallon affair, the complexity of the attitude toward woman revealed in *Paradise Lost* by reference to Milton's wives and his treatment of his daughters, and so on.

We frequently find ourselves here, however, in the same kind of trouble: many writers turn out to have read *Don Quixote*, *The Divine Comedy*, the Bible and to have had mother-fixations and/or father-hatreds; indeed many nonwriters have read the same books and suffered from similar emotional tensions. We are forced to look further still if we are interested in discovering the distinctive *artistic* causes which are able to shape out of all these things—the archetypes, the traditions of an age, and a personality—a poem, a play, or a novel. The final step, therefore, is to concentrate on the work as an independent whole by locating its formal causes within the work itself.

The answer provided by one variety of formalist—the New Critic—is that the organization of a particular work is governed by the author's attempt to balance opposites, harmonize conflicts, fuse tensions. The assumptions here are that imaginative writing is sharply distinct from scientific writing, that the former has ends (the creation of meanings through the reconciliation of contraries) and means (irony, ambiguity, puns, metaphor, paradox, and so on) of its own (as opposed to the communication of information through prose statement), and that each literary work is a self-sustaining organism to be read on its own terms rather than by reference to external and ancillary causes. The difficulty here is that, while some breathtaking analyses have resulted from the reading of novels and plays as poems,[1] and while poetry is seen as different from prose, the form of all of literature is viewed as having its generic cause in the attempt to establish ironic attitudes and ambiguous contrasts (see chapter 3).

There is another kind of internal analysis—the pluralistic—which views each literary work as indeed a unique particular, yet puts its emphasis upon literary forms rather than the Form of Literature. Here the causes of the selection and arrangement of materials in a given work are sought in a determination of what ends it in itself is apparently trying to achieve. The assumption here is that one cannot tell what end a given poem, play, or novel embodies by deciding in advance that literature in general has as its purpose the balancing of opposites. Thus a lyric poem may be seen as a verbal action in which the structure of the utterance implies a dramatic situation in which the speaker is trying to solve a problem, persuade a mistress, or curse an enemy, and it is the effort to effect these kinds of ends which governs the organization of that work. Or a play or novel may be seen as having as its end the achievement of some sort of change in the protagonist's fortune, his state of mind, or his moral character, involving a certain kind of person with a greater or less degree of responsibility for his actions. Here the selection, rendition, and arrangement of parts are seen in relation to one of these sorts of ends.

If one novel—to concentrate henceforth on fiction—is indeed a unique and organic whole unlike any other, it will appear so only from the perspective offered by this last notion of its form. And what I wish to urge here is that the perception of differences is just as important as the perception of similarities for a complete definition of the form of a novel, and that such a definition may be obtained by following in sequence all four of the steps outlined above. In this way we will avoid partial truths and partisan feuds at one and the same time.

Since, as we have seen, an analysis of the specific end which a novel is attempting to effect is the only way in which we can account for the causes which are sufficient to make it the novel it is and not another novel or poem or myth or cultural document or case history in abnormal psychology, it is a consideration of that end with which we must begin if we want a sense of that novel's particularity. The temperament of an author, which stamps all his works, and the quality of an age, which marks all its productions, and the archetypal necessities of the human mind, which characterize all of literature, are indeed causes, but they are merely necessary rather than sufficient in themselves to create a novel. It is the choice of the immediate organizing principle of a novel which determines the channels through which these other causes may operate; it is the crucial choice which limits the range of all the others—which phase of the author's experience will be relevant to that special end, which aspect of the age will pertain to that specific problem, and which of the archetypes will serve appropriately to maximize that particular plot. Although these latter may indeed *suggest* to the author his principle of organization—as, for example, in naturalistic fiction where a change in fortune without a corresponding change in the protagonist's state of mind seems to be dictated by the artistic premises of that particular school—once such a choice is made, it is that principle which takes over and by which we must check any other hypothesis we might frame about its form. By thus discussing the range of factors governing the selection and arrangement of materials, from the most specific to the most general, we will arrive at a more complete definition of the form of a novel than any one of the approaches outlined above in itself will allow.

Great Expectations and The Great Gatsby offer a challenging case for testing these notions because they are so alike—both involve a young man spurred on to immoral ambitions by a woman—and yet so different —the hero of the one survives his catastrophe while that of the other does not. The test will be to show that, while we can account for their similarities in larger terms, we can best account for their differences in formal terms.

II

In attempting to define the specific organizing principle which shapes the development of these novels, we notice in the first place that Pip's career involves essentially the *pursuit* of illusory values, which he never manages to believe in, provoked by his desire to be the social equal of Estella ("The beautiful young lady at Miss Havisham's [is] more beautiful than anybody ever was, and I admire her dreadfully, and I want to be a gentleman on her account" [chapter 17]); while Gatsby's career, although quite similar at certain points (for example, his desire to be worthy of Daisy: "He hadn't once ceased looking at Daisy, and I think he revalued everything in his house according to the measure of response it drew from her well-loved eyes" [chapter 5]), involves essentially not the pursuit of but the *dedication* to the illusion of the ostensible value of its object. Pip, that is to say, is never quite at home in his role as gentleman, never puts his heart into it ("I lived in a chronic state of uneasiness. . . . My conscience was not by any means comfortable" [chapter 34]); whereas Gatsby entertains what amounts to a passionate conviction of the absolute truth of his dream (" 'Can't repeat the past?' he cried incredulously. 'Why, of course you can!' " [chapter 6]).

The specific change, therefore, which the climax of Great Expectations is designed to effect is a reestablishment of a true sense of values in Pip's outlook and hence in his behavior—a change in his moral character. The needs dictated by this end are: to provide a motive for Pip's desire to be a gentleman at the cost of his self-respect and moral feelings (his resentment of Estella's scorn coupled with his love for her), to present the means whereby that desire can be fulfilled (his mysterious inheritance), and then to develop a shock strong enough to make him realize the falsity of his values and change his ways (the successive discoveries that his benefactor is a convict, that this man is Estella's father, and that he—Magwitch—has been treated unjustly all along).[2]

The change effected by the climax of *The Great Gatsby*, however, is the disillusionment of Gatsby's faith in his ideal—a change in his state of mind. And the needs dictated by this end are correspondingly different: to present Gatsby as possessed by his dream (his mysterious mansion), to reveal the causes of its growth and how it came to be identified with Daisy (Dan Cody and officers training school), and then to confront him with a betrayal (Daisy's hit-and-run killing of Myrtle, which forces her to choose in favor of Tom and immunity from the consequences, is the means whereby Gatsby is forced at last to realize the true inadequacy of the star he hitched his wagon to).[3]

It is true that Pip also becomes disillusioned, but it is this disillusionment as to the source of his fortune which is material to his moral regeneration; although it was his love for Estella which originally prompted his desire to raise his social status ("I had never thought of being ashamed of my hands before. . . . I wished Joe had been rather more genteelly brought up, and then I should have been so too" [chapter 8]), he never becomes disillusioned in that love for her, even when he discovers the secret of her parentage, and, particularly in the revised "happy" ending, he is still eager for union with her ("Estella, [he tells her, shortly before the ending] to the last hour of my life, you cannot choose but remain a part of my character, part of the little good in me, part of the evil. But, in this separation I associate you only with the good, and I will faithfully hold you to that always, for you must have done me far more good than harm. . . ." [chapter 44]). Through his discoveries he is forced to acknowledge the essential worthlessness of the values he had come to associate with his love for her; what survives at the end is his love minus his snobbery—a reaffirmation of the true and homely virtues associated with Joe and the forge ("If you can't get to be oncommon through going straight, you'll never get to do it through going crooked. So don't tell no more [lies], Pip, and live well and die happy" [chapter 9]).

With Gatsby, on the other hand, the reverse is true: he had already become addicted to his rosy ambitions before he met Daisy, and it was with some hesitation that he succeeded in identifying their attainment with the winning of her hand ("He knew that when he kissed this girl, and forever wed his unutterable visions to her perishable breath, his mind would never romp again like the mind of God. So he waited, listening for a moment longer to the tuning-fork that had been struck upon a star. Then he kissed her. At his lips' touch she blossomed for him like a flower and the incarnation was complete" [chapter 6]); but when his faith in her was destroyed, everything else went along with it—the world was stripped bare of value altogether—and no subsequent reintegration of values and habits ensued.

Coming now more specifically to the ways in which these two changes —in moral character and in state of mind—served as the principle of selection in choosing the kinds of incidents and characters to be utilized in bringing such changes about, we notice the great care which Dickens took to establish at the outset the positive quality of the relationship between the young Pip and Joe, for it is the values which inhere in such a relationship that Pip must reject in favor of the false ones of social status, and it is these values to which he must return in order that his moral change be made manifest (Joe "was a mild, good-natured, sweet-tempered, easy-going, foolish, dear fellow—a sort of Hercules in strength, and also in weakness" [chapter 2]). We notice further, however, that the presence of his nasty sister serves to make probable and believable his desire to leave the forge ("My sister's bringing up had made me sensitive. . . . Within myself, I had sustained, from my babyhood, a perpetual conflict with injustice" [chapter 8]). Since, on the other hand, Fitzgerald's problem was to effect a final recognition of the utter valuelessness of his ideal in the mind of Gatsby, he took no such pains to establish any affirmative elements in his childhood to which he could return. Indeed the picture we get of his father at the close of the book only serves to promote our sympathy for the young Jimmy's rejection of him.

We notice, in the second place, the different kinds of personality, developed from out of these backgrounds, required of the protagonists to bring about the different kinds of changes. Gatsby was a solitary youth with a great capacity for believing in himself ("His parents were shiftless and unsuccessful farm people—his imagination had never really accepted them as his parents at all. The truth was that Jay Gatsby of West Egg, Long Island, sprang from his Platonic conception of himself. He was a son of God. . . . So he invented just the sort of Jay Gatsby that a seventeen-year old boy would be likely to invent, and to this conception he was faithful to the end" [chapter 6]), and a correspondingly great capacity for deluding himself. There is consequently a pathetic naiveté in his character, an anachronistically eager boyishness which survives in spite of his sinister underworld dealings and which finds its chief dramatic manifestation in his compulsive repetition of the "old sport" form of address. Pip, although he is, to be sure, equally ambitious, has that within him which constantly opposes his ambition; he has, in effect, a much more critical temperament ("Conscience is a dreadful thing when it accuses man or boy; but when, in the case of a boy, that secret burden cooperates with another secret burden down the leg of his trousers, it is (as I can testify) a great punishment. The guilty knowledge that I was going to rob Mrs. Joe . . . almost drove me out of my mind" [chapter 2]). These differences are the natural result of their different childhoods: Jimmy's essential rootlessness as opposed to Pip's early and close involvement with a true and humble Christian man.

Thus, thirdly, the nature of the responsibility involved for their respective misdeeds is radically different. Both become entangled in immoral acts—Pip's boyhood theft of file and food for the convict, his rejection of Joe, his idleness, his involvement with law office and prison, his snobbery, his initial revulsion from Magwitch when the latter returns to reveal himself as Pip's benefactor; Gatsby's lies, his complicity in crime, his irresponsible parties, his maintenance of a magnificent establishment without visible means of support—but Pip is constantly hounded by a sense of guilt whereas Gatsby has never a qualm. Pip practically *allows* himself to be deluded into thinking Miss Havisham is his benefactor because it suits his plans so well (the fact that she encourages him in this delusion works to preserve our sympathy for him—he would be something of a monster otherwise), but Jimmy never knew any better. "I had believed in the forge as the glowing road to manhood and independence," Pip says. "Within a single year all this was changed. Now it was all coarse and common, and I would not have had Miss Havisham and Estella see it on any account. How much of my ungracious condition of mind may have been my own fault, how much Miss Havisham's, how much my sister's, is now of no moment to me or to any one. The change was made in me; the thing was done. Well or ill done, excusably or inexcusably, it was done" (chapter 14).

It is clear that F. Scott Fitzgerald was interested in something else—Gatsby is surrounded by people who are all much worse than he is; he, at least, is sincere, has a noble end in view, and has a twisted kind of integrity in pursuing it—and that we are meant to feel the pathos of such a man being cheated of his dream; his responsibility, therefore, is less. "Gatsby turned out all right at the end," says Nick, after speaking of his hero's "heightened sensitivity to the promises of life" and "extraordinary gift for hope"; "it is what preyed on Gatsby, what foul dust floated in the wake of his dreams that temporarily closed out my interest in the abortive sorrows and short-winded elations of men" (chapter 1). Dickens, on the other hand, wants us to reject Pip in his snobbery (as Pip comes to reject himself), and to feel the justice of his return to Joe and the old values; his personal responsibility is thus made more palpable.

Finally the rendition and arrangement of incidents in these two novels are accordingly of a different nature. *Great Expectations* is narrated by its hero in the first person, and we are thus allowed to follow the rise and fall of his snobbish attitudes, with their accompanying sense of guilt, and to be present as he makes his discoveries and changes his attitudes; *The Great Gatsby* is narrated by a witness in the first person, and we are thereby allowed to trace a sympathetic observer's feelings and reflections about Gatsby, the people he is involved with, the quality of his dream, and the nature of his death. The point here is that the demands of the plot are such in each case that an involved yet critical narrator is required, and Gatsby, even if he had lived, could never have qualified for the job, and have retained at the same time his unsullied capacity for hope; Gatsby himself is unaware of the cultural implications which are supplied by Nick.[4]

Further the chronology of *Great Expectations* is largely that of an extended and straightforward autobiographical account, although there are of course elements of mystery which cannot be introduced in their due order without spoiling the force and point of Pip's discoveries; but since we are meant to follow Pip's rejection of moral values and his subsequent return to them we must be shown his career in its large outlines from childhood to maturity. *The Great Gatsby*, however, covers only the last few months of its hero's life, although knowledge of his background which is essential to the plot is introduced at key intervals (indeed, one of Fitzgerald's chief devices for arousing and sustaining suspense is to raise the question early as to "Where is he from, I mean? And what does he do?" and then to raise it again and answer it bit by bit throughout). What must be done here if we are to see Gatsby's final disillusionment is to present him, with all his meretricious glory and mystery, in the state of illusion from which he must fall, then gradually to introduce his background and motivations so that we may understand and sympathize with his dream (while at the same time being prepared for its collapse), and finally to set in motion the accumulation of incidents which will bring about the climactic situation where he is forced to see through Daisy at last.

If the problem, in sum, is a change in moral character, there must be provided a source of value upon which the protagonist may ultimately draw, and the choice Dickens made in starting at the beginning of Pip's career can be seen as dictated by that end; if the problem is a change in knowledge, we must be shown the state from which the protagonist will change, the reasons why he was in that state, and the factors which bring about that change, and Fitzgerald's choice of a limited time-frame can be seen as governed by these necessities. The one novel, in short, involves two changes, while the other involves only one. We may notice finally that the series of delayed revelations which work their way through both plots are different, in that those in Dickens come as discoveries to the hero, whereas those in Fitzgerald come as discoveries to the witness-narrator.

III

Once all these crucial and sufficient choices have been made, the direction which the other necessary choices—governed by the temperament of the author, his cultural milieu, and universal symbols—may take is delimited and their relevance indicated. We may now ask: what elements of selection and arrangement are accounted for, not by the specific necessities of the shape of the plots in these novels, but rather by the psychological necessities of the individual authors which all their works reveal? In the light of this question, although our two novels will appear more different than they will in relation to History and Archetypes, they will appear more similar than in relation to Form. That is to say, while the works of Dickens and Fitzgerald differ from one another as their authors differ, certain human similarities begin appearing insofar as people are similar. Nevertheless this approach is basically designed to account for similarities among the works of a given author.

The central situation in *Great Expectations*—an underprivileged boy receiving an inheritance from a mysterious benefactor—must have come to the young Charles Dickens many a time in the form of a wish-fulfillment fantasy. We are told by his biographers of his acutely sensitive reaction to the shameful conditions which his father's improvidence reduced the family to, of the necessity for working in a factory which the boy was forced into, of his agonizingly early experience of the need for money and security. His novels are full of orphans who have been the victims of a monstrous betrayal, alienated children cast adrift in the big, unfriendly adult world. There is no special reason why, for the requirements of the plot, Pip need have been an orphan; that fact of course plays its part—he is all the more ready for some fairy godfather or mother—and the opening scene at the grave of his parents where he first meets Magwitch is practically indispensable. Yet there is nothing to prevent a sensitive child with two perfectly healthy parents from imagining a benefactor, nor need the graveyard scene have included the tombstones of his parents—any beloved but deceased relative would have served to bring Pip there at that time. The ubiquity of orphans in Dickens's other novels argues against the supposition that the presence of an orphaned protagonist in this one was dictated by its peculier formal problems alone. Do we have here, then, a symbolic reflection of the anxieties Dickens faced as a boy, a psychological projection of the desire to get rid of one set of parents in favor of another, a relic of the loneliness and humiliation felt by the author when he was a child? Does this also account for the special poignancy of the sense of guilt which haunts Pip throughout his career?

By the same token we may hazard some guesses as to the personal factors, above and beyond the formal needs of the plot, controlling the qualities of Fitzgerald's protagonist. I believe it is commonly agreed that Gatsby is a symbolic projection of certain aspects of the personality of Fitzgerald, who was, as his other works reveal as well, haunted by the problems of wealth and social status. The obsession with money and power, and their relation to love, which *The Beautiful and Damned*, *Tender is the Night*, and *The Last Tycoon* reveal, would appear to indicate that the presentation of such a problem here is not dictated by artistic causes alone. Perhaps Gatsby as the man with a consuming dream which is betrayed by its false associations with wealth, crime, and privilege may be viewed as a paradigm of his creator's deep-seated disillusionment and frustration regarding his own plight as an artist in a commercial society (the tension between integrity and financial-social success) which Fitzgerald, along with Vachel Lindsay, Sherwood Anderson, and Thomas Wolfe, among others, felt so keenly. Gatsby's ambivalent idealization of the rich resembles his creator's; Gatsby's pathetic desire for recognition is a reflection of Fitzgerald's early college days when he tried unsuccessfully to become a big man on the Princeton campus.

If this were all, if Dickens and Fitzgerald were merely letting off symbolic steam, their novels would be of interest merely as case histories. The fact, however, that they also managed to *judge* their fantasies through the medium of art makes them of special interest to the student of literature. This is what is missing from their mere life stories—their superior power as artists for self-criticism. When we come away from reading about Fitzgerald's chaotic life, we feel that he was an ambitious but weak-willed alcoholic. How, we ask ourselves, did he come to write at all? But if Gatsby's dream was Fitzgerald's, we must also remember that Nick Carraway, who passes judgment on that dream, was also created by Fitzgerald. If Pip's dream of a mysterious benefactor was Dickens's, we must recall that Dickens brought Pip to the mature position of rejecting it as false. Perhaps this is what D. H. Lawrence meant when he said an author sheds his sicknesses in his books, projects and dramatizes them in order to master and be rid of them.[5]

IV

The peculiar temperament of a writer then—the pattern of his intellectual and moral qualities—plays its part as a selecting principle in the form of his works. We have now to consider the general cultural causes, over and above artistic and biographical factors, which can account for the similarities found among the novels of two different writers. Of course, since Dickens and Fitzgerald are separated by almost a hundred years and three thousand miles, the surface differences regarding mores and locale between their two novels are quite marked, but in so far as they were both written within what may be called, for lack of a better term, the postromantic—or, more broadly, the postrenaissance—tradition, these differences are more apparent than real. Surely the world of Barnard's Inn is not the world of East Egg, nor are sexual relations therein treated in a similar spirit; but consider, as the most obvious example of similarity within difference which comes to mind, the attitude shared by Pip and Gatsby toward fine clothes: for both of them the proper clothing was a symbol of acceptance in the eyes of their respective ladies —Pip and his gentleman's suit purchased to offset the scorn Estella expressed at his coarse laborer's boots, Gatsby and his excited display of imported shirts to convince Daisy that he was what she wanted. The fact that Pip wears knee-breeches, and Gatsby pink silk slacks, does not obscure this basic resemblance.

Probing a bit deeper now, let us consider the problem of moral values. Notice the degraded position occupied by the Bible in Pip's education (chapter 10), and the whimsical progress of his schooling; the barbarity with which convicts are treated, and the unjust preference given to a "gentleman" in court (chapter 42); the purposelessness of his idle life in London; the dehumanized atmosphere of the law office (chapter 24). Are not these factors paralleled by the pathetic remains of Ben Franklin's code scribbled on a flyleaf of "a ragged old copy of a book called 'Hopalong Cassidy' " (chapter 9) in which Gatsby schools himself; the comfort and ease enjoyed by his early mentor, Dan Cody, the debased heir of the pioneer tradition; the ambiguous means to success offered by American gangsterdom; the superficiality of Gatsby's human attachments and the flashy vacuity of the lavish parties at which he entertained them (chapter 3)? The world of London in the 1820s is only a little less disinherited than that of Long Island in the 1920s: all we are left with there is the natural goodness of the individual which shines from Joe like a halo in the midst of the chiaroscuro of greed, jealousy, envy, spite, hatred, snobbery, and cruelty with which Pip becomes surrounded (see, for example, chapter 32). And Nick, in rejecting the dislocated Midwesterners who make messes for other people to clean up, can find no better course than to reject the East altogether and go back home where he belongs.

In each case, institutions—home, church, school—are found wanting; we have a hero with no proper object for his heroism. In one of the most frightening passages in *Gatsby*, the grief-crazed Wilson looks out at the eyes of Dr. T. J. Eckleburg: " 'God sees everything,' repeated Wilson. 'That's an advertisement,' Michaelis assured him" (chapter 8). Here, in both novels, is a world in which values are either lost or are nonexistent; and, if they are found, they are found only tenuously and at a tremendous cost in human waste and suffering. The time is out of joint, and the attempt to set it right involves either an act of personal redemption on the part of the hero-victim, or his being destroyed in the attempt. The individual vs. society, and the problem of appearance and reality, the two great complementary themes of "modern" literature, are tensions which contribute one order of structure to these novels, tensions which they share in common with such otherwise various works as *Don Quixote*, *The Red and the Black*, and *A Farewell to Arms*.

V

Thus some of the cultural factors governing the form of these novels. We come now finally to an examination of those factors which account for the selection and arrangement of symbolic devices in a novel that serve to universalize its plot—causes which are the least differentiated of all. Among the many heroes whom Lionel Trilling mentions as following what he calls the Young Man from the Provinces formula,[6] are to be found Pip and Jimmy Gatz. The provincial hero "starts with a great demand upon life and a great wonder about its complexity and promises"; he is poor, prideful, and intelligent, standing on the outside of life seeking a way in. Mr. Trilling goes on to stress the source of this motif "in the very heart of the modern actuality" (as we have just outlined it) as well as its roots in folklore (the youngest son of the woodcutter, Parsifal at the castle of the Fisher King), for "through the massed social fact there runs the thread of legendary romance, even of downright magic." Similarly Edwin S. Fussell offers an interpretation, in "Fitzgerald's Brave New World,"[7] of *The Great Gatsby* which sees the object of the Young Man's quest as embodied in the ambiguous archetype of paradise as well as in the fabric of American experience. This archetype represents an image, on the one hand, of release from limitation and the consequent fulfillment of the capacity for wonder and, on the other, of a blasphemous denial of mortality and the consequent search for an earthly Eden (hubris). And was there indeed not something "mythic" itself in the renaissance journey west to the American Hesperides, El Dorado, the land of the fountain of youth?

It remains to explore in greater detail this legendary or archetypal formula, as it appears in both these novels, which such remarks suggest. In the first place the most obvious symbolic element which these two share in common is the youth of vaulting ambition. The problem of adolescence, of the search for something in the adult world—now to be entered —commensurate to the capacity for wonder inherent in the child's world —now to be abandoned—is surely one of the most dramatic loci in human experience. Thus in both Pip and Jimmy we note the characteristic pattern: the dissatisfaction with home-life (the first step toward heroic status and consequently toward hubris is the rejection or loss or substitution of parents, a symbolic denial of mortality), the inexplicable feeling of restlessness, and the frequent and vivid wish-fulfilment fantasies. Along with this are to be found the naive attempts at self-improvement: Gatsby's self-imposed schedule and moral maxims, Pip's persistent attempts to educate himself; Gatsby's efforts to improve his father's eating habits, Pip's vain efforts to teach Joe how to write. And all the while each is waiting for his vague but impetuous destiny to materialize.

We note further that the dream is in each case ironically realized through substitute fathers who are outside the law. The wavering scale of values, teetering now to one side and now to the other, is finally weighted in favor of what seems to be fulfilment, and the protagonist makes the immoral choice for which he will have to pay dearly before his fate plays itself out. Thus Gatsby gets his start through Dan Cody, "the pioneer debauchee, who during one phase of American life brought back to the Eastern seaboard the savage violence of the frontier brothel and saloon" (chapter 6), and he is launched finally by Wolfsheim, the gambler who fixed the 1919 World Series:

> "Did you start him in business?" I inquired.
> "Start him! I made him."
> "Oh."
> "I raised him up out of nothing, right out of the gutter." (Ch. 9)

So, too, Magwitch exclaims, "Yes, Pip, dear boy, I've made a gentleman on you! It's me wot has done it! . . . Look'ee here, Pip, I'm your second father. You're my son—more to me nor any son. I've put money away, only for you to spend" (chapter 39). We see in both instances that the capacity for wonder is accompanied by an equally strong capacity for self-deception.

In the third place the dreams of both our heroes become identified with a woman. Just as Gatsby's dream finds its focus in the remote and mysterious green light at the end of Daisy's dock, so Pip's dream centers upon Estella, the remote and mysterious "star": "Whenever I watched the vessels standing out to sea with their white sails spread, I somehow thought of Miss Havisham and Estella; and whenever the light struck aslant, afar off, upon a cloud or sail or green hill-side or waterline, it was just the same.—Miss Havisham and the strange house and the strange life appeared to have something to do with everything that was picturesque" (chapter 15). Similarly the image of woman as the embodiment of desire, grace, and beauty becomes confused with the leisure class in both cases: "Gatsby was overwhelmingly aware of the youth and mystery that wealth imprisons and preserves, of the freshness of many clothes, and of Daisy, gleaming like silver, safe and proud above the hot struggles of the poor" (chapter 8). Compare this from Dickens: "Truly it was impossible to dissociate her presence from all those wretched hankerings after money and gentility that had disturbed my boyhood—from all those ill-regulated aspirations that had first made me ashamed of home and Joe" (chapter 29).

In both cases the dream becomes objectified in a house. Although Dickens is not content to allow us merely to infer the inner corruption of Satis House and Barnard's Inn (see chapter 21, for example) but rather presents them as literally decayed, there is a palpable similarity in the fact that both Pip's and Gatsby's dreams find symbolic tenancy in mansions. Miss Havisham's and Gatsby's homes are the external emblems of the paradisal vision, which is ironic in both cases since the latter is an imitation old-world castle (chapters 1, 5), and the former is a kind of witch's den into which the abandoned Hansel and Gretel of the novel wander to be destroyed by the child-devouring crone (chapters 11, 38).

On the other side are the corresponding images of hell. The polarizing symbols, counterbalancing Satis House and the star, Gatsby's castle and the green light, are to be found in Pip's marshes (the repeated references to which throughout the novel, on both the literal and figurative levels, form an infernal cluster) and Nick's valley of ashes. From these wastelands emerge Gatsby's nemesis (Wilson) and Pip's (Orlick), demanding vengeance from the hero for his hubris.

As a consequence of reaching too high, each hero becomes involved in a penitential or redemptive journey. Gatsby's tragic self-discovery—"he must have felt that he had lost the old warm world, paid a high price for living too long with a single dream" (chapter 8)—results in no personal purgation: he is simply shot to death by Wilson. But, insofar as there is a moral choice made as a result of his fall from high place, it is made by Nick "Carry Away." In his rejection of Gatsby, Jordan, Tom, and Daisy, and in his decision to return to "my Middle West . . . where dwellings are still called through the decades by a family's name" (chapter 9), Nick is symbolically bringing the purged Gatsby back to where he started and where he belongs. This is a redemptive choice, a return to the moral values and the stable life of childhood; a purification, as far as it goes, of hubris.[8] So, too, does Pip experience his inevitable self-revelation—"All the truth of my position came flashing on me; and its disappointments, dangers, disgraces, consequences of all kinds, rushed in in such a multitude that I was borne down by them and had to struggle for every breath I drew" (chapter 39)—and, at first revolted by the returned convict, he makes the crucial moral choice to devote himself to Magwitch's safety (chapter 54). Although he is not killed, he does suffer physically for his hubris: he is burned (chapter 49), tortured by Orlick (chapter 53), and falls deathly ill. During the period of his sickness and recuperation he is nursed by the ever-loyal Joe, and regresses to the state of childhood ("I fancied I was little Pip again" [chapter 57]) when he and Joe were "ever the best of friends." Soon after his recovery, we note, he makes a pilgrimage to the forge in order to cleanse his conscience completely: "My heart was softened by my return, and such a change had come to pass, that I felt like one who was toiling home barefoot from distant travel, and whose wanderings had lasted many years" (chapter 58).

Finally in both novels the narrator enacts the choric role of moral commentator. Although, as we have seen, *Great Expectations* is told by the "I" as protagonist and *The Great Gatsby* by the "I" as witness, we have in both cases a double perspective. In the former the mature Pip recounts the story of the immature Pip living through a crucial initiatory experience, thus allowing for the narration of immoral deeds in a moral context, after the fashion of Greek tragedy wherein the chorus provides a backdrop of normalcy for the abnormal central action. Thus Pip the narrator can say of Pip the protagonist: "I was too cowardly to do what I knew to be right, as I had been too cowardly to avoid doing what I knew to be wrong" (chapter 6); or, "So, throughout life, our worst weaknesses and meannesses are usually committed for the sake of people whom we most despise" (chapter 27); or, "All the other swindlers upon Earth are nothing to the self-swindlers, and with such pretences did I cheat myself" (chapter 28). Similarly, Nick comments, "They're a rotten crowd. . . .

You're worth the whole damn bunch put together"; but then continues, "I've always been glad I said that. It was the only compliment I ever gave him, because I disapproved of him from beginning to end" (chapter 8). Or again: "They were careless people, Tom and Daisy—they smashed up things and creatures and then retreated back into their money or their vast carelessness, or whatever it was that kept them together, and let other people clean up the mess they had made" (chapter 9).

In progressing, then, from the most central to the most peripheral of selective principles governing the choice and organization of materials in these two novels, we have outlined briefly the ways in which they are unlike as well as the ways in which they are alike. It is only through some such multiple perspective, I submit—some such consideration of different versions of form with a view to their relationships, apart from all partisan debate and vested interest—that the full life of any given novel as an artistic whole will come home to us in its entirety. If we are interested in truth rather than literary politics, in seeing justice done to the facts rather than establishing a favored hypothesis, we have no better way.

PART TWO
THE PROBLEM OF FORM

Chapter 3

Principles of Formal Analysis

Having sketched in and illustrated a variety of critical approaches and their relationships, let us return to formal analysis and begin again in greater detail. I start with form not only because it has received so much concerted attention in the past fifty or sixty years, but also because it controls and limits interpretation, as I have suggested, on other levels. It seems to me necessary in the context of this book to discuss the problem of meaning only after I have discussed that of form.

I

The problem of formal analysis is, historically and logically, to escape the trap of the old form-content distinction; for this distinction tends to be simplistic and reductive, separating form from content and seeing content as the important thing and form as the wrapping. We know, and the New Critics are right in emphasizing it, that something happens to content when it is formed which makes it different from what it was before.[1] It is not simply that hunks of life get reproduced, as is, in art. That is why so many modern movements in the arts may be characterized as nonrepresentational, even though they do not necessarily end up as abstract. On the other hand, the common-sense view of art—which is still that of the man in the street today (or student in the classroom), and which makes as little real sense as those other "natural" ideas which held that the earth is flat or is at the center of the universe, or that heavier bodies will fall faster than lighter ones—is that a work is good insofar as it presents something recognizable or says something we can relate directly to our experience.

Surely the plot summary of novels is as reductive as the prose paraphrase of poems: just as the latter leaves out exactly those elements which are essential to the poem as a whole—the situation in which the speaker is located, the listener he addresses, and the dramatic aim which he is trying to achieve—so too does the former leave out those elements which are necessary to grasp the shaping principle binding the events together—the character and motives of the protagonist, his state of mind, the change he undergoes, and the crucial chain of cause and effect leading him from one condition to another. By way of illustration, we may imagine a given story—say, protagonist meets loved one, wins loved one, and loses loved one—as it might be treated by several different novelists, for instance, Thomas Hardy, D. H. Lawrence, F. Scott Fitzgerald, Ernest Hemingway, and George Orwell. Clearly the same story turns out to be five altogether different things in *Tess of the d'Urbervilles, Sons and Lovers, The Great Gatsby, A Farewell to Arms,* and *1984;* and it is exactly this difference which we are after—the *art* involved.

The reaction against reductionism explains why the New Critics have talked so much against the heresy of paraphrase and the decorative fallacy. Content does not enter a work unchanged—it is subjected to selection, shaping, rendering, and shifts in emphasis—and form is not detachable—it is that in terms of which the content is changed. These two terms are not sufficient to do the job: we need a way of discussing the manner in which they interact.

Thus the New Critics, borrowing certain ideas from certain romantic thinkers such as Coleridge, have attempted to resolve this problem by means of their concept of organic form. Whatever else this protean concept means—and Murray Krieger, among others, has labored mightily to explain it[2]—it is supposed to indicate the essential unity of form and content. Hence the work of art is viewed as separate from life, as forming its own reflexive context, and as being an independent object or structure like a jar or a statue. So far, so good, except that this conception sounds a bit ninetyish, smacks a bit too much of the ideas of the so-called aesthetes and decadents. But I do not think that this flavor is accidental: Pater and Wilde and Whistler (and others of the time) *were* in fact developing certain protomodernist ideas; and certain modernist ideas *do* owe much to the 1880s and 1890s, as well as to Blake, Coleridge, and Keats.[3] Yeats's career offers the perfect case in point.

The emphasis of the New Critics is much different. The aesthetes and decadents talked defiantly of the uselessness of art, for they were reacting against an overly utilitarian society. But the New Critics, while accepting and extending the separation between poetry and prose, art and materialistic society, and literature and science, nevertheless do so only to show that poetry is ultimately *more* useful, *more* real, *more* relevant, and *more* truthful than science and ordinary discourse. Thus certain anti-modernist critics, such as Yvor Winters and Robert Hillyer, are mistaken in accusing the modernist writers of attempting to create meaningless puzzles in a vacuum; and certain promodernist critics, such as Richard Foster, are equally mistaken in assuming that the supposed development of many New Critics from formal analysis to cultural criticism represents some sort of crucial change or even conversion.[4] (I have already suggested and will return to my doubts, however, as to whether the New Criticism *has* in fact succeeded in relating form to life in any logical way).

While I think that this idea of the superior utility of art is implicit even in such men as Pater, Wilde, and Whistler—to divorce art from social utility is not necessarily to divorce it from life—I do think that it is the attempt to work it out explicitly, and to combine it with the organic theory, which sets off the modernists from the 1880s and 90s. Modernists attempt to resolve the dilemma by conceiving of form as meaning, and this is where I think the trouble starts. At first it seems like a good idea: on the one hand they conceive of a work as being an independent amalgam of form and content, and on the other they think of this amalgam in terms of meaning, which in turn brings the work back into focus as part of the human enterprise. Yet I do not think it works out. The trouble with the New Criticism is not that it is too formalistic: it is rather not formalistic enough.[5]

Aesthetically it seeks to avoid the form-content trap by assuming that meaning equals Total Meaning, and thus inheres in the work and cannot be separated from it. Words, phrases, and sentences express denotative and connotative meanings; these together form a context, whose pressure modifies each meaning in turn; the resultant meanings are therefore reflexive—that is, they take on special tones and flavors which apply only in that context; and hence *what* the poem says is a function of *how* it says it, and cannot be detached therefrom. Epistemologically and metaphysically the ultimate sanction of this aesthetics lies in the New Critical notion of reality and imagination: reality is complex and many-sided, and cannot be known or expressed simply via intellectual abstraction, as in science; it can only be known or expressed fully via the imagination, which sees the universal *in* the particular, and which is therefore concrete rather than abstract. Thus, like the very reality it represents, poetry is concrete, complex, and many-sided, and it therefore *is*, on the formal level, what it *means*, on the metaphysical level. That is why poetry is not paraphrasable: we do not derive statements from works of art; we learn instead to become more aware of experience.

Although these ideas seem logical and useful, and I will find them viable in other contexts (especially in the second part of this book), the problem is that they still do not constitute an actual theory of form. While it is true that form and content are no longer separated, it is also true that content is still seen as the governing factor. Meaning is still meaning, no matter how subtle and complex you make it. The notions of reality and art are more sophisticated than those of the old theory, but the basic principle is still the same: art is an embodiment of insight into experience, and hence is governed by the necessities of such insight. But if the governing principle does not come from within the writer himself, in relation to the particular artistic problem he is confronting, then the work cannot be viewed as an autonomous object, existing apart from external necessities.

The New Critical theory of form as meaning, then, is really still only a theory of meaning as it should *relate* to form—and not a theory of *form*. What we are left with is the old message-hunting disguised as formal analysis, having merely exchanged simple-minded platitudes for complicated ones.[6] Even such formal theory as we do have here sees the work basically in static terms, locked in upon itself as it vibrates endlessly between meaning and form, trying to reconcile a polarity it never needed to establish in the first place. In spite of the fact that it points outward toward reality, it does so within itself in terms which see the whole as emerging, somehow, out of coordinate relationships established, somehow, among equal parts. As a result, with the narrative art especially, a sense of the essential flow of cause and effect in time, and the concept of levels of subordination among the parts, one serving as means or material to the next, get lost in the shuffle, with the result that a blind spot remains in exactly the place where we should be looking if we are to find anything like distinctive forms—at the work itself and in its parts and their relationships.[7]

Hence, in opting for Total Meaning, the New Criticism includes too much, failing not only to distinguish art from science, but also to tell one kind of work from another or one example of a kind from another.

II

In order to resolve this dilemma, we must ask the question differently: not what is the relation between form and content, nor how does a poem mean, but what are the parts, and how do they relate to the whole? In order to do this, we must indeed regard the work as a thing in itself, having its aim within itself and displaying as a result a distinguishable structure of relationships among its parts as they are arranged to achieve the end in view. Form and meaning are two separate questions, and we must separate them before we can talk about their relationships; for unless they are different, they cannot be seen as related. In collapsing this distinction, and in attempting to see form in terms of meaning, the New Critics have still left the field open for a real theory of form.

We must in effect go back to where the so-called aesthetes and decadents left off and begin over again. But with this difference: that we accept the autonomy of form without accepting at the same time the polemical context in which it was developed. This is not to say, however, that we are violating the very principles of pluralism explained in our first chapter by wrenching critical ideas out of their logical context. It is to say instead that the logical context not only does not need the polemical context, but also that it is positively harmed by it. To regard form independently is to say neither that it is useless nor that it is meaningful —it is simply to remove it altogether from an irrelevant context, and to regard it as itself. The proper *understanding* of form need not be confused either with the need to *defend* it or with the need to define its *significance* in the broader context of the concerns of men. We certainly can, and in this book we will, proceed to that context, but we should do so only after we have tried to grasp form on its own terms first.

The desiderata for testing a theory of form, in terms of what we have been saying so far, would seem to be five: not only (1) to distinguish the parts of a work and (2) to show how they are related, but also (3) to define the whole thereby constituted, (4) to use this definition as an explanatory principle for analyzing the functioning of the parts and their relationships, and (5) to be able, on this basis, to differentiate one work and kind of work from another. Thus a pluralistic approach sees not only many kinds of criticisms but also many kinds of literary works.

In order to begin over again, consequently, we should now regard the problem of form in its logical or methodological aspects. The problem here clearly appears to be one of how properly to define things, and so we must rehearse the principles of making adequate definitions. The definitions we need for formal analysis, as I have been suggesting, are a posteriori rather than a priori, in that they depend for their meaning upon the prior existence of traits belonging to things in the external world which can be used as the basis of groupings, rather than simply upon mathematical or scientific or philosophical concepts, for example.[8] In an a posteriori definition we must know what we want to define before trying to define it, and therefore we must test our definition by placing it back over the group out of which it arose in order to determine whether it fits or not. The definition, in other words, and the thing defined are two separate things: the latter remains constant, while the former changes to fit it.

The rule for making an a posteriori definition therefore is simply that it must have the power to exclude from the class in question all things which do not belong in it, while at the same time including all those which do. A good definition must contain sufficient differentiae for going about its work. If form and content are not sufficient, neither are language and meaning; certain crucial features of poetic form are still slipping unnoticed through the holes. What those features are will be taken up in a moment, but I must recall here that the intended definitions are not of literature as a whole but rather of the forms of particular works and, on certain levels, of classes of works. Thus it should be clear that this enterprise is not just another version of the old neoclassical genre criticism,[9] since it aims to *describe* rather than *prescribe*, and since it does so in terms of independent variables rather than of predetermined composites (see chapter 9). I hope this matter will become clearer as we proceed.

III

In our search for a theory of form which will meet the stated conditions, filling in the gaps left by the old as well as the "new" criticism by that same token, we turn now to Aristotle's method in the *Poetics*—not because he is an authority, or because we owe him (or the Chicago neo-

Aristotelians) anything, or because of a partisan spirit, but simply because that method seems the best available in terms of the job to be done.[10]

The basic assumption which underlies the argument of the *Poetics* is that a work of art is the artificial product of an intentional process of making. Since *intention* has become a suspicious word in modern criticism, this assumption needs some defending.[11] What Aristotle means by artificial, to begin with, is that a shape is imposed upon material which it does not take in and of itself. Indeed, this concept is the basis for his use of the term *imitation* (see chapter 10).[12] It requires the agency of human will and creative power, and accordingly the artist is a maker in the most literal sense. Language, for example, does not automatically fall into the patterns we call poems, plays, novels, and stories—or, for that matter, into any other significant patterns either (although it does contain, as with most other kinds of material, inherent powers and limitations which will aid or hinder the writer in his attempts to compose: different languages, for example, tend to compose reality in different ways; but the fact remains that actual compositions, in whatever language, require some human agency to do the composing, even if it is only the collective will of a culture in creating oral traditions).

This assumption may seem painfully obvious, but the truth is that theories of organic form, automatic writing, and spontaneous creativity have seriously clouded the issue. To explain Aristotle's conception of intention may help in clarifying it. It does not necessarily mean either that the writer knows what he wants to do before he does it, or that when he does discover it, he can formulate it verbally or intellectually. It simply means that, in order for the work to have reached (relatively) its completed state, it is logically necessary for there to have been *something* which told the writer that he had gotten everything together as well as possible under the circumstances. The creative process, in other words, must be organized by some principle in order to reach completion. This principle is the work's intention.

Such a concept, therefore, need not at all imply that Aristotle regards the work mechanically and in terms of rules. The intention does not come from outside the work, nor need it exist before the beginning of the creative process: the writer may not discover his organizing principle until near the end of that process, and he may not even be able to formulate it, either for himself or others, relying simply on his sense or intuition. The concept obtains nevertheless: in order for there to be a completed whole—that is, an organization of parts into a certain unified set of relationships—there must be something which constitutes that whole and unifies its parts. It goes almost without saying, finally, that such an intention is embedded *in* the work, and is found there, not because the author (or critic) says so or hopes so, but rather because the work itself has a certain design implying a certain principle.

Intention, if it remains a troublesome term, may be replaced by *organizing* or *unifying principle. End effect* or *artistic purpose* will do just as well, so long as we realize that ends or purposes other than artistic ones may be just as operative on other levels, however irrelevant they may be here —the writer's desire for fame, for example, or need to impress a lady, or the pressure of historical circumstances or of the racial unconscious, and so on.

A work from Aristotle's point of view then—and this seems not only true but also appropriate to the problem of formal analysis—confronts us with a design answering to a purpose. The next assumption which we must make, accordingly, is that we can infer the purpose from the design, the effect from the causes. An intelligent being from Mars examining an ax, for example, by noticing the weight and hardness and sharpness of the head, the balance and length and lightness of the handle, the relationship of head to handle, and so on, ought to be able to tell what it is used for, and hence why it is made the way it is. And that is the position we are in when we analyze a literary work, except that we already have a stock of generalizations in our heads derived from prior reading and experience which we can bring to bear upon the question.

The *Poetics* starts from the other end, so we must take this difference into account when we make use of its method. Aristotle is conducting a *productive* argument, saying in effect that if you would write a certain kind of tragic play, then thus and so is the most likely way to construct it, and for such and such reasons. He therefore *begins* with that definition of the whole (in chapter 6) which we normally *finish* with: normally we are reading and analyzing a specific work already in existence, and we want to know what its form is, while Aristotle is talking about a certain kind of work, and he is inquiring into how it may be made. The reader's problem is normally, however, a *theoretical* question of unity: he must arrive at a hypothesis of the whole rather than *begin* with a definition of it.

Nor does this mean that Aristotle is being monistic while we must be pluralistic: he does not begin with a definition of the nature of literature as a whole (contrary to the impression given by most of his interpreters and commentators), but only with a definition of a certain kind of whole to be produced; and he does not reach his definition on the basis of a single differentia, but in terms of his scheme of the four causes seen as independent variables, which he explains analytically and historically in his first five chapters. Furthermore, although he does start with the end or purpose of tragedy—to arouse and allay pity and fear—as a donnée, he then goes on to argue the rest of the problem in terms of the writer's attempt to achieve that specific end in dramatic form. That the end is regarded as a given proposition is simply a necessity of any productive argument rather than a sign of a monistic approach: whether derived inductively from a prior argument, or whether simply postulated as a possible end to use in organizing a whole of a certain kind, the fact remains that such a beginning must serve as the basis for such an argument. Aristotle's formulation, then, need be taken neither as an exact analysis of all the tragedies he was familiar with, nor as a prescription for all the tragedies to come thereafter (least of all for all the plays and novels to come thereafter), but simply as a way of discussing the construction of the kind of work he had in mind at the time—call it what you will, and find it where you will or not, as you please.

Although different in this way, the reasoning involved in a theoretical argument of unity is similar enough to benefit from comparison. Aristotle's reasoning is what Olson calls regressive, going backward from the whole to the parts and their relationships which are needed to produce it.[13] It is a reasoning from the effect back to its causes—if you want to produce that result, then this is the likely method—while the theoretical argument reasons "forward" from the parts to the whole, from causes to the effect—if this is the method, what is its likely end? Either way, however, it is clear that the principles of causal reasoning underlie the process of analysis.

Some possible ambiguity in the use of the terms *cause* and *effect* should be cleared away at this point. From the point of view so far employed in this chapter, *effect* refers to the work's artistic purpose, and *cause* means the design of the work composed to achieve this purpose. On the other hand, when we regard purpose from the point of view of what governs the work and produces its design, then it is the cause and the design is the effect. I trust that my use of these terms in various ways in various contexts, therefore, will not appear inconsistent.

The third assumption is that we can use the inference we have made about the form to go back over the work and explain the functioning or purpose of its parts and their relationships. This procedure, it seems to me, is the raison d'être of formal analysis, its end result—to be able to say that this is there because of that. It is not the primary job of formal criticism to make definitions and classify genres: its job is to analyze works. Here the question of circularity arises: how can we use a definition, which we have made on the basis of analyzing the work, as a way of explaining that very same work? The answer is found in the rules, which we mentioned in chapter 1, for making an adequate hypothesis.

What we do is to inspect the work, come up with several possibilities as to what its form is, and then apply them back to the work in order to determine which fits best. That fits best, we recall, which offers the most complete explanation of its parts and their relationships, in the most economical fashion, and with the greatest degree of coherence. The kind of explanation sought, as I have said, is to be able to say that this is there because of that. *Completeness* means that the hypothesis offered presents us with a unifying principle which relates *all* the parts of the work functionally to the whole, and not just *some* of its parts—that is, those we happen to be interested in or looking for. It is not simply a question, then, of "finding support in the work" for a given hypothesis, for almost *any* hypothesis can find such support if one ignores the rule of completeness.

Economy means, conversely, that this complete explanation should be as small, as simple, as particular, as specific, and as concrete as will cover the case. Again, it is too easy to explain anything in a complex way if one ignores the rule of economy. If we can explain, as I have shown in connection with "A Valediction Forbidding Mourning," an aspect of a work with reference to the particular situation embodied in it, we need not go on to try to find an explanation with reference to some general theory of what literature is or ought to be. And if we can explain the form of a particular work in terms of its own artistic organization, we need not go on, in terms of this particular question, to find reasons in the author's psychology or what have you. The point is not whether we *can* go on to more general causes; it is, instead, whether we *need* to.

Coherence, finally, means that the whole should be explained, in so far as possible, in terms of a single principle of organization, without exceptions and sub-hypotheses. If *mimetic* and *didactic,* for example, can be used in reference to unifying principles (see chapter 6), then it is inconsistent to say that such and such a novel is mimetic in one part and didactic in another. We should see whether the mimetic part can be subsumed under the overall didactic hypothesis, or whether the didactic part can be subsumed under the overall mimetic hypothesis. A unified work, by definition, can only be ruled by a single principle and not two or three: we cannot say, in the same sense and in the same connection, that such and such is "a" central principle among several other "central" principles. If there are two principles of "unity," there must be a third which binds them together.[14] Unless, of course, the work is not, in fact, a unified whole; but we can conclude such a thing only after having tried and tested all the available and relevant hypotheses.

Other things being equal, then, that hypothesis is best which meets these tests better than the alternatives. In this way is the problem of circularity resolved.

We come now to the fourth and last assumption underlying Aristotle's method of formal analysis—the naming of parts. How shall we conceive of artistic wholes and their parts? I do not know of any logical necessity underlying the way Aristotle goes about it, nor do I think that there could be for any formal system. The parts of a work of art, after all, and the wholes they constitute, do not fall open to view upon dissection—as is the case, for example, with a machine or even something organic, such as a body or a flower. Many ways of looking at the question, therefore, are possible, and of course many ways have been devised. The only way of resolving the issue, it seems to me, is to test each method in terms of its consequences, exactly according to the tests outlined above. They are applicable, that is, not only to particular explanations of particular wholes, but also to the general *methods* of explanation which underlie the particular explanations. In either case the basis of choice is that one approach will have superior powers of explanation in relation to the others.

It might be appropriate, before going on, to get a sense of the variety of meanings of many of the terms characteristic of formal criticism, and then to show how they could be stabilized, included, supplemented, and unified by Aristotle's method—not, however, in a spirit of either monism or relativism, but with a sense of various and multiple possibilities.

Content, for example, can mean many different things, but it usually means the ideas and experiences out of which the work is made. *Matter* or *materials,* sometimes used synonymously, can mean the same thing as *content* (*form* and *content, form* and *matter* or *materials*), or they can mean literally, as in Aristotle and (curiously) in the New Critics, language—that is, "a poem is made out of words." *Form* can mean, narrowly, the stanzaic scheme of a poem (for example, the sonnet form); or, more broadly, the plot or argument of a work; or, more broadly still, total meaning, which arises out of the tension and interplay of oppositions. *Structure* can mean anything that *form* means, but it can also mean a pattern of some kind, such as repetition and variation, statement and development and return, cumulative progression, any recurring theme, and the like.

Theme is one of those crucial but shifting terms in contemporary criticism which for the old-fashioned critic means message or moral, while for the New Critic it means total meaning or form. It can also refer variously to the basic problem, issue, or question embodied in the work (the relation of the individual to society, for example); any recurrence in the work, as in motif or leitmotif (the rain theme in *A Farewell to Arms,* for example); any pervasive element or factor (the theme of infection in *Bleak House*); any dominant subject matter or character type (the love theme, for example, or the woman theme); any aspect of content (the theme of religion or travel); or, as in Northrop Frye, the "meaning," "conceptual content," "idea," or "point" of the work. What this latter usage signifies in contemporary criticism is complicated enough in itself, and it will receive further attention at various points in this book.

Technique often means point of view, but it can refer to form or structure as well. *Point of view* here means technique of narration, but it can also refer to the expressed or implied attitude of the author. *Style* refers most commonly to the use of language patterns (diction, rhythm, syntax, and so on), but it can refer more generally to the author's overall way of doing things (as in form, structure, and technique).

Symbol, as contrasted with the more traditional figures of speech, such as *metaphor, parable, allegory,* has no single definite meaning in modern usage, and is indeed often used interchangeably with them (although often distinguished from them as well). Basically it refers to the way in which experience can have significance and can mean anything from a central or repeated image or character or situation which appears to carry the weight of special value, to the way in which the work itself can embody and organize the author's vision and reveal insights into the human condition.

Other terms, such as *iamb* or *full rhyme*, and similar ones from the principles of style and metrics, although certainly not beyond controversy, are for the purposes of formal criticism more or less stable.

If I turn now toward stabilizing the variable terms, it is not because I want to legislate either for critics or writers, or to restrict and mechanize discourse, but simply because I want what I am talking about to be as clear as possible. We come now, therefore, to Aristotle's formal scheme, which is certainly already familiar to any informed reader, but whose actual *use*, I am afraid, is not so familiar. The *Poetics* is naturally taught in every course in criticism, as well as in most courses in drama. And yet, in the light of what I have already said in chapter 1 about its common distortions, it should not seem redundant to go over it once again. Of course, the neo-Aristotelians of the Chicago school, among others, have made an invaluable beginning in such a reinterpretation of Aristotle, and many of my own points rely heavily upon their work, but much still remains to be done.

Aristotle begins by asking a question somewhat like this: what are the factors which must have gone into the making of an object in order for it to be what it is, and which, if we can come to understand them, will tell us how it must have been made? This "must have" phrase is significant, for it directs our attention away from the empirical vagaries of the actual creative process—these vary, after all, from work to work, and from writer to writer—and toward the shaping factors which, as I have said, are derived by logical necessity from the fact that, if a finished whole is before us, it can only be so because its parts are organized according to *some* principle.

The work is the product of a certain process, then, and in this sense is the effect of those shaping factors, which are the causes. Aristotle finds that four causes are both necessary and sufficient to explain a product—in this case, we recall, an artificial product. The final cause is the purpose for which the objejct is made, its functional end, aim, goal, or what have you. The formal cause is the shape of the object. The material cause is that out of which the object is made. And the efficient cause is the maker forming the material in a certain manner. Now one could defend the cogency of this scheme by trying to show, first, that no product can come into being without the operation of these causes (that they are necessary), and that when they are present a product will result (they are sufficient); and, second, that they offer a method of formal explanation which will meet the tests of completeness, economy, and coherence. The point is that there are four causes rather than three or five, for example, simply because these seem to exhaust the relevant possibilities.

Furthermore they must be seen in terms of a logically necessary order or hierarchy; they are related, that is to say, according to functional priorities, in the sense of "what determines what" artistically. Everything must answer to the purpose; material and manner must answer to the form; and material must answer to the manner. Let us take the old example of the pitcher: if it is to hold and pour liquids, then the shape must be such as will allow for container space, hand-holding and -lifting leverage, and pouring over the lips or rim; the manner of making this shape—whether by the potter's wheel, carving knife, furnace, and so on —must be such as will produce these shapes; and the material must be such as will be sufficiently malleable for being so shaped, as well as sufficiently nonporous for holding liquids.

Let us see how these distinctions apply to a literary work. In the *Poetics* the four causes are rephrased as follows: *final cause* is the *end* or *moving power* of the whole; *formal cause* is the *object of imitation*; *efficient cause* is the *manner of imitation*; and *material cause* is the *medium* or *means*. I think these could be rephrased once again in more modern terms: let *end* equal *artistic purpose*; let *object of imitation* equal *structure*; let *manner* equal *techniques*; and let *means* equal *style*. Further explanations will be forthcoming, but I must here illustrate the concept of functional priorities.

If the end of the work is to arouse and allay pity and fear, as is the case with the sort of work Aristotle has in mind, then the object of imitation must be such as will do so—that is, it must show a man suffering undeserved misfortune, for this is what causes pity; and it must portray him as neither markedly better nor worse than we are, since this is what causes fear. The manner of imitation—whether dramatic or narrative— must be such as will most effectively bring out the stated qualities of this action: for example, an action involving a large scope would be best when told narratively, while another action of less scope might be best when shown dramatically, and a third might be best when using combinations. And finally the means must be appropriate to the speaker, the action, and the purpose—as when, for example, the author in using a narrator must adjust his style to the imagined temperament and background of this person.

Notice that this concept of functional priorities is relative, like everything else in Aristotle's scheme, to the problem under discussion, and is not meant to be taken in any absolute sense, least of all as a set of rules. Thus language or style is "least important" here only in the formal sense of being determined by manner, object, and end; in other senses it might be the most important factor—for example, in the reader's coming to know the work or even in the author's coming to write it.[15] But when viewed in terms of the finished product, it seems reasonable to see style as Aristotle does, and this view would require no comment were it not for the fact that the New Critics have viewed language as first in order of formal determination, and so have tried to derive their principles of organization from the qualities of language—with the theoretical and practical drawbacks that I hope I have already shown.

Aristotle's scheme of four causes thus provides differentiae for making formal definitions, and from these definitions we derive in turn certain parts, the whole being a combination of certain parts related in a certain way. These parts, as we will see, cut across the old form-content dichotomy, as well as the new art-reality dichotomy, and provide means whereby we may fill in the gaps left by these oversimple polarities.

Aristotle's definition, opening his sixth chapter, of the kind of tragedy he is analyzing, specifies its end or working power (arousing and allaying pity and fear), its object of imitation (an action that is serious, complete, and of a certain magnitude), its manner (dramatic rather than narrative), and its means (language). He then proceeds to two subsequent distinctions: the naming of parts and the analysis of their order. The parts are six: three comprise the object of imitation—plot, character, and thought; one derives from the manner—namely, spectacle; and two come from the means—diction and melody. Their order, which naturally follows the overall order of the four causes, is as I have listed them—plot, character, thought, spectacle, diction, and melody. The next chapter will take up these matters in greater detail.

Regarding the matter of terminology, there is still some ambiguity remaining in the use of our key term, *form*. *Formal cause* I have explained as shape, object of imitation, and structure. I have also more consistently referred to *form* as the whole, and I think this usage is more appropriate.

Form equals the parts and their relationship to the whole; or, better still, it is the relationship among means, manner, and object as they are governed by the end or purpose. It is in this sense, then, that we can accomplish the basic "this is there because of that" job of formal analysis.

IV

The question of whether six parts are better than two in resolving the form-content or the art-reality dilemma may be answered as follows. It is not simply that we have multiplied distinctions, although up to a point this is an improvement. It is more important that we have shifted our entire basic conception from a simple scheme of polarities to a functional process-product scheme. Because we have separated the question of form from that of content or meaning to begin with, we are free to consider it on its own terms. We need not view artistic form, that is, as a reconciliation of opposing forces—whether of packaging and thing packaged, or of meanings playing off against each other—but instead as a series of means (or parts) related in a certain way, to achieve a given artistic end (or whole). Thus we are also freed from the current static or closed-circle notion of the whole. It is not enough to say that all the parts relate to all the other parts and that the whole equals this relationship. Thinking of the whole as an end, and of the parts and devices as means, brings a sense of developmental progression and hierarchical ordering back into our analysis. Parts and devices are there in the work not just to "relate" but to do a job, to forward a purpose, and that purpose is its end or form.

What we have done, then, is to restore the concepts of end or purpose, of the object of imitation, and of the ordering of parts in relation to that end or purpose, to our theory and practice of formal criticism. In this view nothing is seen as being brought into the work from outside—everything is seen, instead, in terms of the work itself, of effectuating it as an independent thing. Naturally it uses preexisting materials—language, attitudes, ideas, representations of people and situations, and so on—but since these are regarded from the point of view of the particular end being aimed at rather than from their own point of view, there is no problem, on this level of criticism, about their being separate from form, or their implying meanings. They are indeed *materials*, and while it may be true, as we have seen, that materials do contain inherent limits as to how they may be used, it is also true that, within those limits, they are determined by and subordinated to the artistic necessities of the whole. Of course we may then go on to consider meanings and experiences, but only after we have resolved the formal question in its own way, and have moved up on that basis to another critical level.

Consequently, regarding the ability of this scheme to fill in the gaps left by the other theories, it is the lost concepts of end, object, and order which must be restored if formal criticism is to progress at all. Indeed this loss is one of the most curious phenomena in the history of criticism. It is true, of course, that criticism through the eighteenth century was full of talk about genres, decorum, and the unities, but these concepts are really distortions of Aristotle rather than Aristotelian principles. It is no wonder that the romantics—and the modernists—developed the idea of organic form in reaction against this sort of thing. But except for Coleridge, who, as R. S. Crane shows, managed to retain a sense of part-whole relationships varying as the end varied—a sense lost by Coleridge's modern followers[16]—the main drift of romantic criticism was away from the thing made to the maker. The romantics were more concerned with genius and the imagination than they were with genres, decorum, and the unities.[17] And the major Victorian critics developed the romantic concern with "poetic truth" in reaction against the threat of utilitarianism, so that by the time the modern critics were ready to turn criticism back to the poem itself, their whole bias was not only anti-eighteenth-century but also anti-Aristotelian. They set themselves the peculiar task of reinventing formal criticism without the use of formal distinctions. It is not surprising, then, that their formal terms derive from Coleridge's definition of the imagination, the emerging nineteenth-century idea of "poetic truth," and certain developing nineteenth- and twentieth-century theories of language.

Thus the New Critics' view of end or purpose is just as reductive as the eighteenth-century view: total meaning, or the embodiment of complex and concrete insights, is no more useful a tool for formal analysis than the principle of teaching and delighting mankind by imitating nature, to which it bears a strange resemblance. The concept of *specific* ends is still missing, as we have seen, from formal analysis. The New Critics' view of structure is limited either to the general principle of the tension and reconciliation of opposites, or to the tracing of certain general aesthetic or symbolic patterns, or to the curious doctrine of irrelevant texture versus logical structure, or to perfunctory remarks about character and action. Otherwise the notion of *specific* structures is also still missing. The New Critical concept of techniques is limited to a strong concern for point of view, especially in fiction (it still needs to be developed for poetry), but even here, as Schorer's famous idea of technique-as-discovery indicates, there is a typical tendency to invert Aristotle's notion of functional priorities and to see the choice of point of view as governing the end rather than the end as governing the choice of point of view. Such inversion is also characteristic, as we know, of the current view of language, which is the New Critic's focus of attention, and from which he has derived his typical terms for developing a new formal criticism.

It is one of the crucial concerns of this book, then, to explore in some detail the theoretical and practical meanings of structure and end, as well as the entire question of functional priorities, especially as it relates to techniques, theme, symbol, meaning, and so on. It does no more than touch upon questions of style, however, not because they are unimportant, but rather because I have not found anything special to say about them so far.[18]

We turn now to a discussion of structure and end.

Chapter 4

Theory of Structure and End

Having considered the general problem of form, we are now in a position to examine the particulars, especially as they relate to the analysis of fiction. As we have seen, three of Aristotle's parts—plot, character, and thought—derive from the formal cause or object of imitation, or what I am calling structure. It remains to see what these are, how they may be related to each other and to the end effect, and what such distinctions mean for the study of actual works.

I

Since there is some ambiguity, in the *Poetics* as well as in subsequent discussions, concerning the meaning of the ostensibly similar terms *plot*, *fable*, *action*, and *fortune*, let us begin here. Plot, most simply and basically, is the sequence of incidents or external occurrences, that which can serve as the basis of an outline or summary. Fable or action can mean the same thing. It is much more useful, however, and more in accord with Aristotle's overall treatment, to use plot or fable or action to refer not only to the mere sequence of incidents but also to the *composite of causes* making the action what it is—that is to say, fortune, character, and thought.[1] Thus the object of imitation is an action or fable or plot, and its three parts are fortune, character, and thought. Plot, then, equals the sequence of incidents plus its causes, which is not the same thing at all as an outline or summary, for it includes the why and the how as well as the what.

The composite of causes making the action what it is comes from people in situations. People being affected by, and in turn reacting to, situations, bring any line of action into being. Let us refer to situations as *fortune*, which Aristotle also sometimes calls *plot* in the narrower sense and which includes a person's circumstances in relation to nature and society: his physical environment, his goods, honor, status, reputation, relation to others, loved ones, health, well-being—anything which can impinge upon him from without, or beyond his will. Fortune is revealed in what happens to his hopes and plans—success or failure—and to him as a result—happiness or misery.

How fortune affects him, and how he reacts to it, will be determined by the kind of person he is, for different people react differently, of course, to similar circumstances. The kind of person he is may be defined in terms of his thought and character. Now *thought* in the *Poetics* is commonly interpreted to mean theme. Northrop Frye, who is often considered a neo-Aristotelian and is fond of lending authority to his use of Aristotelian terms by transliterating them directly from the Greek, as in *mythos* (plot), *ethos* (character), and *dianoia* (thought), says: "The best translation of *dianoia* is, perhaps, 'theme', and literature with this ideal or conceptual interest may be called thematic."[2] But when this term is thus seen as distinct from plot instead of as one of the three elements which constitute the action—which are, indeed, its basic causal ingredients—it is being wrenched out of its Aristotelian context. In the *Poetics* the action is the principal part of the whole, and plot, character, and thought are parts of the action, organized in a certain order of importance in relation to the end effect. Thought therefore cannot be considered as separate from either the plot or the action as a whole. Most assuredly it cannot be defined as theme or conceptual content, since this notion is not anywhere a part of Aristotle's scheme.

Aristotle himself defines *thought* as "the faculty of saying what is possible and pertinent in given circumstances," and he says it "is found where something is proved to be or not to be, or a general maxim is enunciated" (*Poetics*, chapter 6, Butcher translation). Since this clearly refers to the people in the play, the best translation would seem to be "the conception of things entertained by the protagonist"—his state of mind, attitudes, knowledge, reasonings, emotions, outlook, temperament, and beliefs; and it may be naive or sophisticated, sanguine or phlegmatic, and the like. Thought is revealed either omnisciently, as in many novels, or in what the person says when stating a general proposition, arguing a particular point, or explaining his view of a situation. Clearly a person's reaction to things is in part determined by what he thinks of them, how he sees them.

His reaction is also determined in part by what he wants or would like to accomplish and his determination in pursuing it. *Character*, therefore, refers to his goals and purposes, his motives, habits, behavior, what he seeks or avoids, and his willpower in setting himself to achieve them; and it may be moral or immoral, strong or weak, noble or base, good or bad, sympathetic or unsympathetic, complete or incomplete, mature or immature, and so on. Character is revealed when he decides voluntarily to pursue or abandon a course of action, and in whether he can indeed put his decision into effect, where that is up to him.

Although thought and character are both internal parts, having to do with the traits of a person, they ought not to be confused with one another. Thought is revealed, as we have said, when a person thinks, makes statements, or argues, while character is revealed when he makes choices and decides upon a course of action. And since these may or may not be consistent with one another, they are not the same but are rather two different things. A man may be able to distinguish between right and wrong, for example, but still may choose the wrong—a distinction which is as significant in analyzing fiction as it is in our law courts, for it is the basis of determining whether a man may be held responsible for his acts; and responsibility, as we shall see, is one of the crucial factors in formal analysis.

So much for the parts of an action; next is a consideration of how they may be related to one another. A plot for Aristotle is a sequence of incidents; it is furthermore a *causal* sequence; it is, finally, a *unified* sequence. It is a causal sequence in that it is bound by human necessity or probability. That is to say, the action evolves out of its données, which involve a person with certain traits of thought and character, in a certain situation. In terms of these factors, what evolves, as the action goes from incident to incident, must *follow* what went before in regard to what is likely or inevitable. Place a coward in battle, and he cannot be expected, without adequate preparation, to commit heroic deeds. Thus Aristotle counsels against the use in a tragedy of a deus ex machina, an incident which resolves the action but which does not follow from what went before. A causal sequence then is a series of linked or interlocking incidents, each one arising from what went before and giving rise in turn to what comes after.

This sequence is unified, first, in the sense that it is a completed whole, that it has a beginning, middle, and an end. In other words as it is not simply a series of incidents but a causal sequence bound by necessity or probability, so too is it not simply the story of someone from birth to death but a sequence which raises and resolves a particular issue or problem. That is why the making of plots is the distinctive mark of the poet, and that is why poetry is more philosophical than history. The beginning of the plot is where the problem to be resolved is first raised, the middle constitutes the search for a solution, and the end is where the problem is resolved.

There may be antecedent causes before the beginning, but these will be latent until some initiating factor enters the picture and starts things moving. Sophocles opens his *Oedipus Rex* at the beginning of the plot, which is the oracle's demand that the slayer of the former king be punished: this is the issue around which the action revolves. Since the murder occurred many years ago, however, and as many things preceded and resulted from that act, there are many latent causes going as far back as Oedipus's birth itself, if not before. But the action of the play cannot be brought into being—the latent cannot be made manifest—until the oracle demands retribution, and that is therefore the beginning.

By the same token there may be things which we might be curious about or which occur after the ending, but which do not relate specifically to that problem raised by the plot. Sophocles, indeed, wrote a sequel to *Oedipus Rex* itself, and such things are common without destroying the concept of a completed whole. The ending does not need to resolve *all* of the issues in a person's life but only those which are relevant to the particular issue at hand.

The sequence is unified, secondly, in the sense that the raising and resolving of this issue will be determined principally by one of the three causal ingredients of the plot—whether fortune, character, or thought—and subordinately or mediately by the other two. When Aristotle says that the plot is the main part or the soul of tragedy, he means that everything turns primarily upon a change in fortune for the protagonist from good to bad, with character and thought being subordinate. His reasoning is that you cannot achieve the proper tragic effect—pity and fear—without this change in fortune, but that you can produce it—although poorly, to be sure—without thought and character. That is to say, if pity is aroused by the sight of someone suffering undeserved misfortune, then the primary problem of the poet in unifying his action will be to make sure that it carries his protagonist from good to bad fortune, fortune being defined as what happens to him rather than simply what he wants or does or thinks. Furthermore, if fear results when this person is someone like us—that is, his character is neither conspicuously better nor worse than aver-

age, so that we can identify with him, and consequently feel sympathetically upset when misfortune comes to him—the production of this
emotion by means of this cause is naturally secondary, since *this* kind of
fear depends upon *this* kind of pity being aroused beforehand. Thus, the
issue in *Oedipus* being retribution, the principal part is fortune. The beginning raises this issue, the middle develops it, and the ending resolves it.

There are many sorts of issues, however, and many kinds of plot, and
so thought or character may just as well be the principal part as fortune.
E. M. Forster gave currency to the misconception that Aristotle may
have known about Greek drama but could not have known much about
modern fiction, which has character as its principal part. R. S. Crane has
said what needs to be said on this question, so I will be brief.[3] Although
E. M. Forster distinguishes between story and plot, in that the former is
a mere sequence of incidents, while the latter is a *causal* sequence, he
still regards plot as apart from character and thought and as appealing
to more primitive interests. Interest in character—that is, in motivation
and psychology—is more sophisticated, and so these two interests vie
with one another. There is a conflict, in other words, between character
and plot, since interest in one detracts from interest in the other.

Needless to say, this has nothing to do with what Aristotle is saying.
It is no more the case that all plots have fortune as their principal part
than that they have character. As Crane points out, there may be plots
of fortune, plots of character, and plots of thought, depending upon
what the issue is, how it is resolved, and in relation to what end effect.
It is the task of the next chapter to explore these possibilities in some
detail.

The sequence of incidents is unified, thirdly, in two related senses:
that the action has a certain magnitude or size and that it is either static
or dynamic. Since these distinctions will be treated further in chapter 9,
it is necessary here only to suggest what is involved.

The size of the action does not refer simply to the number of pages
occupied in its telling but rather to the nature and number of its units.
An action may involve but a single scene, for example, or two or more
scenes, or two or more groups of scenes.

The distinction between a static or dynamic action does not refer
simply to whether there is a perceptible passage of time in the story or
not. It refers instead to whether the protagonist undergoes a change or
not, and this may be in fortune, character, or thought. In a static action

one may not properly speak of an issue being raised and resolved so much as its being revealed, completeness here being more a matter of the structure of revelation than of resolution.

II

Thus far we have been talking about unity in a material sense only, the unity of a sequence of incidents. To discuss unity in a more fully formal sense, we must concern ourselves further with the fashion in which the author's desire to move the reader's ideas and emotions in certain specific ways serves as the ultimate governing principle of the shape of the plot. It is possible for any given material sequence of incidents to be conceived of in various ways—as serious, for example, or funny, or ironic, or what have you. The way it appears meant to be taken, then, is its final cause— what Aristotle calls, in relation to tragedy, pity, fear, and catharsis.[4]

Several misconceptions should be cleared away at this point. To say that the end effect is the ultimate governing principle is not to say, as we have seen, that the author *begins* the compositional process with this effect in mind. Poe, in his analysis of how he wrote "The Raven," although otherwise cogent from a formal point of view, creates a dangerous misapprehension when he says he began with the impression he wanted to produce, and then worked backward to the situation which would best produce it.[5] It is much more plausible to assume, it seems to me, that the writer actually begins with a story or a hint of a story which he wants to tell. Then, as he works it out, it becomes clear to him how he wants it to be taken, and it is then and only then that his desire to create a certain impression takes over and functions as a final cause in relation to his materials. This is not to say, however, that he can*not* begin with his end effect if it works out that way: it is merely to point out that the concept of functional priorities varies as the subject of discussion varies, and that order of composition and order of parts are not the same subject.

Another misconception is that the Aristotelian or neo-Aristotelian notion of end effect is monistic, or at best dualistic, in saying that the final cause of literature is to arouse our emotions, or to give pleasure, or that there are two ends—the mimetic and didactic.[6] Elder Olson has even divided mimetic plots into the comic, the serious, and the sympathetic or antipathetic; and he sees serious plots as falling into the tragic and the punitive, and comic plots into the lout-comic and the rogue-comic.[7] In spite of the Chicagoans' repeated protestations to the contrary, and in spite of their constant effort to deal functionally with independent variables,[8] it is this sort of thing which has laid them open to the charge of returning to the old mechanical genre criticism which died a merciful death in the eighteenth century.

To arouse emotions or give pleasure is only a general end (the artist's aim is always to create "beauty" or to suit his means to his end); and if the Chicagoans had left it at that, they would not have advanced at all beyond either the neoclassical prescription to teach and delight, the romantic distinction between pleasure as the end of literature and truth as the end of science (although Coleridge, we recall, said *primary* end, leaving truth as a secondary end in literature and pleasure as a secondary end in science),[9] or the New Critical notion that to embody insight is the end of poetry. The point is that each work, whether mimetic or didactic, generates its own *specific* emotions, pleasures, or moving powers; and it is to these that the formal critic must direct his attention as he tries to define the form of that work.

These may be discussed on two levels, as one may talk of aesthetic emotions or of moral emotions.[10] By aesthetic emotions I mean those feelings of expectation, surprise, and fulfillment which the unified development, variation, and completion of an action embodied in any work of fiction—indeed of any structure whatever in any sort of work—naturally arouse in us. Thus it is an important formal feature of any good plot to move us to anticipate certain things; to mislead us into expecting the wrong things; but to induce us to believe, upon looking back, that the way things actually turn out, however surprising, was nevertheless adequately prepared for and is the only truly appropriate outcome. This it does, of course, by setting up various possible lines of development—possible, that is, in terms of human probability or necessity—and while appearing to favor one, in fact favoring another, which becomes clear only as the possibilities gradually diminish and the resolution approaches, and which should not become entirely clear until the last possible moment.

We spoke of a unified causal sequence being motivated by its données, developing them and exhausting them. Thus the aesthetic emotions are governed by the range of possibilities set up at the beginning, and by the gradual narrowing of this range as the plot proceeds through the middle, until the final remaining possibility has been reached and settled at the end. This effect is a result of the fact that, in literature as in life, choices have consequences, and each choice leaves one facing a narrower range of possibilities than the last.

A unified plot uses itself up, as it were, and is organic in the sense that it does so reflexively and from within. Human probability and necessity, as the principle in terms of which the causes of the action operate and are understood, are in this sense relative to the internal structure of the work itself. In other senses, however, they are absolute in being derived from reality. More will be said on this point in chapter 10.

At any rate the meaning of *catharsis* on this level is that a sequence of aesthetic emotions has been aroused and allayed—a set of possibilities has been generated, explored, and exhausted—or more properly, *catharsis* refers to the end result of depletion. We feel, within the framework of the plot, that nothing more remains to be done. This is what is meant by *pleasure*, and perhaps it is what is meant by *aesthetic distance* (this latter is additionally a somewhat more complex concept). But I am not sure it also means what it is often taken to mean, especially by those who see the *Poetics* as an "answer" to Plato's attack on poetry in book 10 of *The Republic*—namely that the catharsis of poetry drains off in symbolic form the hostilities, aggressions, and frustrations of men, and leaves them thereby more reconciled to the conditions of life and perhaps of society. Surely the catharsis experienced by men in relation to a work of art refers more to that experience than to how they behave in real life, and may or may not have beneficial effects upon their other experiences. If art indeed had such potency, the world would have been cured of its ills long since. All we may justifiably say is that certain tensions are resolved, although they are not simply of the semantic sort, the reconciliation of opposing meanings, discussed by the New Critics; and the reader's feelings, in so far as they have been aroused by the work, are at rest. What remains afterwards is more a matter of individual and social pathology than of formal criticism.

III

The second level regarding a work's moving powers concerns the moral emotions, by which I mean whether the reader is made to like or dislike the people in the story, and consequently which outcomes for them he hopes for and which he fears—and then, whether he feels, in these terms, that the ultimate outcome is justified or not. These emotions are of course generated in terms of the sequence of aesthetic emotions we have just been speaking of; they will be more effective in proportion as the aesthetic emotions are effective; and so they are intimately intertwined with them. But they are nevertheless distinct: the aesthetic emotions are abstract, general, and formal, in the sense of being discussable apart from content, whereas, in this connection, the moral emotions are concrete, particular, and material, in the sense that it is difficult to discuss them apart from individual cases. We can, moreover, have a unified plot, albeit not a very significant one, without many moral emotions coming into play, but we cannot have one without the aesthetic emotions being exercised. Finally it is quite possible, as we shall see, to finish reading a work feeling a sense of aesthetic completion, while at the same time feeling morally unsatisfied.

Thus these two levels are sufficiently distinguishable. We might say that the aesthetic powers of the work lead us into expectations, while its moral powers lead us into hopes and fears. Both effects derive from the operations of human probability and necessity, but the aesthetic emotions are governed more by the logical aspect of probability and necessity in forming a sequence, while the moral emotions are governed more by the human aspect of probability and necessity in being concerned with people in situations. Aesthetic emotions are passive, more a matter of being worked on, while moral emotions are active, more a matter of being involved. This distinction is not, however, to be confused with the old form-content distinction which we have already repudiated: we are talking, whether of aesthetic or moral emotions, about how the artistic effect is produced; and so we are still talking about form and form only. But perhaps this distinction *is* what Forster actually meant when he said that there is a primitive what-happens-next interest, and then there is a sophisticated interest in motivation and psychology. But he need not have set it up as plot vs. character, for the moral emotions, as we shall see, are involved in the plot as a whole—in fortune and thought as well as in character.

Lest we minimize this "liking" and "disliking" issue as being merely a matter of good guys and bad guys, sufficient only for the analysis of popular romances, adventure stories, westerns, and science-fiction stories, let me summarize and explain Crane's principles for assessing the moral emotions of any given plot. We must consider three things, he says, and these are of course parallel to the three causal ingredients of a plot: character, fortune, and thought. The first question is what we are made to think of the moral character and deserts of the protagonist, and consequently whether we wish for him either good or ill. The second is whether we are made to think of the events which befall or seem likely to befall him as having or promising either painful or pleasurable consequences for him, and whether these consequences seem permanent or only temporary. The third is whether we are made to think he acts in knowledge of what he is doing, and therefore whether he is to be held responsible for his actions. "The form of a given plot," Crane concludes, "is a function of the particular correlation among these three variables which the completed work is calculated to establish, consistently and progressively, in our minds."[11]

While we can discuss such principles and even such classes as mimetic and didactic, comic and serious, and so on, it can be seen from this account that the actual working power of any given plot can be specifically defined only by means of a detailed analysis of its sequence of incidents and in terms of its three causal ingredients. Accordingly this part of formal criticism—because it is very painstaking, because it involves a careful assessment of the whole work as it unfolds in progressive stages, and because it is consequently the most liable to find what is in that work only—is extremely difficult to explain, to teach to students, and to accomplish. Crane's analysis of *Tom Jones* is very probably one of the few really detailed pieces of strictly formal criticism of an extended work that we have. Yet, since such criticism provides us with the very principle concerning end effect which we need in order to go back over the work and explain the functioning of its parts in relation to each other and the whole, it is the very fulcrum upon which formal analysis turns. It is fatally easy to analyze a plot structure apart from a consideration of those moving powers which make it a unified whole, and I have not always avoided this trap myself; but without such consideration formal analysis remains indeed mechanical and lifeless.

The relation of moral emotions to catharsis requires comment here. We have seen that one sense of *catharsis* refers to the aesthetic emotions, to the resolving of the plot issue per se. In this sense it does not matter *how* the issue is resolved, so long as it is resolved. The feeling of completion comes, on this level, from the mere playing out of the probabilities. In relation to the moral emotions, however, it does matter how the issue is resolved, and catharsis on this level, as I have suggested, may or may not result, even if it does result on the aesthetic level. To say that the end of literature is pleasure or satisfaction, then, is to say very little if it fails to account for this distinction.

Catharsis of the moral emotions results when we are made to feel, after experiencing the work as it is organized by its plot, that the outcome, however complete it may make the action, is *also*, within its context and under its specific circumstances, acceptable, just, and satisfying in human terms. It is what may be meant by the old idea of poetic justice, and it means simply that what happens to the protagonist at the resolution is in some way deserved. The general principles are, as Aristotle said for tragedy, not to have a merely good man passing from good to bad fortune, or a bad man from bad to good fortune.

It is not always simple in practice, however, as we know from Aristotle's analysis of the tragic emotions, for catharsis on this level may be either direct or indirect. If a good man has good fortune, or a bad man has bad fortune, we feel that the ending is satisfying in and of itself. If, however, a good man has bad fortune, or a bad man has good fortune, then other factors must be called into play, for the ending will not be satisfying in and of itself. Thus tragic catharsis is indirect, and the other factors which must be called into play, it seems to me, are that, although the protagonist is at least partially responsible for bringing about the catastrophe, he is not completely responsible since he acts in the earlier portions of the plot without full knowledge of all the relevant facts; and that he acts in terms of motives which, although they seem mistaken at the end, seemed justified at the time; contrariwise, although he wishes to mend his ways when he does come to a more correct view of things, the fact that he finds out too late prevents him from reversing his impending doom. Thus his anguish, and ours, is an exquisite one, and it is this effect which gives to this sort of tragedy its special flavor. We feel on the one hand that we would like him to escape his doom, for he is, after all, well-intentioned; but we also feel that he has, after all, brought it down on himself, and therefore that he must suffer the consequences.

That he should be neither markedly better nor worse than we are (as Aristotle says) and that his mistake should result from an excess of pride leading to an error of judgment rather than from any viciousness of character, are factors contributing to this mixed effect. Although we deplore his error, we nevertheless wish him well in the long run; yet, although we sorrow at the outcome, we nevertheless see that he did create real harm and must pay the price. Much depends upon his ability to see the truth at last and repent, and much depends upon his seeing it too late. For what could be more tragically moving than for a basically good man to have done harm, and to have been blind or stubborn about it for too long, and then to find it out and repent just after it could have done any good?

The mistake Arthur Miller makes in *The Death of a Salesman*, it seems to me, although he is correct in claiming that modern Aristotelian tragedy can be written in terms of ordinary men rather than kings and princes, is in not seeing that a certain nobility of thought and character is much more important than the protagonist's supposed high station in life.[12] The tragic hero must be able ultimately to recognize his error and he must be able to repent, neither of which Willy Loman can do. Indeed, when he is confronted with the truth by Biff in the restaurant scene and again toward the end, he can only wince, evade, and deny. The catharsis of this play, whatever it is, therefore cannot be of the kind Aristotle had in mind.

And if moral catharsis is attempted, the same sort of principle regarding mixed effect must be applied to any plot whose ending is not satisfying as such.

It should also be remarked that when we talk in this fashion about the effect of the plot on the audience, we are not concerned with whether the supposed effect is actually *felt* by a given audience. This is an empirical question, as W. K. Wimsatt and Monroe C. Beardsley say in their essay on the affective fallacy, and it involves too many extra-artistic and irrelevant variables. It is not the job of formal criticism to discuss the nature, composition, education, and mood of any particular audience at any particular time. It is, however, a perfectly legitimate critical question, although the relation between the work and the reader calls for a different approach. But at this point we are verging on other critical questions, some of which, such as vision and meaning, will be taken up in greater detail in the second part of this book.

IV

We turn, finally, to the mimetic-didactic distinction, which we may phrase as follows: either the plot governs the work, or it does not. If it does, then the work is mimetic—that is, imitative, or organized by and for the representation of a human action for its own sake and for the sake of its moving powers (*imitative* and *representation* do *not* mean here "true to life" or "realistic" but rather an "imagined human action" of any sort, however fantastic: recall that imitation means for Aristotle a form imposed upon some matter which does not naturally take that form, and in this case what is imitated is not nature or life but an imagined action which may exist only in the writer's head). If, on the other hand, the plot does not govern the work, then that work is didactic, that is, "educative," or organized by and for an idea.

By *plot* here I mean the composite of fortune, character, and thought, and the sequence of incidents it gives rise to, plus the moving powers of this action. By *governs* I mean that everything done in the work on the formal level—the way in which the action is conceived, organized, rendered, and embodied, including structure, techniques, and style—is explainable, in formal terms, in relation to the end of maximizing the action and its moving powers. And by *explainable* I mean according to the tests of completeness, economy, and coherence.

As a consequence the plot in mimetic work must be unified, complete, and satisfying. And it must, furthermore, be self-contained in that the persons and incidents must refer primarily to themselves rather than to larger classes or other things. That is to say, the audience must be made to respond to them on a literal and individual level, as if they were actual persons and incidents, albeit imitated or imagined or fantastic.

A plot in a didactic work, on the other hand, may be unified and complete, or it may not. If it is not, then the identification is more easily made, for a work whose plot is not unified and complete cannot by definition be mimetic: it is either badly done, or it is didactic. If its plot is not its organizing principle, either it may not have such a principle, or it may have one of another sort.

The problem is made more difficult if the plot *is* unified and complete. If it is not *satisfying*, however, then it still cannot be mimetic. George Orwell's 1984, for example, presents us with a unified and complete action, but its ending leaves us outraged, depressed, and dissatisfied; therefore we cannot say that its plot is presented for its own sake. It may resolve our aesthetic emotions, but it fails to resolve our moral feelings. In lacking moral catharsis, then, it lacks a dimension of completeness required in the definition of mimetic works.

But a plot may be unified, complete, and satisfying, and still not be mimetic if it is not self-contained, if the persons and incidents do not refer primarily to themselves but rather to larger classes or other things.

It is clear that didactic plots may share many traits with mimetic plots, and thus that differentiation is not simple or automatic. In principle, however, it merely takes a denial of any one of the traits of a mimetic plot for an action to be didactic: mimetic plots require a certain set of traits, while the number of traits required of a didactic plot is variable. I hope it is evident that when I say "required" I am not prescribing anything about literary works, but rather that I am trying to construct usable definitions to serve as hypotheses for explaining and analyzing the forms of works, whatever these forms may be. The essential principle remains: in a mimetic work the plot explains the work on a formal level in and of itself, while in a didactic work it does not; the plot in a didactic work points beyond itself to some other end, and this other end in turn is required to provide a formal explanation of the work. The traits specified in my definitions are merely ways of making this distinction in practice.

Several misconceptions about this distinction may be cleared away, however, before we conclude this chapter. I have already spoken of the mistaken idea that *mimetic* and *didatic* leave us with only two classes into which to place the variety of literary works. Another misconception is that mimetic plots are naive, primitive, and without ideas, and hence lack seriousness, depth, and significance. This notion is related to Forster's distinction between plot and character, but I have already shown how one may think of plot in more than what-happens-next terms. It is also related to the distinction between aesthetic and moral emotions, but significant mimetic plots will have both nevertheless. It is simply not the case that mimetic plots lack psychological, moral, and philosophical interest: to say that didactic plots are organized by and for an idea is not to say that mimetic plots lack ideas. It is to say that the *relationship* between action and idea can vary: a mimetic plot may be full of ideas, and indeed the good ones are, but in terms of formal analysis its ideas are parts of and subordinate to the plot as a whole, while in a didactic plot the action is subordinate to the ideas. Since this distinction refers to such a relationship and not to elements per se, it is a misuse of the terms to say that such and such a work has a didactic passage or a mimetic section. These terms refer to unifying principles and not to materials.

The opposite misconception is that didactic works are inferior because they are preachy, obvious, and abstract, as if to say that they neglect aesthetic emotions in favor of the moral ones. Effective didactic plots will embody both nevertheless: as I have said, moral emotions are most effective when the aesthetic ones are well done, and mimetic plots will contain moral emotions as well. There is no necessary connection between mimetic and didactic and matters of quality and judgment. There is no reason in the world why a work cannot be vivid, concrete, implicit, dramatic, and interesting, and still be didactic. Indeed a didactic work can and should be as exciting to read as a mimetic work; the fact that some of them are not simply shows that writing a good didactic work may be even harder than writing a good mimetic one.

We all know that modern criticism prefers symbolism to allegory, for example, because the idea in a symbol is implicit, while in allegory the image is chosen to suit the idea. This distinction arises from the modern version of the organic-form theory, which says the writer does not begin with a knowledge of what he wants to say, but instead discovers it and leaves it implicit as he writes. As I have shown that this notion is not relevant to the concept of end effect in general, I must point out here that it is also not relevant to the particular concept of mimetic and didactic. A writer may begin without knowing what his final product is to be, or he may begin by knowing it; in either case he may produce either a mimetic or didactic work. To say that the action is subordinate to the idea is to point to a certain kind of formal relationship and not to the fact that the writer began with an idea and then looked around for an action to fit it. As with a mimetic work, he may have begun with the action and only gradually realized what he wanted to make of it. Nor need this realization have been conscious or verbal, so long as it operates in the making of the finished product.

There is, finally, the notion voiced by Virginia Woolf that a didactic work is inferior because it aims at having us *do* something: take steps or write a check. True literature, she suggests in Bloomsbury fashion, presents reality for contemplation.[13] It is correct that a didactic work is not reflexive, that it points to something beyond itself, but what it points to may be an idea and not necessarily steps to take. I do not see why an idea cannot be as much presented for contemplation as a plot, nor do I see why a mimetic plot cannot have an actual impact on our lives. For the empirical effect of a work upon the audience, as I have said, is not a formal question. It may be true that, formally considered, some kinds of didactic work are in fact propagandistic, but it is not necessarily true for all didactic works. Nor, even if they are propagandistic, do I see why this makes them necessarily bad.

We turn in the next two chapters, then, from theory to application, to a further examination in some detail and in a practical way of the problems of structure and end.

Chapter 5

Forms of the Plot

In defining the form of a plot, we must have terms and distinctions for differentiating its structure and end effect from those of other plots. To do this, we must have at our disposal a set of alternative hypotheses indicating the various possibilities concerning structures and end effects. We must avoid, that is, any theory which proposes only a single sort of form, or any merely general notion, or one which does so in terms which decide upon the answers in advance and which does not allow for logical testing.

The bases of our definitions, then, will rest upon a determination of the unifying or principal part of the action, as well as upon an analysis of the sequence of aesthetic-moral emotions aroused in the reader. Since any one of the parts of an action may serve as the principal part, we may have, as we have seen, plots of fortune, plots of character, and plots of thought. Within these categories, we may make further distinctions as to whether the protagonist's situation is better or worse at the end, whether he is responsible and sympathetic or not, and how this combination of factors is calculated to affect our feelings. Except for the initial division, which seems to be exhaustive, there is no reason to consider any of my definitions as final or any of my groups as complete. They are intended to be suggestive, exemplary, and heuristic merely, and are to be used as beginning points of formal analysis rather than as genre-boxes to pack away works in.

In order to keep these variables within control, I have limited myself largely to actions which involve a change and hence are dynamic, as well as generally to those which are unified, complete, satisfying, and reflexive, and hence which are mimetic. I have also felt free, since plots as such are plots wherever they may be found, to refer indifferently at this level to plays as well as stories and novels. Certain practical and less neat problems of structure and end will be taken up at the conclusion of this chapter; the mimetic-didactic problem will be explored further in the following chapter; and static actions will be discussed in chapter 9.

I

Before considering a set of alternative hypotheses for defining the form of a given plot, we must establish the procedure for doing so. Since the unity of an action will naturally revolve around the main character or characters, the first question to ask is: who is the protagonist? The protagonist is the one without whom the structure of the action would cease to function; the one upon whom the causes of the action fall, and from whom its consequences flow; the one who undergoes the major change; the one whose career serves as the chief focus of interest; the one around whom all else in the plot revolves. Sometimes it is a single person, as in *Hamlet*; sometimes it is a pair, as in *Romeo and Juliet*; and sometimes it is a group, as in *The Nigger of the "Narcissus."* Even if it is a pair or group, however, the point is that what happens to one happens to both or all, and so dual or multiple protagonists function ultimately as the collective focus of attention, just as a single protagonist does. (It is not necessary here, as is frequently done, to go on to define the "antagonist," since this is a much more nebulous term and is entirely irrelevant in itself, for a definition of unity.)

Sometimes it is obvious who the protagonist is, as in *King Lear* or *Oedipus Rex*, and sometimes it is not, as in *The Scarlet Letter*, *War and Peace*, *Daisy Miller*, *All the King's Men*, or *The Caine Mutiny*; such cases as these latter require some close reasoning. Sometimes it is the person whose name appears in the title, as in *Tom Jones* or *Oliver Twist*, and sometimes it is not, as in *Julius Caesar* and *Moby-Dick* (I remember an announcement for a television performance of *Moby-Dick* years ago which said that Orson Welles would star in the "title role"!).

The second set of questions is: what is his character, and how do we respond to it? What is his fortune, and do we fear it will become worse, and hope it will become better, or vice versa? And what is his thought, and do we feel he is sufficiently aware of the facts of the situation and the consequences of his behavior to be held responsible for what he does and undergoes?

Since, in any well-organized plot, these three parts—either changing or remaining constant—are inextricably interwoven, one serving as material to another, or as its cause, or as its occasion, or as its sign or manifestation, we must take care not to confuse them. Although they are thus related, they are nonetheless distinct. The protagonist's suicide, for example, as the culmination of a plot, may represent a noble character's decision to atone for the evil he has unwittingly done and the misfortunes he has caused to fall on himself or others, as in *Othello*; or it may represent the last despairing gesture of a protagonist whose character is no longer sufficient to cope with the problems of his life, as in *The Seagull*. And the difference lies in the latitude of choice we think he has in deciding to live or to die. Or a person's goals (character) may indeed be related to his conceptions (thought), and a change in the latter may cause a change in the former, as in *Great Expectations*; but they may also change independently or even in different directions, as when Bernick in *The Pillars of the Community* admits his hypocrisy in private long before he decides to do anything about it publicly. Or again, a person may have a certain goal (character), and yet may be prevented from reaching it because of circumstances beyond his control (fortune), as when Prewitt in *From Here to Eternity* is destroyed by the group within which he has attempted to preserve some measure of personal autonomy. If a person's goal, however, refers to the attainment of some such moral quality, and if his success or failure in this depends upon his own willpower, patience, and self-confidence, as in "The Secret Sharer," rather than upon circumstances, then it is a question of character and not of fortune. More will be said about such problems of interrelatedness in the latter portions of this chapter.

The third question is: not only what these three parts are, but also which is the principal part and how are the other two related to it? This is a matter of what we take the main issue of the plot to be, and how it it resolved. If this issue and its resolution, in terms both of the structure of the action and of our aesthetic-moral emotions, depend upon whether the protagonist succeeds or fails in gaining something outside himself, and if this depends ultimately upon external circumstances rather than upon his will or knowledge, then the principal part is fortune. If the main issue depends upon whether what he thinks and believes is adequate or not, regardless of his circumstances and goals, and if this depends ultimately upon his insight or discovery, then the principal part is thought. Finally, if the main issue depends upon whether he will be able to make the decision called for or not, and if this depends ultimately upon himself rather than upon circumstances or knowledge, then the principal part is character.

In a dynamic plot, it is the principal part which, by definition, undergoes the main change. But if one or both of the other parts also involve a change, as is often the case, we must determine which is the main change and how the others are related to that change. It is not necessarily the case, in other words, that any change indicates what the principal part is, just as it is not necessarily the case that, because we have located a clear causal factor, we have identified the principal part. Analysis of structure in these terms is not so mechanical as that, but rather requires a constantly developing sense of relationships. To locate the main part is not to rule out the presence of other necessary parts; to locate a necessary part is not the same as finding the main part.

We need to appreciate the difference, that is, between necessary and sufficient causes, and how they may be related. If the main change is in character, it may have depended upon antecedent changes in fortune and thought; but it is nevertheless only character, in combination with fortune and thought, which is both necessary and sufficient to resolve the plot, while fortune and thought are necessary merely. We must always think in terms of a complex of causes, then, and we must see this complex as an unfolding and cumulative sequence. One way of looking at the matter is to start at the end and think backwards to the beginning, thereby gaining an effective overall view of the whole, the parts, and their relationships. And it is a fair rule-of-thumb that the final or culminating change is most likely the main one because it is the resolving one—but not necessarily, and we must still test it against the other two possibilities. The best rule-of-thumb, therefore, is that all three should be tossed about in one's mind in the effort to see which actually includes and explains more, and in the most coherent and economical way.

Thus we will define our alternative possibilities in the following manner: we ask first whether the major change is in fortune, character, or thought, and derive therefrom our three main categories; we ask further, within each category, whether the particular change is from a better to a worse state or vice versa; and we ask finally how the remaining two factors are related as material to this end. We will then attempt to define the distinctive power of each type "to move our feelings powerfully and pleasurably in a certain definite way," as R. S. Crane says.[1] This last is not easy to do without going into the details of each plot; but, since such detail would enlarge an already sizable chapter beyond reasonable bounds, we must content ourselves with the barest of hints and suggestions regarding the general range of possibilities. It is sufficiently clear, as we have seen, that a good man achieving good fortune, a bad man achieving good fortune, a good man suffering bad fortune, and a bad man undergoing bad fortune, for example, produce different effects and therefore comprise different kinds of plots.

In the light of the foregoing distinctions and in relation to these variables, let us see what kinds of plots will emerge.

II

PLOTS OF FORTUNE

The action plot. The first and most primitive type of plot under this heading is also, I daresay, the most common in terms of the reading public as a whole. The primary and often the sole interest lies in what happens next, with character and thought being portrayed minimally in terms of the bare necessities required to forward the action. That is to say, we rarely if ever become involved here in any serious moral or intellectual issue; nor does the outcome have any far-reaching consequences for the protagonist, leaving him free to start all over again, it may be, in a sequel (not all sequels indicate action plots, however); and the pleasures we experience are almost wholly those of suspense, expectation, and surprise, since the plot is organized around a basic puzzle-and-solution cycle. There is a gangster to track down, a murderer to discover and apprehend, a treasure to be gotten, or a planet to be reached.

Needless to say, this resembles the idea of plot which E. M. Forster called *plot* in opposition to *character*, and it is the sort which depends more upon what I have called aesthetic than moral emotions. Examples are found most frequently in those classes of fiction called adventure, detective, western, and science fiction.[2] This is not to say, however, that the action plot need necessarily be a subliterary form, since there are many respectable examples which have deservedly become classics of their kind: the novels of R. L. Stevenson, the stories of Sir Arthur Conan Doyle, the mysteries of Wilkie Collins, the work of Ray Bradbury.

The pathetic plot. Here we have a sympathetic protagonist who undergoes misfortune through no particular fault of his own, and hence this type is primarily a plot of suffering. It is frequently the case that his will is in some way weak and his thought naive and deficient. I call it "pathetic" since our long-range fears for him actually materialize, being scarcely alleviated by sporadic and intermittent short-range hopes, resulting ultimately in sheer pity for his suffering. Moral catharsis would depend upon how far we feel that, although he does not actively bring about his own misfortunes, he is nevertheless ultimately self-defeating through weakness of will and naiveté of temperament. It would also depend upon how far we feel that the causes of these deficiencies, as well as the causes of the world's harshness, are in nature rather than society per se.

Although Thomas Hardy, for example, dwells in *Tess of the d'Urbervilles* upon the shameful inadequacy of this heroine's home and school background as a cause of her unfortunate career, he subordinates and absorbs this factor into an overall sense of the rather supine quality of her determination, the irresistible workings of nature's fecund processes, and the fact that she had, after all, murdered her unwelcome lover. This combination is sufficient to produce the desired emotional effect at the end when she is arrested and executed.

Such a plot seems indeed a favorite of those modern or protomodern works concerned with the antiheroic, such as *Tess, The Three Sisters, Death of a Salesman, A Streetcar Named Desire, From Here to Eternity, Maggie: A Girl of the Streets,* and *A Farewell to Arms,* where a brooding sense of human frailty and futility pervades the whole, leaving one with a feeling of pity, sorrow, and loss in the face of the inscrutable steamroller of circumstances crushing the mewling kitten of human hopes. Sometimes, however, a certain ambiguity lingers over these works, as when we are not sure whether it is in fact society or nature which has done the protagonist in. If it is society, then we are not left with the melancholy satisfaction of that's-the-way-things-are, but rather with a disturbing sense of what's-to-be-done. We shall revisit this problem when we come later to distinguish between the universal and the general and to discuss Hemingway in subsequent chapters.

The tragic plot. If, however, a sympathetic protagonist has also strength of will in addition to a certain degree of sophistication or ability to change his thought, his responsibility for what he does or causes to happen may be correspondingly greater, and hence our satisfaction in his downfall is thereby made clearer. When such a man suffers misfortune, part or all of which he is responsible for through some serious mistake or error in judgment on his part, and subsequently discovers his error only too late, we have the tragic plot, strictly speaking. There is here the same long-range fear provoked by threatened misfortune, and pity for its materialization, as in the pathetic plot; but there is also here a more complicated relationship among fortune, character, and thought, resulting in that sort of catharsis, as we have seen, where our fear and then our pity are followed by a sense of justice and emotional release, since the tragic protagonist not only has had a hand in his own downfall but has also come to recognize that involvement. His ensuing agony of spirit therefore, although frequently resulting in the death of an otherwise good man, is somehow deserved; is indeed the best possible end for him, given what he has done or suffered; or is even a necessary atonement for his somewhat imperfect or arrogant nature. Surely this is a complex form, one of the most notable of artistic achievements, and instances may almost be numbered, unfortunately, on the fingers of one hand: *Oedipus Rex, Antigone, Othello, Hamlet, King Lear, Julius Caesar,* perhaps the unfinished *Last Tycoon*—and how many others?

The punitive plot.[3] Here we have a protagonist whose character is essentially unsympathetic in that his goals and purposes are repugnant, yet who may perhaps be admirable for his strength of will and intellectual sophistication, suffering well-deserved misfortune. It is in this type that we most frequently encounter the satanic or Machiavellian hero-villain close to the hearts of the Elizabethan and Jacobean writers, as in *Doctor Faustus* and *The Duchess of Malfi,* or in Milton's Satan, and which was revived by such nineteenth-century romantics as Byron, Huysmans, and Goethe.

At first our admiration and indignation are curiously compounded as the hero-villain sets in motion his immoral schemes and rises above the ineffectual and moralizing fools by whom he is surrounded. But when he succeeds in victimizing truly good and admirable people as well, these emotions give way to horror and outrage, and we finally feel a profound sense of satisfied vindication when he reaches his ultimate downfall. Whatever pity we feel is directed toward his victims rather than the protagonist himself, so that the final emotional equilibrium reached here is not to be confused with tragic catharsis. Other instances, involving various modifications, may be found in *Hedda Gabler, Volpone, Tartuffe,* B. Traven's *The Treasure of the Sierra Madre,* Lillian Hellman's *The*

Little Foxes, Richard III, The Changeling, Arnold Bennett's *Riceyman Steps, The Mayor of Casterbridge,* and perhaps *Moby-Dick* (taking Ahab as the protagonist).

The sentimental plot. Coming now to those plots in which the change in fortune is for the better, we have a very common type involving a sympathetic protagonist who survives the threat of misfortune and comes out all right at the end, although this too, like the pathetic plot, is a plot of suffering. Our emotional responses here are the obverse of those created by the pathetic plot, however, since the long-range hopes which are aroused do ultimately materialize, while the corresponding short-range fears are allayed, the final effect being one of joyous relief at the sight of virtue receiving its just reward. An essential cause of this effect is that, although the protagonist remains steadfast throughout, he is acted upon rather than acting; neither his bad nor his good fortune depends directly upon the quality of his thought or character. *Anna Christie* is a good example of this type, since Anna's final winning of Mat Burke does not depend upon anything she can do or say. *Cymbeline* and *Bleak House* are others, and, of course, we will find instances aplenty in the popular fiction of all ages. This type is also related to such comic plots as are found in *Joseph Andrews* and *Tom Jones,* where sentiment is crossed by laughter.

The admiration plot.[4] A change in fortune for the better which is caused by a sympathetic protagonist's nobility of character results in a somewhat different effect. Here he gains primarily in honor and reputation—and, it may be, even in spite of a loss of some sort in his material welfare. Our long-range hopes are fulfilled, as in the sentimental plot, but with the difference that our final response is respect and admiration for a man outdoing himself and the expectations of others concerning what a man is normally capable of. *The Conquest of Granada* is the prime example of this type, while *Tom Sawyer* and the stage version of *Mister Roberts* provide more recent instances.

PLOTS OF CHARACTER

The maturing plot. It may be more instructive, in dealing with plots which turn upon a change in character,[5] to begin with those types in which the change is for the better, of which there seem, happily, to be a greater number. The most common of these involves a sympathetic protagonist whose goals are either mistakenly conceived or not yet formed, and whose will is consequently rudderless and vacillating. This insufficiency is frequently the result of inexperience and naiveté, as in John Steinbeck's "Flight," or even of absolute wrongheadedness, as in *Emma*, in his or her beliefs and attitudes. If this latter is the cause, some means must be devised for changing his thought; in any case, his character must be given strength and direction, and this may be accomplished through some drastic, or even fatal, misfortune, as when the protagonist in *Lord Jim* gladly accepts death as a way of finally proving his regained strength and purpose (although I am not sure about this, as will be seen below—indeed, this may also be seen as a reform plot, which will be taken up in a moment). Since this type frequently involves the coming-of-age of young people, we may call it the maturing plot, often the same as what we have come to term the Bildungsroman. Our long-range hopes that the protagonist will choose the right course after all are confirmed, and our final response is a sense of justified satisfaction. And it is this crucial element of choice, of coming finally to a radical decision, which is the distinguishing feature of this type. *Great Expectations* is as pure an example as we are likely to find; other various instances are to be found in *The Way of All Flesh, Diana of the Crossways, A Portrait of the Artist, The Portrait of a Lady,* "The Bear," *Sons and Lovers, Huckleberry Finn, The Ambassadors, The Rainbow, Look Homeward, The Magic Mountain,* and *Rabbit, Run.*

The reform plot. Somewhat similar is another form of character change for the better, with the difference that the protagonist's thought is sufficient from the beginning. That is to say, he is doing wrong and he knows it, but his weakness of will causes him to fall away from what he himself knows to be the just and proper path. Faced with the problem either of revealing to others his weakness or of concealing it under a mask of virtue and respectability, he chooses the latter course at the outset. The problem then becomes one of devising the means of forcing his hand, of making him choose the alternative course. Thus, having been led to admire him at the beginning, we feel impatience and irritation when we begin seeing through his mask, then indignation and outrage when he continues to deceive others, and finally a sense of confirmed and justified satisfaction when he makes the proper choice at last. In the maturing plot there is some pity for the protagonist, since he acts and suffers under a mistaken view of things, but it is exactly this element which is lacking in the reform plot. The two chief examples of this type which come to mind are *The Scarlet Letter* (if Dimmesdale is the protagonist) and *The Pillars of the Community*. In certain respects it resembles the punitive plot in that the protagonist is a pious hypocrite or charlatan of some sort, but it is different in that he is reformed at the end rather than merely punished. Other examples are Henry Green's *Loving*, Franz Kafka's "The Metamorphosis" (if the family is the protagonist—see chapter 12 below), and perhaps *Lord Jim*.

The testing plot. The distinctive quality of this type is that a sympathetic, strong, and purposeful character is pressured in one way or another to compromise or surrender his noble ends and ways: he has a choice between losing his nerve and taking the bribe, or holding fast and suffering the consequences. He wavers, and the plot turns on the question of whether or not he will remain steadfast. Our sympathies here are curiously compounded, since he places himself in danger of misfortune if he persists, and the temptation he withstands would, if yielded to, better his material welfare. Thus we feel he should give it up and save his neck, yet if he does he will pay the price of losing his own self-respect and our respect for him as well. When he makes the only proper choice, we end with a feeling of satisfaction that our faith in him has been justified. This type is a favorite, of course, of Ernest Hemingway's, being found in *For Whom the Bell Tolls*, *Across the River*, and *The Old Man and the Sea*. Other examples are William Faulkner's "The Old Man" and Joseph Conrad's "The Secret Sharer."

The degeneration plot. A character change for the worse occurs when we start with a protagonist who was at one time sympathetic and full of ambition, and subject him to some crucial loss which results in his utter disillusionment. He then has to choose between picking up the threads of his life and starting over again, or giving up his goals and ambitions altogether—or, it may be, as in *The Immoralist*, he may end midway between these two alternatives, not knowing what to do next (which may be a sign that the effect is didactic, as we will note in the next chapter).

If he chooses the former course, we have what may be termed "the resignation plot," but since I know of only one such plot, *Uncle Vanya*, I have not reserved a special section for it. Chekhov indeed seems to have been obsessed with the problem of how a person can live after all his ideals, hopes, and goals have been shattered, but he most frequently had his protagonists choose the latter course, as in *Ivanov* and *The Seagull*. There is a sequence of feeble and short-range hopes followed by the materialization of long-range fears, but I am not sure whether the final effect is one of pity or of impatience and contempt for such weakness. It all depends upon how convinced we have become that the protagonist has in fact only one real choice he can make, upon how impossible staying alive for another try seems to be. F. Scott Fitzgerald too was obsessed with this problem, as in *The Beautiful and Damned* (although the conclusion here somewhat complicates things) and *Tender Is The Night*. Other examples are to be found in *The Emperor Jones* and "Death in Venice."

PLOTS OF THOUGHT

The education plot. Since those plots which turn upon a change in thought seem to be a comparatively recent development in the history of the art—and here it would take an Erich Auerbach to trace the cultural causes of this phenomenon, although it clearly has something to do with that modern turning of the mind inward which Arnold lamented in 1853—there are fewer works to talk about. The most common type, however, involves a change in thought for the better in terms of the protagonist's conceptions, beliefs, and attitudes. It resembles the maturing plot in that his thought at the outset is somehow inadequate and is then improved, but it does not continue on to demonstrate or confirm the effects of this beneficial change on his behavior. This inadequacy may be either sophisticated, where the protagonist has been through a series of disillusioning experiences and has therefore become cynical or fatalistic, as in *All the King's Men* and *The Confidential Agent*; or naive, where he has simply not yet been exposed to alternative possibilities, as in Wilbur Daniel Steele's "How Beautiful with Shoes" and Tolstoy's "The Death of Ivan Ilyich." The problem is now to subject him to some sort of change in his conceptions toward a more comprehensive view—or, as the rather verbose Jack Burden expresses it in the closing pages of *All the King's*

Men, "It is the story of a man who lived in the world and to him the world looked one way for a long time and then it looked another and very different way."

The curve of our emotional responses here follows a cycle of short-range fears and long-range hopes, in that a sympathetic person undergoes a threat of some sort and emerges into a new and better kind of wholeness at the end, with a final sense of relief, satisfaction, and pleasure. Other examples of this type are to be found in *Marius the Epicurean, To the Lighthouse, War and Peace, Winterset,* Maxim Gorki's "One Autumn Night," *The Red Badge of Courage,* James Joyce's "The Dead," Katherine Mansfield's "The Garden Party," and *Crime and Punishment*.

The revelation plot. This type hinges upon the protagonist's ignorance of the essential facts of his situation. It is not a question of his attitudes and beliefs but of his knowledge, and he must discover the truth before he can come to a decision. The clearest and neatest example I know is Roald Dahl's "Beware of the Dog," in which the protagonist, a wounded R.A.F. pilot, comes to discover that he is in enemy hands and thereby avoids the danger of unwittingly revealing classified combat information. He wakes from his coma in a hospital which to all appearances is in England. A faint sense of suspicion grows gradually in his mind that he is actually in Germany, which he then manages to confirm beyond a doubt; and at the end he gives only his name, rank, and serial number when questioned. We begin by feeling that everything is fine; our short-range fears develop and then are superseded by our long-range hopes—he is in enemy hands all right, but he has penetrated their masquerade just in time—followed by a final sense of relief and pleasure.

Another example is found in "The Green Fly," a story by a Hungarian writer of the last half of the nineteenth century, Kalman Mikszath. Here a stubborn old peasant refuses to have his gangrenous arm amputated, preferring fatalistically to die quietly instead, until he learns that his young wife is flirting with the hired man and would be just as glad to see the old man die. Once he learns this, the peasant orders the doctor to proceed with the knife.

The affective plot. There is a change in attitude and belief here, but not of the general and philosophical sort which characterizes the education plot. The problem in this type is to come to see some other person in a different and truer light than before, which involves a change in feeling. This change, depending upon whether the discovery is pleasant as in *Pride and Prejudice* or unpleasant as in *The Heart of Darkness*, will leave the protagonist happy and hopeful or sad and resigned, and our emotional responses will vary accordingly. Other examples are to be found in Henry James's "The Beast in the Jungle," Frank O'Connor's "My Oedipus Complex," Jean Stafford's "A Country Love Story," Edith Wharton's "The Other Two," Somerset Maugham's "Mackintosh," Ruth Suckow's "Golden Wedding," August Strindberg's "Autumn," and George Bernard Shaw's *Arms and the Man*.

The disillusionment plot. In opposition to the education plot, we have that type in which a sympathetic protagonist starts out in the full bloom of faith in a certain set of ideals and, after being subjected to some kind of loss, threat, or trial, loses that faith entirely. Such is the case in *The Great Gatsby*, where Gatsby's "dream" depends upon his winning back Daisy, upon whom that dream has come to depend (thus this plot somewhat resembles the affective plot, discussed above). When his grandstand play to do so fails, however, and he sees that she is not worthy of his conception of her, he has nothing left to live for; and his subsequent death at the hands of Wilson is an act of mercy, however mistaken it is in fact. Since this plot leaves its hero at the end somewhat like a puppet without strings, or a clock with a broken mainspring, our long-range fears eventually succeed in thwarting our short-range hopes, and we are left with a final sense of loss and pity—mitigated, however, by our counterbalancing sense that there was something excessive about the protagonist's illusions to begin with, and that therefore he is better off without them. We find in Eugene O'Neill's *The Hairy Ape*, James Joyce's "A Little Cloud," O'Connor's "The Storyteller," and John Barth's *The Sot-Weed Factor* further examples of this type.

III

Having named, defined, and illustrated some fourteen types of plot forms, what have we accomplished after all? Although I have said these categories are not to be regarded as another set of pigeonholes into which we can stuff literary works and forget about them, the fact remains that

I begin with a limited set of three major types and each seems separate from the other. Are they meant to be exclusive, or can they overlap? Can several kinds be fused into a single plot? What about multiple plots and subplots? Episodic plots? Are there novels which do not fit into any of these categories? Such are the questions, and more, which can and should be asked of any such system, and I will attempt to sketch out some answers here in the final section of this chapter.

To begin with, as I have already argued in relation to end effect, it is essential to the concept of form that the parts be related to the whole in a unified way. If the work is unified, then it follows necessarily that there is a principle of unity according to which it is organized: it is a contradiction in terms to speak of more than one such principle in any given work. And this concept applies whether we are talking about unity on the level of artistic purpose or on that of structure. If, then, fortune or character or thought can serve as the unifying principle of the structure of a plot, then we cannot speak of two or three of them serving in this way. They cannot overlap in this sense, for if two or three factors are said to serve as the organizing principle of an action, the question will still remain as to what principle is holding *them* together. There is always one more principle to seek when we find ourselves with more than one on our hands.

However, this principle admittedly may not be either fortune, character, or thought, in which case it will be something else. Such works will be discussed in the next chapter when we take up the question of didactic effects.

If, on the other hand, the plot is unified, and if our terms for the analysis of such plots are adequate for tracing the unfolding sequence of the action, linked by human probability and necessity, and having a beginning, middle, and end, then the principal part of that structure must be—as a way of framing and defining the main issue being established, complicated, and resolved—either fortune, character, or thought, and not some combination.

Of course they are related, as I have explained above, in terms of *some* sort of combination, but that sort means that one is primary and the others are subordinate. Certainly they overlap, but not in an equal way: one serves as a means or as material for the other, and means are formally subordinate to ends.

Or again, it is true that some of my subdivisions within any given category may resemble other subdivisions, as indeed I have taken the pains to point out, but resemblance of this sort is not the same as overlapping of formal or structural principles. Furthermore, as we know, these subdivisions are open-ended, and if one of them actually turns out to be the same as another, then the supposed distinction is easily abandoned.

In the case of those typically Victorian multiplotted novels, such as *Vanity Fair* and *Middlemarch*, it seems to me that careful analysis will reveal formal unity in the midst of profusion. Amelia and Becky form a double protagonist in Thackeray, and they wend their way through their plots, sometimes touching and sometimes not, but related by contrast through a single principal part. The novel as a whole is organized, that is, around their successive changes in fortune: as Amelia sinks, Becky rises, and then as Amelia rises, Becky sinks. Amelia's plot is a sentimental one, while Becky's is punitive. Similarly the plots of Dorothea and Lydgate in George Eliot are related by contrast through a single principal part. *Middlemarch* as a whole is organized around their successive changes in character as they confront the baffling disparity between their dreams and the complex circumstances of life. As Lydgate gradually succumbs to the less noble path of living to please his wife, Dorothea recovers from the disaster of her marriage to Casaubon and chooses the best course available to her in marriage to Ladislaw. The first is a degeneration plot (compare *Tender is the Night*), while the second is a maturing plot.

As for the relation of subplot to main plot, the issue is similar: the former must serve primarily as a means to making the latter more effective, either by similarity, as in the Gloucester plot of *King Lear*, or by contrast, as in the Levin plot of *Anna Karenina*.[6] One could say for example that *Sister Carrie* divides into two plots after Hurstwood and Carrie break up, and that Hurstwood's is a typical degeneration plot, while Carrie's is a characteristic maturing plot (her changes in fortune for the better, as I see them, serve primarily to enlarge the demands she can make on life, the expectations she can learn to have). But unless we can say that the former reinforces, in functional ways, the structure and/or the effect of the latter, as I think we can, we cannot say that the book as a whole is unified in a formal way.

These are matters of logic and method, however; the practical problems are harder to solve.

In practice, some novels are so large and complex as to defy formal analysis altogether; others are so ambiguously organized as to bewilder it; and others are so subtly put together as to tease it out of thought. I have said for example that in many cases it is hard to decide who the protagonist is. One would think that in *The Scarlet Letter* it is Hester, for she seems to be the focus of interest. But it is Dimmesdale's inner conflict, exacerbated by Chillingworth's desire for revenge, which motivates the action, and it is Dimmesdale's decision to reveal himself which resolves it. On the other hand while I once thought that Winterbourne was the protagonist of *Daisy Miller*, since he undergoes a change of thought with regard to Daisy (an affective plot), I now think it is Daisy herself, and that Winterbourne's discovery is a means of revealing her to us. One reason is that his change seems to leave no particular mark on his life, and so the reader is concerned not so much with him as with what can be seen through him.

The question is very much the same in *The Sun Also Rises*. Carlos Baker tells us that Hemingway originally intended Romero to be the protagonist, but then changed his mind to Lady Brett.[7] The novel as we have it, however, begins with Cohn and goes into much detail about him. It quickly becomes evident though that he is not the main character[8] as Jake begins taking the center of the stage, and it is Jake whom most critics take to be the protagonist. It was not until several rereadings and careful analysis, before I read Baker, that I decided that Brett was indeed the motivating force of the action. The trouble is that we are more inside Jake's life and awareness than we are in hers; she seems to pop in and out of the action at odd moments in a peripheral way as merely the source, in combination with his impotence, of his torment. Probably the most adequate hypothesis is that they form a dual protagonist and that the principal part is character, in that they must mutually find ways of resisting with dignity the despair of their frustration. Hers is a reform plot, as she breaks the code and runs off with Romero, then returns so as not to ruin him, while Jake's is a testing plot, as he grapples to hold himself together.

Similarly we can wonder whether Gatsby or Nick is the protagonist of Fitzgerald's masterpiece, whether Jack Burden or Willie Stark of *All the King's Men*, whether Ishmael or Ahab of *Moby-Dick*, and so on.[9] It takes close reading, long experience, and much thought to devise and test hypotheses which will be adequate in such cases. At any rate, it is clear that one's decision concerning form will depend upon one's choice of protagonist, and that difficulty with the one will cause difficulty in the other. But I do not think that troubles of this sort necessarily indicate flaws in the method of approach; they show rather that formal analysis is always a delicate job.

Nor is it necessarily the case that there is an implicit value judgment hidden within this system, which says that if a work fails to yield up the principle of its form, it is therefore inferior. It may be the fault of the critic, or it may be the fault of the approach. But even if it is the fault of the work, formal unity is only one sort of value, and a work may have others of equal or greater importance. I am convinced that *Don Quixote* as a whole, if we include both parts, is not unified—I do not think that even each part taken by itself is unified—and given the circumstances and spirit and method of its composition, I do not see how it *could* be unified. But I am equally certain that it is a great book nevertheless; and as Crane says, if we had to choose between a work that is formally perfect but uninteresting, and one that is vivid and compelling but irregular, we would naturally choose the second.[10] This does not prevent us, however, from also concluding that a work which has *both* virtues might probably rank higher than a work which has only one on our scale of values.

Another practical difficulty I have mentioned is that of distinguishing among fortune, character, and thought when they are so closely intertwined as to be easily confused. *Lord Jim* for example is deliberately ambiguous. I do not hold with Wayne Booth, if I understand him correctly, and however brilliant I feel his book to be in other respects, that the novelist must not leave moral ambiguities unresolved. This is not the place to analyze his argument, but it seems clear to me that a plot can be unified and still be morally ambiguous—and I mean unified in relation to both our aesthetic and our moral emotions.

The ending of *Lord Jim* resolves the plot in that it brings its protagonist face to face with the consequences of his mistakes, as well as bringing to a conclusion in a unified way the underlying issue of his courage which has been developed all along. It also resolves the plot in such a way as to involve a catharsis of our moral emotions in that, since he undertakes to face the consequences voluntarily, it produces in us a sense of justice and satisfaction, even though we feel pained at the fact that this involves his death. In other words, he *has* made a fatal mistake, but he also accepts the responsibility for it. So we can feel sympathetic toward him, even though he has been somewhat self-deluded; and at the same time we can feel his death is deserved, even though we wish it could have been avoided.

The problem in *Lord Jim,* when seen from the point of view of structural analysis, is whether his acceptance of death at the end signifies his final accession to the courage he has been trying to regain from the beginning, or whether it signifies his ultimate realization that it is impossible to impose his romantic dream upon life (the point about Stein, I think, is that he is more flexible in having a set of alternative dreams to try). If the first, then the principal part would be character, but if the second, it would be thought—a disillusionment plot resembling that of *The Great Gatsby.* I do not think it is a tragic plot since I do not see that his change in fortune for the worse controls the resolution of the whole: he has in other words, in spite of catastrophe, various choices still open to him, as Jewel urges; and it is his voluntarily going to Doramin which resolves the action.

The moral ambiguity then is more understandable once we have defined the structural ambiguity. But it is still not likely that resolving the latter would entirely clear up the former. We could agree that it is a reform plot and still not be sure that courage retains any positive definition in view of what Jim has gone through and of how he has had to regain it. Or we could agree that it is a disillusionment plot, and feel even more, of course, that his "heroism" is undercut by life's perversity. Which way we went, however, *would* have some effect upon our definition of this plot's catharsis, as well as upon our conception of Conrad's vision of life.[11]

Yet another practical difficulty I have mentioned is that, although we may be able to specify the protagonist and distinguish his fortune, character, and thought, we may still find it hard to decide which is the principal part. This difficulty may stem from the fact that there appear to be several important changes, as in *Great Expectations,* or that several parts are very closely related.

An interesting problem of the second kind involves the various close connections between character and thought found in such books as *Emma, The Ambassadors, The Nigger of the "Narcissus,"* and "The Pastoral Symphony." In each of these plots we find a protagonist (in Conrad's novel the crew forms a group protagonist, as we have seen) whose thought keeps undergoing significant changes but whose change in character is really the main issue. In other words it is not that there appear to be several important changes, but rather that the subordinate one appears on the surface to be the main one. Emma, for example, keeps learning all along how mistaken she has been about others, but she fails to abandon her conceit that she sees truly, until the end. That is, her changes in thought, which do in fact occupy a prominent place in the plot, are not the determining issue of the whole; it is rather her coming to a more humble acknowledgement of the natural limitations of her own powers of insight which is the main issue, and this is a matter of character rather than thought. Thought then would be both material and means in relation to the form as a whole.

Similarly, both the crew in Conrad and the pastor in André Gide's story actually *see* the truth—the former concerning Waite, and the latter concerning Gertrude—long before they are willing to *acknowledge* it. Since repeated shocks of revelation are required to move them out of their conceit, it may seem that thought constitutes the main issue, whereas in reality it is a matter of stubbornness and arrogance, which is a matter of character (although I am not sure that the indicated character change actually *occurs* in Gide—see the next chapter). Not exactly the same but somewhat similar is Strether's story in *The Ambassadors*. The issue here is for him to come to a true understanding of the nature of Chad's life, and especially of his love life. But this issue is absorbed by a larger one, and that is the question of what Strether will *do* in relation to Chad, and also in relation to his own life, once he does achieve this understanding.

It is a measure of James's artistry and inventiveness, incidentally, that he resolves this plot in a way that we could not have anticipated, but which does impress us as most effective once we have come to the end. The knowledge Strether achieves of Chad is not what he was expecting or hoping for, and yet he still decides to take Chad's part; and his reaching for his own freedom at the end takes the form of rejecting rather than accepting Maria's availability, since this rejection signifies his ability to achieve a truly disinterested act. Helping Chad without gaining anything for himself, without using Maria to protect himself against the loss of Mrs. Newsome, puts to the test his new and larger conception of life as being true to himself, being bold, taking risks: being in short truly free. His final gesture is not one of those ostensibly typical Jamesian renunciations; it is rather an affirmation of the self and is fully in accord with his earlier advice to little Bilham that one should live all one can, which scene James said served as the original seed of his novel.[12]

Other interesting character-thought combinations are found in *Madame Bovary* and John Updike's *Rabbit, Run*. Both of these works display protagonists whose characters are stronger than their thought: rebels who break away from the stifling conventional life around them yet without any real vision of what they are doing, why they are doing it, and what alternatives they may strive for. It is as if their authors were being cruel in endowing their creations with their own individualism and contempt for society yet depriving them of their own insight. Or perhaps they are being self-critical, as if to indicate, à la Gide, certain dangers inherent in their own positions if carried to extremes, or if followed unintelligently. Either way the net effect is ironic, distanced, and ambiguous[13]—are we to criticize the position taken or the person taking it? What is accomplished by making the protagonists seem so small, so marionette-like? Are we fooling ourselves if we feel sympathy for them? Are such works critiques of the romantic who uses the idea of doing something above the ordinary as a mere escape from dissatisfaction and an incapacity to deal with the ordinary?

Contrariwise, the protagonists of "Notes From Underground" and *The Seagull* have more insight than will, and hence they are tormented by knowledge they cannot act upon. The effect here is also ironic (are they tortured modern heroes of insight rather than action, or are they self-pitying complainers neurotically in love with suffering?) but less distanced, more sympathetic, perhaps because one senses the authors are not taking so superior and condescending a stand vis-à-vis their own creations (when Flaubert said that Madame Bovary was himself, he must have meant she was a *part* of himself, for *she* could never have written *Madame Bovary*).

Yet another set of problems is found in the close fortune-thought relations of such works as *The Great Gatsby, To Have and Have Not,* and *Lord Jim.* In each of these instances, insight is followed by death, and the question remains as to whether the insight or the death is the resolving factor of the whole. I have already shown why I think fortune is subordinate to thought in Fitzgerald and Conrad, but I am not quite sure whether the insight of Hemingway's Harry Morgan about brotherhood before his death is simply a way of mitigating the mixture of sorrow and satisfaction we feel at his dying (he has been a sympathetic but violent man), or whether it is the culminating factor. I tend toward the former, since in the other two cases death followed disillusionment, whereas here it follows a positive gain in insight. It is more difficult, that is, to argue that death merely supports an affirmative insight than it does a negative one.

These are three sorts of practical problems one might confront in formal analysis, as well as some of the ways they may be handled. Let us conclude now with a brief consideration of the more general question of works which are apparently under- or overorganized.

There are the loosely jointed plots, such as in the picaresque plots of *Don Quixote*, *Joseph Andrews*, and *Huckleberry Finn*;[14] there are the plots made of different strands, as in *Tom Sawyer* and *This Side of Paradise*; there are those comprised of distinct, almost separable sections, such as *To Have and Have Not* and *To the Lighthouse*; there are those with elaborate interchapters, such as *Tom Jones*, *Moby-Dick*, and *War and Peace*; and so on. Generally speaking, although one may fail to find a tight "Aristotelian" plot in such works, one may nevertheless find plot unity of a less rigorous sort; and if so, one may try to explain the various ingredients and sections in terms of it, provided one is prepared to distinguish between those few portions which are necessary and the many which are elaborations of one sort or another. Either that, or it may be poorly done in this respect. Or it may be didactic.

But what of the opposite case, where works are overorganized? *Ulysses* has been faulted on this point,[15] while *Finnegans Wake* has been praised for the same reason.[16] I think that the excessive number of secrets, revelations, closet skeletons, ghosts, reversals, and the like in such books as *Tom Jones*, *Joseph Andrews* (the same work can, of course, be underorganized in some respects and overorganized in others), and *Lafcadio's Adventures* can be defended on comic and/or satiric grounds, but what of similar features in such noncomic or nonsatiric works as *Great Expectations*, *Bleak House*, *Henry Esmond*, and *The Mayor of Casterbridge*? One may seek grounds in the concept of genres—such as the influence of mystery, folk, and adventure tales, gothic romances, and melodramas—but I think it is much sounder formal criticism to judge the work in terms of its own structure and end rather than of its author's supposed subservience to certain conventions, although the conditions of serial publication may be more of an exoneration.

At any rate, the problem of evaluation here is that the work does more than is needed to bring about the desired structure and end. In *The Mayor of Casterbridge*, as I shall explain more fully in chapter 17, the opening section in which Henchard sells his wife at the fair seems to have more effect on the ensuing plot than it actually does. Of course Hardy's obsession with fate and chance can be used to explain his frequent use of hidden influence and coincidence, but one would expect at the same time that his plots be consistent with such devices. It is not the wife-sale which ultimately brings Henchard down, however, but rather his conflict with an entirely unrelated element, namely, Farfrae. So too in *A Farewell to Arms*, also discussed in chapter 17, the treatment of the war episodes seems somewhat disproportionate in relation to the main line of the story. It is not war which kills Catherine, but rather the biological mischance of her having narrow hips when giving birth. On the other hand, it is a mark of some very good writers that they not only do what is necessary but also what is more than merely necessary, and it takes a nice judgment to distinguish between what is creatively abundant and what is simply excessive. As Thomas Wolfe wrote to Fitzgerald, there are the great putter-inners as well as the great taker-outers,[17] but Wolfe's own practice as a great putter-inner, as we shall see shortly, is not always successful—other great putter-inners, after all, did not need a Maxwell Perkins to boil down their manuscripts into publishable shape.

Another sort of overplotting is found in works where a person reaches what appear to be climactic moments of insight, of decision-making, or of turns in fortune, again and again, so that their effect as climaxes becomes dulled and absorbed into an overall sense of futility—at least until the end, which, if it resolves the issue, may finally bring relief. "Notes From Underground," *Crime and Punishment*, *The Red Badge*, *Sister Carrie*,[18] *The Rainbow*, and *Look Homeward, Angel* produce this effect characteristically, and it may be a flaw or it may be effective. Some writers give the appearance of simply writing out straight ahead without looking back, so that their repetitiousness results from a lack of planning and revising. Dostoevsky, D. H. Lawrence, and Wolfe certainly did not conceive of themselves as chiselling Jamesian jewels or fashioning well-wrought urns. Moreover, whether by intent or by accident, their plots do sometimes capture the felt quality of life by means of this effect —its desperation, its lack of clear pattern, its indecisiveness, its open-endedness, and so on. Carelessness, however, is not tantamount to truth in art, and one does not necessarily capture the true rhythms of experience by simply being heedless.

There is, finally, the problem of plot structure posited by such family chronicles as *The Way of All Flesh, War and Peace, The Rainbow,* and *Look Homeward,* where several generations are followed over an extended period of time. Usually there is one protagonist emerging, as well as a fairly unified plot line; but since there is also an enormous amount of background material, one may well wonder once again about over-elaboration.

The more I think about these questions of under- and overorganizing, the more I can see the possibility of developing principles to explain them which, although they would differ from those of a strictly unified plot, would nevertheless indicate, by carefully relating devices to effect, formal unity of a kind. And the more obvious kinds of plots I have outlined in this chapter may still be used as convenient starting points. I am convinced that *Look Homeward,* for example, contains a maturing plot, but I am also sure it contains much more—especially as it portrays the other members of the Gant family, going back to the youth of the father and mother, in such great detail—both of effective as well as ineffective elements. Much of the novel lacks focus and direction, but much, even of the overelaborated material, coheres. Perhaps there is a certain kind of maturing plot which requires us to see the hero emerging biographically out of his antecedent conditions: when he comes to that decision which ultimately resolves the plot, the whole weight of his life up to that point rests in the balance. And without his origins and development, this weight would not be there.

I say these things as mere suggestions, for the question of mimetic and didactic principles awaits us now as a further way of resolving problems of formal unity.

Chapter 6

Mimetic and Didactic

We must now discuss not so much the plot of the work as the way in which the plot relates to the work as a whole, and so we must consider in some detail the question of ends. For it is really only in connection with structure and end together—and, of course, with techniques and style as well—that the question of formal unity can be fully resolved.

Let us remember what *mimetic* and *didactic* refer to: that principle which can explain the organization of the work formally. Thus, although it deals with the parts as they relate to the whole, it does not deal with the "whole work" in the sense of "everything about it," but only in the sense of its artistic organization. Nor does it deal with genres, since it cannot deal with all facets of works, even when considered formally, but only with the way in which these facets are related. The same kinds of plot structures, techniques, and stylistic devices, that is, may be found in didactic as well as mimetic works; the difference is to be found in a difference of end and consequently in how this end causes the organization of the whole to look and feel somewhat different.

On the other hand, there is a certain sense in which the genre concept applies—namely, that we do not analyze, interpret, and judge didactic works in the same way as mimetic works, and vice versa. If similar parts and structures and elements may be found in both, they nevertheless play different roles in each, according to different principles of organization, and hence should be studied differently. If it is monistic, as Wayne Booth implies, to require the objective point of view in all good novels, it is also monistic to require, for example, round rather than flat characters—and even more so in didactic works.

At any rate, since we have already discussed the *theory* of mimetic and didactic ends, we need only summarize it briefly here. The basic point is that when the action and its moving powers can explain the work as a whole in formal terms, then that work is mimetic; when the action and its moving powers cannot, then that work may be didactic. If the latter is the case, it follows that we must look outside the action itself for our organizing principle. Its organization, its meaning, and its effect are not fully intelligible within itself, even allowing for the fact, as we have said, that mimetic works *do* in some sense require outside points of reference. Thus there must be something about the action in a didactic work and the way it relates to the whole which distinguishes it from the action and its relationships in a mimetic work. I have suggested what such distinguishing marks are: the action may not be unified and complete, or it may not be satisfying, or it may not be self-contained, or some combination. It remains now to discuss these principles in practice.

I

Let us begin by trying to distinguish didactic from mimetic works.[1] It is useful to begin with a rule-of-thumb: assume the work is mimetic and try to analyze the work in that way. There are two reasons for this. Both New Critic and old look for meaning as the principle of a work, and this bias, which we all share in one way or another, predisposes us to give all works a didactic slant; and so regarding them as mimetic first will help counteract this tendency. Further, when considered methodologically, such a question as this benefits from making a negative definition: if a work is not mimetic, it may be didactic. When we say a work is didactic if we have to look outside its action for its unifying principle, we must first look *inside* its action in order to determine whether that principle is to be found there or not. Let us see in other words how far an analysis of its plot will take us. In that way we will be able to tell whether it is unified and complete, or satisfying, or self-contained.

We could analyze the plot of "Billy Budd" as a change in fortune for Billy for the worse, and we could trace the unity and completeness of this change in terms of its beginning, middle, and end. But at least three things will turn up, as we do so, to cause us to wonder whether this work can be explained formally in terms of this plot. In the first place there is no motivation for Claggart's hatred of Billy—indeed, Melville is at great pains to explain that this antipathy has no realistic basis—and thus the sequence of incidents which should be bound by necessity or probability is missing one of its crucial links. Secondly and similarly, the origins and developments of Billy's and Claggart's lives are purposely shrouded in mystery, which serves further to de-individualize them and to make them counters in a drama of ideas rather than imagined persons in a literal action. And finally the ending is far from cathartic, since Melville has gone to great lengths to show that Billy has not personally deserved such a fate.

In fact what Melville seems to intend—what the work seems to be formally organized to do—is to show that even under the *most* extenuating of circumstances the rule of law must prevail during a state of emergency.[2] It is the situation rather than individual responsibility which governs the outcome. Why else would he have set up such an obviously innocent lawbreaker? Why else would he have set against him such an obviously unjust accuser? Why else would he have had Capt. Vere choose against his own officers—indeed, his own heart—in deciding to execute Billy? The point is that if this particular idea is to be conveyed, it must be conveyed in terms of the most difficult case imaginable, for no one would be surprised if the rule of law prevailed in an easy and obvious case; the true force of this idea is realized only if it is shown that no exceptions can be allowed.

It is this principle then, rather than the action and its moving powers, which explains the unity of the whole. We do not understand the whole in a formal sense until we understand that the action points to or exemplifies this idea; if we remain only with the action as our principle, we shall continue to feel both aesthetically and morally dissatisfied, for it is neither unified, nor self-contained, nor cathartic. And the fact that the crew, the officers, Vere, and the reader all sympathize with Billy merely reinforces the governing principle of the whole. If they had not so sympathized, the end effect would have been greatly undercut.

So far, I hope, so good: we could proceed inductively, according to these principles, from work to work in the attempt to determine the end effect of each. We can also, however, make a few generalizations which may serve in a heuristic way to assist this rather tedious process, much in the way that we made generalizations about plots in the preceding chapter.

Another way of defining didactic works, as we know, is to say that the action is subordinate in a formal sense to the idea. It may be unified and complete, and it may be satisfying, but it will not be self-contained. It points to something beyond itself, something without which, unless it be defined, we cannot satisfactorily explain the relation of the parts to the whole. Elder Olson has suggested three ways in which an action may be subordinated to the idea and defines accordingly three types of didactic actions: as like to like, or by analogy, which constitutes the *parable*; as concrete to abstract, or by personification, which constitutes the *allegory*; and as member to class, or by exemplification, which constitutes the *exemplum*.[3]

It is easy to recognize parables and allegories, but it is harder to find novelistic examples of them. They are easy to recognize because they are obviously not literal, and that is also perhaps why it is hard to find novelistic examples. Parables and allegories are, of course, found commonly enough in poetry and in homiletic literature, but I can think of at least some novelistic examples of each: Bunyan's *Pilgrim's Progress* is an allegory (or at least it is allegorical, for these categories may be mixed without damaging the usefulness of the distinction); and George Orwell's *Animal Farm* and John Barth's *Giles Goat-Boy* are parables.

The structure of an allegory is one in which the settings, the characters, and the actions are concrete embodiments of abstract ideas; or, when looked at the other way around, in which ideas are personified in terms of human or humanized settings, characters, and actions.[4] The definition is familiar enough: the only point to make here is that the action is not formally intelligible in and of itself. Bunyan's Slough of Despond, Vanity Fair, and the Delectable Mountains make no more sense on a literal level than do Spenser's Una, the Redcross Knight, and the Dragon of Error. Seen apart from the religious and moral doctrines which inform and govern them, these elements cannot be formally accounted for.

Modern critical fashion rates allegory as a literary mode inferior to symbolism, but I can see no necessary reason for this, any more than I can see why they must be viewed as comparable at all. I shall have more to say about symbolism later on, but suffice it to say here that I do not find it useful to conceive of it as a formal term, as I do with allegory. Pluralistically they exist on different levels of meaning. Symbolism on the formal level more properly refers to certain sorts of images, devices, patterns, and relationships than to kinds of forms—that is, means governed in a certain way by ends. Nor do I see why useful distinctions among these terms—parable, symbol, allegory—should be collapsed, as they frequently are.

The structure of a parable is one in which the settings, characters, and actions are parallel to an analogous set of situations, are governed by that parallel, and so are grasped formally only in terms of their parallel.[5] The presented action is always concrete, but the real action may be either concrete or abstract. It is the parable which may most truly be called an extended metaphor: in the biblical parables, for example, planting and reaping refer to spiritual actions; in *Animal Farm* animals are like humans and make sense only in terms of their counterparts; and in Barth's novel all the accoutrements of academia are used as parallels to America's situation during the cold war period.

The didactic art extends far beyond what we normally consider to be the sphere of fiction, so this is hardly the place to explore the whole of it. The really significant question here, as well as the most difficult, is to be able to distinguish exemplary plots from mimetic ones, for exempla are the most commonly found didactic forms in fiction and are also the most similar to mimetic forms. The reason is that exempla normally can be read and understood on a *literal* level, just as mimetic works can; the difference, however, is that they are not fully intelligible in formal terms on the *individual* level and so are still not self-contained.

Orwell's *1984*, for example, is much more like a regular novel than *Animal Farm*. In fact, as we have seen, it is a boy-meets-girl, boy-wins-girl, boy-loses-girl story like many others, and so is much more like *The Great Gatsby* or *A Farewell to Arms* than *The Divine Comedy* or *Paradise Lost*. It is, however, formally different from *Gatsby* or *Farewell*, and it is this difference which we must define.

The first thing we should notice is that, although the plot is unified and complete, it is not resolved in a satisfying way. Orwell has taken much trouble to make it as morally unsatisfying as possible: a sympathetic man is forced, through no fault of his own but rather by means of irresistible mental and physical torture, to betray his beloved. One point of this plot rests upon literally breaking his will. There must be something, we begin to suspect, that Orwell is trying to tell us over and above the story.

The next thing to notice is that Winston C. Smith (even his name is indicative) is not, as Aristotle says, merely a man like us or slightly better than we (for comedy he would be slightly worse, in some respect, than we are)—the problem is more than that of arousing sympathy or fear or indignation with respect to this protagonist. Smith rather is an average man, a typical man, a representative man. The other point of this plot, then, rests upon his being not only like us but also like almost anyone. While it is true that he takes more than ordinary risks, it is also true that anyone, given the same circumstances, would have probably taken the same risks. And when he gives in, he is doing what anyone would have done. There is very little that is distinctive about him, and we can easily imagine someone else from the same general class as being in his shoes without spoiling the plot or its effect at all.[6]

What he does, what he gets involved in, how he fares—all these things are explainable, not in terms of who he is, but rather in terms of Orwell's intention to arouse our repugnance for what a viciously repressive and totalitarian society can do to an ordinary, decent man. In order to accomplish this, Orwell had to bring this man somehow into conflict with his society—hence Smith's rebellion. But it is a pitiful rebellion, and he never has a chance; the very person to whom he turns for help turns out to be an agent of the state and ultimately his very nemesis. There is nothing remarkable here, nothing to distinguish the protagonist. Indeed, if there had been, the effect would have been lost: in order to make us hate this state, Orwell had to convince us that it could destroy anyone and not just heroes, malcontents, and rebels.

How, it may be asked, is *Gatsby* (to confine ourselves to but one example for the sake of brevity) any different from 1984? Here the protagonist also loses the girl at the end, and so it could be said that the resolution is not satisfying. Let us see, however, what the various causes of these unhappy endings are. The ultimate break between Smith and Julia is due to his will's being broken by the machinery of the state. He has done nothing in our eyes to deserve this, and we cannot by any stretch of the imagination blame him either for rebelling or for not being stronger: it is not only a totally evil state, but is also a totally omniscient and omnipotent one. Neither his unhappy misfortune nor his giving in can be said to be morally his fault: anyone could have rebelled; no one could have done more; and no one could have held out. The point is that it is the fault of the state, and any suggestion of individual responsibility would have weakened this point. Such a state is not inevitable: it could have been otherwise; it should have been otherwise; and we had better correct any tendencies in that direction which we see in our present society before they go too far.

In *Gatsby*, on the other hand, although some criticism of American society is involved, the fact is that the protagonist, because he is self-deluded, has hitched his wagon to an unworthy star—Daisy and the life of wealth and ease which she represents—and so must be held responsible. He has also of course chosen to reach his goal via the ambiguous means of gangsterdom, and this increases his responsibility. Indeed, he acts, according to his own rather pathetic sense of chivalry, as if he *were* responsible. That is why Nick concludes at the end that although he disapproved of Gatsby, he nevertheless considers him to be better than the others—at least he had the dignity of his dream, however misled, whereas the others are merely selfish and careless.

The immediate cause of his loss of Daisy is her lack of responsibility, and the mediating cause is his groundless belief in her. It is true that the ultimate cause is something meretricious about American culture, which encourages the use of immoral means for reaching noble ends and even confuses noble with ignoble ends, therefore easily misleading and thwarting idealistic and ambitious men, denying adequate goals to potential heroes; but it is also true that F. Scott Fitzgerald conceives of his people as acting within those limits as individual moral agents and not just as victims of society. That is why Nick can repeatedly and consistently take moral stands; that is why his narration places the plot in its moral context; and that is why he chooses at the end to return to the Middle West. The critique of society, then, plays a formally subordinate role here—the same story could conceivably have taken place in some other society—whereas in 1984 it is the primary factor, and this difference controls and is revealed in the differences in plot structure.

Furthermore, where Smith is a representative man, the average citizen, Gatsby, although embodying certain characteristic features of American culture, is an individual rather than a type. That is to say, in the formal sense, he is motivated as much if not more by his own personal history and temperament and circumstances as by his place in the history of his country or in an imagined utopian or antiutopian society. One cannot conceive of someone else like him as a substitute for him without spoiling the plot and its effect. Indeed, one of the features of this plot is that he *is* different from those around him, in his peculiar combination of innocence and corruption—not only from gangsterdom and the leisured rich, but also from Nick as well. What he does, what he gets involved in, how he fares—all these *are* explainable in terms of who he is.

As we have seen, the difference between mimetic and didactic works is not that the latter have ideas and the former do not; the difference is rather that the ideas in mimetic works are subordinate, while in didactic works they govern the whole; this difference should be perceptible in examining plot structures. Thus both 1984 and *Gatsby* involve social criticism, but this criticism plays a less direct structural role in *Gatsby* than in 1984. Perhaps this difference can be further clarified by defining and distinguishing among individual, general, and universal traits.

Individual traits of course are the unique aspects of a person. General traits are societal, those which a person shares with other members of his class, his culture, his time, and his history. Universal traits are natural, those which he shares with all of mankind, regardless of time and place—these are elemental, basic, fundamental, mythic, permeating. Any work may portray its protagonist in terms of all three sets of traits, except that difference in form will involve differences in proportion and relation. Individual traits will be emphasized in mimetic works, with general traits subordinate; general traits will be emphasized in exempla, with individual traits subordinate; while universal traits are usually involved as the substratum of both kinds.

In a mimetic work, although the individual traits are dominant, pure individuality would not be intelligible to the reader without at least some universal and probably general traits as well, for the reader would have very little to relate to in the protagonist and hence would be unable to respond to him. Individual-universal works with a minimal amount of general traits, such as *Wuthering Heights*, give a timeless and mythical effect; whereas individual-general works, such as *Sister Carrie*, give the effect of being exempla by virtue of their high degree of documentation. We must be careful, however, not to assume that a work is an exemplum simply because of either a strong general or a strong universal flavor, for it is quite possible and common to find works which, even though they seem general or universal, are nevertheless primarily individual and self-contained and hence mimetic. It is all a matter, as we have said, of relationships rather than simply of elements.

Sister Carrie, for example, is in many ways an ordinary small-town girl coming to the big city, and her experiences are in many ways representative. Dreiser also introduces a palpable tone of social and cultural documentation and criticism. Yet the fact remains that there is something about Carrie which is more than ordinary, and that, I take it, is one of the points of the plot—to bring her by a series of stages to an awareness of a gradually rising sense of values and goals. No other girl like her could be satisfactorily placed in her shoes, for she has too much that is strictly her own: not only her talent and her attractiveness, but also her restlessness, her insight, her sensitivity, her ambition, and her need to find a meaning in life.[7] Thus in spite of the typicality and "realism" of much of the plot, the individual-universal outweighs the general, and hence the book is mimetic.

The exemplum, on the other hand, emphasizes the general and builds its plot according to its needs, but its action would not be as interesting without a sufficient dash of the individual, or as moving without enough of the universal.

Although there is a strong flavor of the general in *Gatsby*, it is absorbed into the primary workings of the individual-universal. Not only could we not substitute another man like Gatsby, we also could remove the general altogether without damaging the basic structure of the plot (although it would most certainly make it less of a book). That *Gatsby*, although strongly American, is not essentially so, is shown by our comparison of it with *Great Expectations* in chapter 2; and when we discussed the archetypal-mythic level in these works, we were implying an interpretation more consistent with a mimetic-individual than a didactic-general analysis, since the general level, however significant, is not formally determinative in these works. Indeed, at the end Fitzgerald deliberately transcends the societal and absorbs it into the mythic.

Neither will the presence and proportion of the universal, therefore, indicate in and of themselves that a work is didactic. A work which is individual-universal will not be an exemplum, for an individual who represents something universal will not usually do so literally. For a person to be a type, he must actually *be* a member of the class represented, and the class must actually exist. Molly Bloom is not a type of earth mother,[8] for example, because she is not in fact an earth mother, nor is there any such thing as an earth mother. What is involved is rather a trait which we imagine certain women may have, or which we may personify in the figure of a woman. Bloom himself is not exactly a wanderer, but rather is *like* a wanderer in certain ways. Similarly, although there may have been sacrificial rituals at one time, the one in Shirley Jackson's "The Lottery" is more parabolic than literal, for it is *analogous* to rather than *typical* of what we do today. We may not actually stone people to death, but we do in fact oppress them in one way or another out of blind and superstitious adherence to outmoded traditions.

Thus Gatsby is not a Dutch sailor or man yearning for the Hesperides, but rather resembles or embodies this idea in some ways. The universal, that is, tends more toward concepts and therefore will be less literal, while the general tends more toward types and therefore will be more literal. An individual-universal work, then, will be either mimetic if the individual dominates, or a parable or allegory if the universal dominates. If the universal does dominate, in other words, both the personal and the societal will tend to diminish to such an extent that both the mimetic and the exemplary will be excluded; and parable or allegory, where nothing is literal or individual to begin with, will tend to emerge. I say *tend* here because nothing prevents a didactic work from being exemplary in certain parts, allegorical in others, and parabolic in still others.

We may conclude that it is the function of the individual to arouse and sustain interest in an imagined human action, of the general to develop historical texture and relevance, and of the universal to maximize the moving powers of the action, whatever they may be. The general and universal meanings of *Gatsby*, then, are subordinate to the plot, whose structure depends more upon a particular man losing his faith in his beloved and hence in the dreams he associated with her than upon the fact that his love and this dream were given their present flavor by our history up to the 1920's and by man's immemorial quest for an earthly paradise.

II

Having approached the problem of definition and classification from the point of view of distinguishing didactic from mimetic works, we may now consider the problem of distinguishing mimetic from didactic works. There are many works which, although I take them to be mimetic, might because of their rich idea-content be mistaken for didactic works. Those intercalary chapters, for instance, in *Tom Jones*, *Moby-Dick*, and *War and Peace* might be difficult to account for strictly in terms of the respective plots of these books, but neither do I think these plots are, formally, illustrations of the ideas expounded in the intercalary chapters. In each case, the plot is unified, complete, satisfying, and self-contained. What we have, it seems to me, is more authorial wit, brilliance, and restlessness than can be confined within any given form. If we deleted the "extra" material, we would have more unified works, but we would also have somewhat less interesting ones.

I prefer to leave the question open, however: a detailed analysis *might* be able to relate these ideas to their plots, or it might show these plots as exemplary of their ideas. As I speculate in chapter 8, Tolstoy's obsessive philosophizing about the causes of war seems to me to be contradicted by the lesson of acceptance learned in the plot by Pierre, and so I am not sure how to handle this problem. On the other hand, I feel that much of Herman Melville's expository writing about whaling is an attempt to make Moby-Dick more real, more convincing, and less of a mere symbol or personification.[9] Much formal work remains to be done on such books.

Other didactic-seeming mimetic works are perhaps less difficult on second thought. James Joyce's *Ulysses* does have a fairly perceptible plot, in spite of its symbolic intricacy, and S. L. Goldberg, apparently working independently of Chicago theories, has analyzed it in terms which seem very Aristotelian to me.[10] The question would be whether the elaboration of patterns is meant to serve this plot, or whether the elaboration is simply overdone (as Goldberg concludes), or whether the plot is an illustration of the symbols. To put it another way: is Bloom primarily another Odysseus, or is the *Odyssey* meant to help universalize Bloom's story?

Although I can hear many a critic saying, "It is both," I do not think this sort of flexibility and ambiguity can take us very far toward real formal analysis, which requires, as I have already argued, a hierarchical principle of unity in terms of which to relate the parts to each other and to the whole. Thus if Joyce wanted Bloom to be a modern Odysseus, he would have written the book one way, and if he wanted the *Odyssey* to throw light on Bloom's story, he would have written it another. Surely, different intentions must have different consequences, or else the whole game of formal analysis becomes a shambles. And so it must also be the case that seeing the book in one way makes more sense out of it than seeing it in another. Formally, therefore, it cannot be both, although in other respects —reading Joyce, for example, can throw as much light on Homer as reading Homer can throw on Joyce—it may very well be.

Again I would like to leave the question open, since I am more concerned at the moment with method than analysis, but I do have an opinion which I could proffer, so long as it is understood that it needs further testing. I think that the concern of *Ulysses* is with Bloom's relationship with Stephen on the one side and Molly on the other (the individual aspect), with their coming to know and understand each other and the catharsis which this knowing and understanding produces in their lives and hence in the reader. The plenitude of local and historical detail (the general aspect), as well as the abundance of the mythic and symbolic (the universal aspect), serve primarily to reinforce that reality and that catharsis. Historical relevance, that is, and universal appeal are both subordinate to and supportive of the imagined human action. Bloom is modern man, he is Odysseus and the Wandering Jew, and he is much else besides; but he is primarily a particular individual with a particular problem concerning a dead son and an adulterous wife, and I do not see how this problem represents anything but itself—I see rather that history and myth are called upon to render it more vivid, relevant, and moving.[11]

Although Molly most certainly takes on aspects of the earth mother, as I have noted, she too is primarily a particular individual with a particular life history. So also with Stephen: he is Hamlet, he is the artist, he is Telemachus, but he is no more a type here than he was in A Portrait. Although certain typical traits clearly appear—the rebellion against family and environment, the sexual problems, the philosophic discussions, the witty and serious and cynical friends—it is equally clear that Stephen is exceptional, both in his negative as well as in his positive traits. His brilliance, his coldness, his guilt over his mother, his shame over his father and his consequent need to look for a father-substitute—the combination of all these traits and many more mitigates against our taking him as representative of anything but himself.

No: it is only in Finnegans Wake, where Joyce deserts the individual altogether for a mishmash of the general and the universal, that he becomes didactic; and I am constrained to agree with Goldberg that in this case the change is for the worse.[12] It is neither the excessive word-play nor the overwrought intricacy of the repetitive patterns which defeats this book, but rather the lack of any specific and particular situation—in spite of the fact that Dublin is once again supposed to figure in here somewhere —to sustain the great superstructure. The movie version does counteract this lack somewhat by necessarily dealing with concrete images and recognizable actors and actresses; and of course, although it made use of subtitles, it could not come anywhere near reproducing the verbal-symbolic superstructure. Nevertheless it too suffers from the same difficulty in sustaining interest, since it denies the audience any particular situation to fix its mind on.

Another sort of problem occurs in certain books which we might agree are mimetic but seem not to be clear or consistent or effective in the presentation of their values. Since values in a mimetic work are what we might call the content of the action and hence are in some way responsible for its effect on the reader, an inconsistency in them might very well cause an inconsistency either in the structure of the plot or in the effect on the reader, or both.

Now since I have already defended the ambiguity of *Lord Jim*, when I imply that values should be clear, consistent, and effective, I hope I will not be mistaken as saying that a novelist needs to formulate a definite philosophy and take a definite stand before he can write well. All I mean is that the significance he finds in his materials, and which helps him organize the whole, should be sufficiently focused in order to serve the purpose. Certainly, especially if he is writing a mimetic work, he need not simplify his materials down to black and white, good and bad. He is writing about life and not just ideas. But even complexity and ambiguity—*particularly* complexity and ambiguity—need a firm focus in order to be fruitful.

In William Faulkner's "The Bear," for example, although there are large elements of history and myth, especially in part 4, the action seems to me to be mimetic—a particular young man coming to repudiate his heritage as a result of what he has learned in the woods—and this interpretation is borne out by the fact that Faulkner follows Ike's subsequent career in *Go Down, Moses*. The question is not clear, however, and critics have been aware of the problem as to whether Ike's repudiation represents a positive act in choosing natural and humane values over those of property and possession, or a negative one in avoiding responsibility in favor of personal quietism.[13] How we answer this question will, of course, determine how we define our response to the action. I think Faulkner meant it to be a positive act, and hence that he intended Ike to be sympathetic and admirable, but I also think he got tangled in the coils not merely of his rhetoric but also of his ideas.

There is a similar problem in *The Scarlet Letter*. The effect here, it seems to me, depends on our accepting, for artistic purposes, the values governing the world of the action—seventeenth-century, Puritan New England. We have to feel, that is, that Dimmesdale's struggle within himself is, for *him*, a meaningful conflict; and we cannot feel this unless we willingly suspend our modern disbelief in the values causing the conflict. *We* may feel that Hester is right in urging him to run away with her; *we* may feel that their sin was negligible; and *we* may feel that Roger, the wronged husband, is much worse than they are—but we must not feel that *they* feel these things too. If they do, then the action becomes a mockery, and they all could have saved themselves the trouble.

I do not think it *is* a mockery, but I do think that Hawthorne did not always keep his attitudes clear. The book reveals to me a wavering overlap between nineteenth- and seventeenth-century values: on the one hand, a deep and sympathetic insight into the rigors of Puritanism, and on the other, a more rational and liberated view of the case. Indeed, Hester's toying at the end with very modern views on male-female relationships makes us feel that Dimmesdale was more silly than noble in bringing himself at last to face the music and purge his guilt. He really need not have felt so guilty: if only he had waited a few years, he need not have lacerated himself so, and the whole problem would have been forgiven and forgotten by a more enlightened community. Why, they could have even gotten Hester a divorce, and married and lived happily ever after. . . . But what has all this got to do with the story Hawthorne set himself to tell? Either Hester's liberalism is the work of the Devil, or it is prophetic of more humane and rational times to come; but if it is the latter, as it seems to be, then the effect of the story itself is undermined. Nor can I see that this implies a didactic effect, for the purgation of Dimmesdale seems intended as a noble act, and it is an act which conforms to rather than criticizes his society.[14]

III

Having distinguished didactic from mimetic works, and mimetic from didactic works, let us conclude by trying to define in more positive terms the traits of didactic works, and problems—such as that of confusions in value and of the nonliteral—related to that attempt. In the first portion of this chapter we approached didactic works from the point of view of what was left over if a work proved not to be mimetic, but now we must discuss didactic works in themselves. Aside from the more obvious cases of parables and allegories, the clearest positive marks of the didactic work are the open-ended plot and the typical character.

André Gide is a master of the open-ended plot.[15] At the conclusion of *The Immoralist*, the protagonist has become free but rudderless; at the end of "The Pastoral Symphony," the pastor has come to see the terrible consequences of his unacknowledged love for Gertrude, but he has not come to see the real truth about himself or to experience any catharsis; and at the end of *Lafcadio's Adventures,* the narrator concludes with a series of questions about his hero's motivations. In the first two instances, I think Gide is more interested in the problem than in the action per se: in each case Gide presents a man acting according to values Gide himself holds, but a man who holds them without self-awareness or a sense of responsibility. These books are in the nature of warnings to himself and to would-be disciples. They can almost be read as antiliberation works, except that the positions of their protagonists are shown too sympathetically: it is not the ideas that are wrong but rather the men who act upon them. In the case of *Lafcadio,* the point seems to be that the action, in being a reductio ad absurdum of the intrigue plot, is a parody of itself.

"Notes from Underground" is another fine example of the open-ended plot, and the attack on the reader at the end is meant to be just what it seems, an attempt to wake us up, to force us to acknowledge what fools and hypocrites we really are, and to stop hiding from reality behind a wall of poses and literary attitudes. Nothing cathartic or self-contained here.

Of course the effect of such plots is to leave us dissatisfied in one way or another and hence to lead us out from the action toward something beyond it. Such a didactic effect can also be produced, as in 1984, by resolving the plot unhappily and without any counterbalancing sense of the protagonist's responsibility. Which is exactly what happens in Shirley Jackson's "The Lottery," where the woman finally chosen to be stoned to death by the community has even less to do with it than Winston Smith had in Orwell's book. Outraged horror is the effect certainly, for there is not even as much reason for her to suffer as there was for Smith. And the point is precisely that men *can* be so mindlessly destructive out of blind obedience to purposeless habit and tradition (compare the discussion of William Golding below).

Although "The Lottery" is a parable by virtue of its action, as we have seen, it is also an exemplum by virtue of its characters. Tessie Hutchinson is like Smith in being a type. Typicality can be produced in at least five ways. The first and most obvious is simply to reduce or practically eliminate individual traits in the characters, which is the method used in 1984, "The Lottery," Stephen Crane's "The Open Boat," Sinclair Lewis's *Babbitt,* and in Walter Van Tilburg Clark's "The Portable Phonograph."

Tessie, for example, is simply another housewife—any other would have done just as well. In such works the characters are so truly dominated by their circumstances that they become almost mere figures seen in shadowy outline against some ominous landscape. Hence the whole is dominated and shaped by what that landscape represents: the state, community, society, nature, doom, fate, or what have you.

Another obvious way is to make the various characters mouthpieces for various ideas or positions, as in *Brave New World*, *Darkness at Noon*, *Lord of the Flies*, and *Saint Joan*. Of course, this technique can become very stilted, but as at least some of these examples illustrate, it is not a necessary consequence.

A third method is to portray characters who represent the essential aspects of an historical situation, as in *The Grapes of Wrath*, *Cry, the Beloved Country*, and *Uncle Tom's Cabin*.

There is, fourthly, the method given currency by Aldous Huxley in *Point Counter Point* and taken up by John Dos Passos in *U.S.A.* and Norman Mailer in *The Naked and the Dead*. Here the technique is to construct the action out of a composite of characters representing different backgrounds or attitudes and to piece them together by means of cutting, splicing, alternating, inlay-work, and the like, with the result that it is clearly the design and what it represents rather than any action per se which governs the whole.[16]

A fifth sort of typifying is somewhat more complex. Billy and Claggart, for example, in Melville's novella are not types in the sense of being average, typical, or representative of a class of people. Nor are they mouthpieces for ideas or positions, or essences of the historical or social situation. They are almost allegorical in standing for, personifying, good and evil, and yet they are too literal, too much like actual people, really to form an allegory. But neither can they be taken, as I have shown, as individuals: the motivation of the action has too little to do with who they are and too much to do with what they are. This sort of typifying, then, we may call *epitomizing*, wherein a character stands for a markedly intensive, albeit literal, trait rather than representing a group of people. Billy is not simply like anyone; he is *better* than anyone, just as Claggart is worse. So too with the protagonists of John Steinbeck, Alan Paton, and Harriet Beecher Stowe, for these methods may, of course, be mixed: these are excessively noble, patient, long-suffering, and idealized men.

As with mimetic works, confusions in value in didactic works can produce inconsistencies in structure and effect, except that in such cases the results, since the ideas govern the whole, can be even more damaging. I find such problems in *Brave New World* and *Lord of the Flies*.

In Huxley's early novel, it seems to me, the Savage, who embodies the criticism of a plastic paradise, also embodies as much antihuman absurdity as does the scientific utopia itself. But William Golding presents an even more confusing ambiguity. It is clear that many readers have taken *Lord of the Flies* to be a revelation of the savagery which lies just beneath the veneer of civilization, and there is much in the book and in certain of Golding's remarks which lends support to this interpretation. Indeed, that seems to be what most of the plot is about: the conflict over the group of boys between Ralph and Jack goes in favor of Jack, and almost all of them revert to savagery, except for Ralph, the man of good-will; Piggy, the man of reason; and Simon, the mystic. Furthermore, the choice of children as the agents of his plot makes Golding a real pessimist, for children are naturally thought of as more innocent and less violent, at least in terms of the romantic tradition he seems to be satirizing. He also might be thought of as using children because the veneer of civilization is more shallow in them, and their inherent viciousness lies closer to the surface. This is an almost Calvinist case for the natural depravity of man.

However, there are other elements in the book which thoughtful consideration sees as directly opposing this interpretation. These boys are refugees from an adult world at war, and it is the dead parachutist and his descent which serves as the focal point of the young savages' superstitions. As we pursue this line of inquiry, we come to see that it is civilization rather than nature which is causing the violence of the action. These boys are acting out only what they have learned from their fathers. And certain of Golding's other remarks on his book support this interpretation: inherited prejudices are the cause of war, and it is the exposure and criticism of this idea which governs the work.[17] Indeed, one of his original impulses was to satirize the idea found in typical boys' adventure stories that white Christian fellows are somehow superior to the painted savages found on tropical islands.

But the book fails to be wholly intelligible in terms of this interpretation as well. I think the trouble lies somewhere in that gap between intention and execution. If Golding wanted to satirize civilization, why did he have his boys act like savages? Perhaps to show that civilization, not nature, is savage underneath. Fine. But savages are not civilized: they are primitive and live close to nature. Why could he not have shown Jack standing for law and order instead of Ralph and Piggy and then have portrayed Jack and the rest as forming fascistic bureaucracies and battalions the way their fathers do? Are Ralph and Piggy as parliamentarians representatives of nature or of civilization? In what way is civilization violent? In what way is nature rational? Where does Simon and his rapt contemplation of that fly-bitten pig's head come in? Maybe nature versus civilization is the wrong polarity either way. Maybe true civilization is rational and false civilization is violent, but what does that officer, the deus ex machina who rescues Ralph just as he is about to be destroyed by all those little savages, represent at the end? The focus is blurred.

Last is the problem of plots which use the marvelous or the fantastic as part or all of the action. Since one of my criteria for mimetic plots is that the action be literal, it would seem on first thought that the use of marvels and fantasies is a clear mark of the didactic. And so it is in allegories and parables, where we encounter dragons, unicorns, talking animals, and more. How can these be organized around the representation of an imagined human action where so much is not human?

On second thought, however, we must beware as usual of making our definitions on the basis of a single differentia when many variables are involved and multiple distinctions are needed. I cannot help but think that many science-fiction stories are innocent of didactic intent, even though they make large use of nonliteral characters, events, settings, and vehicles. One answer to the problem is that they still follow certain conventions of probability, avoiding phenomena which cannot be extrapolated from what is already known and accepted.[18] Yet they nevertheless, it seems to me, often portray nonexistent monsters, creatures, and forces which are not based on the already known or accepted.

Then again there is a whole repository of myths, legends, folk tales, nursery stories, and so on, which is characteristically full of what does not exist. Are all of these, or works based on them, necessarily didactic as well? And there are many quite literal works which employ fantastic elements as parts of the whole, in the action itself or in dreams, visions, nightmares, and hallucinations.[19] Do these become automatically didactic too?

Although these questions raise again the whole vexed issue of just what *probability* actually means—whether merely internal consistency, conformity with external experience, or some degree of each—I think it can be resolved for the time being by means of a somewhat simpler distinction. Marvels and fantasies may be used either for themselves or for the sake of some idea. In the former case, something which does not really exist may be presented as if it did in fact exist, and it will function in the plot on those terms. Thus a weird monster in a science-fiction story could be just a weird monster—something which threatens the safety of the space travellers, and which they must somehow deal with—and the emotions aroused in the reader would be the usual ones concerning hopes, fears, and expectations of their safety. The monster need not stand for anything else, either symbolically, allegorically, typically, or parabolically.

The same would be true of folklore and works based on them. Men with wings may be simply men with wings; enchanted forests may be simply enchanted forests; lovely queens transformed into ugly witches may be simply queens becoming witches. Our definition of *mimetic* then has to be slightly modified on this count to read: literal, if not in substance, then in function. As regards the question of probability, perhaps it is enough to say that such creatures, although they may be based on nothing known in external reality, must be portrayed in terms of how, if they *did* exist, they would naturally behave, rather than merely in terms of some idea.

Of course, I do not mean to rule out the possibility of reading such stories symbolically. Surely "Little Red Riding Hood" lends itself remarkably well to a psycho-sexual interpretation,[20] but that is not saying the same thing as that such an interpretation concerns the *form* of that story. It may rather concern the implications, suggestions, or latent content of the story. Any work may be mimetic and lend itself at the same time to "larger" interpretations. I hope I have made this point clear, not only in my theoretical chapters so far, but also in my comparative study of *Gatsby* and *Great Expectations*.

Literal works which use fantastic elements as parts of the whole must not be automatically identified as didactic works either. The case is particularly clear if it is the characters who dream, have nightmares, hallucinate, and see visions. Although in themselves such phenomena may involve distortions of or departures from external reality, their occurrence is indeed quite literal. That is to say, people in real life literally *do* dream, hallucinate, have nightmares and visions; and so there is no doubt at all of the probability of these events.

On the other hand, what of such cases as Franz Kafka's *The Trial*, *Amerika*, and *The Castle*, and many other similar works, where we get not simply a character's hallucinations but rather the author's dreamlike vision? The story as a whole, although apparently human, involves such consistent distortion as to look like one vast nightmare, where things bloat or shrink, appear or disappear, look real one minute and eerie the next, without seeming to follow the laws of probability or necessity as we have come to define them so far.

I think it still depends: works of this sort are not any more necessarily didactic than the kinds discussed above. An action can look thoroughly nightmarish yet still contain an organizing, self-contained, literal plot. I think *The Trial* is a didactic work, however, but not because it is nightmarish—rather because, as in 1984, which it surely influenced, its protagonist is barely individualized at all; because he is in no way responsible for what is happening to him; because he is up against the state; and because the ending, although it concludes the plot, does not resolve the issue or produce any moral satisfaction in the reader.

"The Metamorphosis," on the other hand, to which we shall return in greater detail later, even though it involves a similar nightmarishness, seems to me to be mimetic. As I hope my subsequent discussion will show, it does have a self-contained and satisfying plot, and its characters are much more individualized. In certain important ways, the Samsas *are* a typical family, and their problem is a typical family problem, having to do with the unhealthy aspect of dependency in love relations. But they are not merely, or mainly, typical: we know too much about each of them as individuals, both before and after the transformation, and what they suffer and how they survive are not at all representative.

The role of Gregor's fantastic transformation, although this transformation is certainly not literal, is likewise understandable in mimetic terms, functioning to make him so loathsome to his family that they must find a way of getting rid of him. What this revulsion accomplishes in turn is to free them from being his dependents. Thus while Gregor's becoming a giant insect may symbolize something, it symbolizes meanings which belong entirely within the plot itself: that they find him repulsive, and that they must free themselves. Indeed, his metamorphosis not only symbolizes these things, it also brings them about. And regarding probability, he acts as a man would naturally act if he *were* turned into a bug, and his family in turn react as people would if someone in their midst suddenly became a bug.

Thus while allegories and parables are necessarily built on the non-literal, the nonliteral is not necessarily allegorical or parabolic. In mimetic works, the nonliteral may very well be serving as a means or device, functioning literally even while appearing to be nonliteral.

We turn now to a consideration of how structure and end determine and are served by techniques.

Chapter 7

Theory of Techniques

We come now to that aspect of the whole which Aristotle considered under the heading of efficient cause or manner. In the case of a jar, the efficient cause is the agency by means of which the material (clay) is converted into the desired shape, that is, the potter's hands and his wheel. In the *Poetics*, however, manner refers to whether the action is shown by means of narration or the characters' own voices, and in the drama it refers additionally to spectacle or all that pertains to stage presentation. It would seem then that in literature the efficient cause refers to the way in which the action is presented to the audience—in a sense, as we shall see, a question of how the material is shaped. Furthermore, although Aristotle does not specifically develop the point, we would seem to be justified in referring other devices of representation to this question as well—such as selection, scaling, and order[1]—and in calling them by the more familiar name of *techniques*.

I

The entire idea of techniques depends then upon making a basic distinction, not between form and content, but rather between the action per se on the one hand and its actual presentation on the other. What we have in the finished work is not necessarily the same as the whole action, that is, but is rather a particular presentation of it embodying one set of choices from among a range of alternatives. So if we wish to discuss the techniques of a finished work, we must think our way back to the whole action in order to be able to compare it with its final method of presentation. The concept of a series of artistic choices, in other words, from the raw materials to the finished product, is central to technical criticism as well as to formal criticism generally. Let us therefore place this matter in the broader context of our discussion in this book up to now.

Envision a story about Oedipus which is to begin with perfectly neutral or inert. This story contains a certain set of incidents, beginning at least as early as his birth and ending with his death, including the high points in between. Although a certain causal sequence will inevitably begin suggesting itself, the fact is that it is still up to the writer who would construct a plot out of these materials to decide what the main issue is around which he wants to organize his materials, to pick the appropriate incidents, and to relate them in a unified causal sequence. In Sophocles' play, as we know, that issue is the call to right the wrong of King Laius' murder, but this is certainly not the only issue which could serve as the unifying principle around which to organize a plot based on these same materials.

The first choice the writer makes, then, concerns his object of imitation—or what we have been calling formal cause, structure, plot, or action —and this choice has to do with the beginning, middle, and end of that plot, as distinguished from the entire life story of Oedipus. That is why, as I have shown, Aristotle says that the poet is distinguished by virtue of his ability to construct plots and that poetry is more philosophical than history.

Next, although he may now have a unified action, the writer must still decide how he wants the audience to take it, whether seriously, comically, satirically, ironically, and so on. Just as the story of Oedipus' life is neutral in relation to the plot any given writer wants to make out of it, so too is the plot neutral in relation to the effect any given writer wants it to have.[2] That this is true becomes clear when we reflect that, while many different writers can and do make different plots out of the same materials, they also can and do evoke different effects out of the same plots. Sophocles' use of myth is an example, as are Chaucer's and Shakespeare's uses of their sources, and it is interesting to see what changes are made in film versions of novels in this connection.

Thus the second choice the writer makes concerns the final cause, end effect, *dynamis*, or moving power of the whole. This is his organizing principle, his governing conception, and it will tell him what he must do, over and above the requirements of mere mechanical sequence, to make his action produce the moral emotion desired—that is, how he wants the audience to feel toward his characters in their situations, whether favor or disfavor, sympathy or antipathy, praise or blame.

Finally, although he may now have his governing conception, he still must decide how to embody it in language: as a play or a novel, in prose or verse. He must make choices, in other words, about what we are calling techniques (efficient cause) and style (material cause or means). And here too the same governing conception could conceivably be embodied in different ways and is therefore neutral in relation to that choice. A novel may be transformed successfully into a film without changing its original effect, for example, or into a play, and vice versa.

In Aristotle's scheme, then, the writer does not take some content and put it into a form, but rather shapes and embodies his material on four different levels, of which techniques are the third. Form, strictly speaking, is a product of the second level, and it is not content which techniques and style embody, therefore, but rather form itself.

II

On what basis are the writer's technical choices made? According to Aristotle's approach, they are made in the light of the desired effect of the whole, and this effect, as I see it, may be discussed both in general and particular terms.

It is common enough to find discussions of general effects, and this is the chief difference between the *Poetics* and, say, Horace's *Ars Poetica*: Horace's suggestions concerning devices depend entirely upon such general criteria as vividness, harmony, decorum, and so on, while Aristotle's depend upon the particular moving power of the specific form he is analyzing. Horace's definition of the end of the poetry as teaching or delighting, which is not only general but also monistic (that is, it sees all of literature as having the same ends), persisted well into the eighteenth century (compare Sidney, Dryden, Johnson, et al); and even the romantics wrestled mightily with the question of whether poetry had as its end truth or beauty or some combination. When Arnold said that poetry should enspirit and ennoble the reader in his 1853 Preface, he was working in the same critical tradition, as was Wilde when he said that art is perfectly useless. Finally, as we have seen, the same is true of the New Critics when they talk of the reconciliation of opposites and total meaning, and of most of the contemporary handbooks on writing when they speak of concreteness and objectivity.

Now there is nothing inherently wrong with dealing with general effects, so long as one realizes that he can derive only general criteria of artistic choices from such principles. One cannot, in other words, derive a criticism of specific forms in this way, but he can discuss features which are common to all literary works—indeed, often to all artistic works, or even all human products. But we can have better and worse general criticisms, depending upon whether they are rigid or flexible and upon whether they are being combined with specific formal analysis.

Even a general criticism can be monistic or pluralistic, that is, but since general criticism deals with features which are common to all literary works, the dangers of monism are especially great. If we say, for example, that a novelist's use of point of view should always be objective, or that he should always show rather than tell, or that his characters should always be round rather than flat, we are being not only general but also monistic, for we are denying the function of independent variables—that is, the possibility that in some cases it would be better to use an editorializing narrator, or to tell rather than show, or to portray flat rather than round characters. We must find a way of defining general criteria which will allow us to see each technical choice in the light of the context of the whole.

This can be done, I think, by discussing the various things an author may try to accomplish, and the various powers and limitations of the devices available to him for accomplishing them, while at the same time suspending judgment about their possible combinations, balancings, emphases, and proportions, until we have a particular case before us. In these terms, then, I can see the usefulness of a model constructed as follows: a work must strive for optimal intelligibility on the one hand, while working simultaneously for optimal vividness on the other, and it must do so in terms of the optimal economy of means overall.

This model is based, of course, on the dialectic principle so dear to the New Criticism, which derived it from Coleridge, who derived it in turn from Schiller and Hegel. We are seeing general principles in terms of the tension and reconciliation of opposites, but we are doing so not in terms of meanings but rather in terms of effects. At any rate, if one is concerned explicitly with general criteria, it is a useful scheme; where it breaks down is in being used in place of specific criteria.

Intelligibility means simply that the writer must present his conception in such a way that it will be understood or grasped somehow by the reader. Other things being equal, it is better to be clear than obscure, for what the audience cannot grasp, it cannot effectively respond to. Omitting connecting links where they cannot even be inferred results in obscurity, while overclarifying something which can be inferred results in tedium. What can be inferred and what cannot is of course a relative matter depending upon the particular context, but the principle remains.

Vividness is in certain senses an opposing principle and is therefore implicit in what has just been said about clarity. Other things being equal, it is better to show than to tell, to suggest than to state. Not only does the audience receive more pleasure from a dramatic presentation, but it also receives a greater impact. And that is because, as we know, it is more effective to involve the reader actively than to reduce him to passivity by doing all the work for him. On the other hand, deny him sufficient clarity of presentation, and he will become frustrated and lose interest that way. Thus showing may have to be balanced with telling.

The reconciling principle is that of economy, and this refers to the proportions of the whole. In relation to the end effect, the writer should not do any more than is needed, either by way of making his conception clear or of making it vivid. Whereas intelligibility and vividness were seen as controls upon one another, economy is a control upon both—to be neither too clear nor too vivid—in relation to the total context. All other things being equal, it is better to do no more than is enough, to achieve the most by means of the least, because this course is more striking, surprising, pleasing, and admirable than redundancy and inefficiency.

Our model provides a flexible and rational scheme, then, making allowances for individual cases, and without undue prescriptiveness. But it is still a bit oversimple when one considers the multitude of literary facts it must confront, and so certain additional conditions and exceptions must still be made.

Intelligibility is relative not only to vividness, economy, and the particular case, but also to the audience and its historical situation. The fact is that the mysterious, the complex, and the suggestive, from the time of the romantics, have become established as primary artistic values, and this is due to a fundamental shift in metaphysical and aesthetic outlook. The world seems less clear and ordered, and the artist's function is to portray and explore its chaos and emptiness.

There is nothing in the principle of intelligibility, however, which is necessarily hostile to paradox, irony, and ambiguity, or which is inherently antimodern or pre-Freudian. It does not ask William Faulkner to write more like Jane Austen, or T. S. Eliot to be more like Alexander Pope. Educated readers of the twentieth century have been trained in the mysterious and the suggestive, and what would have been unintelligible to eighteenth-century readers is quite intelligible to us (although one wonders about *Tristram Shandy!*). But the principle remains: the artist must adopt those means which will best achieve his effect, and if his effect is to be ambiguous, then his means must be chosen accordingly. Intelligibility is not a prescription about orderliness and clarity, but is rather a principle which says be as clear as you need to be in terms of what you are trying to do.

If, on the other hand, the principle of showing versus telling becomes prescriptive, it degenerates into a mere fashion and produces frustration and boredom. The abrupt beginning, the unexplained transition, the ambiguous dialogue, the murky stream-of-consciousness, the primordial symbol, the shifting point of view, the superfluous distortion, the omitted exposition—any and all of these may be governed, not by the need to render the true impact of an existential universe, but rather by the need to appear sophisticated and up-to-date. This is especially true of such plays as Thornton Wilder's *By the Skin of Our Teeth* and *Our Town*, and Archibald MacLeish's *J.B.*, where old-fashioned sentimental values are embodied in modern techniques, as well as of many current movies using hitherto experimental techniques to embody insipid and philistine plots. Even in many genuinely avant-garde plays, novels, and movies, essential plot-links are often dropped out for no apparent reason, as the meaning of the action, which would have been easier to grasp had they been put in, is merely obscured rather than deepened by leaving them out. If depth is sometimes obscure, that is, obscurity is not always deep.

Nothing I am saying, however, should be construed as a philistine attack on modernism, particularly when one considers the relation of an uninformed audience to avant-garde works. As Randall Jarrell has pointed out, one has no right to complain about obscurity in twentieth-century works if he is unpracticed in the more traditional classics, which are themselves often complex enough.[8] Works which appear frustratingly opaque at first, often become clearer upon further study. Works whose end is to puzzle and suggest should not be rejected because they are not simple and direct. The basic question is, as I am implying, whether there is in fact a deep and complex insight being aimed at, or merely a set of dazzling but functionless tricks.

Nor am I saying that if a writer is modern, he must portray the existential universe; or if he wants to portray the existential universe, that he must use modernist techniques. Neither must he avoid such techniques if he does *not* portray the existential universe. There are certain general correlations which make some sense here, but there is nothing necessary about them, nothing which tells the writer that if he seeks a certain end, then these are the means he must use. What I object to in the Wilder plays, for example, is not that the means and the end are inconsistent with one another on the basis of some criterion I have in my head, but rather that the end is made to seem something it is not by these means. Perhaps a sentimental view *could* be embodied by means of modernist techniques so long as it recognized itself as sentimental.

The question of economy involves similar considerations. Excessive bareness and excessive fecundity can be equally ineffective. But it all depends upon what we mean by excessive and upon its relation to the whole. We have seen Thomas Wolfe saying to F. Scott Fitzgerald that there are the putters-in and the takers-out: the genius of certain writers works one way, and that of others in another. We do not ask Stephen Crane to write like Henry James, or Faulkner to write like Ernest Hemingway; we do not ask Emily Dickinson to write like Walt Whitman, or Wallace Stevens to write like H. D. What is excessive is relative to the style of the author concerned.

But even a relative principle can be used as a yardstick. We would not wish away Wolfe's torrential recall, although it could have been more disciplined; we would not want to divest James of his moral and psychological subtleties, although he could have been a trifle less fussy and wordy; we would not desire to strip *Moby-Dick* of its lore, but it could have been somewhat less tedious. By the same token, Emily Dickinson would be something else than she is if she were less bare, but she is often too skimpy altogether; and the same could be said of H. D. *War and Peace* would be a big book even without the interchapters, but it would have been a more beautiful one; *Ulysses* is a marvel of the fictional art, but it is perhaps overdone. Faulkner is less limited in many ways than Hemingway, but he could have pruned some; Hemingway is cleaner and straighter than Faulkner, but less insightful in some ways (see chapter 14).

Then again there are different kinds of excess, even within the same category. Bareness can be the result of feeble inspiration, or of successful discipline; fecundity can be the effect of a plodding and dull temperament, or of a vital and overbrimming one. The starkness of Emily Dickinson is more brilliant than that of H. D.; the verbosity of Shakespeare is more exciting than that of Sir William Davenant.

And there is ultimately a sort of excess in any great work of art, in the sense that the artist has not only done effectively what he set out to do, but also has done it in such a fashion as to amaze us by his resourcefulness and penetration. Once we see it, we feel its rightness, but we also feel we could never have thought of it ourselves. I think of the ending of *The Ambassadors* as a striking example, and it seems to justify the sometimes tedious subtilizing which precedes it.

To discuss the writer's technical choices in terms of the particular effect of the work in question, on the other hand, is to see them in terms of their specifically individual formal context; and it is this context, as we have been suggesting, which provides the controlling framework within which to apply the more general principles. The reason is that vividness, clarity, and economy, while partly applicable in themselves, are also partly dependent, as we have just seen, upon a given context for their meaning. The only thing we can say is always true for a good work of art is that it should achieve its intended effect in the best way possible; we cannot say it should always be clear, or objective, or ironic, or concrete, or whatever, because all these things depend upon particular cases. Thus round characters might be fatal in a satire, for example, or a limited point of view in a panoramic novel.

But the particular end effect of a given work provides more than a mere limiting framework in relation to general ends; it provides as well a positive principle for determining technical choices. The writer, that is, does not choose a given device simply because it is appropriate to his end effect, but also because it helps bring it about in the most efficient way. Fitzgerald did not choose Nick as his narrator for *The Great Gatsby* merely because he could not have used the protagonist—for Gatsby is dead, of course, before the book ends—or merely because the choice of Nick is more suitable to the development and revelation of Gatsby's aura of mystery—for Gatsby himself, or even an omniscient narrator, would not have been able to do that as effectively—but more because the use of Nick helps place Gatsby in the desired moral light vis-à-vis the reader.

By its very nature, however, such formal criticism of technical devices cannot be discussed for very long on a theoretical level, and so we will have to move on to other matters at the moment, reserving more practical analysis for ensuing chapters.

III

It remains to outline the writer's actual range of technical choices, and this entails the classification of the devices at his disposal, the display of his toolbox.

The choice of narrator, or of the point of view from which to tell the story, is, I think, the basic or determining choice of all these devices, as the others seem to depend upon or derive from it. So let us first sketch out the possibilities of point of view: it is useful to see them in terms of the two extremes and the range in between, and this means either that no one tells the story, or that the author tells it, or that one of his characters tells it. The most objective method of presentation is the dramatic point of view, where the characters speak in the present in their own voices— that is, the action is shown by means of dialogue and/or interior or exterior monologue and soliloquy. At the other extreme is pure authorial narration, which is the least objective method. In between, but closer to the dramatic point of view, is protagonist-narration, which means that the main character tells the story; closer to the omniscient point of view is witness-narration, in which a secondary character tells the story. Further details of these and similar matters will be taken up in the next chapter.

It can be easily seen why the writer's style would be governed by his choice of narrative method, for the language of the story must suit its supposed speaker. And it is almost as easy to see why his choice of the remaining technical devices would be similarly determined. Using a dramatic point of view normally limits the amount of compressing and the like the writer can do, for example. Using a witness-narrator may naturally involve time-shifts, for he will often tell the story as he experienced or came to know it, and this will not necessarily be in the order of its chronological occurrence.

And there are certain inherent powers and limitations involved in each choice of point of view regarding the nature of the plot being presented, as we shall see, and hence that choice will be governed in turn by the needs of that plot. The dramatic point of view, for example, is not suited to the portrayal of large actions, involving many incidents, characters, years, and settings—unless, of course, it could portray these selectively and representatively. Nor is it easy to present mental states directly by this means, except via monologue and soliloquy. On the other hand, the omniscient point of view, while it can present mental states directly, is not especially suited to the depiction of small actions—unless it is appropriate to amplify upon them. Nor can the protagonist-narrator be easily used, as we have seen, if the main character does not live past the end of the story, or if part of the point of the story is that he is imperceptive—unless things can be revealed through him ironically. Nor can a witness-narrator be used if the protagonist's states of mind are crucial —unless the witness can draw upon the protagonist's conversations, letters, and diaries. Nick, for example, has to make inferences and speculations about Gatsby's disillusionment just before the latter is killed, for Nick was not present at the time and must therefore draw upon what he already knows and what others can tell him.

We have already discussed the writer's choice of an action, from all the possibly relevant story materials involved, which will have a beginning, middle, and end. The question of selection here refers to a further step, where the problem is to decide how much of that unified action needs to be actually shown, how much may be best left to inference, and how much extra may need to be added. Let us call the parts of the action itself structural parts and those which are added representational parts, since the former are essential to the causal sequence, whether they are shown or not, while the latter, although not essential, are useful in helping to bring that sequence about and/or to produce the desired effect upon the audience.[4] Henry James's notion, for example, of the *ficelle*, a character in whom the protagonist can confide,[5] is a representational device, as is the current notion, given impetus by E. M. Forster and E. K. Brown, of patterns of balance and repetition and variation,[6] wherein this character or incident is brought in to throw light by way of comparison or contrast on that character or incident (which also may be seen in terms of order and sequence).

Of those parts which are to be shown, the next question is whether they are to be shown on an expanded scale, a condensed scale, or somewhere in between. *Scaling* refers to the degree of detail in which a given incident is rendered, and there are no apparent limits to the extremes on either side. A lifetime can be summarized in a sentence, while a moment can be expanded to many pages. It all depends upon the nature and effect of the plot. D. H. Lawrence's *The Rainbow*, which covers several generations, is not quite five hundred pages long, while James Joyce's *Ulysses*, which covers less than twenty-four hours, is over 750 pages long, and the choice of each method is governed by a different artistic purpose. Lawrence is concerned with the formation of character in the historical context of values in transition (from agrarian-communal values to industrial-individual ones), while Joyce is concerned with a few key moments of insight, recognition, and communion, plus all that they imply, in the dense context of the quotidian.

We must distinguish, finally, between the temporal or chronological sequence of incidents in the plot, and the order in which they are actually presented to the reader in the book. Often of course they are the same, but frequently they are not. And thus this question of order involves a fourth area of choice regarding technical devices which confronts the writer. Certainly the use of flashbacks, for example, which is also often related to the point-of-view device known as stream of consciousness, is a characteristic especially of modern fiction, and must be treated in that connection.

Let us turn now to the more specific issues and practical problems of technique in greater detail. Matters of point of view will be given extended consideration in the next chapter, while the remaining technical questions will be taken up during that chapter and the subsequent discussion of short story forms.

Chapter 8

Point of View

It is no longer necessary to show that point of view has become one of the main concerns of those who want to fashion an aesthetics of fiction comparable to that aesthetics of poetry which marked the early development of the New Criticism. Even Wayne Booth, whose *Rhetoric of Fiction* appeared over a decade ago, while conducting an extended attack on the principal dogmas of this new poetics of fiction, and arguing for a more pluralistic approach to the question, served primarily to confirm contemporary interest in the technique of point of view. Although I hope that one of the thrusts of the present book will be to return technical questions to their proper perspective in the range of formal questions as a whole, there is no doubt, as I have already suggested, that point of view is first among problems of fictional technique.

The main issue seems to be whether the authorial presence should make itself known directly or not—plus the related question of whether the scale should be expanded or condensed—and the answers have been varied indeed, with the New Critics following the lead of Henry James in preferring an objective method of presentation, where *subjectivity* refers to the interfering and summarizing authorial narrator and *objectivity* means the disappearance of the author. It seems to me that since those who attack and those who defend the objective method both have much right on their side, attempts at resolving the issue would benefit from a reconsideration of first principles. Let us glance at the aesthetic background of this concept of point of view and its emergence as a critical tool before going on to outline and exemplify its basic principles and discuss its implications and problems.

I

Perhaps the objective-subjective problem can be profitably framed in terms of the general criteria of intelligibility, vividness, and economy already established in the preceding chapter. The art of literature, as opposed to the other arts, is by virtue of its verbal medium both cursed and blessed with a fatal capacity for talk. Its vices are the defects of its virtues: on the one hand, its range and depth of significance far exceed the scope of painting, music, or sculpture; on the other, its ability to project the sensory qualities of person, place, and event is correspondingly less. While it can express more ideas and attitudes, it presents qualitatively weaker images. It is enough for the painter to attend to his palette, to get the proper shade in the proper place; but the writer is torn continually between the difficulty of showing what a thing is and the ease of telling what he thinks and how he feels about it. The sculptor can only show; the musician, program music notwithstanding, can rarely tell. But literature derives its very life from this conflict—which is basic to all its forms—and the history of its aesthetic could in part be written in terms of this fundamental tension, to which the particular problem of point of view in fiction is related as part to whole. For the general distinction was being made, from Plato and Aristotle to James Joyce and T. S. Eliot, in order that the specific one could take shape. From the ancient rhetorician's directions regarding vividness (*enargia*) to the modern aesthetician's study of projection (empathy), the relationship between the author's values and attitudes, their embodiment in his work, and their effect upon the reader, has been and continues to be of crucial concern.

For our purpose it will suffice to fix the two opposite points in time between which the history of this concept may be plotted. Plato to begin with made a distinction, when discussing the style of epic poetry, between simple narration on the one hand and imitation on the other (*The Republic*, book 3). When the poet speaks in the person of another we may say that he assimilates his style to that person's manner of talking; this assimilation of himself to another, either by the use of voice or gesture, is an *imitation* of the person whose character he assumes. But if the poet everywhere appears and never conceals himself, then the imitation is dropped and his poetry becomes *simple narration*. Plato then illustrates this difference by translating a passage from the beginning of *The Iliad* out of the direct form of discourse into the indirect—chiefly by substituting "he said *that*" or "he bade him *to*" for quoted dialogue—thus changing an imitative passage to simple narrative. He goes on to note that the opposite extreme, dialogue only, approaches the style of the drama, which is wholly imitative (with the exception, we might add, of choral comment and messenger-narration). Homer of course mixes the two, as do most of his successors. We have, on the other hand, that form which uses the poet's voice only: for example, the dithyramb (lyric). As we shall see below, however, dialogue is not the only factor which distinguishes imitation from narration.

Coming now to the opposite end of the curve of history, we recall a similar distinction developed by Joyce in the person of Stephen between the lyric and the dramatic forms, with the epic as intermediary (*Portrait of the Artist*, chapter 5), which in no way differs in its essential outlines from that of Plato. He is speaking here of the evolution of literature from the lyric cry to the impersonalized dramatic projection: "The narrative is no longer purely personal. The personality of the artist passes into the narration itself, flowing round and round the persons and the actions like a vital sea. . . . The dramatic form is reached when the vitality which has flowed and eddied round each person fills every person with such vital force that he or she assumes a proper and intangible esthetic life." There follows the by now famous passage about the disappearance of the author: "The personality of the artist, at first a cry or a cadence or a mood [lyric] and then a fluid and lambent narrative [epic], finally refines itself out of existence [drama], impersonalizes itself, so to speak."

Let us now consider briefly the emergence of the specific application of this basic distinction to the analysis of point of view in fiction, for point of view provides a modus operandi for distinguishing the possible degrees of authorial extinction in the narrative art.

Regarding the particular problem of the relation between the author, the narrator, and the story subject, Edith Wharton complained in 1925, "It seems as though such a question must precede any study of the subject chosen, since the subject is conditioned by the answer; but no critic appears to have propounded it, and it was left to Henry James to do so in one of those entangled prefaces to the definitive edition from which the technical axioms ought some day to be piously detached."[1] As it turns out, she was more nearly correct than she knew, for not only have James's prefaces become the source and fount of critical theory in this matter, but also no fewer than two full-length interpretations of them had already appeared before she wrote these words—that of Joseph Warren Beach in 1918 and that of Percy Lubbock in 1921. But first let us examine some of the pronouncements of the master himself.

James in his prefaces (1907–09) tells us he was obsessed by the problem of finding a "centre," a "focus" for his stories, and that he in large measure solved it by considering how the narrative vehicle could be limited by framing the action inside the consciousness of one of the characters within the plot itself. "A beautiful infatuation this," he comments, "always, I think, the intensity of the creative effort to get into the skin of the creature." Thus, since the irresponsible illusion-breaking of the subjective omniscient author, who tells the story as *he* perceives it rather than as one of his characters perceives it, is eliminated by this device, objectivity is equated with intensity, vividness, and coherence. "There is no economy of treatment without an adopted, a related point of view, and though I understand, under certain degrees of pressure, a represented community of vision between several parties to the action when it makes for concentration, I understand no breaking-up of the register, no sacrifice of the recording consistency, that doesn't rather scatter and weaken."[2]

Beach undertook to organize the theory of this method and to apply it to James's own fiction. He distinguishes among several kinds of points of view and discriminates between James's calculated shifts in focus and "that arbitrary and unconsidered shift of point of view within the chapter, within the paragraph, that visible manipulation of the puppets from without, which is so great a menace to illusion and intimacy." The problem as a whole, however, "is a most complex and difficult one, and the practice of story-tellers is manifold. It would be impossible to give a brief summary of the common usage, even if one had made a sufficiently careful survey of the field to feel certain of all the facts."[3] The time was ripe, apparently, for the next step.

It remained to Lubbock to apply the general distinction between direct and indirect presentation—a distinction common, as we have suggested, throughout the history of aesthetics and criticism—to a discussion of James's particular concern with point of view in fiction. "The art of fiction," he claims, "does not begin until the novelist thinks of his story as a matter to be *shown*, to be so exhibited that it will tell itself [rather than being *told* by the author]. . . . The thing has to *look* true, and that is all. It is not made to look true by simple statement." If artistic "truth" is a matter of compelling rendition, of creating the illusion of reality, then an author speaking in his own person about the lives and fortunes of others is placing an extra obstacle between his illusion and the reader by virtue of his very presence. In order to remove this obstacle, the author may choose to limit the functions of his own personal voice in one way or another: "The only law that binds him throughout, whatever course he is pursuing, is the need to be consistent on *some* plan, to follow the principle he has adopted; and of course it is one of the first of his precepts, as with every artist in any kind, to allow himself no more latitude than he requires." One of the chief means to this end, the one James himself not only announced in theory but followed in practice, is to have the story told, albeit in the third person and the past tense, as if by a character in the story in the present. In this way the reader perceives the action directly as it impinges upon the consciousness of that character; he perceives it without superimposed commentary; and he perceives only what that character perceives, thus avoiding that removal to a distance which results when either the author or the character tells it retrospectively: "the difference is that instead of receiving his report we now see him in the act of judging and reflecting; his consciousness, no longer a matter of hearsay, a matter for which we must take his word, is now before us in its original agitation."[4] Mental awareness is thus dramatized directly instead of being reported and explained indirectly by the narrator's voice, much in the same way that words and gestures may be dramatized directly (*scene*) rather than being summarized by the narrator (*panorama*). And implied here is that *scene* involves the expanded scale, while *panorama* involves the condensed scale.

Although one may find many shrewd observations on this point scattered through the writings of novelists and critics before the prefaces of James served to crystallize the main issue—for his notions did not spring full-blown from the head of Jove[5]—we must perforce limit ourselves to a brief consideration of what happened to them after they were expounded by Beach and Lubbock. An exception may be made, however, for the work of Selden L. Whitcomb, entitled *The Study of a Novel* (Boston, 1905), the first to my knowledge which devotes a formal section to the rubric, "The Narrator. His Point of View." Here it is claimed that "the unity of a passage or a plot depends largely on the clearness and stability of [the narrator's] position."[6] This notion, coming as it does a year or two before James's prefaces, seems remarkably prophetic of things to come, since from this point on almost every manual published on the art of fiction contains a similar section. During the next ten years or so we find a spate of such manuals which soon grows into an avalanche, and the specific analysis of point of view becomes common property.

The most significant work in the field after Beach and Lubbock, although as we have seen she seems curiously unaware of them, is that of

Wharton herself in 1925: "It should be the story-teller's first care to choose his reflecting mind deliberately, as one would choose a building site . . . and when this is done, to live inside the mind chosen, trying to feel, see and react exactly as the latter would, no more, no less, and, above all, no otherwise. Only thus can the writer avoid attributing incongruities of thought and metaphor to his chosen interpreter."[7]

The remainder of the second decade is distinguished by the demurral of E. M. Forster in 1927, who glances briefly at our problem only to pass it up as a trivial technicality. Allowing Lubbock full credit for his "formulae," he prefers to regard the novel otherwise: the novelist's chief specialty is unhampered omniscience whereby "he commands all the secret life, and he must not be robbed of this privilege. 'How did the writer know that?' it is sometimes said. 'What's his standpoint? He is not being consistent, he's shifting his point of view from the limited to the omniscient, and now he's edging back again.' Questions like these have too much the atmosphere of the law courts about them. All that matters to the reader is whether the shifting of attitude and the secret life are convincing."[8] Aldous Huxley, speaking through Philip Quarles's "Notebook" in 1928, agrees: "But need the author be so retiring? I think we're a bit too squeamish about these personal appearances nowadays."[9]

The third decade is graced chiefly by Beach's monumental study in 1932 of the technique of the twentieth-century novel, which is characterized, he says, mainly by virtue of the fact that "the story tells itself; the story speaks for itself. The author does not apologize for his characters; he does not even tell us what they do but has them tell us, themselves. Above all, he has them tell us what they think, what they feel, what impressions beat in on their minds from the situations in which they find themselves." Apparently encouraged by the work of Lubbock, which followed shortly after his own early study of James, Beach now makes a concerted and massive onslaught upon the telling-showing problem as it appears in hundreds of modern novels.[10]

In an essay dated 1941 we find Allen Tate taking up the gauntlet cast down by Forster: "The limited and thus credible authority for the action, which is gained by putting the knower of the action inside its frame, is perhaps the distinctive feature of the modern novel; and it is, in all the infinite shifts of focus of which it is capable, the specific feature which more than any other has made it possible for the novelist to achieve an objective structure." Accordingly, Phyllis Bentley in 1947 is constrained to remark: "The gradual decline in the use of direct comment, till at last heaved overboard with a splash by the twentieth century, is a fascinating study which should be attempted by a contemporary critic in the interest of [that rather neglected aesthetics of fiction] I mentioned in my introduction."[11]

The really notable advance in the theory of point of view which occurred in the forties is the work of Mark Schorer in 1948. If Lubbock was concerned with the point of view as a means to a coherent and vivid presentation, Schorer takes it one step further by examining "the uses of point of view not only as a mode of dramatic delimitation, but, more particularly, of thematic definition." A novel, he says, normally reveals a created world of values and attitudes, and an author is assisted in his search for an artistic definition of these values and attitudes by the controlling medium offered by the devices of point of view; through these devices he is able to disentangle his own prejudices and predispositions from those of his characters and thereby to evaluate those of his characters dramatically in relation to one another within their own frame. He was here anticipated by Ellen Glasgow, who wrote in 1943: "To be too near, it appears, is more fatal in literature than to be too far away; for it is better that the creative writer should resort to imagination than that he should be overwhelmed by emotion." The novelist must "separate the subject from the object in the act of creation"; he does this by total "immersion" or "projection" into the materials of his story.[12]

Most of the fifties were devoted to refining the Jamesian distinctions and extending them inward toward clearer and fuller definitions of the modes of rendering mental states, chiefly the stream of consciousness, as the work of Robert Humphrey, Leon Edel, and Sisir Chattopadhyaya makes evident. A warning of things to come, however, was sounded by Kathleen Tillotson, who wondered in 1959 why the old-fashioned omniscient narrator was not appropriate to the art of fiction after all. That this bit of nonconformity was not simply a throwback to Forster's talkative narrator who "bounces" us along, was shown by the thoughtfulness of her argument. The tradition of story telling, she said, is not the same as that of the drama; the omniscient narrator is not the author but rather a second self; and the technique of omniscience is complex, various, subtle, and worthy of careful study.[13]

In one of those more than coincidental sequences we have noticed before in this survey, Booth wrote his influential *The Rhetoric of Fiction*

(1961)[14] as if in answer to Tillotson's suggestions, developing the larger framework for discussing point of view which Schorer introduced. But instead of talking about point of view as a mode of thematic definition enabling the writer to objectify and master his conflicts, Booth sees it as a matter of moral definition enabling the writer to control the reader's responses and impress upon that reader his vision. The basic thrust of this wide-ranging and patiently worked out study is to substitute a pluralistic approach to the problem for the then reigning monism: the narrator need not disappear, the manner of telling need not be objective, and the effect need not be ambiguous—various devices may be used in relation to various ends. What Booth accomplished was threefold: he refined the usual distinctions concerning point of view, he reinstated the talkative narrator as a possible artistic choice, and he brought the whole problem back into focus as one of means and ends. But he may be faulted in his strictures on ambiguity for attacking not only critical monism but literary modernism as well; and, in his eagerness to relate technique to effect, for underplaying the essential mediating role of plot (more will be said on these points below).[15]

Whatever else may be said for or against *The Rhetoric of Fiction*, however, it is certain that the study of point of view will never be the same. Henceforth the concepts of rhetoric and of the implied author are everywhere to be reckoned with. In 1962 Shiv K. Kumar explored the whole question of the stream-of-consciousness novel from a Bergsonian perspective. Kenneth Graham showed in 1965 that the Victorian critics themselves were not so naive about the intrusive narrator and had indeed anticipated James's notion of the indirect and oblique approach. Michael J. Tolley argued in 1966 that the narrator of *Vanity Fair* is not Thackeray the man. Robert Scholes and Robert Kellogg, also in 1966, refined the distinctions between interior monologue and stream-of-consciousness, and introduced terms of their own for analyzing various points of view. In 1967 Louis D. Rubin, following Tillotson and Booth, urged that we put the novelist back into the novel, not in the sense of using the author's biography but rather regarding his role as the teller of the tale. J. Hillis Miller in 1968 developed the notion of intersubjectivity as it applies to point of view. And in 1969 Gordon O. Taylor analyzed intensively the representation of mental states in the late nineteenth-century American novel.[16]

So far the seventies have been a time of penetration, reconsolidation,

and sophisticated new directions. Françoise Van Rossum-Guyon outlined in 1970 an international perspective, while Edith Kern applied
existential concepts to the problem of author-narrator-character-reality
relationships. In 1971 Sharon Spencer approached the question of modernism in fiction afresh and analyzed distinctions among human, photo-
graphic, and typographic perspectives. Although Franz Stanzel's work
goes back to 1955, it did not appear in this country until 1971, and it
represents an extended treatment of point of view, revealing that the
subjective-objective debate was going on in full force in Germany during
the early years of this century. Finally, also from an international perspective, Paul Hernadi's work in 1972 attempted to place the whole issue in
the context of genre concepts and promises fruitful applications.[17]

II

Having traced the development of this key concept, we may now attempt
a concrete and coherent definition of its parts and their relationships.
Such a definition will, I think, be produced if we can manage to codify
the questions of which these distinctions are answers, and if we can arrange these answers into some semblance of logical sequence.

Since the problem of the narrator is adequate transmission of his story
to the reader, the questions must be something like the following: (1)
who talks to the reader? (author in third or first person, character in first,
or ostensibly no one); (2) from what position regarding the story does
he tell it? (above, periphery, center, front, or shifting); (3) what channels
of information does the narrator use to convey the story to the reader?
(author's words, thoughts, perceptions, feelings; or character's words and
actions; or character's thoughts, perceptions, and feelings); and (4) at
what distance does he place the reader from the story? (near, far, or
shifting). Since our major distinction is between subjective telling and
objective showing, the sequence of our answers should proceed by degrees
from the one extreme to the other: from statement to inference, from exposition to presentation, from narrative to drama, from explicit to implicit, from idea to image.

No value judgment is intended here, however, in thus going from less
objective to more objective points of view: I of course agree with Wayne
Booth that one method is not inherently better than another. We are

more aware now that the issues are not as simple as they at first appeared: narrative intrusions may be dramatic, while even the most objective mode implies an authorial stance. My procedure is purely descriptive and analytical. The way I frame the question nevertheless differs from Booth's approach. Where he is concerned primarily with the way in which the author imposes his values upon the reader, I am mainly concerned with how he embodies his plot in effective form. Booth's framework is, as he clearly shows, rhetorical, while mine is, as the organization of this book makes evident, technical. It is certainly legitimate to relate techniques to meanings as he and Schorer do, which is why he is interested in the moral and intellectual qualities of the narrator; but for my purposes it is more useful to treat such larger problems after considering the more strictly artistic questions first. In this way I shall be able to bring to bear upon the problem of meaning a fuller and more coherent theory of form, involving not only point of view but also other techniques, and not only techniques but also structures and ends.

Regarding the modes of transmission of story material, we have first therefore to define concretely our major distinction: summary narrative (telling) vs. immediate scene (showing). This distinction is based on whether the point of view is subjective or objective and on whether the scaling is condensed or expanded. The tendency of the objective point of view, as we have seen, since it brings the reader closer to the story, is toward the expanded scale, while that of the subjective point of view, since it takes the reader away from the story, is toward the condensed scale. That is, when there is a narrator telling the story, he naturally leans toward summarizing, but when the story "tells itself," there is a natural leaning toward step-by-step presentation. Thus *telling* is equivalent to subjective summarizing, while *showing* is equivalent to objective detail. *Objectification* implies concrete particularity, while *subjectification* implies abstract selection. Further, *telling* implies retrospective removal from the action in time, while *showing* suggests being present within it.

Ben Franklin on his way as a lad to Philadelphia came across a copy of *Pilgrim's Progress* in Dutch and commented somewhat unhistorically: "Honest John was the first that I know of who mix'd Narration and Dialogue, a Method of Writing very engaging to the Reader, who in the most interesting Parts finds himself, as it were, brought into the Company, and present at the Discourse. De foe in his Cruso, his Moll Flanders, Religious Courtship, Family Instructor, and other Pieces, has imitated it with Success. And Richardson has done the same in his Pamela, etc." While this is our distinction, I am not so sure that for our purposes dialogue is the crucial factor. Edward Overton, the narrator in Samuel Butler's *The Way of All Flesh*, informs us in the opening chapter that "My father's face would always brighten when old Pontifex's name was mentioned. 'I tell you, Edward', he would say to me, 'old Pontifex was not only an able man, but he was one of the very ablest men that I ever knew.' This was more than I as a young man was prepared to stand. 'My dear father,' I answered, 'what did he do?' " [18] It can hardly be said that the dialogue here constitutes a scene; other factors would seem to be required. Notice that the verb form is past imperfect, and that as a result the time and place are indefinite.

In order then that the event be placed immediately before the reader, there is required at least a definite point in space and time. The chief difference between narrative and scene is accordingly of the general-particular type: summary narrative is a generalized account or report of a series of events covering some extended period and a variety of locales (the condensed scale) and seems to be the normal untutored mode of storytelling; immediate scene emerges as soon as the specific, continuous, and successive details of time, place, action, character, and dialogue begin to appear (the expanded scale). Not dialogue alone but concrete detail within a specific time-place frame is the sine qua non of scene.

Butler again will supply us with an example of pure summary narrative: "Old Mr. Pontifex had married in the year 1750, but for fifteen years his wife bore no children. At the end of that time Mrs. Pontifex astonished the whole village by showing unmistakable signs of a disposition to present her husband with an heir or heiress. Hers had long ago been considered a hopeless case, and when on consulting the doctor concerning the meaning of certain symptoms she was informed of their significance, she became very angry and abused the doctor roundly for talking nonsense" (opening of chapter 2). Notice here that, in spite of the specific date (1765), it is the narrator's tone rather than the event itself which dominates: "unmistakable signs," "certain symptoms," and such phrases reveal Overton's delight in the irony of the situation rather than the situation itself. We are not shown Mrs. Pontifex's appearance directly (although we can of course infer its general outlines), nor her visit to the doctor, nor her words of anger and abuse.

For an example of immediate scene we might as well select the obvious

—Ernest Hemingway is its master: "The rain stopped as Nick turned into the road that went up through the orchard. The fruit had been picked and the fall wind blew through the bare trees. Nick stopped and picked up a Wagner apple from beside the road, shiny in the brown grass from the rain. He put the apple in the pocket of his Mackinaw coat" ("The Three-Day Blow"). Here, although no one has yet spoken, we have Hemingway's typically patient presentation of sensory detail: setting (weather: rain, wind; background: road, trees, apple, grass); action (Nick turned, stopped, picked up, put); and character (Nick and his Mackinaw coat). The event itself rather than the overt attitude of the narrator dominates.

EDITORIAL OMNISCIENCE

These modes of rendering, the one second hand and indirect, the other immediate and direct, rarely occur in their pure form. Indeed the chief virtue of the narrative medium is its infinite flexibility, now expanding into vivid detail, now contracting into economical summary; yet one might hazard the loose generalization that modern fiction is characterized by its emphasis on the scene (in the mind or in speech and action), while conventional fiction is characterized by its emphasis on narration. But even the most abstract of narrations will have embedded somewhere within it hints and suggestions of scenes, and even the most concrete of scenes will require the exposition of some summary material. The tendency, however, in editorial omniscience is away from scene, for it is the author's voice which dominates the material, speaking frequently as "I" or "we." (Let it be understood here that by *author* I mean the authorial narrator, in order to preserve Booth's valuable distinction between the literal person who wrote the book and the disembodied narrative voice which tells the story.)

Here *omniscience* signifies literally a completely unlimited—and hence difficult to control—point of view. The story may be seen from any or all angles at will: from a godlike vantage point beyond time and place, from the center, the periphery, or front. There is nothing to keep the author from choosing any of them, or from shifting from one to the other as often or rarely as he pleases.

The reader accordingly has access to the complete range of possible kinds of information, the distinguishing feature of this category being the thoughts, feelings, and perceptions of the author himself; the author is free not only to inform us of the ideas and emotions within the minds of his characters but also of his own. These may or may not be explicitly related to the story at hand. Thus Fielding in *Tom Jones* and Tolstoy in *War and Peace* have interpolated their essays as separate chapters within the body of the work, and hence they are easily detachable. Hardy makes no such formal distinction, commenting here and there in the midst of the action as he sees fit.

One may indeed investigate this sometimes ambiguous relationship between the author's commentary and the story itself. The results are almost always interesting, if not enlightening. Hardy in *Tess of the D'Urbervilles* indulges in one of his characteristic editorializing passages: "In the ill-judged execution of the well-judged plan of things, the call seldom produces the comer, the man to love rarely coincides with the hour for loving." He continues on the general unlikelihood of this uneven situation ever improving and then attempts explicitly to relate this observation to the story at hand: "Enough that in the present case, as in millions, the two halves of an approximately perfect whole did not confront each other at the perfect moment. . . . Out of which maladroit delay sprang anxieties, disappointments, shocks, catastrophes—and what was called a strange destiny" (1891: chapter 5).

We may therefore expect the story to illustrate this cause and effect relationship: if Tess's misery has its source in plain bad luck, then it should properly have no cause in her temperament; either the fault is in ourselves or in our stars. Yet Hardy in his analysis of the motivation of his people seems at times to be implying something quite different. Tess has screwed up her courage, for example, to tell Angel the horrible truth, but ends (as usual) by ducking the issue: "At the last moment her courage failed her, she feared his blame for not telling him sooner; her instinct of self-preservation was stronger than her candor" (middle of chapter 30). Here is an internal conflict, one which she cannot resolve. Apparently it is more than mere clumsy mischance. Again, she decides to visit his parents in an effort to settle things, but again quails at the crucial moment: "She went her way without knowing that the greatest misfortune of her life was this feminine loss of courage at the last critical moment" (chapter 44).

Things need not have been so bad for her, on the other hand, if Angel's character had been different: "Within the remote depths of his constitution, so gentle and affectionate as he was in general, there lay hidden a hard logical deposit, like a vein of metal in soft loam, which turned the edge of everything that attempted to traverse it. It had blocked his way with the Church; it blocked his way with Tess" (chapter 36). If the moment had been correct—that is, if Tess and Angel had come together before her seduction by Alex—would their relationship, given their respective character defects, have been any more successful? Or would the right moment perhaps have attenuated the damaging effects of these weaknesses? Or would their defects, dormant during the successful establishing of their relationship, have been made manifest by means of some later difficulty? Either way, it is certainly more than blind luck or mischance; it is rather, as usual, a combination of character and circumstance.[19] It is obviously an open question whether a novelist can create characters wholly devoid of significant motivation, even in the service of a naturalistic fatalism.

At any rate, it is a logical consequence of the editorial attitude, in addition to such commentary, that the author will not only report what goes on in the minds of his characters, but he will also criticize it. Thus Hardy depicts poor Tess wandering disconsolately about the countryside after her disastrous encounter with Alex, imagining natural sights and sounds as proclaiming her guilt. He then overtly informs the reader that the unfortunate girl was wrong in feeling this way: "But this encompassment of her own characterization, based upon shreds of convention, peopled by phantoms and voices antipathetic to her, was a sorry and mistaken creation of Tess's fancy—a cloud of moral hobgoblins by which she was terrified without reason" (chapter 13). Because *she* never discovers this, all we can say is that it is just too bad she has less perception than her creator.

Editorializing need not, of course, have such unfortunate effects, and Booth and others have shown how it may make for an accuracy and consistency of its own. Fielding, Thackeray, Dickens, George Eliot, George Meredith, Theodore Dreiser, and even D. H. Lawrence, among others, often make successful use of this device, not only to clarify and reinforce the meanings of a story, but more significantly to develop an ironic tension between the mind of the narrator on the one hand and the characters in their situations on the other. Commentary and analysis need not merely be a substitute for dramatizing, but may also be part of what is being dramatized. In *Joseph Andrews* and *Tom Jones*, as Robert Alter shows, all the devices of editorial omniscience—wit, irony, parody, style

—are bent toward the objective rendering of the action and its significance. It would seem then that narrative commentary and analysis may
not necessarily be detachable but rather should be read, as in the case of
the story materials themselves, within the formal context of the whole.[20]

NEUTRAL OMNISCIENCE

The next step toward objectification differs from editorial omniscience
only in the absence of direct authorial intrusions: the author speaks im-
personally in the third person. The absence of overt intrusions does not
mean that the author necessarily denies himself a voice when using the
neutral omniscient frame: such people as Mark Rampion and Philip
Quarles in *Point Counter Point* are obviously projections of one or another of Huxley's own attitudes (at that time), as we know from the
external evidence, even though Huxley never editorializes in his own
voice.

Although an omniscient author may have a predilection for scene and
consequently may allow his people to speak and act for themselves, his
predominant tendency is to describe and explain them to the reader in
his own voice. Thus Tess meets Alex for the first time, hesitating uncertainly before him: "a figure came forth from the dark triangular door
of the tent. It was that of a tall young man, smoking." Although Tess is
standing there and observing, Alex is described as seen by Hardy and not
by his heroine: "He had an almost swarthy complexion, with full lips,
badly moulded, though red and smooth, above which was a well-groomed
black mustache with curled points though his age could not be more
than three- or four-and-twenty. Yet despite the touches of barbarism in
his contours, there was a singular force in the gentleman's face, and in
his bold rolling eyes" (chapter 5).

By way of illustrating this characteristic indirection concretely, I have
rewritten the passage by placing this description more directly within
Tess's sensory frame: "*She saw* a figure come forth from the dark triangular door of the tent. It was that of a tall young man, smoking. *She
noticed* his swarthy complexion, his full lips, badly moulded though red
and smooth, and above them a well-groomed mustache with curled
points. Though he cannot be more than three- or four-and-twenty, *she
thought.* Yet despite the apparent touches of barbarism in his features,
she sensed a singular force in the gentleman's face and in his bold rolling
eyes."

Similarly the mental states and the settings which evoke them are narrated indirectly as if they have already occurred—discussed, analyzed, and explained—rather than presented scenically as if they were occurring now. If we return to the passage where Tess is wandering guiltily about the countryside, we read: "On the lonely hills and dales her quiescent glide was of a piece with the element she moved in. . . . At times her whimsical fancy would intensify natural processes around her till they seemed a part of her own story. . . . The midnight airs and gusts, moaning among the tightly wrapped buds and bark of the winter twigs, were formulae of bitter reproach." In contrast, I have again tried revising the scene by showing it occurring directly within Tess's mind: "At times *she felt* the scenery as part of her own story. *She heard* the midnight airs and gusts, moaning among the tightly wrapped buds and bark of the winter twigs, *reproaching her* bitterly."

Of course in both of these illustrative revisions the changes have been merely mechanical, and in order to bring out the real difference I would have had to imagine—and rephrase accordingly—how things would look in terms of Tess's *own* sensibility. Alex, no doubt, would not have appeared to Tess exactly as he appeared to the authorial narrator, nor would the styles appropriate to each be the same. So, too, when she feels the scenery as a part of her story, her awareness of what she sees and how she sees it would no doubt have been different. And that to be sure is precisely the question: the difference between one point of view and another is not simply a matter of changing a few words and phrases—it is more a matter of what sort of sensibility shall serve as the medium through which the reader receives the story.

Finally, since summary narrative and immediate scene are equally available (the latter largely for external speech and action), the distance between the story and the reader may be near or far, and it may shift at will, often whimsically and without apparent design. The prevailing characteristic of omniscience, however, is that the author is always ready to intervene himself between the reader and the story and that even when he does set a scene, he will render it as he sees it rather than as his people see it.

Here again it is not necessarily the case that the sensibility embodied in omniscient narration is an obstacle between the story and the reader, for it may be an essential part of the whole, not only for greater flexibility and range but also for a more encompassing evaluation of things, as in

Tender is the Night or *The Lord of the Flies*. The difference between successful and unsuccessful techniques is not a matter of objectivity versus subjectivity *per se*, but rather of whether the objectivity *or* subjectivity is an effective part of the whole or not. And effectiveness here is a question of which point of view is needed to get certain things done which must be done, as well as of whether it relates dramatically to the story itself. In *Lord of the Flies*, for example, we need not only access into the minds of Ralph, Piggy, Simon, and others, but also a narrative medium embodying a more inclusive awareness of things than that found in any one of the boys. Objectivity and subjectivity, then, must refer not merely to some aspect of the whole but rather to the whole itself. If subjective narration is expendable, inconsistent with the story, or an impediment, then it is subjective in the bad sense; if it is not these things, then its subjectivity fits into a larger objective pattern.

"I" AS WITNESS

Our movement toward more direct techniques charts the course of surrender; one by one, as the concentric rings of an onion are peeled, the author's channels of information and his possible vantage points are given up. As he denied himself personal commentary in moving from editorial to neutral omniscience, so in moving to the "I" as witness he hands his job completely over to another. Albeit the narrator is a creation of the author, the latter is from now on denied any direct voice in the proceedings at all. The witness-narrator is a character on his own right *within* the story itself, more or less involved in the action, more or less acquainted with its chief personages, speaking to the reader in the first person. The witness has no more than ordinary access to the mental states of others. The reader, having available to him only the thoughts, feelings, and perceptions of the witness-narrator, views the story from what may be called the wandering periphery.

What the witness may legitimately transmit to the reader is not as restricted as may at first appear: he can talk to the various people within the story and can get their views on matters of concern (notice how carefully Joseph Conrad and F. Scott Fitzgerald have characterized Marlow and Carraway as men in whom others feel compelled to confide); particularly he can have interviews with the protagonist himself; and finally he can secure letters, diaries, and other writings which may offer glimpses of the mental states of others. At the utmost limit of his tether, he can draw inferences as to how others are feeling and what they are thinking. Thus Nick Carraway speculates, after Gatsby's solitary death, about what went on in Gatsby's mind before he was shot: "No telephone message arrived. . . . *I have an idea* that Gatsby himself didn't believe it would come, and *perhaps* he no longer cared. If that was true *he must have felt* that he had lost the old warm world, paid a high price for living too long with a single dream. *He must have looked up* at an unfamiliar sky through frightening leaves and shivered as he found what a grotesque thing a rose is and how raw the sunlight was upon the scarcely created grass" (chapter 8; italics mine).

On the other hand, Fitzgerald is much less certain in his use of the witness-narrator in *The Last Tycoon*, but perhaps had he lived to complete this novel, he would have ironed out some of the more obvious difficulties. What he did complete, however, in combination with his notes, does serve to indicate very well what is involved in this technique. Cecilia Brady's point of view was to have provided the book with a combination of first-person immediacy plus a certain amount of omniscient detachment, but her personal involvement with Stahr is much greater than Nick's with Gatsby, and her handling of material of which she has no first hand knowledge is much more clumsy. Maybe she was indeed a poor choice to begin with, and Fitzgerald would have had ultimately to recast the whole in some other terms.

Samuel Butler also wanders uncertainly beyond his limits in *The Way of All Flesh* more often than one could wish. His witness-narrator does, in fact, explicitly inform us of his boundaries: "But what were the feelings of Theobald and Christina when the village was passed and they were rolling [in their honeymoon carriage] quietly by the fir plantation? . . . For some time the pair said nothing: what they must have felt during their first half-hour, the reader must guess, for it is beyond my power to tell him." What, then, are we to make of this passage immediately preceding? "Christina and he [Theobald] had got on, *he thought to himself,* very nicely for a great number of years; why—why—why should they not continue to go on as they were doing now for the rest of their lives?" (chapter 13). Or again, " 'I hope,' *said* Theobald *to himself,* 'I hope he'll [Ernest] work—or else that Skinner will make him' " (chapter 24; italics mine).

It is true that Overton is a contemporary and close friend of Theobald, as well as the godfather and guardian of Ernest, and that Theobald in these instances might have told him later about what went on in his mind, but Overton too frequently gives us no clue whatever as to his authority for such information.

Since the witness-narrator can summarize his narrative at any given point as well as present a scene, the distance between the reader and story may be either near or far, or both. We may note here that the scenes are usually presented directly as the witness sees them, although he may, like an omniscient authorial narrator, summarize and comment as well. Other examples are *The Good Soldier, The Sun Also Rises* (if Brett is the protagonist), *Moby-Dick* (if Ahab is the protagonist), and *All the King's Men* (if Willie is the protagonist). Also here and in the next category are found, of course, such various first-person modes as the memoir novel, the diary novel, and the epistolary novel.[21]

"I" AS PROTAGONIST

With the shift of the narrative burden from a witness to the chief character, who tells his own story in the first person, a few more channels of information are given up and a few more vantage points are lost.[22] Because of his subordinate role in the story itself, the witness-narrator has much greater mobility and consequently a greater range and variety of sources of information than the protagonist proper, who is centrally involved in the action. The protagonist-narrator, therefore, is limited almost entirely to his own thoughts, feelings, and perceptions. Similarly the angle of view is that of the fixed center.

But since the protagonist-narrator can summarize or present directly in much the same way as the witness, the distance may be near or far, or both. One of the best examples of this mode is to be found in *Great Expectations*. Others are *Huckleberry Finn, The Heart of Darkness* (in combination with the nameless narrator who introduces us to Marlow), *Farewell to Arms*, "Notes from Underground," *The Catcher in the Rye, The Stranger,* and *Pastoral Symphony.*

MULTIPLE SELECTIVE OMNISCIENCE

In spite of the fact that both the "I" as witness and the "I" as protagonist modes are limited to the narrator's mind, there is still *someone* doing the talking. The next step toward the objectification of the story material is the elimination not only of the author, who disappeared with the "I" as witness frame, but also of any narrator whatsoever. Here the reader ostensibly listens to no one; the story comes directly through the minds of the characters as it leaves its mark there. As a result, the tendency is almost wholly in the direction of scene, both inside the mind and externally with speech and action; and narrative summary, if it appears at all, is either supplied unobtrusively by the author by way of "stage direction" or emerges through the thoughts and words of the characters themselves.

In effect, as we have seen, it is as if the character were talking in the first person and in the present tense, although grammatically it may be related in the third person, past tense. Mental states of people in the story, that is, may be presented directly or indirectly, but either way are the medium through which action is rendered. The appearance of the characters, what they do and say, the setting—all the story materials—can be transmitted to the reader only through the mind of someone present. Thus Mrs. Ramsay's age and appearance are rendered in Virginia Woolf's *To the Lighthouse:* "They must find a way out of it all. There might be some simpler way, some less laborious way, *she sighed.* When *she looked* in the glass and *saw* her hair grey, her cheek sunk, at fifty, *she thought,* possibly, she might have managed things better—her husband; money; his book" (Harbrace ed., pp. 13–14). Although this is in the third person and past tense, it is also rather direct. The point is that it represents Mrs. Ramsay's way of seeing and thinking rather than the unobtrusive narrator's, who is limited to giving stage directions (which I have italicized).[23]

As we have seen, selective omniscience differs from normal omniscience in that in the latter all is seen through the sensibility of the authorial narrator, and when he chooses to dip into the minds of his characters, he reports what he sees there in terms of his own idiom and awareness. In the former, all is seen through the sensibility of the characters, and thus all—including, of course, mental states—is rendered in terms of their idiom and awareness. There is no detached angle of vision above the story in selective omniscience, in spite of the third-person, past-tense construction which it sometimes may have in common with ordinary omniscience. A "translation" of another passage from Mrs. Woolf will illustrate the precise point of difference: "Such was the complexity of things [thinks Lily Briscoe]. For what happened to her, especially staying with the Ramsays, was to be made to feel violently two opposite things at the same time; that's what you feel, was one; that's what I feel, was the other, and then they fought together in her mind, as now. It is so beautiful, so exciting, this love, that I tremble on the verge of it" (p. 154). Notice here that grammatically the style progresses toward the first person and the present tense. A normally omniscient author, on the other hand, would have summed it all up (condensed the scale), and would have put it in his own terms (rendered it subjectively): "Lily felt ambivalent about love, especially with the Ramsays."

Other conspicuous examples of the use of multiple selective omniscience are found in *Mrs. Dalloway* and *Ulysses*.

SELECTIVE OMNISCIENCE

Here the reader, instead of seeing the story through several minds, is limited to the mind of only one of the characters. Instead of being allowed a composite of viewing angles, he is at a fixed point, whether center, periphery, or somewhere in between. The other questions are answered as they were for the previous category.

Let us explore this matter of selective omniscience a bit further. A vivid example of exactly how the story materials are transmitted directly to the reader through a character's mind is found in Joyce's A *Portrait:* "Consciousness of place *came ebbing back to him* [Stephen] slowly over a vast tract of time unlit, unfelt, unlived. The squalid scene *composed itself around him*; the common accents, the burning gasjets in the shops, odours of fish and spirits and wet sawdust, moving men and women. An old woman was about to cross the street, an oilcan in her hand. He bent down and asked was there a chapel near?" (chapter 3).[24]

The abrupt beginnings and much of the distortion characteristic of modern stories and novels are due to the use of multiple and selective omniscience; for if your aim is to dramatize mental states, the logic and syntax of normal daytime public discourse begin to disappear as you descend farther into the mind. Indeed, one may chart the stages through which the rendering of mental states may go in terms of whether direct or indirect discourse is used, whether the present or past tense is employed, and whether the expanded or condensed scale is called upon. Generally, the closer one comes to actual mental states, the more characteristic will be direct discourse, the present tense, and the expanded scale (scene), while the farther one goes from actual mental states, the more characteristic will be indirect discourse, the past tense, and the condensed scale (summary narrative or panorama). "Such was the complexity of things" is more direct, while "Lily thought that things were quite complex" is less direct.

What is called the stream-of-consciousness technique, it seems to me, is simply a sustained effort to render mental states from as much within the mind of the character as possible—directly and in his own style, in the present, on an expanded scale—and at a level of awareness somewhere below that of the rational, verbal, intellectual, conscious mind. Stream of consciousness is merely a subdivision of selective omniscience. Filtering the story through the sensibility of a character may be direct or indirect, conscious or subconscious, but it will still be selective omniscience. All that is needed is seeing the story through a character's awareness. James, staying on the upper levels of his characters' minds, which are usually of the highly articulate type anyway, and using the third person, past tense, although he practically invented selective omniscience, cannot be called a stream-of-consciousness writer.[25] Woolf, who might be said to dwell on the middle level of her characters' minds, which are typically chaste, and using a mixture of first and third person, present and past tense, is relatively more difficult. While Joyce, who knows no bottom, and using the first person and present tense extensively, is most difficult.[26]

Other examples of the use of varying degrees of selective omniscience are found in *For Whom the Bell Tolls, Across the River and Into the Trees*,[27] and "The Metamorphosis" (at least until Gregor dies).

THE DRAMATIC MODE

Having eliminated the author and then the narrator, we are now ready to dispose of mental states altogether. The information available to the reader in the dramatic mode is limited largely to what the characters do and say; their appearance and the setting may be supplied by the author as in stage directions; there is never, however, any direct indication of what they perceive (a character may look out of the window —an objective act—but what he sees is his own business), what they think, or how they feel. This is not to say, of course, that mental states may not be inferred from action and dialogue.

We have here in effect a stage play cast into the typographical mold of fiction. But there is some difference: fiction is meant to be read, drama to be seen and heard, and there will be a corresponding difference in scope, range, fluidity, and subtlety. The analogy, however, does largely hold, in that the reader apparently listens to no one but the characters themselves, who move as it were upon a stage; his angle of view is that of the fixed front (third row center), and the distance must always be near (since the presentation is wholly scenic). Hemingway comes into his own here (mainly in short stories such as "Hills Like White Elephants"), and mention might be made of James's *The Awkward Age* (1899), which is something of a tour de force, the gains in immediacy hardly compensating for the difficulties of sustaining a full-length novel within this mode (compare also his *The Europeans* [1878] and *The Sacred Fount* [1901]). Henry Green, however, in such works as *Loving* has revealed the possibilities of this technique for novels a bit more flexibly and successfully.[28]

III

Having sketched out the principles underlying the problem of point of view, traced its emergence as a critical concept, and examined the range of its possibilities, let us see if we can sum up our results as a solution to that problem. Contrary to the general impression created by those on either side of the question, objectivity and consistency are really not the shibboleths only of a parochial and monistic New Criticism. "Homer, admirable as he is in every other respect," said Aristotle, "is especially so in this, that he alone among epic poets is not unaware of the part to be played by the poet himself in the poem. The poet should say very little *in propria persona*, as he is no imitator when doing that. Whereas the other poets are perpetually coming forward in person, and say but little, and that only here and there, as imitators, Homer after a brief preface brings forthwith a man, or woman, or some other Character—no one of them characterless, but each with distinctive characteristics" (*Poetics*, chapter 24, Bywater translation). As we have seen, it has all along been a commonplace of aesthetic theory that effective presentation and objectivity go hand in hand.

The application of the principles of objectivity and consistency, however, *has* tended to become monistic and parochial in modern criticism, as indeed any principle tends to become when means are seen apart from ends. Whether an author is being an imitator cannot be resolved simply in terms of point of view alone. Thus Wayne Booth is certainly correct in attempting to frame the question in a larger context. There should be nothing merely automatic about using more objective points of view as opposed to less objective ones. What is truly crucial, as always in formal criticism, is whether the end effect—seen both generally and particularly—is best achieved by this technique or that, in combination with everything else in the whole.

The basic assumption of those who are seriously concerned over technique, as James himself so long ago pointed out, is that the general end of fiction is to produce as complete a story-illusion as possible. Given material potentially interesting, concentration and intensity, and hence vividness, are the results of working within limits, albeit self-imposed; and any lapse thereof is in all probability the result either of not establishing a limiting frame to begin with or of breaking the one already established. Surely this is one of the basic principles of artistic technique in general. Even breaking the limiting frame, if it is done deliberately for the sake of calling attention to the artificiality of art—which is, curiously, as characteristic of earlier as of modern novelists—may be subsumed under this principle, for the breaking of a frame implies the existence of a frame in the first place.[29]

Thus the choice of a point of view in the writing of fiction, although it does not in and of itself determine the degree of objectivity, is at least as crucial as the choice of a verse form in the composing of a poem: just as there are certain things which cannot get said in a sonnet, so each of the categories we have detailed has a probable range of functions it can perform within its limits. The question of particular effectiveness, therefore, is one of the suitability of a given technique for the achievement of certain kinds of effects, for each kind of story requires the establishment of a special kind of illusion to sustain it. Editorial omniscience, for example, may be called the free verse of fiction: its limits are so wholly internal that an unwary novelist has more opportunities for illusion-breaking here than with the others. How much of Whitman, Carl Sandburg, or Edgar Lee Masters is flat and dull? And how much of *War and Peace*—to take the highest achievement—could easily be dispensed with? On the other hand, as I have suggested, when the personality of the author-narrator has a definite function to fulfill in relation to his story— say of irony, compassion, philosophical range and depth—he need not retire behind his work, so long as his point of view is adequately established and coherently maintained. It is more a matter of consistency than of this or that degree of impersonality.

But the author-narrator has a more complicated problem on his hands here, and had best look to his devices. Free verse is not "free" after all, as Eliot has somewhere remarked; but to establish a pattern within it is more difficult and hence more liable to disruption. In this respect, Fielding's *Tom Jones* is more successful than *War and Peace*: the intellectual tone and pedantic material of Tolstoy's interchapters are often at variance with the tenor and impact of the story itself, which has as its issue the discovery (in Pierre, Kutuzov, Karataev, Nikolay, Natasha) of the instinctive and intuitive forces in life and the adoption of an attitude of negative capability toward experience. There is thus revealed, for all its majesty, a fatally unresolved ambiguity at the core of this novel: it is commonly agreed that Andrey and Pierre are symbolic projections of Tolstoy's own ambivalence; and it is as if, having killed off Andrey, the author-narrator could not allow Andrey's irritable reaching after fact and reason to disappear altogether from the story and so kept it alive, as it were, in the interchapters. However we may view them, they are basically undramatic.

It is necessary, in other words, to relate the choice of point of view to the needs of the plot and its effect rather than simply to an abstract set of prescriptive criteria about objectivity, and for this we must discuss more than either technique as discovery or technique as morality. Thus if it is essential to an author's purpose that the minds of many be revealed freely and at will—to achieve, for example, the effect of a social milieu in the manner of Huxley—and if the author's superior and explanatory tone is to dominate the perception and awareness of his characters—to achieve that typical Huxleyan effect of smallness and futility and indignity—then neutral omniscience is the logical choice. If the element of suspense is to be foremost—as, say, in mystery stories and detective fiction—if a situation is to be gradually built up and revealed piecemeal—as in *Lord Jim*—then the witness-narrator seems more likely than any other. If the problem is one of tracing the growth of a personality as it reacts to experience, the protagonist-narrator will prove most useful—as in *Great Expectations*—assuming that he has sufficient sensitivity and intelligence to develop and to perceive the significance of that development (a naive protagonist may, of course, be used for an ironic effect). If the author is concerned with the way in which personality and experience emerge as a mosaic from their impingement upon the sensibilities of several individuals, then multiple selective omniscience provides a way—as in *To the Lighthouse*. If the intent is to catch a mind in a moment of discovery and decision—as in *A Portrait of the Artist*—selective omniscience is the means. And finally, if the author's purpose is to produce in the reader's mind a moment of revelation—as in Hemingway's "Hills Like White Elephants"—then the dramatic mode, with its tendency to imply more than it states, provides the logical approach.

Nor need any given point of view be used consistently throughout, for this would indeed be requiring a merely mechanical kind of consistency. I have said that my categories are simply reference marks, and that often in practice they are found in combination. There are many different first-person points of view in William Faulkner's *As I Lay Dying* and varying first-person points of view plus omniscience in *The Sound and the Fury*, but such composites are not effective or ineffective per se. Michael Millgate praises the former book, noticing its fifteen first-person narrators, but he mentions certain reservations. "This diversification and multiplication of point of view has often been praised, but it seems at times both excessive and irritating, as when Darl is presented as clairvoyant and made to report events (such as the finishing of the coffin in the rain) at which he is not present. Richard Chase has commented on the tendency of a multiple point of view to become 'simply the point of view of the omniscient author.'"[30] It would seem that a more limited point of view which fails to stay within its limits is tantamount, in effect, to omniscience.

Or again, Hemingway uses omniscience, the protagonist-narrator, and a witness-narrator in different parts of *To Have and Have Not*; while these shifts may not in themselves be the cause of disunity, they may indeed reflect the disunity of the book's origins and manner of publication. Conrad uses an omniscient narrator to begin *Lord Jim,* and then shifts to Marlow's witness-narration. Marlow himself, of course, relays various other witnesses' accounts to us in addition, and this is surely quite effective.[31] An anonymous witness introduces us to the protagonist-narrator in *The Heart of Darkness*. Although Fitzgerald's *Tender Is the Night* is selectively omniscient in focusing on Dick Diver's consciousness, it begins by focusing on Rosemary's, but the problem that Fitzgerald had with this book was more one of order than of point of view.

Consistency in the larger sense and not cold-bloodedness is all; for consistency, within however big and diverse and complex a frame, signifies that the parts have been adjusted to the whole, the means to the end, and hence that the maximum effect has been rendered. Point of view is, however, a necessary rather than a sufficient cause; the overall consistency of a great but clumsy novelist may emerge in spite of his technical inadequacies, while the consistency of a lesser talent will not in itself produce masterpieces, succeeding within a smaller frame than that which genius may attempt. Sometimes a noble failure is more exciting than a petty victory. But how many of our most ambitious and brilliant novels would have been even more successful if closer attention had been directed toward these matters? There is surely no necessary contradiction between genius and technical mastery.

I have in mind here the obvious inconsistencies in the narrative of *Don Quixote* as well as the often burdensome references to Cid Hamet, the author of the "original" manuscript;[32] or Melville's continual bursting of his basic witness-narrator frame in *Moby-Dick*; or the frequent absurdities engendered by Samuel Richardson's epistolary technique in *Pamela*. These are not merely matters of changing points of view, or of not using a point of view which is objective enough; they are more matters of lack of care, or of failing to realize the limits and potentials of whatever point of view or combination of points of view the author himself establishes as his basic medium of presentation.

Moby-Dick also presents us with another sort of problem which I have mentioned in a different connection, and that is the case in which the witness-narrator (or reflecting consciousness, in the case of third-person selective omniscience) becomes so central as almost to usurp the role of the protagonist. That is to say, the use of a technical device can become disproportionate enough to threaten a disruption of the plot structure itself. If the protagonist is defined as the one around whom the causes of the action operate—upon whom the causes work, and from whom they flow—then Ahab and not Ishmael is the protagonist of *Moby-Dick*. It is Ahab and his monomania which motivate the action and bring about its culmination. But Ishmael is so much more often present, he does so much talking about himself, and he does indeed go through such significant changes, that it is difficult not to think of him as the main character and of Ahab as simply grist for his mill. Similar questions arise, as I have shown, in *Gatsby*, *The Sun Also Rises*, *Daisy Miller*, and *All the King's Men*.

An even more basic sort of inconsistency is found in Lawrence's *Sons and Lovers*, and Schorer has outlined the underlying cause of the curious restlessness with which this book leaves the reader. In spite of its "modern" concern with sex and the unconscious, it is still narrated within the frameless frame of old-fashioned editorial omniscience, and the danger of authorial identification with the protagonist—and hence of partisanship and dice-loading—has not been obviated. The author-narrator thus analyzes Miriam's thoughts: "So in May she asked him [Paul] to come to Willey Farm and meet Mrs. Dawes. There was something he hankered after. She saw him whenever they spoke of Clara Dawes, rouse and get slightly angry. He said he did not like her. Yet he was keen to know about her. Well, he should put himself to the test. She believed that there were in him desires for higher things, and desires for lower, and that the desires for the higher would conquer. At any rate, he should try." And then Lawrence adds, "She forgot that her 'higher' and 'lower' were arbitrary" (chapter 9).

Both Schorer and Diana Trilling point out that there is consequently a contradiction in the book's theme: Paul Morel cannot achieve a satisfactory sexual relationship either because of his enervating mother-fixation or because Miriam can encompass only the "spiritual" aspects of such a relationship.[33] Since these two themes are mutually exclusive—the fault is the mother's or Miriam's—the trouble is that Lawrence has been unable sufficiently to dissociate himself from Paul to tell one from the other, with the result that he tries to have it both ways. The reader remains frustrated; lack of consistency means loss of effect. Yet the irony is that Lawrence himself believed in the efficacy of dramatic projection as a way of clarifying and understanding his own emotional problems: "One sheds one's sickness in books—repeats and presents again one's emotions, to be master of them." E. T., however, the original of Miriam, knew that in this case he had failed: "he burked the real issue. It was his old inability to face his problem squarely. His mother had to be supreme. . . . So instead of a release and a deliverance from bondage, the bondage was glorified and made absolute. . . . The best I could think of him was that he had run with the hare and hunted with the hounds."[34]

By way of contrast, we may note Joyce's presentation of Stephen in *A Portrait*, where, in spite of the common tendency to treat it as autobiographical, the story of the hero's coming of age is completely objectified. Because Joyce has strictly limited the flow of information only to those scenes, perceptions, thoughts, and feelings which Stephen's mind records, he has minimized the possibility of authorial partisanship which so vitiates the structure of *Sons and Lovers*. As a result, we get so clear a picture of the protagonist that near the end of the book one of his friends can say to him: "It is a curious thing, do you know—Cranly said dispassionately—how your mind is supersaturated with the religion in which you say you disbelieve." One cannot conceive of Lawrence, given his lack of control, as allowing Miriam to say to Paul: "It is a curious thing, do you know, how your rather excessive love for your mother causes you unwittingly to seek a sexual outlet with younger women which will be devoid of spiritual content. Passion and devotion are split in your mind by guilt, and therefore you react violently when a woman asks you for both together, accusing her of wanting to draw the soul out of you. Your soul has already been given to your mother. So you misconceive me completely when you say I want only your spiritual love." (Due allowance will, I hope, be made for the fact that I am not a novelist; but I believe, from the evidence in E. T.'s book, that Miriam was fully capable of such penetration. Lawrence, however, renders her as agonizingly inarticulate.)

Such is the success of Joyce's projection that, in spite of the fact that both he and his hero deliberately rejected Catholicism, literary Catholics can nevertheless relish his portrayal of religious life in the book. Thus Thomas Merton comments regarding the famous Hell passages: "What impressed me was not the fear of hell, but the expertness of the sermon. . . . So then I continued to read Joyce, more and more fascinated by the pictures of priests and Catholic life that came up here and there in his books." Similarly, Caroline Gordon can say, "I suspect that this book has been misread by a whole generation. It is not primarily a picture of the artist rebelling against constituted authority. It is, rather, the picture of a soul that is being damned for time and eternity caught in the act of foreseeing and foreknowing its damnation." While I think that this is perverse sophistry, I think also that it is a tribute to Joyce's dramatic genius that a Catholic can sympathize with the portrayal of Catholic values which the hero rejects.[35]

When we talk of objectivity and consistency, then, we should be careful not to confuse questions of overall organization with mere matters of technique. Schorer is surely right about the somewhat muddled effect created by *Sons and Lovers*, but I do not agree with him about its cause. It seems to me that he takes hold of the problem by the wrong handle:

finding the right technique will not enable the writer to be objective; it is rather being able to be objective which permits him to find the right technique. Lawrence's lack of success with the omniscient point of view is a symptom rather than a cause of his overidentification with Paul and his special pleading in relation to Miriam. Fielding, using editorial omniscience in *Joseph Andrews* and *Tom Jones*, is as detached and ironic in relation to his characters as one could wish. A writer can use an objective point of view, and use it consistently, and still not produce a successful work; or he can use a subjective point of view, and then shift around, and still produce an effective work. For the real criteria are control and unity rather than simply objectivity and consistency. The writer may use a subjective point of view, so long as it is the most suitable to the whole, and he may vary it, so long as he does so with a sense of what he is doing. It is the arbitrary and self-indulgent which are to be avoided, rather than the subjective and the shifting.

But if Booth has made out a similar case for underlying unity of focus as opposed to mere technical objectivity and consistency, he raises more problems than he solves, I think, in his strictures against moral ambiguity. In opposing the technical dogmatism of modern critics, who require objectivity and impersonality in rendering, he has substituted a dogmatism of his own, in requiring a moral focus and consistency. In other words, if the New Critics do not want the author to be confused or overidentified with his characters, Booth does not want him to be too separate from or underidentified with them, for this will be, as he argues, both aesthetically and morally irresponsible.

While I do not think it is necessarily wrong to treat technical and moral problems together, as I have said, I do think it is better to separate them before joining them. Booth, in concerning himself on the technical level with the moral and intellectual qualities of the narrator, has in reality painted himself into a corner. It is one thing to castigate modern critics for conceiving of objectivity in terms which are too narrow, but it is quite another to conceive of it in terms which are too broad. Overall formal control and unity are not necessarily the same things as either technical objectivity on the one hand, or moral clarity on the other, although all three levels of inquiry are indeed related. A work, that is, can be formally unified and still be morally ambiguous without diminishing its excellence—indeed, as I hope I have already made clear, formal unity and moral ambiguity may stand in positive and healthy relation to one another. Or, at least, a profound concern for form may help make our approach to moral questions more profound. Having related technical to formal objectivity, then, let us see if we can relate formal control to the question of moral control.

One of the reasons Booth dislikes dogmatic technical objectivity is that it encourages the writer to adopt a laissez-faire attitude toward his materials, abdicating his responsibility for shaping them somehow into a pattern whose moral significance is ultimately clear. The writer, he says, should not leave the reader rudderless in a sea of moral ambiguities; a deadpan, noncommittal presentation of evil, for example, is both aesthetically and morally vicious.[36]

Although I am certainly against sin, I am not sure I always know what evil really is, whether fundamentally or in particular cases—except, perhaps, not seeing another as a human being—and I would like to see the problem constantly being explored. And even if I did know, I am not sure I should impose my knowledge upon others, or legislate how it should relate to art. Booth confuses, it seems to me, art and life rather badly: as a man, I must make up my mind about such matters, however tentatively, in order to function in society, however restively; but as a writer and reader, I must be constantly experimenting and inquiring (recall Keats's ideas about negative capability and the chameleon poet).[37] Things which were once thought good—the accumulation of property, for example—are now seen to be not so good, while things which were once thought to be bad—sexual pleasure, for example—are now thought to be not so bad.

I do not mean to take a relativist position any more in moral questions than in critical ones, however, and claim that nothing is true or false but thinking makes it so. I think that in certain ways things may be called good or evil, but I do not think we can very often know in advance which is which. Here, as in criticism, I am a pluralist: knowledge and values are possible, but we have to work hard to get them, and we must be careful to distinguish between principles and applications. Thus, just as technique must be judged in the context of the plot rather than simply in terms of abstract criteria, so too must a real act be judged in the context of its situation rather than merely in terms of general rules. There are standards, certainly, but they must be applied in relation to the whole rather than to the parts only. Life, even more than art, of course, involves the working of many independent variables, and so we must beware even more of taking parts for wholes here. And, just as plot supplies the context for analysis of technique, so too does it supply the context for discussion of morality—for the plot is the situation in terms of which we must judge the moral and intellectual qualities not only of the narrator but also all the other characters as well. Only after this has been done can we say either that the technique is effective or that the values of the author are healthy. Aristotle again has suggested the basis for solving this problem: "As for the question whether something said or done in a poem is morally right or not, in dealing with that one should consider not only the intrinsic quality of the actual work or deed, but also the person who says or does it, the person to whom he says or does it, the time, the means, and the motive of the agent—whether he does it to attain a greater good, or to avoid a greater evil" (*Poetics*, chapter 25, Bywater translation).

Furthermore, art neither affects us directly nor leaves us unaffected: we do not pattern our lives after books, nor do we read merely for amusement or distraction. Art enlarges our minds, broadens our feelings, and deepens our sympathies. It contributes to that process of exploration which Shelley says is the basis of morality; it is one of the ways we have of remaining free from practical decisions while attempting to see what the possibilities really are. It affects our lives ultimately, after being absorbed and assimilated, but not necessarily immediately. My practical life must always remain less full of possibility than my artistic life, but at the same time it should always be open to change and growth, and change and growth can be partially fostered by my artistic experience. The relation between art and life, then, is vital but indirect.

Thus I can read about an "evil" man, and he can be presented either unfavorably, neutrally, favorably, or in some combined way. Either way, however, I am not a schoolboy learning his catechism: I can learn that what I thought was evil is not necessarily so; or even if it is still evil, I can see more clearly how it looks from the inside. And if the author is genuinely trying to corrupt me, whether intentionally or inadvertently, resisting his influence can be a healthy exercise. But the ambiguity of many modern writers is more a shouldering of moral responsibility than an evasion of it, for exploring complexities honestly is more moral than making rigid categories. The "morality" of art is not that it should conform to the values of daily life, but rather that it should remain open and honest.

Aesthetically, though, the question is whether a work can be ambiguous and still be unified. Here a distinction between controlled and uncontrolled ambiguity will prove useful. Multiple meanings may either add to or detract from one another. If a writer wants to create an impression of the complexity of life, and if he does so in terms of the interplay and overlap of meanings, then his work may be perfectly unified—whether generally or particularly—around this intention. There is nothing either morally or artistically vicious about it; he need not take a definite stand or make up his mind; all he needs to do is to relate varying meanings together in such a way that they build a greater whole which is "truer" than any one meaning, while at the same time being difficult to express without all of them. If, on the other hand, he creates an impression of chaos rather than complexity, and if his meanings, such as they are, fail to relate, or if they contradict one another, instead of interplaying and overlapping, then his work will be lacking in control and unity.

It is in this sense that objectivity and consistency can be used as valid criteria, so long as it is understood that they do not refer simply to this device or that technique. Any amount of technical subjectivity and shifting is allowable so long as it contributes effectively to the whole: a writer may be ultimately quite objective, even while using a subjective device, just as he may be ultimately quite subjective, even while using an objective device. Thus, I agree with Booth as against the New Critics in saying that objectivity is a larger matter, but I agree with the New Critics as against Booth in saying that objectivity is an aspect of the moral freedom of art. And I can occupy this mediating position, I think, because I can interpose between technique and meaning, as neither he nor they appear to do, a more specific concept of artistic form, the validating context.

Chapter 9

What Makes a Short Story Short?

I

A pluralistic formal criticism, although concerned with distinctions among different works and kinds of works, is not interested in the definition of genres as such but rather in the varying ways in whch the forms of works and kinds of works may be defined. On the one hand, as we have seen, it believes in the uniqueness of individual works and distrusts a priori definitions of forms and kinds; on the other, it strives to develop principles for the analysis of forms and the definition of kinds. But the resolution of this apparent contradiction is found in its concept of independent variables. Substantively, if we cannot know in advance just what makes any given work what it is, we *can* know in advance the general principles of its making; that is to say, if we know what sort of variables to look for, we nevertheless do not know what they will be or how they will be combined. Thus, while the principles of a work are general, their application and combination are unique. And procedurally, the concept of independent variables is related to the logic of making adequate definitions, in that we must decide what facet or facets of a work we are referring to, we must base our definition on multiple differentiae, test it according to the rules of exclusion and inclusion already discussed, and judge its use in terms of what it is designed to do.

That this approach is not a version of the genre-criticism of the eighteenth century, I hope I have already suggested. The mistake of neoclassic genre criticism was to have specified elements and combinations of elements in advance, and thus it thought of epic, satire, pastoral, elegy, tragedy, comedy, lyric, and the like, as preexisting forms, whereas in reality they are merely rules-of-thumb based on a loosely assorted variety of aspects and on certain conventional and traditional conveniences. Epic, for example, refers to a certain sort of hero involved in certain sorts of situations and to an action of a certain magnitude. Satire, on the other hand, refers to a certain sort of end, and allows for a variety of sorts of

By permission: *Modern Fiction Studies*, © 1958 by Purdue Research Foundation, Lafayette, Indiana.

actions—one may have a satirical poem, a satirical play, a satirical nar-rative, and so on. But the pluralist would make his distinctions, for any given purpose, on the same level of differentiation, and he would apply them in relation to that purpose and in terms of multiple differentiae. Thus he would see that if certain works are alike in some respects, they are different in others, and therefore there are in reality no such things as preexisting forms or even "inductively" derivable types of any fixed sort.

The usual distinctions among poetry, drama, and fiction are similarly convenient rules-of-thumb rather than logical categories. Poetry refers loosely, in Aristotle's terms, to the means of imitation, or language; drama refers to the manner;[1] while fiction refers to the manner and object of imitation. Poetry, while keeping constant a certain use of lan-guage called "verse" (whatever that may be), can be dramatic, epic, lyric, narrative, elegiac, satirical, or what have you. Drama, while keeping constant a certain manner, can involve different sorts of means, objects, and ends. And fiction, while normally dealing with certain sorts of action by means of certain sorts of narration, can be in verse or prose, short or long, and so on. Worrying over the question What Is Poetry? for ex-ample is therefore usually fruitless. The concept of poetry does not in-clude within itself sufficient differentiae to do the job, and even if it did, it is too general and loose a concept to begin with for it to be useful in actual instances.

The multiple differentiae upon which we must base our definitions are thus means, manner, object, and end; or as we have rephrased them, style, techniques, structure, and purpose. We will draw, in other words, upon what has been done so far in this book in our attempts to define the short story. And we will do so in terms of what we need in order to get the job done. The basic variables involved in this particular defini-tion, as we shall see, have to do with structure and techniques; for these are the ones, rather than style or purpose, which are primarily determi-native of length, and it is with length that we must necessarily concern ourselves. A story may be short or long, that is, and still have the same style or end. And the inquiry as a whole has been framed in the context of the attempt to show that a pluralistic approach to definition will bring into view a type which is more subtle and complex than the usual monistic definitions reveal.

II

Although the short story as a literary type gets a fair share of attention in classroom texts and writers' handbooks, it is still—tainted by commercialism and damned by condescension—running a poor fourth to poetry, drama, and the novel in the books and journals devoted to serious theoretical criticism. It is in the hope of making a beginning toward the evaluation of the short story as a worthy and noble art that I should like to attempt a frontal attack upon its basic problem, that of its shortness.

But it is not a question merely of defining shortness, of fixing the upper and lower limits in terms of the number of words a work of fiction should have in order to be called a short story. Common sense tells us that, although the exact dividing lines cannot, and need not, be determined, we can pretty well distinguish, apart from marginal cases, between long, short, and medium fiction.[2] We shall not argue, then, about length in strictly quantitative terms, for most of us know what a short story is and can pull down from our shelves at a moment's notice a dozen anthologies containing stories of varying lengths, all called "short." To haggle over the borderlines is almost always fruitless, and that is one very good reason for not trying. I shall simply assume without proof that the examples discussed in this paper as specimens of the type are indeed commonly regarded as short stories.

Nor is it a question of defining a different form, if by form we mean, as we usually do, certain materials unified to achieve a given effect; for the materials and their organization in a short story differ from those in a novel in degree but not in kind. To say, as has frequently been done, that short is distinguished from long fiction by virtue of its greater unity is surely to beg several questions at once. A fossil survivor of Poe's aesthetic,[3] this notion confuses wholeness with singleness, unity with intensity. If unity implies that all the parts are related by an overall governing principle, there is certainly no reason why a short story should have more unity than a novel, although it may naturally have fewer parts to unify—a matter we shall examine in due course.

Nor may we say that a short story cannot deal with the growth of character, as has also been frequently done, or that it focuses upon culminations rather than traces developments, because the simple fact is that many stories do portray a character in the process of changing—

Ernest Hemingway's "The Short Happy Life of Francis Macomber," for example, or William Faulkner's "Barn Burning." Similarly, there is no reason why a story cannot deal with a change in thought, as in Wilbur Daniel Steele's "How Beautiful With Shoes," or with a change in fortune, as in F. Scott Fitzgerald's "Babylon Revisited." (Of course, some stories *are* static, and we shall discuss them below.) Nor may we say that stories are more commonly organized around a theme than novels, for some are, like Shirley Jackson's "The Lottery," and some are not, as Edith Wharton's "The Other Two" (see chapter 6). A story may arouse suspense and expectation, pity, repugnance, hope, and fear, just as a novel may, and may resolve those emotions in a complete and satisfying way, just as a novel may.[4]

There is, of course, much truth in the approaches we have just touched upon, but none of them manages to include enough of the actual possibilities to be finally useful. Surely short stories contain fewer words than novels, but that measure is a misleading one because it centers on symptoms rather than causes; surely a short story may make a singular impact upon the reader, but that is an effect having to do with questions other than simply unity as such; and just as surely a novel may deal at greater length with dynamic actions than a story, but there are ways in which a story may handle changes within its own sphere. Most of these principles, in brief, are too prescriptive. In order to understand how and why a short story gets to be short, therefore, I would like to propose a way of answering these questions which will apply to all examples of the type without prescribing beforehand what the characteristics of that type should be.

A story may be short, to begin with a basic distinction, for either or both of two fundamental reasons: the material itself may be of small compass; or the material, being of broader scope, may be cut for the sake of maximizing the artistic effect. The first reason has to do with distinctions as to the object of representation, and the second with distinctions as to the manner in which it is represented (see chapter 7). We will thus discuss the size of the action (which may be large or small and is not to be confused with the size of the story, which may be short or long), and its static or dynamic structure; and then the number of its parts which may be included or omitted, the scale and order by means of which it may be shown, and the point of view from which it may be told. A story may be short in terms of any one of these factors or of any combination, but for the sake of clarity and convenience we shall discuss them separately and give cross-references where necessary.

III

Elder Olson has provided us with a useful set of terms for discussing the question of the size of the action with some degree of clarity and precision.[5] A *speech*, he says, contains the continuous verbal utterance of a single character in a closed situation; the speaker is either talking to himself without interruption (soliloquy), or if there are others present they neither reply nor make entrances and exits while he speaks (monologue). This is the kind of action shown in most short poems commonly called lyric, as in Marvell's "To His Coy Mistress," or Keats's "On First Looking Into Chapman's Homer," and many many others. A *scene* includes the continuous chain of utterance engendered between two or more speakers as one replies to the other (dialogue) in a closed situation, while an *episode* contains two or more such scenes centering around one main incident. A *plot*, finally, is a system of two or more such episodes.[6] And a short story may conceivably encompass an action of any such size.

Naturally a large action, such as the plot of *Great Expectations*, although unified in terms of its overall size, will contain smaller subactions, such as speeches, scenes, and episodes, unified in terms of their particular sizes; and these smaller subactions may be and often are detachable for certain purposes, as when an episode is extracted from a larger work for inclusion in an anthology. Actions of different sizes, that is to say, dovetail the smaller into the larger. The point is, however, that a speech, scene, or episode which is designed in itself to serve as the unifying basis of a single complete work must be fully independent, whereas in a larger work it is only partially so, necessarily containing elements binding it to what has gone before and what is to come after.

Why an author makes a certain initial choice regarding size we can only guess, except that he probably senses that he has a whole and complete action in itself and that this will suffice as a basis for separate treatment. This is a matter, then, of the original conception, and all that we can say is that a writer chooses to treat actions of different sizes because he feels, either by habit or deliberate choice or intuition or some combination, that any given one embodies all that is relevant to his purpose. An action of any given size, then, may be whole and complete in itself, and the smaller the action, the shorter its presentation may be.

The relevant parts of an action which is whole and complete, therefore, include those incidents which are needed to bring about and then display whatever necessary or probable consequences the writer wants to show his protagonist enacting or undergoing (structural parts), and such other incidents as may be useful in casting these in their proper light (representational parts). The size of that action, then, will depend upon what he wants his protagonist to do or suffer and upon how far back, correspondingly, he must go in the protagonist's experience to find those causes which are both necessary and sufficient to motivate and make credible that action. Clearly, a dynamic action will call into play a larger number of causes than a static one, and a more inclusive change will require a longer chain of causes than a less inclusive one. An action of whatever size is thus whole and complete whenever the delicate interlinkage of causes and effects encompasses whatever is enough to make that action both understandable and likely.

The speech is best suited, obviously, to render a single moment or a brief succession of moments in any given chain of cause and effect. An immediate response, whether static or dynamic, to an immediate stimulus is the special province of lyric poetry. In Keats's "Chapman's Homer," for example, the speaker responds with an expression of wonder to the fact that he has just discovered a magnificent poem, while in Robert Frost's "Stopping By Woods" the speaker responds to the mysterious attraction of the dark and snowy woods by first yielding to their temptation and then by resisting it. In the first we have a single but complete moment of feeling, while in the second we have a longer but equally complete succession of moments during the course of which the speaker makes up his mind about something, in the sense of choosing between alternatives. Either way, these particular actions are inherently small, and whatever is needed to make them clear and likely may therefore be encompassed in a rather short space.

As a result, such actions are rarely treated in fiction, even short fiction. We all know that the devices of the poetic art are especially capable of handling this sort of thing in an intensified manner, and that narrative prose, being especially flexible, is much better suited to larger actions where more has to be shown. I do know of three or four such actions in fiction, but they are rather the exceptions which prove the rule. Dorothy Parker's "A Telephone Call" presents a young lady in the throes of anxious anticipation as she awaits her boyfriend's belated phone call. And that is all there is to it: as far as we are concerned here, the entire story comprises her interior soliloquy as she waits for the phone to ring. E. B. White's "The Door" similarly presents practically nothing but the continuous mental states of its one and only character—shown sometimes indirectly by way of narration and sometimes directly by way of interior soliloquy—who is portrayed in a state of uncertainty and frustration regarding the contradictory values of modern civilization. Hemingway's "Big Two-Hearted River" is rather unusual in presenting a single character going through successive stages of thought and feeling in response to an unfolding series of situations containing no one else but himself. Jack London's "To Build a Fire," finally, is somewhat similar in this respect, except that the isolated protagonist there does interact with and respond to the reactions of his dog.

To present a single scene is much more feasible in short fiction, although even here pure examples are not as common as one might think. The best and clearest specimen with which I am familiar is Hemingway's "Hills Like White Elephants," which shows a young American couple waiting in an isolated train station in the valley of the Ebro for the express from Barcelona. Except for the waitress who brings them drinks, the story encompasses only the single and continuous interchange of dialogue which occurs between the man and woman as they wait. The point of this story, which deals with a static situation, is, I think, to reveal to us by degrees the cause of the girl's plight and through that to arouse our pity. Apparently unmarried, these two are on their way to get the girl an abortion. This is not, however, the source of the story's pathos; it lies rather in our discovering as the conversation progresses that her lover has no real feeling for her and her incipient need to extend their relationship to its normal fruition. Since that is all we need to know to get this particular effect, and since it can all be done within the bounds of a single conversation, that is all Hemingway had to show to unify this particular story.

And it is done, of course, with consummate skill. We read toward the end, for example: "He did not say anything but looked at the bags against the wall of the station. There were labels on them from all the hotels where they had spent nights." From this small detail we are allowed to infer worlds about the situation of this couple: the shallowness of their relationship, its rootlessness and its transiency. This allusion to the immediate past, although not formally a part of the whole action being shown (since the causes of the pathos are shown as the scene itself progresses), helps to place the situation in its proper light in the reader's mind. And notice how artfully it has been incorporated into the fabric of the present scene itself without authorial intrusion.

The episode is an even more commonly found size in the short story; indeed, its frequency may warrant our calling it the typical sort of action dealt with by this art. Hemingway's "Ten Indians," for example, contains five scenes centered around Nick's discovery of his Indian sweetheart's infidelity, his subsequent depression, and his final forgetfulness of his sorrow. He is, after all, rather young to allow amorous heartbreak to affect him for more than a few hours at a time. This is a dynamic action involving changes in thought and feeling, and therefore requires, other things being equal, a larger action than a single scene for the establishing of its chain of cause and effect. It does, however, all take place within the span of a few hours, and each of its scenes leads up to or away from a single central incident: (1) Nick is driving home late one afternoon from a Fourth of July celebration in town with the Garners, and they kid him about his Indian girlfriend; (2) they arrive at the Garners, unload the wagon, and Nick strikes out for his own home; (3) Nick is walking home; (4) his father gives him supper and tells him how he saw Prudie "having quite a time" in the woods with another boy, causing Nick to feel bad; (5) Nick goes unhappily to bed, but awakens contentedly later in the night to the sound of the wind and waves, having forgotten his sorrow.

Thus a scene or episode requires less space in the telling, other things being equal, than the plot.

Another question regarding size is whether the action involves a change, and if so, whether that change is major or minor, simple or complex. I hope it is clear by now that a short story may be either static or dynamic; but, as we have seen, an action which is static normally requires fewer parts than one which is dynamic and will therefore normally be shorter in the telling. That is to say, a static story simply shows its protagonist in one state or another and includes only enough to reveal to the reader the cause or causes of which this states is a consequence, while a dynamic story brings its protagonist through a succession of two or more states, and thus must include the several causal stages of which these states are the consequences. Thus a static story will normally be shorter than a dynamic one.

Therefore, although not all short stories are static, most static actions are likely to be found in short stories. Static situations expanded and elaborated to novel length are comparatively rare, and again the few that come to mind are exceptions that prove the rule. *Mrs. Dalloway* is an instance which I will discuss in more detail in chapter 17, and some of the characteristic works of Alain Robbe-Grillet depend for their peculiarly viscous effect upon the use of this device. In *Jealousy*, for example, the structural principle I take it is the revelation of the protagonist's anxious state of mind as he obsessively goes over and over the circumstances of his wife's overnight trip into town with their neighbor. Normally material for a short story, this situation is made relatively longer—a little over 100 pages in the American edition—in three basic ways.

First is the fact that Robbe-Grillet, in line with his critical pronouncements,[7] has chosen to filter the story strictly through his main character, and not only through him alone but also strictly through his sense perceptions rather than his ideas and feelings. The protagonist-narrator speaks in the present, rarely participates in dialogue, and never mentions himself.[8] The result is that we are given facts merely and must infer his mental states from these facts—just as he himself must infer whether his wife was unfaithful or not merely from the facts. Since it takes more space to give the causes of mental states than the mental states themselves the story is longer in the telling.

Second is the fact that the nature of the protagonist's mental state is indeed obsessive, and he must mull repeatedly over the same incidents time and again, seeing them from different angles and in terms of varying contexts, imagining those he did not witness and fantasizing about some he did. Third is the related fact that these repetitions do not follow their normal chronological order and are shown as if they are taking place in the present. Not only repetition,[9] then, but also presentness occupy more space in the telling.

There are, nevertheless, general correlations between static and dynamic actions and their various sizes. To achieve in fiction a change in the protagonist in a single speech or scene is possible but not likely, and to extend a static situation through an entire independent episode or complete plot is also possible—as the examples above show—but also unlikely. I would say, as a rule, that most static actions require but a scene or a small episode.

Another example of a static story, in addition to "White Elephants" already discussed, is Sean O'Faolain's "Sinners," which reveals a Catholic clergyman's mental anguish over the lies of a servant girl at confession. The priest is shown first twitching irritably at her stories during the confession, and then crying out in positive vexation later when he happens to overhear her admitting her lies at confession to her mistress. His emotional state is announced, as it were, in the first phase of the story and confirmed in the second phase (because of transitions there are slightly more than two scenes here). Thus the reader is made to see his frustration and then to understand it as having ample justification. In order to achieve this effect, the writer showed as much as he needed, two scenes or so, and no more.

Of course, by introducing a whole new line of causes he could have continued this story to show us the canon going through a subsequent change in feeling for the better; but if he had merely gone on with the same line of causes, he would have blundered in exceeding the needs of his effect. It is this effect and the amount of action required to achieve it which determine the shortness of this story, when considered in itself as an independent work.

"Francis Macomber," "Barn Burning," "How Beautiful With Shoes," "Babylon Revisited," and "The Death of Ivan Ilyich" are short stories which comprise, on the other hand, dynamic actions. In the first, a cowardly man becomes finally courageous in the face of danger; in the second, a young boy decides to oppose at last his father's vindictive destruction of their landlord's property; in the third, an ignorant mountain girl becomes aware that man can be more than an animal; in the fourth, a reformed drunkard is frustrated temporarily in his plans to regain his estranged daughter; and in the fifth, a dying man sees his empty life truthfully for the first time. But there is a difference regarding magnitude even among dynamic actions, for all but the last are minor changes, not in the sense that they are unimportant or that their consequences are not serious or far-reaching, but rather in the sense that they call into play and require for their representation only one phase of their protagonists' lives. Thus a minor change will normally require less space than a major one.

Here again there may be a general correlation between inclusiveness and the size of an action, for most minor changes will involve but an episode, while a major change will involve a complete plot. In this sense, "Ilyich" has more in common with *Great Expectations* than with the other stories just mentioned; indeed, it covers even more aspects of its protagonist's life than the Dickens novel. Some episodes, then, are static, and some are dynamic, but plots tend almost always to be dynamic. And one of the differences between a short story plot and a novel plot need not, as we shall see below, be a difference in the intrinsic size of their actions but rather in the manner in which their actions are shown. In this sense, "Ilyich" is of course much closer in length to a short story than to a novel.

On the other hand, there is no reason why an action covering several episodes may not involve merely a minor change. We have thus to distinguish, on the basis of inclusiveness, minor and major plots (and I suppose an episode may deal with a major change, but I do not think this is likely). Fitzgerald points to this distinction as he narrates the experiences of Dexter Green in "Winter Dreams": "It is with one of those denials [the mysterious prohibitions in which life indulges] and not with his career as a whole that this story deals." And again, toward the end of the story: "This story is not his biography, remember, although things creep into it which have nothing to do with those dreams he had when he was young. We are almost done with them and with him now." Fitzgerald is saying, in effect, that this particular story finds its unity in treating only as many episodes as are required to show the reader the causes of Dexter's infatuation with Judy Jones and his subsequent disillusionment in her and the youthful possibilities she stands for in his mind, and that Dexter's other experiences (probably his business ventures and the like) are not particularly relevant thereto. He has guided himself, in consequence, largely by this original choice in matters of where to begin and end, and how much to include and omit. It is this limitation as to what phases of the protagonist's life are relevant to a given change which accounts for the shortness of this story.

The action of *The Great Gatsby*, although it is strikingly similar in its general outlines, is a major plot because it deals with Gatsby's entire life. The obsession of Gatsby with Daisy and what she represents to him consumes all aspects of his career and indeed costs him his very life at the end. The disillusionment of Gatsby therefore cannot be understood except in terms of his life as a whole, and that is why his story takes longer to tell than Dexter's. To have added Dexter's other interests to "Winter Dreams" would have been just as bad an artistic mistake as to have omitted Gatsby's from *The Great Gatsby*: the former would have resulted in irrelevance, while the latter would have caused a lack of clarity. Indeed Fitzgerald was aware that some critics of the novel have argued that it is too short even as it is to produce the requisite sense of probability or necessity in the reader,[10] but that is quite another matter. (A rather different complaint has been raised against *For Whom the Bell Tolls*, which seems to some critics too *long* in proportion to the size of its action.)[11]

There is a second difference regarding magnitude among dynamic actions which cuts across the one just examined between major and minor changes. A simple change brings its protagonist gradually from one state to another without reversals and is thus, since it calls into play only a single line of causation, a smaller action than a complex change, which brings its protagonist from one state to its opposite and which thus calls into play several lines of causation. The former, having consequently fewer parts, may be shorter in the telling.

All of the dynamic actions discussed so far are examples of the complex type, while Joseph Conrad's "An Outpost of Progress" illustrates a simple change. The moral characters of Kayerts and Carlier, weak and shallow to begin with, deteriorate swiftly and surely when brought to the acid test of prolonged and intimate contact "with pure unmitigated savagery" in the heart of Africa. If a short story can deal with the development of character, it can also deal, apparently, with its degeneration. It is interesting to contrast this story with *The Heart of Darkness*, for there, in making Kurtz a paragon of moral character *before* his surrender to the abyss, Conrad set himself a much harder job. But he also achieved more vivid results, because if the fall of Kayerts and Carlier is more probable, it is also by the same token less interesting. The second story, however, is almost three times longer than the first (the greater length of *The Heart of Darkness*, incidentally, may also be explained in terms of its ruminative narrator—a topic to which we shall return below).

Thus because it requires more "doing," a dynamic action tends to be longer than a static one; a major change, because it includes perforce more aspects of the protagonist's life, tends to be longer than a minor change; and a complex change, because it has more parts, tends to be longer than a simple one. But our principles must be continually qualified at every point because, as we shall see, we are dealing with a set of independent variables. A story which should be long in one way may actually be short in another; a story involving a major change, for example, which should be longer than one involving a minor change, all other things being equal, may actually turn out to be shorter because those other things are not equal.

IV

A short story may be short, then, because its action is inherently small. But, as I have indicated, a story may encompass a larger action and still be short. If a writer has decided to show a plot, he has a further option as to the manner in which he shall do so. And here, as we know, he will be guided by his desire to maximize the vividness of his effect on the one hand, with the optimal degree of intelligibility on the other, in combination with the greatest economy of means. He may decide that although a given part of the whole action is relevant, he may best omit it and leave it to inference. A whole action is, as we have seen, an action of a certain size—whether a speech, scene, episode, or plot—containing whatever is relevant to bringing the protagonist by probable or necessary stages from the beginning, through the middle, and on to the end of a given situation.

The question now under examination concerns selection, or how many of these parts are actually shown to the reader and how many are merely alluded to or left to inference. In John Steinbeck's "Flight," a young and hitherto rather shiftless boy, as a result of his first visit alone to the city, is forced to prove himself a man—even to the point of facing death bravely. In the actual telling of the story, however, Steinbeck chose to omit the boy's trip to Monterey entirely, bringing it in only later when the boy returns and tells his mother what happened there before he sets out for the mountains.

We are dealing with a complex dynamic action: what are the parts required for such an action to achieve its proper effect?

A complex change involves bringing the protagonist from one state to its opposite by means of a reversal. What is required for clarity and belief, therefore, is (1) a precipitating cause to bring him into his first state, (2) a counterplot action to represent the consequences of that state, (3) an inciting cause which will serve to bring him out of the counterplot and on toward the opposite state, (4) a progressive action to represent him in the process of change, and (5) a culmination where the process is completed.[12] A simple change, as we have seen, involves bringing the protagonist from one state to another without a reversal and therefore requires only the last three parts outlined above. And similar principles regarding selection may be applied to static actions in terms of the single states and relevant causes which they reveal.

Let us see how this scheme works for "Flight": (1) the boy is sent to Monterey for medicine by his mother; (2) he dons his father's hat and rides in his father's saddle, boasting of his newfound manhood, and in Monterey drinks too much wine and gets into a fight; (3) he kills a man and must now either face the consequences like a man or run and hide "like a chicken"; (4) he returns home, tells his mother what happened, prepares himself for his journey, and suffers untold hardships for four days among the mountains; and (5) he dies finally with honor by facing, in his last extremity, his pursuers and accepting their vengeance. Most of phase two and all of three are omitted. Why?

We may say in the first place that, because probability demands that the protagonist tell his mother what happened anyway, Steinbeck simply acted in the interests of economy by avoiding repetition. That, however, is a rather mechanical explanation, although pertinent enough in its own way. More importantly, we may infer that Steinbeck intended to leave us with feelings of mingled pity and admiration for this boy as his story unfolds—pity for his suffering and death, and admiration for the noble manner in which he suffers and dies. This being the case, we may infer further that he left out most of the counterplot and the inciting incident because in his effort to arouse our sympathies he wanted consciously to avoid showing us his protagonist acting senselessly, without thought, and fatefully. By omitting these portions he also impresses us more vividly with the startling contrast between immaturity and maturity in his protagonist's behavior from the time he leaves in the morning till the time he returns at night. He is thus free to concentrate the greater portion of the reader's attention upon the boy's suffering and nobility rather than upon his rashness and immaturity. We must still know, however, what happened in Monterey, why the boy is taking to the mountains, and in what light to regard these events. And this we get from the boy's narration to his mother: the very fact that he tells her without hesitation and evasion is a sign of his real manhood. He was insulted, and so he killed before he knew what he was doing. Thus his ultimate death is made acceptable on the one hand and admirable on the other.

An instructive contrast to Steinbeck's wisdom in this matter is provided by a television adaptation of this story which I happened to see some years ago. Faced with wholly different technical problems, the television writer sought to enlarge his script not only by including those parts of the action which were left out of the original, but also by elaborating upon and expanding them. The young boy is shown in Monterey —it was fiesta time and he got mixed up with a girl—and we see him getting insulted and killing his man. The fiesta allowed the insertion (intrusion would be a better word) of some dance productions as well as of some flicker of romantic interest. The flight itself was handled as honestly as possible, but even there the limitations of the medium necessitated the awkward device of having the boy talk to himself as he suffered, since he was, of course, alone and the fictional narrator was denied his function. The overall effect was distracting, to say the least: the only really relevant parts are the insult and the murder, so that the dancing and the girl, even though they were trumped up as the causes of his being insulted, simply came to nothing in terms of the rest of the story; even with the insult and the murder, it was quite upsetting actually to see our young hero draw blood, and the subsequent effort to elicit our sympathies for his suffering in the mountains was correspondingly weakened. Perhaps because of the brevity of the original and its corresponding dependence upon narrative flexibility, the dramatized version of "Flight" was doomed from the outset.

The point to be made here is that a story may be short not because its action is inherently small, but rather because the author has chosen in working with an episode or plot to omit certain of its parts. These gaps may be at the beginning of the action, somewhere along the line of its development, at the end, or some combination. Correspondingly, an action may be longer in the telling because more than its relevant parts are included.

Once he has decided what parts, of those which are relevant, he will include, the writer has a second option as to the scale on which he will show them. A given action may be made longer in the telling by expanding its parts, or shorter by contracting. The contracted scale, as we know, tends to cover a long timespan of action in a relatively short space, while the expanded scale tends to cover a short timespan in a relatively long space. And all this is, of course, actually a question of degree.

James Joyce's *Ulysses* goes to one extreme by expanding a single day into a full-length novel comprising many episodes, while Tolstoy's "Death of Ivan Ilyich" goes to the other in being as good an example of a whole and full-sized plot condensed down to the length of a short story—albeit a rather long one—as can be found. It contains twelve numbered sections of varying lengths and, with some backtracking, takes its protagonist all the way from his childhood to his death in late middle age, including his schooling, courtship, marriage, career, and children. The whole action culminates in Ivan's first and final awareness, as he dies, of the reality of death and consequently of the hollowness of his entire life up to that point. Clearly, in order for this change to strike the reader with the proper intelligibility and force, Ivan's entire life has to be shown. The impact, that is to say, of Ivan's discovery depends for its point upon a knowledge of how his life has been lived previously and in terms of what values and attitudes. But "Ivan Ilyich" is short (relatively) because, although the whole plot and more is shown, it is shown largely on a condensed scale. Likewise *Ulysses*, although it covers so much smaller a timespan, is so much longer because its action is expanded to the last detail (apparently).

Economy is still the general principle in these cases, however. Even though Ivan's whole life must be shown, it is of such a repetitive and shallow character (which is exactly the point, of course) that to have shown it on a full scale would have bored the reader to extinction—although Tolstoy naturally does represent the more important parts of his plot on an expanded scale. Joyce, too, did what he had to do to get his effect, although it is of an altogether different sort. Since the work turns, as we have seen, on Stephen and Bloom and Molly's becoming aware of and accepting each other's reality, it is exactly these realities which Joyce must emphasize. In addition, of course, to particularizing the historical and expanding the mythical, he also manages to include much material from the past, which is outside the frame of the present action. Such inclusions naturally also help increase the length of the book. It follows therefore that while an almost infinite expansion serves Joyce's purpose, it would have hampered Tolstoy in the achievement of his.

Another instructive contrast between the two extremes is found in comparing "Ivan Ilyich," which utilizes a high degree of contraction, with "White Elephants," which is almost as expanded as a single scene between two people covering thirty minutes or so can be. The reasons for this difference should be clear by now: Tolstoy has a large action to show, but most of it is important only as it throws light upon the final few scenes; while Hemingway has only one scene to show, and show it he does. Thus a story may be short, even if it encompasses a large action, because much of its action is best shown on a contracted scale.

We have seen how the question of order or sequence may also be involved in this matter of length—the question of whether the order of presentation follows the time-sequence of the events in the story or not. It is clear that an action whose limited timespan would ordinarily call for a short presentation may be made longer in the telling by the use of time-shifts or the bringing in of material from the past into the present of the action, as is the case in *Jealousy* and *Ulysses*.

Time-shifts may be seen in terms of a scale which runs from minor changes to major ones. Small shifts may occur almost inevitably in the telling of any story which involves more than one set of characters and incidents. Actions which are in fact occurring simultaneously cannot be presented simultaneously, and therefore one must be dropped while the other is turned to and brought up to date, as in *Vanity Fair*, which is a characteristic example. Slightly larger shifts may occur by means of the abrupt and dramatic opening and the subsequent looping back to fill in the needed expository material, as in "The Metamorphosis." Then there is that sort of delayed, piecemeal revelation characteristic of *Oedipus* and *Gatsby* and of course of mystery and detective stories. And there are the major chronological transpositions, where large blocks of time are simply rearranged in the presentation, so that we have not simply overlapping, looping back, or delayed revelation, but a basic disruption—commonly called the flashback—in the unfolding of the present action itself, as in *Lord Jim*. Here, past incidents are not merely explained, brought in, or referred to, but are also actually portrayed in the same manner as the present action and so produce effects which are on a par with that action.[13]

Let us look at the related problems of selection and order in "The Bear," as a case in point. Although each of the sections involves major disruptions of the normal chronological sequence, it is the fourth section—almost half of the entire story—dealing with the talk between Ike and his older cousin over the plantation ledgers, which involves the problem of selection as well.

One of the major effects here, it seems to me, is that of the archetypal and timeless pageantry of the hunt and of the mode of existence of the old bear. Disruptions of chronology function not only to create the usual effects of suspense and expectation, but also to produce a sense of timelessness by juxtaposing present events against past and future events —a technique most fully developed, of course, by Joyce in *Ulysses* and *Finnegans Wake*, T. S. Eliot in *The Waste Land*, and Ezra Pound in *The Cantos*—thereby minimizing the sense of change and development, while maximizing the sense of sameness and recurrence. In a way, it is a denial of history, of mortality, and of the human world (the general); and yet in another, it is an interpretation of history and human life (the universal).

The fourth section of "The Bear," however, is also easily detached, for while the other four sections, if thought of chronologically, are parts of a relatively continuous narrative concerning the hunt and its aftermath, this section is removed not only in time—a "flashforward" taking place some three years after the conclusion of the main action—but also in place and mode—occurring on the plantation rather than in the woods, and being much more of a debate and exposition than an actual "action." Faulkner himself lends support to this view when he says that, although the fourth part is appropriate when the story is seen as belonging to the larger *Go Down, Moses*, it is not appropriate when the story is seen as a whole in itself.[14]

On the other hand, many critics have felt that this part gives to the story, which they usually see as a relatively independent unit, its ultimate profundity and significance; for it is here that Ike comes to understand history and to relate the wisdom he learned in the woods to that understanding.[15] The result is a decision, fed by his experience in the forest, to repudiate his inheritance and to live the simple life of a carpenter and woodsman—thereby putting him in that long line of "dropouts" in American fiction analyzed so pungently by Leslie Fiedler in *Love and Death in the American Novel*. Thus the question of part 4 is not one of techniques merely but finally one of basic structure as well as meaning: without it the action forms an education plot, while with it the action forms a maturing plot—a change in thought, or a change in character.

Although the other four sections read marvelously well without this part, and although certain obscurities of vision emerge in it, I do not feel that, once having had this story with five sections, we can be content with only four. It is true, as Faulkner indicates, that part 4 relates more directly to the rest of *Go Down, Moses* where Ike's subsequent life as a carpenter and woodsman is shown, but it is also true, as most critics have thought, that part four grows naturally and necessarily out of the rest of the story itself. Furthermore, I feel it is in fact best that part 4 be placed unchronologically as it is because it does help to produce thereby the requisite air of repetitive foreknowledge essential to the whole. Despite its faults, then, and even though it makes the presentation almost twice as long, this section does make the story per se more rich, profound, and moving; and I do not see how we can put it out of our minds when confronted by the abridged version.

We may consider, finally, how the choice of a point of view is related to the question of length. If a writer decides, for example, to allow his narrator complete omniscience, then several things will naturally follow. His narrator may editorialize, as in *Tom Jones* or *War and Peace*, and this of course will add significantly to the bulk of the work. Or, given omniscience, his narrator may analyze his characters' motives and states of mind at some length, and such commentary and exposition will also increase the bulk of the work. This is the reason why Thomas Mann's "Disorder and Early Sorrow" seems to cover so much more ground at first sight than it actually turns out to encompass upon close study: although it takes almost two hours to read, it actually includes an action whose timespan runs only from the afternoon to the evening of the same day. Because the action is shown through a screen of exposition and commentary regarding the professor's states of mind, even though the external action itself is rarely, as a consequence, shown directly and on an expanded scale, this short story is a lengthy one in proportion to the time covered in the action.

Omniscience involves, on the other hand, features favorable to brevity. That is, a narrator who exists over and above the action itself may exercise, as they say, wide discretionary powers in matters of scale and selection. Because he is bound by no mortal limitations, he can manipulate his material at will. Thus he may shift the scene of the action in time and place, and, more importantly for the question in hand, may omit and/or sum up parts of the action which do not merit more explicit and detailed treatment. In the long run, then, omniscience is characterized by its flexibility and is equally at home in novels and short stories.

A character-narrator may also be given to commentary and speculation, as is Marlow in *Heart of Darkness*, and this too may add to the bulk of the work. The dramatic point of view similarly, because it is committed by definition to an expanded scale, as on the stage, tends toward length. Thus an author who chooses the dramatic method for a short story had best work with an action of small size to begin with or, dealing with a larger one, omit certain of its parts.

To sum up, a story may be short because its action is intrinsically small; or because its action, being large, is reduced in length by means of the devices of selection, scale, order, and/or point of view. No one can tell in advance that, if a story is short, it is short because it has a certain number of words, or because it has more unity, or because it focuses upon culmination rather than development. All we can do, upon recognizing its shortness, is to ask how and why, keeping balanced simultaneously in our minds the alternative ways of answering these questions and their possible combinations. And then we may win increased understanding and hence appreciation of the specific artistic qualities of this curious and splendid but vastly underrated art.

PART THREE
THE PROBLEM OF MEANING

Chaper 10

Theory of Meaning

Having sketched out and illustrated a theory of form and of formal analysis, we must inquire now into the question of meaning and of the interpretation of meaning—or, better still, of the relations between form and meaning, art and life—no small order, of course, and I approach it with a full sense of the many difficulties involved. But perhaps if we retain a firm grip on what has been said in the preceding chapters about form, and if we can use this sense of form as we work in this large amorphous area of meaning, we might be able to find our way toward a somewhat clearer conception of what is going on here.

I

As R. S. Crane points out, since the Aristotelian notion of form is that certain materials are being shaped in a certain way to achieve a given end, there is no separation between form and content in this approach. If form is "shaped content," then it is impossible to discuss form apart from content. When we discussed structure and end, we could not do so apart from considerations of the protagonist's circumstances, his moral goals and purposes, his attitudes and beliefs, and the reader's moral and emotional reactions to these things. There is, as we see, a necessary and inherent connection here between literature and life, art and reality. The job of discussing form and the job of discussing meaning, as Crane says, are not two tasks but one.[1]

Yet when we look at a work from the point of view of formal analysis, it has strictly speaking no meaning at all. We have all learned from the New Critics—who seem not to follow their own teachings—that a poem should not mean but be. Of course, neither they nor Archibald MacLeish (whose poem is apparently contradictory, a didactic work against didacticism) are, in their own terms, necessarily contradicting themselves: as we have seen, although a poem has something to say, it should do so implicitly, suggestively, dramatically, and by means of images rather than directly and overtly. The meaning thereby embodied is more rich and various than direct statement can be. This doctrine goes significantly beyond Sidney's, which says merely that poetry makes meaning more affective and vivid; for the New Critic poetry makes a different sort of meaning altogether.

I do not need to rehearse my objections to this theory—that even though it thinks in terms of differing means in relation to a different way of thinking about the end, its end is still meaning, and therefore it is a theory of meaning rather than of form—I merely want to show that the question can best be handled by separating the problem of form from that of meaning and then by discussing their relationships. And I shall do this by trying to distinguish between *meaning* and *meanings* and between the particular end of a work and its whole or form.

Formally speaking, then, a work has no meaning; it simply *is*. And I take this much more literally than the New Critics, for I do not believe merely that, while the end is meaning, the devices of embodiment are dramatic and concrete and implicit—even if I agree that these devices *do* create another order of meaning in the process. I believe that the work as a form does not mean anything at all (unless one wants to quibble about the meaning of the word as implying intention, as in "What do you mean by doing that?"); it does not "have" meaning, nor does it "say" anything. It is rather *doing* something: it is structuring parts in relation to a whole. And this includes didactic as well as mimetic works, prose essays and discursive poems as well as dramatic ones. To look at any work formally is to examine its organization, not its meaning. It may *have* meanings; it may *use* meanings; but it does not *mean*. Of course, as we shall see, a meaning may emerge from its meanings, and its organization may imply meaning, but the first step is to see its organization as organization.

It is worth emphasizing here that this distinction concerns what we do at a given level of analysis; it does not concern the nature of the object itself. A work of literature is everything at once, but in terms of a given approach it is only one thing at a time. The problem of criticism, as I have said, and the problem of this book, is to make useful distinctions and then to work out effective ways of relating the things thus distinguished. So it is perfectly valid on one level to say with Oscar Wilde that all art is quite useless, but it is perfectly silly to say it on another level. From the point of view of form, it *is* in fact a matter of internal relations, and there is nothing precious or perverse or paradoxical about it; from other points of view, it is not, and there is nothing utilitarian or vulgar or philistine about it. (Although, as we shall see, even such useful distinctions are more complex than they seem, for form involves questions of external experience, while meaning involves questions of form.) Both the aesthetes and the moralists make the same mistake of confusing criticism with art, the aspect of the whole which serves as the critic's subject matter with the whole work itself, the thing said with the thing spoken about.

Thus if we talk about form, we talk about ends and means; it does not matter to us at this point what meanings it may contain, or even if its end *is* to say something. What does matter is that it *has* an end, no matter what it is, and how its parts relate to that end, how its meanings relate to the whole. Even in a didactic work, where the end is specifically a meaning, the problem of form is to see how its means relate to that end, its parts relate to the whole; even in a didactic work, meanings are to be interpreted contextually, and meaning is a function of form. We concern ourselves, that is, not with the meanings as such but rather with their functioning. This is what we imply when we tell students that to summarize is not the same as to analyze, and if we can encourage the latter we need not fear the heresy of paraphrase. In a didactic work or prose essay, we want to know not simply what the meaning is but more that it is the end governing the whole; indeed, the end itself is not so much the meaning as it is the principle which controls the functioning of all the meanings, and the meaning is what the New Critics say it is—a Total Meaning, a matter of the whole context. In this sense, meanings are among the givens of our analysis: as with any elements of the whole, they are what we start with rather than what we conclude with. The end of the work is not the end of the inquiry; it is rather an item of analysis, for form is a composite of means, manner, object, and end.

This separation of form and meaning does not contradict what I said at the opening of this chapter about Aristotelian analysis not separating form and content. The sense in which this is true is the sense in which meanings are parts of the whole: to analyze the whole is willy-nilly to analyze meanings. Meanings are a part of form: meaning is a matter of the whole.

But in just what way are meanings a part of form? And exactly *how* do we know what they are? In fiction, some set of human values must go into motivating the action, and so we can reasonably expect to infer those values from an analysis of that action. Specifically, since the plot sets up and resolves a human problem, and since this problem-solving process necessarily involves right and wrong answers, it follows that we can infer an underlying value system which explains the distinction. Another way of putting it is to say that we can infer the nature of the causes from the nature of their effects. The course and outcome of the action, as we know, are determined by external circumstances in combination with the moral and temperamental qualities of the protagonist, and the outcome is, in effect, a judgment upon those causes. Events evaluate motivation: the consequences of an intent are, in the total context, a judgment of that intent.

This is a principle which may be less difficult to illustrate than explain. When Pip embarks upon his career as a "gentleman" in *Great Expectations*, we know he is pursuing false values, and we know this for several reasons. It produces bad effects in him, for one thing: he becomes ashamed of his former life, but his new life is idle and aimless, and it brings him no happiness. Furthermore, it springs from rather suspicious causes: he thinks he is the beneficiary of Miss Havisham's largesse and is intended to marry Estella, but we know that the old lady cannot be trusted and that her standards are arbitrary and ambiguous. Finally, the fact that it is this career which he must abandon in order that the plot may be resolved "proves" that it belongs on the negative side of the scale of values.

Of course, a resolution itself may be negative, as is clearly the case in works which are didactic because their culminations produce no catharsis, but such endings are distinguishable from cathartic ones in terms of the total context of the action. Thus we know that Pip's return to the forge is a positive act because, although it takes a good bit of suffering to accomplish, it makes him feel better about himself and his life, and he is a basically well-meaning chap. On the other hand, while Winston C. Smith, in 1984, must abandon his beloved in order that his plot may be resolved, we do not take his love for her as belonging on the negative side of the scale. And we know this because the state which breaks his will and wins him over has been portrayed in decidedly negative terms. Indeed, that is the artistic purpose of the book, as we have seen, and it is reinforced and culminated in the destruction of the protagonist's spirit.

Thus it is not so much the *way* in which the plot resolves as it is the *fact* that it does which tells us about the values embodied, for a resolution puts two or more forces in opposition; and it is this contrast which defines, or partially defines, meanings. That is to say, since a plot works by setting up and then eliminating alternative courses of development until one has been fixed upon and the others have been denied, we can tell in the context what is positive and what is negative in terms of human evaluation. Even if the resolution is ambiguous, and even if there is no resolution—or even if a work is so impassive as apparently to deny any evaluation—these possibilities too tell us about the values embodied.

There are such values, then, embodied in almost any plot—often even in mere adventure stories—simply by virtue of the structure of the action, and these are meanings which it contains. They have gone into the motivation of the sequence of incidents. An analysis of how they function in the whole results not in a statement about what the work means, but rather in a hypothesis about how the means are related to the end. They exist not to be interpreted but to be analyzed.

II

But if meanings are formal, it is also true that form itself is dependent upon life and experience. For the establishment and resolution of a conflict are not sufficient in themselves to imply a system of values—they must also be consistent, both within themselves (coherent) as well as with reality (congruent). And it is in relation to reality, of course, that form is not autotelic.

I have already explained what I think Aristotle's *necessary* and *probable* mean, but I must develop these terms a bit further for the present argument. There is first their purely aesthetic meaning: the writer must remain true to his own givens as he works out the sequence of incidents and brings it to a close; he must have one incident follow another in terms of what is inevitable or likely in relation to what has gone before. We understand and accept certain things happening in a certain way, therefore, because they have been prepared for, we have been led to expect them. This is a matter of internal consistency, of coherence, and from this point of view the work *is* self-contained, organic, reflexive, contextual; and verisimilitude or credibility regarding correspondence to actual life is not primary. Aristotle even says that factual distortion, if it aids the effect, is permissible. Lord Macaulay, who has many interesting things to say on these matters, throws further light on this concept: "Truth, indeed, is essential to poetry; but it is the truth of madness. The reasonings are just; but the premises are false. After the first suppositions have been made, everything ought to be consistent; but those first suppositions require a degree of credulity which almost amounts to a partial and temporary derangement of the intellect" ("Milton" [1825]). This is somewhat exaggerated, but it is true as far as internal consistency goes.

On the other hand, there is the moral meaning of necessity and probability: since the author is trying to prepare *us*, to develop *our* expectations, he cannot concern himself with establishing probabilities and necessities merely in terms of *his* givens. He must also depend upon his knowledge, and his estimate of our knowledge, of actual life and experience in order to know how to handle these probabilities and necessities. He can show that a certain character is a coward and prepare us for his cowardly behavior at the crisis; but what cowardice is, and how cowards behave, are matters to be determined in terms of the community of experience and values which the writer shares in a society with his readers.

This shared community is a matter of external consistency, then, of congruence, and it derives from observation, beliefs, and judgments.[2] Observation tells us whether certain things generally happen or not; beliefs tell us that certain acts have certain causes or motives in certain contexts; and judgments tell us that certain acts have certain meanings, significances, and values. Again, Macaulay's exaggeration is illuminating, although I am not so sure that he shows how it squares with his earlier statement: "A fiction may give a more impressive effect to what is already known; but it can teach nothing new. If it presents to us characters and trains of events to which our experience furnishes us with nothing similar, instead of deriving instruction from it, we pronounce it unnatural. We do not form our opinions from it; but we try it by our preconceived opinions. Fiction, therefore, is essentially imitative. Its merit consists in its resemblance to a model with which we are already familiar, or to which at least we can instantly refer" ("History" [1828]).

Even in the case of plots based on fantasy, as I have argued, the writer must follow a principle of what would be probable or necessary if such things existed. We have to be able to extrapolate, that is, from what we do know to what we do not know, and to put them into some sort of analogous relationship, before we can understand, appreciate, and respond to any supposedly self-contained plot. While internal consistency is a direct principle, then, external congruence is an indirect one; but the first depends upon the second, since the links between what is given and how this leads us to have certain expectations come from outside the work. In other words, internal consistency provides the *form* of our expectations, while external congruence provides the *material* in terms of which they operate. This is a specific way of explaining the "shaped content" concept or, better still perhaps, "content-ed shape."

And this concept applies both to the aesthetic and the moral emotions aroused by the action. In order to play upon our expectations—involving intelligibility, or what we will accept as having been prepared for—and then upon our sympathies—involving the artistic purpose, or what we will accept as plausible and what will make us feel and react in certain ways—the writer must be able to know or intuit how we will respond to certain things; he can do this because of this shared community of experience and values about life and experience. He does not have to agree with these assumptions, but he has to be aware of what they are in order to bring about his desired effect. Nor does he have to remain bound by or limited to them, contrary to Macaulay, but he must either work *from* them or lose us altogether. Indeed, the meanings of a work exist in this tension between what we already know and what the author needs to get us to see.[3] And in the case of works which exist outside of our culture, either because of removal in time or place, it is one of the functions of historical scholarship and of the study of comparative literature, as we shall see, to show us what other sorts of writers and audiences could be assumed to know, particularly in terms of the functioning of the general and historical level.

Even in the case of works which exist within our own culture, it is one of the functions of teaching to bring the world of the student and that of the writer into some sort of congruence. The job, then, of analyzing "content-ed shape" has broad implications, and is no mere academic exercise. Technically and formally, we must talk about this shared community of values in order to discover how an artistic structure functions, but once we do this, we have opened the door to all those complex problems of meaning. Nor need this be a cause for alarm: form is form, but it also involves meaning, and ultimately implies meaning.

III

Even congruence with the external word, general and/or universal, is only a consistency by analogy. If measured against strict standards of verisimilitude, literature is self-contained in another and further sense. It can never really transpose directly what we know from life: we must accept its verisimilitude in relation to the powers and limitations of the medium, in relation to the conventions of the art. Art cannot function at all apart from some frame, some foreshortening, some exaggerating, some distorting, some selecting, some manipulating, some arranging. Even spontaneous art—chance composition, action painting, happenings, environments, audience-involvement theatre, and the like—in trying to abolish the separation between art and life, can only do so to a degree.[4] Nothing can be actual experience except actual experience itself: when it is duplicated directly, by film and tape-recording for example, it becomes flat and dull; and when art tries to imitate it literally, it becomes confused and aimless. And, of course, even film and tape-recorder inevitably involve selection and distortion.

In actual dialogue, for example, normal repetitions of phrases are filtered out as we listen to and participate in the talk: they establish tone, manner, attitude, and so on, and we attend more carefully, within that context, to the substance of the talk. In written dialogue, the novelist can suggest this repetitiousness, but he cannot duplicate it exactly, for it will then appear, by force of the written as opposed to the spoken word, more repetitious than it actually appears in real life. We do less filtering out, on this level, in reading than in living. Compensatorily, he must also introduce in his words somehow the equivalents of tone, manner, and attitude which are the products of physical confrontation in real-life dialogue—voice, posture, gesture, facial expression, and a dozen other similar phenomena. That is why Wordsworth, when he was arguing in favor of the use of common life and common language in poetry, also had to keep insisting that the poet should use a selection and organization of common life and language in order to produce poetry of value.

We are dealing here with the principle of mental sets made familiar by Gestalt psychology: different media imply different intentions, evoke in us different modes of attention, and arouse different expectations, so that where a given element will affect us in one way in a given medium, that same element will affect us in another way in a different medium.[5]

That is why something happens to content when it enters a form, and that is why meaning is a function of form. If we want to transpose a certain effect from one medium to another, therefore, we must use different means to produce that same effect. And this principle applies not only to the transposition of elements from one artistic medium to another, but also to the transposition of elements from the medium of actual experience to any of the media of art.

And not only to the transposition from life to art, but also to any shift from one situation in life to another. The sound of a phone ringing affects us in one way when we are in a crowded restaurant, for example, and quite another when we are at home. People dressed in scanty bathing suits produce different reactions on the beach than they would if they showed up dressed that way in the city. Friends sometimes fail to recognize us if they see us in unfamiliar circumstances; strangers react differently to us if we wear unaccustomed clothing. Behaviors permitted at ball games, in boxing rings, and in war are forbidden in other contexts. War itself seems intolerable if we view it in personal terms, but may prove acceptable if we view it in political ones. We feel differently about children when we become parents than we did when we were children. Indeed, we ourselves change in different contexts, acting in terms of the structure we become a part of, as when we achieve a portion of authority, for example, in an institution where we were previously subordinate.

On the other hand, as I shall point out later in my discussions of Albert Camus and Ernest Hemingway, often these frames outlive their functions; and we feel the need to challenge them, change them, or transcend them, doing something out of context or thrusting something new into a context, in an effort to make life less routine, less abstract, less dehumanized, more full, more natural, more real. Many features of the so-called hippie, youth, counterculture, and peace movements are based on the need of young people to experiment with behaviors—in dress, in sex, in school, in politics—that were eschewed by their parents. The satirical device in literature of the innocent or foreign observer also serves to bring into view new perspectives upon old frames. A similar principle provides a rationale for such various avant-garde devices as the collage, juxtaposition, found objects, environmental art, pop art, the nonfiction novel, and the like. But there is built-in obsolescence in all frames, whether old or new, and both life and art go through cycles of convention and revolt, as certain ways of seeing become routinized and new ones take their place. The new ones then become absorbed back into our modes of attention, and the process must begin again.[6]

Thus if art cannot imitate actual life, it can still give the effect of actual life, as Dr. Johnson said in his preface to Shakespeare; and it can do this by an imaginative transposition—by finding equivalents in its media for those aspects of life it is trying to render which exist in *their* medium. That is why art, even though it is not purely formal, is like life only by analogy; and that is why it is always, first and foremost, formal, a matter of means and ends. The New Critics are right then in saying that language is all, but not so much in the sense that it governs *what* the writer wants to say as that it governs *how* he may say it. How literature can be both reflexive and referential at the same time is not particularly mysterious: it *means* in relation to life, but *what* it means, for the reader, is a function of the context. But the New Critics are wrong in saying that this is the differentia of literature, for all meaningful experience is a matter of context, of media structuring elements; therefore the study of such structures is the basis of understanding meaning and is indeed the true meta-study, the mother of the sciences. It is our basic chance to free ourselves from that crippling human prejudice which identifies what is right with what we are used to; and it is the basic reason why theory, and the theory of theories, in life as well as art, far from being the sterile, arid, and abstract pursuit it is often taken to be, is in fact fruitful and liberating.

Just as we must go by analogy in dealing with the implied system of values in a work, from what we know in life to understanding what is in the work, so too must we make the transfer, in dealing with a shift in medium, from the way life actually appears to its representation in art. There is, as Macaulay suggests, a model in each case against which we test art in terms of its resemblance to that model. The model in the first case is more a material matter—a picture of the world which we have in our heads—while the model in the second case is more a formal matter—a sense of effects and how they may be produced. But in both cases these models are ultimately based upon how the mind reacts to and acts upon experience: we notice patterns in life by filtering out the distractions, and we make observations and come to beliefs and judgments by means of generalizations upon those patterns.

Thus the writer, when he wants us to grasp the fact that one of his characters is a coward, for example, and so to prepare us to expect a certain sort of outcome, must not only incorporate into his characterization enough of what we understand cowardice to be in order to produce the appropriate effect on us, but also must not confuse us by putting in as much noncowardice as we might find in a similar situation in life, in order not to weaken the desired effect—for we will pay much more attention to the opposing evidence in literature than we do in life. In order to realize that a man is a coward in real life, we do not expect that he will be cowardly in everything that he does; we expect only that he will be cowardly basically, in important situations calling for courage. Now the writer, in order to get the effect of versimilitude, would do well to include in his portrayal some of his character's noncowardliness. Otherwise, he will be open to the charge of being overschematic, shallow, and naive. But he would also do well not to include as much of it as might be found in real life, for our sense of what is important and what to pay attention to differs in life and in art. And this limitation applies, as we shall see, even to modernist writers who want to convey a much less fixed sense of character and a much less contrived sense of plot.

What we can see in our own lives only in in the midst of a thousand distractions, the writer highlights for us in a more accessible way. We respond to his story, except that we are free for the moment from literal involvement, just as we would respond to it in real life—if we could recognize it there. The difference is that if we do recognize it there, we ignore the distractions as the pattern emerges for us—we know they are irrelevant. But if the writer puts in the distractions along with the pattern, we tend to take the distractions as relevant. The force of the medium— the experience of words rather than the experience of life—compels us to attend equally to all that is said, thereby causing us to risk losing the pattern.

It is clear that critics have been developing this argument all along, but I am not sure that they have done so in the same way or in terms of the same reasoning. It is common to argue in favor of the abstracting process of art in the sense of art as an idealization of life, an improvement, a typification, a transcendence, an essence, even as—for Wilde—a deliberate falsification or lie. In this view, art is more real than reality and presents a golden nature, in Sidney's terms, rather than actual nature. When this view attains ascendency, it then becomes necessary to rebel against it in the name of realism, naturalness, or aimlessness. But the point need not be put in this way, and so the polarization is—logically, at least—fruitless. Another usual way of putting it is that art needs to create the illusion of reality by means of selecting and arranging but does not necessarily need to idealize it. This is closer to my own position, except that I think the theory of the altered mode of attention appropriate to different media offers a more specific rationale for the position. The question then becomes, if we accept the fact that we must willy-nilly come to terms with the powers and limitations of our media, not whether art should be more like life or less like it, but rather which means will best produce the desired effect in a given medium. And so we come to the realization that an artist may have to alter reality in order to be more realistic:[7] the real element may have a false effect in the new medium, while an unreal element may have a truer effect. Formal and representational theories of art are thereby reconciled rather than opposed.

This is what I think Aristotle meant when he said that a probable impossibility is more effective than an improbable possibility (Poetics, chapter 24), for what actually happens in life may not be plausible. A contradiction between what we think we know and what actually happens is not automatically implausible: it may involve either an unassimilable freak occurrence or a meaningful element which causes us to reorder our hitherto inadequate system of knowledge. If it is the former, then Aristotle is right; and if it is the latter, he is also right, for then we will simply be operating as before, only on the basis of a broader system of probabilities. Truth may be stranger than fiction, as the old saw has it, but fiction may be truer than truth.

IV

This seeming paradox is not as contradictory as it may sound, and I suspect that it lies at the bottom of the many nineteenth- and twentieth-century attempts to define art as an order of knowledge different from that of science. We realize that we do not get factual accuracy or literal congruence with reality from art, but we also sense that art is nevertheless a form of knowing. In order to avoid the opposing traps of regarding art as either an inferior brand of science (Zola) or a harmless toy (Bentham), we have become enmeshed in a variety of rather murky cognitive doctrines about "total meaning," "nondiscursive language," "prescientific consciousness," "wholism," "mythic awareness," and "emotive vs. referential meaning." Thus, instead of being poor science, art becomes a superior form of religion or morality or philosophy.

I do not think that I can settle this difficult question once and for all, but I do have a simpler explanation which might serve as a beginning. In experience we come to knowledge about life just as we do in science, by hypothesis, by experiment, by trial and error, by abstracting, by seeing relationships, by accumulating data and ideas, and by building and growing. The differences are mainly two: our knowledge of life is hampered by inherited cultural patterns which are imposed on us as we grow up and which tend to limit the number and kind of hypotheses we can apply to experience; and our control over the relevant variables is much less than it is in the laboratory. Consequently our knowledge of life is much less accurate and certain. On the other hand, our scientific knowledge is limited, even though theoretically it should not be culture-bound, to those relatively few matters whose variables can be controlled.

Nevertheless, just as we get our knowledge of life by abstracting and relating, which is a process similar to that of science, so too does the artist, by virtue of shifting the medium, have to select and arrange in order to interest, move, and illuminate us. The difference here is that, while in life we must come to our insights in the midst of distractions which we cannot control, in art we must eliminate or at least reduce them. The reason is that our mode of attention is different when we read a novel as opposed to when we are in experience. It is this felt pattern in the midst of distractions which art imitates, and it is this which we may call its inner truth. It is true because it is there; it happens.

Although structures do not inhere in reality, we cannot know anything without them. When it comes to the inner truth of art, it is a fact that patterns of relationships do occur to people—the effects of causes, the results of acts, connections and intersections, similarities and differences.[8] These may not be what they were expecting or looking for, and indeed much may be said in favor of a more undifferentiated awareness as a healthier approach to life, but these are patterns nevertheless. Nor do they emerge only if we have the support of some traditional value system beforehand. They emerge because of the way things happen in relation to the way the mind reacts to things. I can agree with Alain Robbe-Grillet in saying that the universe does not reflect human consciousness, but I cannot agree that this necessarily means we must abandon plot, character, introspection, and all the rest. Even Robbe-Grillet's characters see objects in terms of their own obsessions, while at the same time the implied author is presenting these objects in his deadpan way.[9] It is this subjective-objective tension which organizes his presentation, as indeed it did for art before the new novel, however more conscious he wants us to become of it.

The truth of art is the truth of experience, of the world as it impinges on the mind, and if there is no guarantee that that is the way the world *is*, there is nevertheless a sense that that is the way the world is to *us*. One frame is neither better nor truer than another, but we need not conclude from this that all is relative. Frames serve certain reality functions in certain contexts, and then, as the contexts change, the frames become outmoded. If we can never achieve experience apart from frames, we must nevertheless be continually testing them in relation to the functions they are supposed to serve in their respective situations. Each writer who shows a pattern of significance gives us a hypothesis to test on our pulses, whether he shows us a familiar or an unfamiliar one, and it is up to us to use it accordingly. If it occurred to *him*, however, it is authentic, and we begin by accepting that fact.

Art is more like science, then, than different; and Aristotle was right when he said that poetry is more philosophical than history, Sidney was right when he said that it refines upon nature, and Dr. Johnson was right when he said art creates the illusion of life rather than life itself. Art is different from science only if we take science either to be merely the observation of facts and the accumulation of data, or the only way to obtain meaningful knowledge.[10] Indeed, it could be said that Aristotle sees history as the mere chronicling of facts and thus distinguishes it from poetry which orders facts, but I do not think he is best interpreted in this way. If poetry consists in the construction of plots—that is, in the making of a causal sequence—this does not necessarily mean that the historian finds no sequence of his own.

The poet finds what is there, as I have been saying, but it need not be literally there in the facts as they present themselves—it need be there only in the sense that we can recognize that life is like that when we see patterns in experience amidst the distractions. Thus the poet is freer to select and arrange: he need not treat the entire life-span of Achilles, nor the whole of the Trojan war, nor even all of Achilles' involvement in that war, but only (say) Achilles' wrath and its consequences. He is bound only to establish and resolve that issue.

The historian, on the other hand, is more closely bound to the facts as they present themselves, but he too is looking for a principle of organization. The difference lies, I think, in a different relationship between fact and principle. As Macaulay puts it: "In fiction, the principles are given, to find the facts; in history, the facts are given, to find the principles. . . . The talent which is required to write history thus bears a considerable affinity to the talent of a great dramatist. There is one obvious distinction. The dramatist creates; the historian only disposes. The difference is not in the mode of execution, but in the mode of conception. Shakespeare is guided by a model which exists in his imagination; Tacitus, by a model furnished from without" ("History" [1828]). In other words, although both form their materials, the poet fits his materials to his form, while the historian fits his form to his materials. Each has a different standard of validation; each refers to a different court of appeal. For the poet it is artistic unity and truth-seeming; for the historian it is factual accuracy and cogency of interpretation in those terms.[11]

Although science is like history in being bound to the facts as they present themselves, it is also like poetry in being more selective than history. The laws of science deal like poetry with what is generally and probably so, while history must deal with what actually and literally happened in any given situation. Thus it is that history must deal, unlike poetry and science, with the possible improbability. Macaulay explains it this way: "Hence it is that the anecdotes which interest us most strongly in authentic narrative [history] are offensive when introduced into novels; that which is called the romantic part of history is in fact the least romantic. It is delightful as history, because it contradicts our previous notions of human nature, and of the connection of causes and effects. It is, on that very account, shocking and incongruous in fiction" ("History"). This notion, of course, is subject to my previous distinction between improbabilities which are freaks and those which make us enlarge and reintegrate our conceptions of what life is actually like.

The basic difference, on the other hand, between science and art, conceiving them both as structures of knowledge, is that one of the variables which science strives to eliminate or control is precisely the one which art tries to center upon, namely, the observer himself. It is not that science is objective and art subjective, but rather that art is concerned with the interrelations between object and subject, while science—even the so-called human or social or behavioral sciences—is concerned with the objective in itself. Art is concerned, as I have suggested, not only with external reality, but also with how it appears to the observer and how he feels about it, which might with justice be called "internal reality."

Thus the writer gives us not simply ideas and insights but how it *feels* to have ideas and insights, as Sidney implies and as Arnold and Eliot have said.[12] It is not that he depends upon critics and philosophers for ideas and insights: those which he deals with, at that intersection between external and internal reality, are his own province and arise from his dwelling upon his own distinct and legitimate subject matter. Understanding experience as it is felt by a person living it is another form of knowledge, different from that of science, and it is this which I think is meant by all that talk about nonrational discourse.

Only there is nothing mythical or preconscious or mystical about it. It is true that literature depends largely upon dramatizing insights rather than upon simply stating them, but the reason is that it is difficult if not impossible to render the feeling of experience merely by explaining it. It must be shown in such a way that the reader will feel and not just understand it, for if he does not feel it, he will not really understand it. This is what Keats meant when he said that truth is not truth until it is tested on the pulses, and this is what present-day organicists mean when they talk about the objective correlative, contextual or reflexive or total meaning, and nonparaphrasable content.

Thus there is in fact another kind of truth and another form of presentation for expressing it, but this doctrine can be explained much more simply than has hitherto been done. We can come to understand scientific truths by intellectual means, but when it comes to understanding life and experience, we have to be somehow inside life and experience ourselves. And this is what art attempts to do: it gets inside of people, and it induces us to feel their feelings. What is the use of defining love—or even jazz, as Louis Armstrong or Fats Waller is supposed to have said— unless we can somehow feel it for ourselves?

V

Meanings are a part of form, then, but they come from life and experience; on the other hand, although they refer to something real, they must be adapted to the medium. They exist at that intersection between external and internal reality, between art and life. What of the meaning of a novel? How do we actually relate it in practice to formal analysis?

We have what is commonly called a "created world of values" in a novel, and this pattern is there both because the writer needs to know his audience's assumptions in order to play upon its expectations and sympathies and because he wants to freshen and extend these assumptions. His knowledge of life and experience and the overlap between his knowledge and his audience's are drawn into the structure of the work in order to enable it to function. Then we extrapolate and generalize from that implied system of values in order to compare it with our own notion of the world as well as with that of other writers. The result is a juxtaposition of pictures of the world, and herein lies the interpretation of meaning. The problem, as we know, is to extrapolate and generalize in terms of the functioning of meanings *within* the work, rather than in terms of abstracting them *from* it.

To say that the writer wants to freshen and extend our assumptions, however, is not to say that he has didactic designs upon us: *Great Expectations* is an absorbing and moving tale, and it would be foolish to say that it teaches us anything. Even if it does, what could it be teaching, except that it is wrong to become a snob? Surely we knew that before. Even 1984, which is formally a didactic work, is not simply teaching that totalitarianism is wrong. We also knew that before. What we have in each novel, whether mimetic or didactic, is a tension, conflict, and adjustment established among values; and, as we experience the unfolding of this pattern, we become aware not simply of ideas but rather of their relationships to people and situations and feelings. It is this sense of relationships, as we have been saying, which constitutes a novel's area of knowledge. It is not merely the knowledge but rather the ingestion and internalization of insight which make the difference, because it not only comes to us through the medium of an observer, but it also places *us* in the position of an observer (*observer* in the context of this chapter, since it refers to the intersection between subjective and objective, could be read equally as *participant*).

This is the sense in which art may be regarded as reflexive, autotelic, and unique: the knowledge it embodies cannot be found elsewhere, except in those moments when we respond as artists to life and feel a pattern emerging in the midst of the irrelevancies. And yet we are not actually artists until we have mastered some medium for transferring that pattern into another form so that it can be felt by others. That is what Aristotle meant by regarding art as artificial, as a form imposed upon some matter which does not naturally take that form, and that is what the New Criticism means by emphasizing that art is not just its content.

That is how I have been trying to reconcile the apparently rival claims of art and life, for art is not merely reflexive either, and reference to the outside world is inevitably involved in the very terms we have been using to analyze form. The knowledge we get from literature is unique to art, but it is at the same time a knowledge of life. Poetry is both reflexive and cognitive; it means, but what it means is a matter of its context. It must be what Arnold meant in saying that serious poetry is at bottom a criticism of life, and what everyone means when he talks about theme and vision and what the writer has to say. We naturally sense a difference among writers in this respect, not only in that one may have a different sort of vision from another, but also in that one may have a larger and/or deeper vision than another. Thus we may say that Dostoevsky's vision differs markedly from Fielding's, William Faulkner's from Henry James's, and that all of these writers have more of a vision than that of the standard best-selling novelists, such as Herman Wouk, Leon Uris, and Frank Yerby. It is not simply that the lesser novelists are worse writers qua writers—John Updike, for example, a lightweight among serious novelists, is certainly a skillful and clever writer. It is not difficult to distinguish, as Faulkner has suggested, between writers who can do what they set out to do extremely well and those who try to do more but succeed less consistently.

This is what is wrong with the extreme aesthetic position which, in healthy rebellion against representationalism, philistinism, didacticism, and utilitarianism, claims that a writer writes language, a painter paints paint, a movie-maker makes film, and so on. Mastery of a medium is mastery only of means: all arts, when considered from the point of view of meaning, have an end beyond themselves, and that is somehow to heighten, broaden, and deepen our awareness of life. But they must do so—and this to me is the true significance of aestheticism—in their own way, in terms of their own special kind of knowledge, and by means of their own unique devices. When the great precursors of modern formal criticism—Gautier, Flaubert, Baudelaire, Mallarmé, Swinburne, Pater, Whistler, Wilde—speak of the nonutilitarian freedom of art, they do so in terms of the larger vision which thereby ensues, and not in terms of any sterile encapsulation of art apart from life. To divorce art from society is not tantamount to divorcing it from life, and that is why the New Critics have been at such pains to develop a formalistic approach in terms of "total meaning."

It is in the context of these familiar issues that I have been trying to establish two points of my own: first, that although meaning is a valid critical question, it is not to be confused, as the New Criticism does, with form; and second, that if it is to be handled clearly and precisely, it must be done in terms of form. This is how I hope to do what all sensible critics have tried to do: preserve the autonomy of art while at the same time insisting upon its human importance. For we must reconcile the double need of any significant theory of literature, which is to respect the demands of form and reality at one and the same time.

The first point hinges upon the distinction I have been making between *meanings* and *meaning*. The formal critic must perforce deal with *meanings* even as he analyzes parts and wholes, means and ends; but his job is completed when he has a hypothesis in terms of which to explain the function of the parts in relation to the whole, the means in relation to the end. The critic of *meaning*, on the other hand, following upon the formal critic's findings and hypotheses (needless to say, they may of course be one and the same person), asks another and different sort of question—namely, what do all these meanings, in combination with everything else in the work, a work which is partly self-contained and partly not, imply about the author's vision of the world? In other words, how do the meanings relate to each other and to the whole to suggest meaning? It is here that it is relevant to go outside the work—not merely in terms of how it relates to our common assumptions about experience —to relate it to other works of the same author, other authors of the same period, and other periods. Thus we become logically involved in the study of vision, history, and archetypes.

But (this is where the second point hinges) he cannot do this either by ignoring formal analysis,[13] taking it for granted, or collapsing the distinction between form and meaning. If form and meaning are not the same, meaning is most certainly a function of form. We all know that meaning cannot be properly interpreted apart from its context in the work, but it is not always clear that this context is form and not meaning, and that form may involve meanings but is a question independent of meaning. Otherwise it would make little logical and less practical sense to say that one thing depends upon another if they are really both the same.

"Meaning is a function of form," as I have pointed out, might be considered a contemporary critical catchword, just as "form is the relation of parts to the whole" is; but just as the latter has not always been thought through clearly, so too has the significance of the former not always been fully worked out. In certain obvious cases, its meaning is clear enough, as when we know that Gloucester's lament is a contextual expression of his own anguish rather than of Shakespeare's cynicism. And yet we are not always so specifically aware of dramatic contexts and plot structures when we interpret the parts of a work as standing for the whole. Indeed, the latest feminist interpretation of D. H. Lawrence, Henry Miller, and Norman Mailer as male chauvinists confuses the ideas of characters with those of their creators in a very inconsistent way.[14] Because modern criticism has tended to underplay the role of literal actions in its analyses of fiction (as well as poetry), it is likely to come up with favored hypotheses without any sense of the need—or of the method—for supporting these hypotheses.

Thus I attempt to show in certain of the chapters which follow that to interpret symbols and symbolic structures apart from explicit plot analysis frequently results in misreading, that one cannot really discuss the meaning of a novel until one has specifically analyzed its plot. We cannot look first, in other words, for structures of meaning: if the meaning inheres in the plot, it is the plot which must be analyzed first.

Formal analysis may be simply routinely corroborative of our interpretation of meaning, confirming what we have already sensed. But even if formal analysis turns out to tell us nothing new, we cannot really know in advance that this will be the case and so must look for confirmation of hypotheses anyway—if only to develop good interpretative habits. How else can we actually know that we are not simply favoring a certain interpretation because it corroborates something in our heads rather than because it is consistent with the evidence in the work?

But formal analysis is necessary, of course, when the plot is so subtle and complex as to defy easy generalizations, when it is hard to settle on a satisfactory interpretation of meaning among competing interpretations, when the reigning interpretation seems to be accepted without adequate scrutiny, or when it seems to exceed the evidence. And it is necessary, finally, if we are really to avoid the heresy of paraphrase and retain the essential quality of artistic knowledge—that which inheres in the intersection between the subjective and the objective. Meanings must not be seen merely as relating to other meanings, but rather as functioning within an action of a certain kind.

The principle here is that an element in a set of relationships has its meaning only or basically in terms of that system. Effects are best understood in the context of their causes: an act is best interpreted in terms of its motives, intentions, and consequences. But, as I have said, cause-effect relations may be regarded from either end, and if an effect results from what the writer does, it may at the same time also be said that his attempt to achieve that effect is the cause of what he does. Thus if formal analysis determines our interpretation of meaning, it may also be said that our knowledge of meaning—of the writer's vision, of the assumptions of his age, of the historical influences working on him, of archetypal patterns—can aid us in the creation of hypotheses for formal analysis and can even be seen as causes of elements in the work. It is reasonable to assume, as we have seen, that what it shares with many different works over a long period of time has archetypal causes, what it shares with other works in its tradition or period has historical causes, and what it shares with other works by the same author has temperamental causes.

What it shares as a whole with no other works has, of course, only formal causes. Indeed, all the other causes must be pressed into the service of the formal causes: if the former do not originate in the form, they must at the very least be appropriate to it. All must be shaped, in other words, toward one end; formal causes funnel and dispose all other causes *toward* and *within* the work itself. Content, as we know, is changed when it gets into a form. If the writer must find an equivalent in the new medium of the original impulse in an attempt to preserve that impulse, then the reader must resist the temptation to see the whole in terms of that content, but rather must see the content in terms of that whole. That is why meaning is a function of form, why we should not read out of context, why paraphrasing is heretical. If an element had an independent existence before entering the work, it no longer has it after entry. It has entered a new system of relationships and has now a slightly or greatly different meaning.

The form-meaning relationship, then, is reciprocal: meaning may cause certain elements of the work, while form causes the whole and determines our interpretation of everything in it on whatever level—*determines* in the sense of "limits," "controls," "guides," "serves as the basis of," "provides the context for." That is why, if we can see historical causes operate in a work, it is also true that we can get our best idea of the period by close formal analysis of many works. Then this improved idea of the period can be applied to other works as a help to analysis and interpretation, which can then be reapplied to improve our period concept further. Thus formal study can be used to improve the study of meaning, the study of meaning can be used to improve the study of form, and so on, each reinforcing the other in a mutual way. But only if they are seen as separate questions to begin with, and then appropriately related.

We turn now to the body of part 3, wherein the problem of meaning is explored first in relation to artistic vision, and then in relation to the interpretation of symbols and archetypes, with the historical level of interpretation serving as a point of reference throughout.

Chapter 11

Theory of Vision

Having discussed the general interrelationships between form and meaning, literature and life, we are in a position now to talk about looking at a work and interpreting its particular created world of values, the author's way of regarding life embodied there. If a system of values is implicit in the structure of the action, in other words, we need categories and procedures for making them explicit; and if these values derive from the overlap between the work itself and our experience of life outside the work, we need methods and approaches for relating the work to other things. We want, that is, to be able to trace the actual connections between form and meaning, and then, with these in hand, to go on to larger contexts which will throw added light on them and bring them into areas of concern for us as human beings living in the extra-artistic world.

I

Beginning with the work itself, we must proceed from the meanings embedded in the work to an analysis of the meaning which they, in combination with the form and their role in the form, add up to. R. S. Crane suggests three categories, derived from Longinus (whose criticism was aimed in part at defining the quality of an author's mind), for getting at this question: "namely, thought, in the sense of the author's distinctive conceptions of things [and it will be noticed here that this is not the Aristotelian term, being actually closer to what Northrop Frye mistakenly interprets Aristotle to mean by it]; emotion, in the sense of the characteristic qualities of his sensibility; and expression, in the sense of all the devices of language by which his thought and emotional responses are realized in his works or particular passages thereof."[1]

Let us develop these suggestions further. Regarding thought, there is at hand a commonly used scheme which might prove useful; it asks in turn three questions: what is the author's view of the relation between man and himself, between man and society, and man and nature? The first might be termed the area of the author's psychological assumptions; the second the area of his moral, political, cultural, economic, sociological, and historical assumptions; and the third that of his religious and metaphysical assumptions. The first and third deal with what I have been calling the universal, while the second deals with the general.

Regarding emotion, in addition to such commonplace categories as optimism and pessimism, or even such archaic ones as the sanguine, the bilious, the phlegmatic, and the like, I once developed a scheme which is partly a matter of thought and partly a matter of emotion, but which does bring out some useful distinctions concerning attitudes.[2] One can conceive of the relation between nature and society, freedom and control, in four different ways. The Philistine sees nature as dangerous and chaotic, and wants human forms to order and contain it (James Gould Cozzens, for example). The Anarchist sees nature in terms of its own order, and wants human forms merely to allow that order to express itself (Henry Miller, for example). The Reformer sees society's forms as being too limited, and hence wants to open them somewhat (Dickens). And the Utopian wants a radical change in the forms altogether (George Bernard Shaw). There are, consequently, four attitudes one can take toward this problem. The Discipline Paradoxer, who resembles the Philistine, believes that one can achieve freedom only through control (T. S. Eliot), while the Freedom Paradoxer, who resembles the Anarchist, sees control as arriving only through freedom (Blake). On the other hand, the Discipline Ambivalent, who resembles the Reformer, chooses order while loving freedom (Capt. Vere in *Billy Budd*), and the Freedom Ambivalent, who resembles the Utopian, chooses freedom while loving order (Aschenbach in *Death in Venice*).

Regarding expression, apart from his particular formal, structural, technical, and stylistic practices, which will be taken up in a moment, we may ask about an author's expressed or implied aesthetic and critical assumptions, and here we may go the round of critical questions as outlined in the first chapter of this book: what is his view of the relation between the parts and whole of a given work, of the relation between the writer and the work, between literature and history, literature and the audience, literature and reality? The first, of course, pertains to his assumptions about artistic form; the second to his assumptions about biography, psychology (certain overlappings here are natural and logical), imagination, and the creative process; the third about historical criticism and all that it implies about genres, traditions, movements, influences; the fourth about fame, education, morality, politics; and the fifth about metaphysics, imitation, science, truth.

As far as the use of these categories is concerned, Crane suggests two procedures: first, that we test our generalizations about an author's vision against what formal criticism tells us, and second, that we specify "in the details of the texts the particular devices through which the felt qualities of the writer are made manifest."[3] These procedures involve deriving meaning from meanings, and meanings from form, as well as relating the expressive power of the aesthetic aspects of the work themselves to meaning.

Again, the implications of these remarks need to be developed. The real issue at this level is how form reflects vision and how vision affects form—or, if you will, what the reciprocal relations are between thought and emotion on the one hand and expression on the other. We can define meaning on the basis of three steps: making explicit the meanings implied in the structure of the action, interpreting them in terms of their role in that structure and in the form as a whole, and seeing them in terms of the meaning of the writer's characteristic artistic devices. Expression, in other words, is expressive in itself. Patterns and qualities in the medium inevitably, if loosely, suggest implications above and beyond the medium.[4]

The field of aesthetics commonly takes this third matter as one of its principal concerns: how balance implies rest, imbalance unrest; rapid rhythm excitement, slow rhythm peace; closed couplet certainty, run-on line hesitation; red passion, white purity; and the like. If we saw in the preceding chapter that similar effects in different media require different devices because different media affect us in different ways, we see now that media have intrinsic and specific powers and limitations of their own, that they are not aesthetically and emotionally neutral. This is not to say that the medium is the message—but it certainly contributes to and affects that message. And these powers and limitations derive from the relation between the human body and mind and from facets of external experience—sometimes literally, as when the heart beats faster when excited so that rapid rhythm means excitement, and sometimes figuratively, as when the unpleasant feeling we have when touching something rough with the hand leads us to equate other kinds of roughness—visual, stylistic, intellectual—with difficulty and disagreeableness. As we have seen, it is unreasonable to expect ideas from music, and it is hard for language to be direct and immediate. Certain media are more bound to temporality, while others are more bound to spatiality, and it is difficult to get the effects of one in the other. And, cutting across these distinctions, we find that certain qualities of composition, such as symmetry and asymmetry, have certain affective powers in all media.

We want to know therefore not simply what a writer's view of man, nature, art, and society is, but also what difference his view—and our knowledge of it—makes in the way he writes and in our interpretation of the way he writes. Correspondingly, we want to be able to infer, if vision does make such a difference, the meaning of various visions on the basis of various ways of writing. The orderly way in which Jane Austen's plots work out, her rational conception of character and motivation, the balanced quality of her style, the level tone of her narrator's voice—these imply a largely reasonable, commonsense, and conventional view of life (not necessarily, however, a dull or ordinary or uninspired view). Similarly, if we know anything about her vision of life, we would expect to be able to appreciate the fact that the artistic qualities of her works represent not simply a certain bag of aesthetic tricks but rather a specific way of looking at life. The aesthetic aspects of her work embody a kind of meaning in themselves and apart from any more direct implications of value to be found in the characteristic human issues, problems, situations, and milieus of her novels. It is at the point of intersection between these two mutually related levels of meaning—what the plot tells us about the author's values, and what the way it is handled tells us about these same values—that the study of vision should find its center, and it is here that it can proceed reciprocally in two directions—how the whole reveals meaning, and how meaning affects the whole.

This approach is not as circular as it may sound. In the first place, we do not simply go from form to get meaning and then from the same meaning to interpret form. There is a crucial intermediary step aimed at getting the meaning right on the basis of formal analysis, which implies, as Crane says, testing one's generalizations against the facts. This test means that one can come up with better and worse interpretations, so there is nothing self-proving about it. It is also the case that the relation between form and vision is not automatic; what an author means and how he embodies it may not be positively related at all. A poor poet may embody an intensely vivid and personal experience in a slack and mechanical style. More subtle questions of this sort are found in Baudelaire's use of a balanced style to embody rage, disgust, and hallucination; in Hart Crane's use of the fragmented method of *The Waste Land* in *The Bridge* to achieve a vision of integration; or in Thornton Wilder's being inspired by *Finnegans Wake* to write *The Skin of Our Teeth.*[5]

In the second place, and correspondingly, going in two directions does not simply represent the asking of the same question in two different ways, but rather two different questions. When we go from form to meaning, as I have said, we are asking how our interpretation of meaning is based on and limited by our analysis of form, whereas when we go from meaning to form, we are asking how meaning affects form; that is why our interpretation of meaning must be controlled by form to begin with. The two questions are different by virtue of asking about two different causalities: what governs interpretation, as opposed to what governs things in the work being interpreted. So the former should be governed by the latter.

II

We know that on a formal level a work is complete, self-contained, and autonomous. We concern ourselves here with internal systems of relationships, and—particularly if the work is successful—we do not need outside information. We also know that, even on the formal level, we must necessarily bring to the work assumptions about life and experience in order to follow it at all, however unaware of these assumptions we may be. And we know that, if we are not familiar with the particular set of writer-reader assumptions embodied in a given work, we do need outside information. But these points have already been developed in the preceding chapter: I want to explore here the question of using outside information over and above them. Even after we have gone through formal analysis and a discussion of vision as outlined in the first section of this chapter, and even after we have stressed the necessity of outside information on these levels, there is still a sense in which, from the point of view of meaning, no work is complete in itself and will therefore benefit from being placed in larger contexts for the sake of clarifying, deepening, and broadening our interpretation of its vision, and for the sake of evaluating the relative scope and profundity of this vision.

This inherent incompleteness has two causes: either the human problem serving as the basis of the plot is shown only in terms of selected facets, or it is shown more fully but still not sufficiently in terms of human life as a whole. Meaning, in other words, is a matter of relationships in experience, and since such relationships have no boundaries or limits or ends, no book—not even *Finnegans Wake*—can include them all. What we must do then is to fill in the missing links and/or supply larger contexts. In the first instance, we can find that the problem presented in the plot can be clarified, for example, by following out its implications beyond the confines of the book and then by returning to it with a fuller grasp of the weight and significance of the issues. This is what I will try to do in my interpretation of *The Stranger* (chapter 13), whose problem I see as one of the intrusion of public values into the realm of private values; there I consequently hope to illuminate the meaning of this problem by developing the other side of the issue not developed in the book— namely, how private values affect (or ought to affect) the realm of public values. In the second instance, the problem can be clarified by relating it to different but similar things outside the book and thereby achieving a fuller sense of its magnitude and importance. This is what I intend to do in my analysis of Ernest Hemingway (chapter 14), whose vision I place in the context of a certain notion of transcendence which elevates his concern for sport and ritual above the level of the mere boyishness which it is sometimes taken to be (an intention which also guided my earlier studies of E. E. Cummings's vision). And we must do these things for two reasons: first, the better to understand, define, and place the nature of an author's vision; and second, the better to judge and evaluate its value. We are able to discuss an author's vision in terms of his thought, emotion, and expression as they are embodied in any single work, but we are not able really to place and judge it merely in those terms.

Let us look a bit further at the various sorts of framework available to us for this kind of inquiry. These are, as we have seen, first, the context provided by the author's other works as well as by his personal life; second, that provided by the works and biographies of other writers of the same period as well as by the cultural context of the period itself; third, that of the historical sequence of different periods; and fourth, that of universal symbols and archetypal patterns. (These contexts represent a modification, for the sake of discussing meaning, of the schemes outlined and developed in the first two chapters of this book, since *vision* is seen here as relating to the period concept, literary history, and archetypes, as well as referring simply to the biography and works of a given author.) Indeed, as we thus broaden the scope of our study, the most basic context of all may be made more and more explicit: a form of partisanship, as we shall see, on the part of the interpreter for or against the artistic vision he is defining and evaluating, so long as it is relevant to that vision and is based on objective analysis, acknowledged assumptions, and coherent reasoning. Critical and scholarly objectivity need not result in uncommitted and lifeless analysis.

In the context of the other works by the same author, we find not only confirmation of what we find in a single work by seeing it treated again and again throughout the canon (which is what R. S. Crane means by "characteristic")—abandonment in Dickens, for example, or betrayal in Joseph Conrad, or guilt in William Faulkner, or crime in Dostoevsky— but a sense of how it relates to other different problems in that writer's vision as well. Thus for example I find that, although "The Metamorphosis" is assuredly part of Franz Kafka's world, it is best treated as a problem in family relations rather than as the more usual one of the individual vs. society (chapter 12). Indeed, if we can aid our interpretation of the meaning of a book by assimilating it into larger categories, we can by the same token damage it as well. On the assumption that an author must be doing here what he was doing there, we are endangering our interpretation of any one of his works by predisposing it to mean something in particular before we have read and studied it.

In "The Metamorphosis" it is common to regard Gregor as the victim of his family, just as the protagonists of so many of Kafka's other works are victims of society, and naturally evidence can be found in the novella to support this interpretation. But I find that a close analysis of the story itself suggests a rather different way of looking at it, and if we then relate this fresh look to Kafka's vision, we do not only the story but also the vision itself greater justice. Similarly, we must be on the lookout, when dealing with the ostensibly coherent framework of an author's world, for shifts and even contradictions, as in D. H. Lawrence or André Gide, and for developments and even conversions, as in Tolstoy or John Dos Passos. We want to be able to allow an author to change his mind; we do not want to find more consistency than the facts warrant. If formal analysis can be supplemented by the interpretation of vision, the interpretation of vision must be controlled by formal analysis.

Also, as I have suggested, we want to be able further to confirm our interpretation of vision by reference to the aesthetic aspects of the work themselves, to be able to see what difference such knowledge makes—in the context now of all his works—for our understanding and appreciation of the writer as artist. It is not enough to say that Faulkner's vision involves an obsessive awareness of the impingement of the past upon the present, or that his writing is characterized by long and involved sentences: we want rather to see if there is an intelligible reciprocity between vision and art, and this applies to other facets of form as well—technique and structure, in addition to syntax and diction. Thus we might hypothesize that Faulkner's sentences are multifaceted and multileveled because he is trying to convey a sense of temporal simultaneity, and it would be foolish to wish he wrote more like Hemingway, who in his turn is much more concerned with the directness and immediacy of the present.

Negative evidence must be taken into account here too, however, as when F. Scott Fitzgerald's great success with the spare dramatic method in *Gatsby* is "contradicted" by his not quite so successful attempt in *Tender is the Night* to press on toward a fuller and more philosophical method. Having mastered one mode, Fitzgerald deliberately chose to strain his resources in an effort to achieve something more rich and profound in another mode. Predetermined readings must be avoided on this level as well, just as we must be careful to notice when an author continues to use a style and approach he developed in response to the pressures of his vision long after those pressures have ceased to operate—as perhaps is the case, alas, with the later Faulkner—when manner becomes mannerism.

Another aspect of this framework is the writer's personal life. That Dickens' childhood was what it was certainly throws light on certain recurring key situations in his novels, and I find similarly that I can make large use of Kafka's problems with his father in interpreting "The Metamorphosis." But here too one must be careful about variations and negative evidence. Many novels, of course, involve very little relation between the author's life and his art, or even an inverse relation, so we cannot work simply according to prior assumptions. Certain writers are much less obsessive than Dickens or Kafka, Lawrence, Dostoevsky, Conrad, James Joyce, or Thomas Wolfe about turning the things that haunt them in life into art. The novels of Fielding or Austen or James are naturally affected by their lives, but a study of their lives is much less directly relevant to a study of their artistic visions because, although they wrote out of themselves, as any good author must, they rarely wrote about themselves.

The problem of negative evidence is an especially interesting one on this level. Why are Jane Austen's plots, for example, so often based on the question of getting married, while she herself, of course, lived and died a spinster? Perhaps one does need, at this level, theories as involved as Freud's analysis of dreams as wish-fulfillment fantasies to do justice to such issues. But it may be that the case of Victorian women novelists, who were not themselves particularly doll-like, writing about shrinking-violet heroines, is more easily explained in terms of the pressures of fashion and the marketplace than of anything so personal as depth psychology. A related problem is how authors can write about things they have no personal knowledge of, as with Stephen Crane and his *Red Badge*, which was written, as we know, before he had experienced any actual warfare for himself. How can men write about women, or women about men? How can anyone write about the distant past? Can a celibate write about sex? Simple-minded connections between biography and art ought to be avoided.

Another similar question is that of the writer who goes out into life so that he may have material for his books, or who—à la Oscar Wilde—makes his life a work of art, or writes books about his life as a man writing books. Here an element of calculation enters, and again the critic must risk illuminating novels in the context of biography warily. It may be safely assumed that Hemingway developed his interest in the outdoor life and the life of sport, action, and adventure early and naturally, but we can suspect that some of his later doings—his involvement in the Spanish Civil War, for example—were at least partly motivated by his desire to get a book out of them. Which is not to say, of course, that he was not sincere, either about the action or the book, but merely to raise an aesthetic question about interpreting novels in the context of an author's life. We know, alas, that often Hemingway had a tendency to act in person like someone from his books, so that it became hard—perhaps for him, certainly for us—to tell where one left off and the other began. Wolfe, too, was writing himself into a corner, I believe, when each successive book became the story of the man writing the preceding one.

When we *can* use biography, however, the question is just how to do so. The larger context which we may use to fill in links and/or place in perspective must come not simply from a knowledge of the facts of an author's life but more from an interpretation of their significance, and this interpretation comes inevitably out of the application of a certain psychological-moral theory to those facts. It is certainly necessary, when interpreting Kafka's vision in "The Metamorphosis," to realize that the author's peculiarly severe father problem informs the meaning of this work, as well as most of his others (as he himself acknowledged). But it is not sufficient as an interpretative framework until we come to some understanding of the meaning of his father problem, for it is only then that we can see how it informs the meaning of the work.

Now for this purpose we may use any one of the common psychological-moral theories available today—most notably, of course, the Freudian, according to which we would almost be constrained to see Kafka's problem in terms of the Oedipus complex, interpreting it as an incestuous desire for his mother accompanied by the usual need to get rid of his father. We know by now, however, the usual objections to this sort of flat application of psychology to literature, and that we should beware of taking imagined characters as if they were real, of confusing their problems with the author's, of forgetting that a successful work of art is not simply the product of neurosis. Furthermore, even if we are not reductive on this level, just as we ought to be pluralists in criticism, so too ought we to be pluralists in psychology and morality (as well as in general).[6] Just as there is no single explanatory principle for literature, even more is there no single theory to cover human behavior. Most phenomena are the result of multiple causes, and many of these causes operate in individual cases as independent variables. So if it is true that in a given case one explanation will meet the canons of evidence better than another, it is by the same token equally true that we cannot know in advance which one it will be. What we need is a variety of available causal principles and a keen sense of which is most appropriate in a given context.

We will be aided in this inquiry, naturally, when we are dealing with those authors who happen themselves to have written on psychological-moral theories, as did Lawrence,[7] or who happen to have written auto-biographically, introspectively, or self-analytically—even though such writings may, of course, have to be taken sometimes with a grain of salt. But with Kafka, for instance, I did find my interpretation greatly enhanced by studying his "Letter to My Father," which provided me with a clarification of some of my key terms and insights. I had been analyzing

"The Metamorphosis" itself in terms of the problem of dependency in love relations and of becoming free of that dependency, when reading his "Letter" helped me to see by means of Kafka's own self-realization that such dependency is brought about more by the dependent one than the dominating one, and this in turn helped me to interpret the meaning of the story more clearly.

The problem is to avoid applying either preconceived principles or preconceived personal concerns to the original search for the most adequate explanation: this search must be conducted objectively—that is, in terms most appropriate to the work rather than to the critic—and verified according to the appropriate rules of evidence. But as I have said I see no reason why scholarly objectivity must keep our interpretations in a vacuum. The objective scholar can easily relate his findings to both public and personal concerns without damaging in the least his objectivity. Indeed, in this sense, objectivity is itself a passionate principle and a most radical or revolutionary stance, most essential to bringing about a better world. For it is just as important to understand life as it is to improve it— in fact, understanding is necessary to effective improvement.

III

The second sort of framework available to us for filling in and giving perspective to the interpretation of vision is that provided by the works of other authors of the same period. The principle is, of course, that treating writers of the same period—even more specifically, of the same country—gives us a basis of comparison similar to that provided by treating the various works of a given author, only somewhat broader. Similar problems of variation and negative evidence obtain in relation to this question as well, for neither should we assume here that there is any predetermined relationship between the age and the work.[8] But if we are to know what a vision is in its own terms rather than simply in our terms, this larger context will enable us to understand and evaluate it more adequately. As R. S. Crane says, "the method of procedure is comparative, inasmuch as the only way in which particular literary qualities can be defined is through a consideration, supported by references to other authors and works, of what they are not."[9] A definition, as we know, involves placing the item in an appropriate class of similar things and then distinguishing it from some of them and identifying it with others (per genus et differentiae). We must know and judge an artistic vision in the framework of its conditions and in terms of what other related authors can do along similar lines, rather than according to some favored standard such as maturity.

Even such a general and flexible standard as freshness, intensity, and immediacy of insight[10] can only be applied comparatively, for these qualities too are relative to the context. Yet I suspect that the quality of an author's vision is more important than its nature, that *how* he sees cuts across distinctions regarding *what* he sees. That is why we can respond deeply to an author whose ideas we do not share or even disagree with: if he transcends the individual and general levels to reach the universal, he leaves questions of ideology and belief far behind. Thus an author's politics, religion, morality, and so on move us less than the freshness, intensity, and immediacy by means of which he embodies them. I think it is in underplaying this effect that Wayne C. Booth troubles me, and it is in their hard focus on the political that radical critics make me hesitate to join them. In answer to the standard objection that an evil work can be well-written, I can only answer that any work which encourages harm to others or insensitivity to the downtrodden cannot display freshness, intensity, and immediacy of insight, as I understand these qualities. One can hurt or ignore others only if one becomes desensitized—not merely to their humanity but also to one's own—and this is the opposite of freshness, intensity, and immediacy. Ezra Pound ranting about kikery is not writing well. Conrad's attitude toward imperialism and primitive peoples is not everywhere enlightened, but it is at least ambivalent and conditioned by intense self-awareness. Many great writers are less concerned with feminist rights than we are becoming today, but only the very greatest are able to push through all of their inherited mental sets at once. Thus although quality of vision is to some degree relative to the context, it does provide a more flexible and just criterion than favored ideological standards.

Another way of using the framework of the age is to relate an author's vision not so much to other writers of his time as to the cultural background of the period itself and some interpretive hypothesis concerning that background. This relationship may be implicit and indirect, as when modern cultural fragmentation and alienation find their counterparts in the fragmentation and alienation of modern fiction, whether in form or content or both; or it may be explicit and direct, as when modern cultural issues form the problems themselves of certain novels. We find inter-relationships between the work and the age, that is, either on the psychological and metaphysical level of the universal, in combination with the aesthetic level, or on the political and historical level of the general.

The first instance provides us with a way of being concerned not simply with vision but more with how vision and art are interrelated. Joseph Warren Beach's fine *The Twentieth Century Novel* (1932), for example, is an extended analysis of how the modern world view and many modern fictional devices go together. Thus an objective point of view and/or a studied multiplicity of points of view, the stream-of-consciousness, the antihero, discontinuity, juxtaposition, ambiguity, and symbolism are all reflections, in one way or another, of the modern, post-Freudian, relativist, existential sensibility. Supporting evidence is of course found by examining the works of many authors of the same period, but the context is no longer simply other works but rather the age itself. Similarly Richard Chase in *The American Novel and Its Tradition* (1957) and Roy Harvey Pearce in *The Continuity of American Poetry* (1961) see relationships between the peculiarly American sensibility and the "open" forms developed by writers living in an "open" society.

We must be pluralists here as well, however, for although many modern writers seem to form a coherent group in these terms, many do not.[11] Very few modern writers have all of the traits of modernism; most have only some of these traits; and they have them in different combinations. Therefore we have to limit and control our discussion of the effect of the age on them by means of a prior study of their individual forms and visions. We cannot deal, that is, with a fixed definition of a period concept, nor with a direct causal notion of how the age influences writers.

It is useful nevertheless to try for large generalizations, so long as they are flexible and broadly-based. There is *something*, after all, which genuinely distinguishes most characteristically twentieth-century art from earlier periods, and it applies to Lawrence, for example, as well as to Joyce. It is not a given combination of aesthetic features, nor of thematic features, least of all of aesthetic plus thematic ones. There is, however, a common situation and certain varieties of ways of responding to it. These ways, however much they may differ, are still governed by that situation, in combination with the unique sensibility of a given writer. Each modern writer who responds in an authentic way to the modern age is bound to be a modernist in some way. If Hart Crane strove for a more affirmative view of an industrial society than Eliot's, he nevertheless felt constrained to do it by means of Eliot's techniques. And when Eliot comes to a more affirmative vision of his own (albeit religious rather than historical), he still feels the need to do it by means of symbol, suggestion, paradox, and experimental structures.

Trying to come to grips with the twentieth century will somehow leave its mark on the writer, and that mark is, as I see it, a characteristic tentativeness somewhere—if not in this aesthetic aspect, then in that one, and if not in this thematic aspect, then in that one. Or, if not in aesthetics, then in theme, and if not in theme, then in aesthetics. And if not in any obvious interrelationship between aesthetics and theme, then in some less obvious way. Thus, Lawrence is more modern in certain thematic aspects than Virginia Woolf (notably in his treatment of sexuality), while he is less modern in certain aesthetic aspects (notably in his use of more regular narrative, which is, however, not quite traditional either). Yet they both share a defining sense of areas of human awareness which the traditional novel was either in ignorance of or was unable to embody.

And the same may be said in relation to many others. An inductive definition, then, will be fashioned to fit the facts rather than imposing a programmatic pattern on them. It will be based on an operative awareness of multiple distinctions and independent variables, as well as upon a filtering process whereby what is truly held in common by a variety of things will emerge by itself without preconceptions. In this way, we shall be prevented from forming specious canons in terms of which Hemingway or Fitzgerald or Lawrence will be excluded, and from forcing simplistic causal hypotheses upon writers in their relation to the age.

When the issues of the age affect the work more explicitly and directly, so that they form the problem itself of its plot, then the critical question becomes additionally not merely one of how the cultural background helps shape the work, but also one of how the work reflects the political and historical background on the level of the general. It is here, of course, that matters of "relevance" become most explicit and clear, and it is here consequently that interpretive hypotheses concerning the meaning of such relevance are most appropriately called for.

What I have in mind in this instance are utopian and dystopian novels, political novels, novels of social consciousness, novels whose plots are based on specific problems of our culture[12]—*Brave New World*, *1984*,

Grapes of Wrath. But I also have in mind such works as *The Trial, The Stranger,* and *Billy Budd* which deal with problems of our culture but in a less specific way. Both of these types are often didactic in form, but I do not take this as essential. What is essential, as I see it, is that they are all based in some important way upon the explicit conflict between man and his institutions, and that therefore they express or imply a view of and/or a judgment upon the nature and meaning of that conflict.

Certainly any serious novel will reflect its cultural background, *Mrs. Dalloway* as authentically as *The Grapes of Wrath,* and that is one reason why any good work is as relevant as any other, regardless of whether it deals directly with the problems of oppression and injustice or not. Indeed, it could be argued that in the long run we get more of a sense of the reality of the twentieth century from Woolf than from John Steinbeck. She is as aware of the more universal problems of consciousness in our time—what is a person? how do we get to know him? how do we balance our love of living against our awareness of its meaninglessness?—as he is of the more general problems of oppression and injustice; and who is to say that solving the latter will automatically help us to solve the former? We might even say that solving the former just might help us solve the latter.

Yet when we want to place works more in the historical and political context of their age than in the psychological and metaphysical context, it is useful to deal with certain works reflecting more explicitly that historical and political context. Not that these contexts are unrelated: although I see "The Metamorphosis" primarily in psychological terms, it could also be seen in societal terms, for the family is an institution as well as a psychological nexus. Thus I could talk additionally about patriarchal forms, sibling relations, and the like, all in the proper context of authority patterns, economic roles, and legal structures, and it would be quite appropriate to do so. I feel, however, that such inquiries are more common for Kafka critics and that I have another light to cast upon this particular story. Contrariwise, perhaps we have had enough studies of modes of consciousness in Woolf and are now ready for more work on the sociological aspects of her novels.[13] An inquiry into the economic base of the Ramsay family or into its sexual patterns might prove revealing. That certain aspects are implicit rather than explicit is no reason to forget them.

Man in the setting of his institutions, however, is the explicit subject of books like *The Stranger,* and to interpret them in the context of the reality they reflect requires, as I have suggested, a hypothesis about the meaning of those institutions. According to my earlier distinctions, there are various attitudes we can take toward this problem: at one end of the spectrum, at the "right," we can assume that man is inherently disorderly and destructive and hence that he needs the control and discipline of institutions to get whatever good out of him he is capable of; at the other end, at the "left," we can assume that he is inherently orderly and creative and that institutions should either serve him or be replaced. As we have seen, there is a variety of intermediate attitudes and combinations possible.

IV

The third sort of framework for interpreting vision is found in the chronological unfolding of history and of literary history, rather than simply in any given period per se. What we want, as R. S. Crane puts it, is not simply to develop "a rounded scheme of periods, movements, literary schools, and the like, with definitions of their respective dominant traits." We want "to build up, informally and bit by bit, through our discussions of particular authors and texts, first of all a grasp of essential chronology; then what I should call a sense of period styles; . . . and finally a habit of asking questions about works which will yield such information concerning their occasions, their sources or models, the philosophic 'commonplaces' or artistic conventions they use, and the traditions they carry on, as will directly promote our . . . understanding and appreciation of them in their aspect as permanently valuable works of art produced at a given time." He then suggests a causal analysis of a number of works whereby we hold their form constant and vary the period in an effort to see what the difference in period is responsible for: we may take works having the same form (plot structure and end effect) but written in different periods, and compare and contrast them in this way.[14] It is not just a matter of developing period concepts and concepts of influence, but more one of putting these concepts in vital relation to aesthetic concepts. Let us trace the implications of these ideas a bit further.

What the historical framework can do for us is twofold: it can show us the thematic and aesthetic differences among the periods, without which there would be no historical concept to begin with; and it can bring out their similarities, without which there would be little point beyond antiquarianism for studying history. We can see, in other words, who we are in contrast to who we are not, and we can also see where who we are came from. The result in the first instance ought to be, ideally, to prevent us from interpreting the works of one period in terms of those of another[15] —and particularly, of course, from interpreting earlier periods in terms of our own—while the result in the second instance ought to be an interpretation of the works of any given period in terms of the relations between it and other periods. It can be seen that we are still dealing with classification and division, or, if you will, with definition; that the value of proper definition is to reveal that if things are different in some ways they are similar in others; and that we must always avoid oversimplified categories and seek pluralistically contextual definitions based on multiple differentiae.

Perhaps it is best to say that, while insight into the human heart and certain of its basic emotional workings remains the same from age to age, ideas and certain feelings and ways of expressing them do change—even progress. Otherwise, the whole notion of literary history and period concepts is nonsense, which is clearly not the case.

Similarities from period to period are found not only on the basis of the primary emotions but also of other sorts of continuities. If the twentieth century in some ways rebelled against the nineteenth, it is also in some ways similar, in that it shares certain societal and cultural problems with it, which neither shares with the eighteenth century. Concerning the novel, the nineteenth and twentieth centuries are closer than the eighteenth and nineteenth. The differences between *Tom Jones* and *Great Expectations* are more marked than those between *Great Expectations* and *The Great Gatsby*, and the sequence formed by all three is especially instructive. It is crucial that *Tom Jones* have a happy ending, not only formally in being comic, but also historically in showing a young man, however rascally he may be, achieving harmony with his society. Dickens himself preferred his original, less happy ending to the official one in which Pip and Estella are to be reunited;[16] and the ending of *Gatsby*, in which the protagonist is killed by mistake, is of course peculiarly modern. By the same token, the nineteenth century is no longer to be thought of as simply the producer of long and shapeless novels presented by garrulous and self-indulgent narrators. Our Jamesian prejudices are being questioned, and the application of more flexible standards to nineteenth-century novels is revealing that they are much more artistic —much more consciously structured and objectified—than we had supposed.[17]

An extremely interesting, if at times slapdash, approach[18] to novelistic traditions and their periods and their large interrelatedness is found in Leslie Fiedler's *Love and Death in the American Novel* (1960, revised 1966). By means of shifting his categories, Fiedler can show how romantic emotionalism is related to eighteenth-century rationalism, how Victorian "white" romanticism is related to the corresponding "black" romanticism, how the courtly love tradition is related to later conceptions of love, how sentimentalism is related to diabolism, how sexuality is related to violence, how modern fiction is related to gothic, and so on. Fiedler's book is basically a study of romanticism somewhat in the manner of Mario Praz's *The Romantic Agony*, but its distinguishing feature is its expansion of the periods and traditions included in the term; hence it is a good example of the advantages of blending various periods together under the aegis of a single interpretive framework.

But it is also a good example of the disadvantages, for Fiedler is as obsessed with types and genres and traditions as Frye, and he soon has the reader's head spinning with genres evolving out of genres like rabbits out of a hat, traditions and countertraditions, modifications and qualifications, complexities within complexities. Surely too many things are being seen as similar here; surely the approach is finally too facile; surely a detailed formal analysis of a few of his examples might begin to throw the scheme off somewhat. A mind like this is insatiable in its pursuit of the generalization, the type, the abstraction, the category. But there is no question that Fiedler has opened up a fertile field for further investigation and that the problem he raises is a most crucial one for the study of American fiction and culture.

Another example, even broader in scope if somewhat more theoretically reasoned, is *The Nature of Narrative* (1966) by Robert Scholes and Robert Kellogg. By widening their genre concept to include narrative rather than simply the novel, they emerge with a picture of modes and traditions, their blendings and separations and rises and declines, which throws literary history into a rather new light. But here again I feel bewildered and not a little bored by the proliferation and intermingling of genres, as well as respectful of fresh areas being opened up.

V

Fiedler, Frye, and Scholes and Kellogg bring us naturally to the fourth and last framework for filling in and giving perspective to the study of vision: that provided by the archetypal patterns. Here the concern with the general—with time and the age and history and politics—vanishes, or at least becomes subordinate, and we enter the area of the universal, of the psychological and metaphysical and transcendent, of the timeless itself. Or at least the expansion of our focus becomes so much broader and more inclusive than that of a period or sequence of periods that it seems to transcend the temporal level altogether. I have spoken of certain primary emotional loci which enable us to link various periods together, and now we turn our attention almost exclusively to them and to their characteristic manifestations in the human imagination: birth, coming of age, sex, marriage, parenthood, and death; producing food, clothing, and shelter; and experiencing this planet, its landscapes, its seasons, and its weathers. As we shall see, this approach involves us in the study of anthropology, myth, ritual, psychology, and dreams, but this is not yet the place for an extended analysis, which is reserved for the concluding section of this book.

Suffice it to say here that it helps to understand what Melville, for example, means in *Moby-Dick*, to see the chase after the whale not only in formal terms, Melvillean terms, nineteenth-century terms, and in terms of the various traditions—Biblical, Elizabethan and Jacobean—it reflects, but also in terms of the archetype of the night journey under the sea and what the anthropological and psychological implications of this archetype are (initiation, death, rebirth). So too does it help to understand what Hemingway means, as I hope to show, to see his "adolescent" passion for sport and the hunt in archetypal terms. It is true that his limitations are much more evident from other perspectives: he makes little sense in sociological terms, as there is very little indeed of ordinary living portrayed in his works; and he makes even less sense in Fiedler's terms, for there is, of course, very little adult heterosexual love portrayed in his works either, and there is a good deal of very suspicious male camaraderie.

But from another perspective—that of living in a society whose conventions are becoming more rigid as they become more empty—it is healthy and productive to break through these dead forms; to strive, however futilely, for contact once again with reality itself; and to see what may be built afresh. Hemingway was very brave, it seems to me, to try this; and if he lacked complete self-awareness, if he fell into absurdities, and if his manner became a mannerism, why then it only goes to show that a man may use himself up very easily and quickly in trying to touch reality, so long a distance have we to go and so unused are we to the journey.

We turn now to a study of the vision of three novelists in the perspective of larger frameworks: Kafka primarily in a biographical context, Albert Camus primarily in the political and historical context of his period, and Hemingway primarily in terms of history and archetypes.

Chapter 12

Self and Family in "The Metamorphosis"

No better demonstration that our interpretation of meaning is significantly enlarged by means of biographical and psychological contexts can be found than in the attempt to explain Franz Kafka's "The Metamorphosis," for it is a story whose connection with the author's life and emotional problems is obvious. On the other hand, no better case for showing that meaning is a function of form can be made, for it is a story whose meaning appears obvious until one begins to analyze its structure, and its structure is not obvious at all. The procedure is to use larger contexts for filling in links that are absent in the story itself, but not to use them precipitously and prescriptively. What I propose to do accordingly is to show how certain biographical-psychological approaches are inadequate because they fail to fit the story itself, then to construct a viable hypothesis of the story's form, and finally to interpret its biographical-psychological meaning on what I hope will be a firmer basis.

The question that teases us in this story is how to explain Gregor Samsa's mysterious and disgusting change. Normally we could attempt to solve such a problem by asking two questions: how and why did he become an insect in terms of the probabilities of the action, and what are Kafka's reasons for handling it in this way? The first question can usually be answered directly by examining the incidents in the story and their causes, while the second may be answered only indirectly by making inferences about what the author wanted to accomplish in so arranging things.

Now the trouble with this story is that we can never answer the first question, simply because no clues are either stated or implied as to how and why this change came about. His family, in spite of all their anguish over how to handle this bizarre situation, never once ask themselves how or why it happened. Nor does Gregor, however alarmed he is at the outset and however unable he is later to adjust to this new state, think of asking such obvious questions. Indeed, Kafka himself seems not at all concerned with the matter, and the critics have been unanimous in their praise of his skill in creating an aura of reality around so fantastic a beginning. For, as we know, the story begins after Gregor's change has taken place.

This transformation must be accepted as a fait accompli, and so all avenues of explanation regarding the first question are closed. The story, however, deals exclusively with Gregor's and his family's reactions to this change, and it stands to reason that unless we understand the meaning of this change we shall fail to understand the meaning of their reactions to it and hence of the story as a whole. We must rely solely on exploring the possible answers to the second question, and here at least two avenues of approach are open to us as we pursue Kafka's motives: the psychological and the artistic. Let us consider them in turn.

I

The search for psychological causes is the most common approach followed when dealing with this story, and it seeks to find in it an intelligible pattern by building on Kafka's biography, the Freudian hypothesis, and some scheme of literary or archetypal symbolism. Generally speaking, such an interpretation runs along the following lines: we know, to begin with, that Kafka felt inadequate in relation to his efficient and successful father, and therefore he was ambivalent about him, feeling ashamed at not measuring up while at the same time feeling resentful that he had to measure up, and admiring his father and wanting to please him to boot. Since Gregor's father plays a characteristic role in the story, wanting no nonsense from his buglike son and even wounding him at the end, it seems plausible to attribute to the Samsa situation the factors involved in the Kafka situation (even the names are alike). Thus Gregor has turned himself into a bug, however unconsciously, in order to spite his father and at the same time to punish himself for being an inadequate son. By becoming something nonhuman or subhuman, he has symbolically allowed his hidden and suppressed self to emerge: his need to escape responsibility, his wish to hurt his father, his desire to express guilt. Some critics even see an element of clinical hysteria in this creation of Kafka's, "the neurotic's horror of losing control, . . . hints of fear of the lower depths of sleep, night, and dream, and also of existence in death without the release of death—a mythical echo of Tantalus."[1]

A curious consequence of this kind of interpretation is that it ends by setting us against Gregor's family. Stodgy bourgeois vs. sensitive artist becomes inevitably the story's formula, just as it is the formula of Kafka's life. Thus the ending, where the family is happily released of its dread burden and looks toward a better and healthier future with renewed hope and strength, has either to be wished away as an artistic mistake or to be read ironically as Kafka's final indictment of a sterile society returning once more to its superficial routines of marriage, work, and respectability after an unlooked-for encounter with the profound forces of life and death in the unconscious. Charles Neider, who argues in both of these directions, fails to notice that in deploring the ending he is forced to misread the story itself, for he talks of "the gradual physical degeneration of the family under the impact of disaster, and their re-generation after Gregor's death."[2] The fact is that Gregor's family was disintegrating before the disaster of his metamorphosis and is regenerated during and because of its efforts to face up to it, a fact which Gregor himself notices well before the middle section is over: he had "been unaware of a certain change of character in his family"[3] until his father appeared before him in the uniform of his new job in a banking house.

And there are other details of the story which the usual psychological interpretation fails to explain or has to explain ironically. There is the crucial fact that it is not the son who is inadequate, at least to begin with, but rather the father. Gregor has been supporting the family for the past four years, while his father has been lying around the house and growing fat ever since his business failed five years before. Now this could very easily be interpreted as a psychological displacement or inversion, so that inadequate Franz becomes adequate Gregor by way of wish fulfillment. And this is indeed Neider's strategy: "This is a wish projection of a Kafka depressed by his economic dependence on his father." But why then does the story proceed to reinstate the father's power over the son by rendering that son incapable of meeting his responsibilities? Can we have it both ways—a Kafka who is placing himself beneath his father by means of a story which begins by literally placing the son above the father, or who is symbolically placing himself over his father by means of a story which eventually places the father over the son?

Perhaps the question can be rephrased in terms of whether we need to have it both ways, regardless of whether it is possible. What I want to suggest, in short, is that an answer may first be sought within the story itself, regarded as an artistic whole, for the significance and function of any given element in that story are in the last analysis to be interpreted primarily in terms of that story. If such a literal approach fails to provide an answer, then it can only be concluded that there is none. Unless, that is, we are content to accept the story as a dream, and that I am not prepared to do.

I do not mean to suggest that we must blind ourselves to symbols when they appear in the story, or to hidden motives, or to our knowledge of family life; I mean only that we must interpret these things in terms of assumptions which are directly relevant to the story, and of hypotheses whose ultimate justification lies within the story and its internal relationships. Nor do I mean to say that such a literal reading will provide exhaustive and final answers: I mean only that such a reading may supply a sound basis for further inquiry. This is a powerful and mysterious and puzzling story, and it works on us in many ways. It is doubtful whether it can ever be fully explained, but in so far as it is a story it ought to be interpreted as such.

II

Just what is the story, and what is the function of Gregor's transformation in it? The basic problem Kafka set for himself, as I see it, was to show the family gradually freeing itself from its moral dependence upon Gregor, and the solution he hit upon was to turn Gregor into an insect in order to accomplish this. This will take some explaining.

The action is built on two changes: the first is Gregor's gradual deterioration and death, and the second is the family's gradual mobilization and recovery—the two together forming something of an hourglass pattern. The inciting cause of both changes is, of course, Gregor's unexplained metamorphosis. Its immediate effect is to cut off Gregor from normal life and his family from their sole source of support. This creates in Gregor a pathetic but inevitably frustrated yearning to be recognized, to be understood, to be taken care of, and in his family an opposing disgust and revulsion. This in turn produces in Gregor a selfish unconcern for his family, and in them the need to support themselves combined with an evergrowing desperation as to how to get rid of this monster who was once their son and brother. (The family members, I realize, each react in different ways to his metamorphosis—the mother helplessly, the father tyrannically, and the sister charitably at the outset—but in the end they are united in their resolve to get rid of him.)

Now since we are told nothing about the probabilities of Gregor's change and cannot therefore interpret it in terms of its causes, perhaps we can interpret it in terms of its effects. Why to begin with does his family react so negatively after he becomes a bug? The obvious answer is that he is repulsive. I still think with horror about the insect when I force myself to dwell upon its appearance and movements, although Kafka's manner of treatment softens this horror with pity. And I believe that indeed is part of the point, for the reader sees the story largely from within Gregor's point of view, while the family sees him entirely from without.[4] This means that they are of necessity less sympathetic than we are toward the creature.

But is it not possible, a Freudian might ask, that their hostility toward this bug is in reality a symbolic disguise for their hitherto suppressed hostility toward the son? Surely there is loathing aplenty here, and it is certainly possible within the framework of the story to infer that they have been storing up against him a good deal of resentment for being his parasites. Similarly it is quite possible to compound the symbol by having it stand for his disguised hatred of them for having to support them. Both family and son have been frustrated enough, and, as we all know, frustration leads to aggression.

This is possible, but again I ask whether it is necessary. The only reason for us to postulate a prior mutual resentment between them is our assumption that there must have been bad feeling in such a situation. But the only expressed hostility regarding the circumstances prior to Gregor's change we can find in the story is that which Gregor feels toward his boss, the manager, the other salesmen, and his job itself. He does not blame his family for his hard life as a salesman, nor do they blame him for their dependence on him.

It is possible that Kafka was psychologically unable to confront such hostilities openly and that this device was a means by which he could deal with them covertly, so that this story is a disguised incest-fantasy with the bug symbolizing Kafka's suppressed desire to become a child again and the sister standing cryptically for the mother whom he wishes to wrest from his father. But since such theories postulate a degree of control of the story over the author which I am unable to accept, I would prefer to continue my search for more literal causes. Relegating this story to the limbo of neurotic nightmare does little for it as a work of art, suiting it more to the analyst's couch than the reader's enjoyment.

I reject on the same grounds the possibility that the change represents Gregor's desire to escape from his responsibilities. It is true of course that he has been working for four years already and has five or six years to go before his father's debt is paid off; but, disagreeable as he has found his job, there are no expressed signs of any desire on his part to chuck the whole business. The only reason to think so is our assumption that he must want to get out of it. But why choose such a disagreeable way to escape? Is not being a bug even worse than being a travelling salesman? There is surely no pleasure in it for Gregor.

But, says the Freudian, he is also punishing himself: are you so simple-minded as to be unable to see how he can gratify himself and punish himself for this gratification at one and the same time? No one wants to be thought simple-minded, but I wonder whether such a heads-I-win-tails-you-lose assumption covers too many things and hence fails to be sufficiently clear when applied to a particular case. Besides, why couldn't Gregor have merely developed some psychosomatic ailment and thereby have accomplished his purpose much more effectively? A convenient paralysis of the legs, for example, would have given him enough of an excuse for stopping work while at the same time providing him with enough pain for self-punishment. I'm sure the true hypochondriac suffers genuinely for his imaginary afflictions.

But this sort of solution would have hardly suited Kafka's purpose, for then the family would have had to care for him and pity him instead of rejecting him as they do. Robbing the family of their hostility would have robbed Kafka of his story. And that is just the point: not that they have hated him for having been his parasites, but that *they* have fallen into a psychosomatic torpor as a result of their dependence on him and no other way could be found to bring them out of it.

I reason as follows: Gregor is changed into an insect through no evident fault of his own, nor through any fault of theirs either. It seems to me that Kafka omitted any clues as to the how and why of Gregor's change precisely because he sensed the necessity of preventing the reader from assigning responsibilities in this matter. I believe he wanted us to sympathize with both Gregor and his family: with Gregor, because the story would lose the seriousness of its impact if we were made to feel simply disgust at his transformation; with the family, because without their anguished reaction we would never see for ourselves that Gregor was once human. A moral problem would become for us merely a housecleaning problem. (For the charwoman at the end, remember, it *is* merely a housecleaning problem.) Kafka wants us to sympathize with the family, because we must be prepared for the beneficial transformation they are to undergo: they are about to be released from a trap, and we are to feel the force of their rescue as having some positive significance in their lives.

Indeed, if my analysis is correct, it may be that the title refers as much to their charge as to his. Some readers have been so moved by Gregor's suffering, however, that they have lost sight of the family's anguish. Recall that Gregor's family do not see this bug as we do. As far as they are concerned, he is no longer their Gregor but a hideous monster with a claim on their affections. And they have every right to feel this way, for who among us would have acted differently in the same situation? "I will not mention my brother's name when I speak of this monster here," his sister says. "I merely want to say: we must find some means of getting rid of it. We have done all that is humanly possible to care for it, to put up with it; I believe that nobody could reproach us in the least." It is the function of the lodgers' presence in the house to precipitate the Samsas' need to reject him, for his continued existence is now a threat to their very livelihood.

What they *are* accountable for, however, is the torpor into which they have fallen as a result of their dependence on his support. The father "had become very fat and moved with great difficulty. And the old mother . . . passed a good deal of her time each day lying on the sofa, panting and wheezing under the open window." The sister "only" seventeen years old, was well "suited to the life she had led, . . . nicely dressed, getting plenty of sleep, helping in the house, taking part in a few harmless little entertainments, and playing her violin." And it is this torpor out of which the shock of Gregor's transformation wakes them, and with that awakening, it seems to me, we can only sympathize. The father gets a job, and his appearance improves: "his white hair, ordinarily untidy, had been brushed till it shone." The mother does needlework at home for a lingerie shop, "and the sister, who had obtained a job as a shop assistant,

would study shorthand or French in the hope of improving her position."
At the end we read: "On careful reflection, they decided that things were
not nearly so bad as they might have been, for—and this was a point they
had not hitherto realized—they had all three found really interesting oc-
cupations which looked even more promising in the future."

They have been, in effect, redeemed. The only trouble is that poor
Gregor has been sacrificed in the process. Kafka mitigates the pathos of
this necessity in two ways: first, he has Gregor get more callous and buglike in his attitudes as the story progresses (although music retains its
power to move him); and second, he has him die peacefully: "He thought
of his family in tender solicitude. He realized that he must go, and his
opinion on this point was even more firm, if possible, than that of his
sister. He lay in this state of peaceful and empty meditation till the clock
struck the third morning hour. He saw the landscape grow lighter through
the window; then, against his will, his head fell forward and his last feeble
breath streamed from his nostrils."

Gregor was turned into a bug, then, because there was no other way
to free his family from their moral degeneration, and he died because
there was no other way to free them for the future. But granted they had
to be freed by means of some external agency, it might be objected that
Kafka showed poor artistic judgment in choosing so desperate and fantastic an expedient. Consider, however, the alternatives. Had Gregor
continued working, they would have continued as his parasites. Had he
simply quit his job and left them, they would have been able to blame
him and feel sorry for themselves. Had he gotten sick or lame, they would
have had to pity him. Had he simply died, they would again have been
able to feel merely sorry for themselves. My thesis is that, given the situation, they have to be made to want to be free, and the solution Kafka
chose was to make Gregor repulsive to them, for only then could they
reject him. All avenues of self-defeating escape from their decision are
thus closed: blame, pity, remorse—any such emotion would have hindered
their desire for freedom. Only by being made to reject him could they
be made to want to be free.

It might be further objected that their having to be freed by means of
some external agency places Kafka's conception of the situation in a
rather poor light. Why were they not capable of rising to the challenge
of their lives by drawing upon their own inner resources? Why were they
not capable of undergoing an inner change? Why are they worth saving

at all, and at so great a cost? The answer lies partly in the fact, I think, that the father and mother are both washed out. The former is "an old man who had ceased to work five years before," and this was "his first holiday in a life entirely devoted to work and unsuccess." The parents simply have no internal resources left, and the sister, just on the threshold of maturity, is too young and inexperienced to promise great things. They are ordinary people, the victims of a hard life and of a trap they do not know how to escape. And this, I think, heightens the sympathy we are meant to feel toward them. I doubt though that the parents are in themselves worth saving: it is rather the rescue of the sister which, if anything can justify the cost, explains the sacrifice of Gregor. And that is exactly the note on which Kafka ends: "And it seemed to them that their daughter's gestures were a confirmation of these new dreams of theirs, an encouragement for their good intentions, when, at the end of the journey, the girl rose before them and stretched her young body."

It was a difficult artistic problem which Kafka set for himself, for he had to retain the reader's sympathy for both parties. Gregor was not to be blamed for turning into a bug, nor was the family to be blamed for rejecting him in this new shape. We were to be made to see both sides and to recognize the inevitable suffering involved in this family convulsion; neither side asked for trouble, but both were caught in a trap not of their own devising. But Gregor has to be destroyed to get them out of it, and the cruelty of this necessity, mitigated or not, cannot be put out of mind. Thus, when the family breathes freely once again at the end, our pleasure is crossed by our knowledge of the price of their redemption. A characteristic aura of Kafkan ambiguity remains as we look back over the whole, for the disagreeable shock of Grete's erotic health when seen in the light of her poor brother's miserable fate, coupled with our memory of the family's miserliness in having withheld some money from his hard-won earnings, of his mother's servile helplessness, and of his father's selfish vanity, prevents us finally from resting content with any simple attribution of sympathy.

The only thing which ultimately allows the story to produce its proper moral satisfaction is our recognition of the fact that of the two possibilities—Gregor continuing on as the sole support of his family, or Gregor being transformed and dying so that they could be reborn—only the second could do any good to any of them. For Gregor was not really alive at all in his role as provider—that pathetic picture on the wall which he tries to save represents the closest he had been able to come as a man to normal sexual experience—and ironically his continued success in that very role could only have reduced his family further in their moral degradation. Even if he had paid off that impossible debt, they all would have lost in the end, he wasted by overwork and they wallowing in indolence. As it turns out, he paid off the debt after all.

III

What then can such a story mean, and in particular just what can Gregor's transformation into a bug symbolize? So far we have constructed a viable hypothesis about its functioning in the whole—formally, this metamorphosis is a way of freeing Gregor and his family from a vicious cycle of dependency—but we did not, indeed cannot, explain why he was turned into a bug in the first place, how it happened, and what it means, by limiting ourselves to the story as an autonomous artistic object. Specifically, if we want to know why Kafka chose to have Gregor turn into a bug of this sort (variously interpreted as a dung beetle or cockroach) and not into some other kind of creature—for there are many sorts of parasites, and some others could have functioned equally well from a strictly artistic standpoint—we have to go outside the aesthetic donnée and consider the biographical-psychological context. Similarly, if we want to know what the bug symbolizes and what its implications are in relation to the problem of family love—of how dependency comes about and how it is fostered—we have to consider them in a slightly broader moral-psychological context than that provided by the story. Luckily the facts of Kafka's life, as well as another piece of his writing, provide ample clues both to the meaning of the bug and the significance of its symbolism. And they do so in terms that are quite consistent with what we have said so far about the story's structure. In fact, they corroborate a stubbornly literal reading remarkably well.

In 1919, when he was thirty-six, Kafka wrote a long "Letter to My Father" in which the meaning of his life becomes painfully clear. His mother, who was to act as intermediary, returned it undelivered to her son, and nothing more was said about it. But Max Brod, Kafka's friend and biographer, published some parts of it after Kafka's death, and in reading these selections we can see that Kafka's whole soul was warped from childhood by feelings of inadequacy. He felt and was made to feel that he could never measure up to the standard of manhood set by his father, and so he went through life haunted by an endless and unendurable shame. The attempt to come to terms with this shame, to get out from under it, governed the entire course of his career. This task was made doubly difficult by two more twists of the knife: first, he actually loved his father and remembered their good moments together with nostalgic tenderness; second, he had intelligence enough to see that what was torturing him was completely senseless and irrational, yet he still could not free himself of it.

Here are a few central passages from this letter:

> Courage [he writes to his father], resolution, confidence, joy in one thing or another never lasted if you were opposed to it, or even if your opposition was only to be expected—and it was to be expected in nearly everything I did. In your presence—you are an excellent speaker in matters that concern you—I fell into a halting, stuttering way of speech. Even that was too much for you. Finally I kept still, perhaps from stubbornness, at first; then because, facing you, I could neither think nor speak any more. And since you were the one who had really brought me up, this affected me in everything I did.

The result of this upbringing was—and here he quotes at the end of this passage the closing words of his novel, *The Trial*—that "I had lost my self-confidence with you, and exchanged a boundless sense of guilt for it. Remembering this boundlessness, I once wrote fittingly about someone: 'He fears that his feeling of shame may even survive him.' "[5]

The rest of his life, Brod comments, Kafka then reconstructs as a series of attempts to break away from his father's influence. He even planned at one time to call his writings *The Attempt to Escape from Father*, and he says:

> My writing was about you, in it I only poured the grief I could not sigh at your breast. It was a purposely drawn-out parting from you, except that you had forced it on me, while I determined its direction. [And so, too, with his life:] My self-appraisal depended on you much more than on anything else, such as, for instance, an outward success. . . . Where I lived, I was repudiated, judged, suppressed, and although I tried my utmost to escape elsewhere, it never could amount to anything, because it involved the impossible, something that was, with small exceptions, unattainable for my powers.

He went to the German elementary and secondary schools, and when he was eighteen he went to the Prague University. After a few false starts in literature and then chemistry, he decided to study law, sensing the need for a profession which would not involve him personally, which he could master in a routine way, and therefore at which he could succeed without fear of failure. As he himself explains, in the "Letter": "The point was to find a profession which would most readily permit me [to be indifferent] without injuring my ego too much. And so law was the obvious choice. . . . At any rate this choice showed remarkable foresight on my part. Even as a little boy I had sufficient strong premonitions concerning studies and a profession. From these no salvation was to be expected; I resigned myself to that long ago." And this course seemed to offer hope of a post where he might at least have some time for himself. He became a Doctor of Law in 1906, and after a short period as a clerk in an insurance office, he obtained a position in the semigovernment office of the Workers' Accident Insurance Institute for the Kingdom of Bohemia in Prague in 1908. The work proved to be trying, however, and he found it difficult to live the double life of an official and a writer.

In 1912 he met a girl from Berlin, and they became engaged a few years later, but Kafka could not face up to the consequences of such a decision and broke off with her several times. He blames this vacillation, too, on his subservience to his father: "The most important obstacle to marriage is the already ineradicable conviction that, in order to preserve and especially to guide a family, all the qualities I see in you are necessary —and I mean all of them, the good and the bad. . . . Of all these qualities I had comparatively few, almost none, in fact. And yet what right had I to risk marriage, seeing, as I did, that you yourself had a hard struggle during your married life, that you even failed toward your children."

After the outbreak of World War I, he was exempted from military service as the employee of an office doing essential work. In 1921 he began to have lung trouble and spent most of his remaining years in sanatariums. He died of tuberculosis in 1924 at the age of forty-one.

Very little of his work, as we know, was published during his lifetime; and so diffident, so morbidly inadequate did he feel, that before he died he ordered Max Brod to destroy the unfinished manuscripts of his three great novels, *Amerika, The Trial,* and *The Castle.* Luckily for us, his friend took upon himself the terrible burden of disregarding Kafka's wishes and published these works posthumously.

The weak son of a strong father; a German Jew in a Slavic world; an official in a government bureau; a citizen in a feudal empire; an artist trying to find time to write in the midst of the grinding business of making a living; a modern man whose life was lived in the shadow of two world wars—what sort of vision of life would the writings of such a man reveal? What *could* they reveal? Guilt, and the search for freedom from guilt. And since he perceives the personal and the public as mirror images of one another, when Kafka writes of his own life, he writes—although never directly of current events—of the condition of twentieth-century man. Alone, homeless, and anxiety-ridden, outsiders, exiles, and aliens, Kafka's strange heroes are at once projections of their creator's neurosis and of our own, for he felt in an especially acute form what we all feel in one degree or another. We are in a nightmare world which is all too real, where forces beyond our control or comprehension are massed de-structively against us, and where our love never seems to go right. And nowhere can we find whoever or whatever is responsible, for the enemy is so close to us that we cannot see him—he is inside us, he is ourselves. It does not matter whether this leader or that one is in power: the rush of our doom seems to menace us always. So we are sick, sick with fear, shame, and paralysis of the soul. The more we try to do something about it, the more involved we become in the sticky web of defeat and despair.

The world which we find in his books then, when regarded from the standpoint of vision, is a symbolic world in which the inner nightmare finds its images in terms of the outer nightmare, a world in which lonely men wander down endless corridors trying to find a way, a door, to the answer of the riddle of their existence, trying to make sense out of a senseless life. They are obstinately rational in the midst of irrationality, and they patiently and desperately and stubbornly go from clerk to official, from office to bureau, in an endless quest to discover what crime they have been accused of, who the judges are, and how they can defend themselves. They are faced with an enormously and mysteriously pro-liferating social structure where those at the bottom do not know who is at the top, or whether anybody is at the top at all. In this respect, as in so many others, George Orwell's 1984 shows the influence of Kafka (just as Kafka shows the influence of Charles Dickens, another writer con-cerned with the clash between the homeless ones and the cruel and monstrous structures of society), for no one knows whether Big Brother actually exists or not—and it probably does not very much matter. It is like playing a game—a grim game of life and death—without knowing the rules, or a game in which only your invisible opponent knows the rules and changes them at his will (which reminds us of even so stubbornly "literal" a writer as Hemingway).

It is with a shock that we realize that what looks like a nightmare is actually our world. For Kafka is justly celebrated as the master of the art of serious fantasy: he treats the fantastic literally, and as a result we can see that the literal world is fantastic. The point is not to provide us with an escape from our world, but rather to bring us closer to it. Starting with some weird and impossible occurrence—as, for example, a man turning into a bug one gray morning—he proceeds soberly and realistically to show how this man feels, how he worries about being late for work, how it is difficult for him to turn his doorknob, how his family is horrified but never incredulous. Beginning with a completely unnatural event, he treats it so naturally thereafter that all seems perfectly logical and real. The result is that we soon begin to recognize that the literal is not only symbolic, it is also literal. Kafka sees what is happening to the inner reality of our world—he sees the threats developing beneath the surface of our lives because they are closer to the surface of his life than of ours—and by means of the special catastrophes of fantasy brings them vividly to light, making visible the hidden and known the secret. The exaggerations and distortions are poetic license, but the threats they reveal are palpable; they are there, dwelling within the lives of us all. But when we return to the "real" world we know after reading his fables and fancies, we are able to see it more clearly. The real world *is* fantastic and is becoming more so every day. And so it is that we see that Kafka's fables are not so fabulous after all: we have come full circle, from the real to the fantastic, and back again to the real.

It remains now to show how our discussion of Kafka's life and vision can clarify and deepen our interpretation of the story's meaning. We have come from the projection of his family problems into a social vision back to a concern with family life itself, the root and source of that vision. Only something has gotten turned around in the process, for the personal situation has been reversed: in this story, at least to begin with, it is the father who is weak and the son who is strong, and it is the family which must be freed from the son rather than the son from the family. This reversal of roles makes the issue more universal and less personal, and it makes it less stereotyped by showing that the dependency problem works both ways. It is an artistic tour de force thus to turn the son's inadequacy into the family's. Of course the story itself, in detailing Gregor's change from breadwinner to parasite, reverses these roles once again and thus does reflect more immediately Kafka's personal sense of inadequacy, his sense of being indeed a bug, and his feeling that it would be better for all concerned if he did die.

I remarked earlier that Kafka not only feared his father but loved him as well. He writes in his "Letter":

> when I used to see you, tired out on those hot summer noons, taking a nap after lunch in your store, your elbow stemmed on the desk; or on Summer Sundays, when you arrived exhausted on a visit to your family in the country; or the time when mother was seriously ill, when you leaned against the bookcase, shaking with sobs; or during my recent illness, when you came softly into my room, remaining on the threshold and stretching your neck to see me in bed, and then, out of consideration, greeting me only with a wave of your hand. At such times I would lie down and cry with happiness, and I am crying again while writing it down.

But it is as if he were saying in this story that only by freeing himself from this love could he become free of this fear.

In his life, however, he could not manage such freedom, for he could not find it in himself to reject his father as Gregor's family had to reject him, perhaps because he could not see his father as a revolting insect—only himself. In his letter he puts these imagined words of reproach against the son in his father's mouth:

> You have simply made up your mind to live entirely on me. I admit that we are fighting each other, but there are two kinds of fight. There is the knightly battle, where equal opponents are pitted against each other, each for himself, each loses for himself or wins for himself. And there is the struggle of vermin, which not only stings, but at the same time preserves itself by sucking the other's blood. . . . Such are you. You are not fit for life, but in order to live in comfort, without worry or self-reproach, you prove that I have taken away your fitness for life and put it all into my pocket.

Max Brod speculates that this is a crucial passage for the understanding of "The Metamorphosis," and I think he is right.

It was the tragedy of Kafka's life that he could see the way to freedom but could not bring himself to take it. Although he wanted desperately to free himself from his dependency on his father, he could not surrender the comfort of his love for his father, a love which enslaved him because it enabled him, in a twisted and neurotic way, to avoid self-reproach for his inadequacies, inadequacies of which he was somewhat too exquisitely aware and on whose bitter fruit he had to feed in order to live at all. It is in the nature of dependency to need the approval or disapproval of the other as a substitute for the risk of confronting one's own life and of taking one's own responsibility. By thus convicting himself of defeat in advance, he simply did not have to try to succeed, for if he tried and then failed, he would have had only himself to blame. To try is to put one's efforts to the test of experience, and this Kafka could not risk, for then the failure would be his and not his father's at all. That is why he purposely sought out a dull profession, that is why he could not marry, and that is why he wanted his manuscripts burned after his death. He made a career out of failure by refusing to risk success.

But he also made great art out of it, so that in a paradoxical way he succeeded after all. What he could see but not act upon as a man, he could, as a writer, have his characters both realize and do something about. In this way, he has left us the legacy of a partial victory at least. By making a fantasy out of the problem of family love, and then by treating the fantasy as real, he has shown us that the inner reality is fantastic indeed. The metamorphosis of a man into an insect symbolizes parasitism: Gregor becomes literally what his family had become figuratively—a vermin, a creature which not only stings, but which at the same time preserves itself by sucking the other's blood.

The point is that this loving, which enables you to nourish your feelings of inadequacy instead of seeing that the other's love may be at fault, may be a cover-up for your fear of failure, for it allows you covertly to make the person you love responsible for your own inadequacies. Your love for him has made his smiles or frowns the cause of your joys and despairs. If you did not care about his approval, you would not be able to feel he was responsible when you feel you have failed. The attribution of responsibility is the vermin's sting, and the love is the bloodsucking of the parasite—the love which makes your whole emotional life dependent on him and which in turn allows you to hold him responsible in the first place. Thus does your dependency become a form of domination, and thus does the person you have placed in the commanding role become your prisoner, the prisoner of his victim. For you are asking him to give you what no one can give you except yourself: security, self-confidence, and self-esteem. Your success or failure depends on his approval or disapproval and so is not a knightly battle where "each loses for himself or wins for himself." That is why it is a dependent love, and that is why such a love is wrong: it allows you "to live in comfort, without worry or self-reproach." When you cannot win security and self-esteem by trying something on your own, this love becomes a substitute for independent risk-taking and so prevents you from growing. The answer is easy to see but hard to do: you must free yourself from this love in order to become yourself; you must cease to care about the person who has reduced you—whether because of your fear or your love—to ineffectuality; you must purge yourself of your concern for him. (Or, better still, transcend the problem by freeing him of responsibility for yourself, thereby freeing yourself of dependency on him, and then loving him anyway.)

That is why Kafka had Gregor turn into a bug: so that his family would be able to stop caring about him. Once they see that he is no longer their son and brother, they no longer feel responsible for loving him and so are free to grow and prosper for themselves. It is almost as if Gregor, in seeing that they had become his helpless parasites, decided unconsciously to exchange places with them in order to free them, for they could not find it in themselves to break away from their dependency on him any more than Kafka could find it in himself to break away from his dependency on his father. Thus he made himself their dependent, becoming the bug in fact that they were becoming figuratively, so that they could no longer depend on him even if they wanted to. They are forced by his subservience to become independent, but they must also stop loving him in order to stand on their own feet. And they cannot love a bug—no one can—so they are free.

His support of them was ruining them all anyway; it is as if he chose to sacrifice himself quickly rather than drag the ordeal out endlessly. In this way they can be free of him without guilt. They would have earned from us even less sympathy than they do now if they had rejected him when he was still in human form: his metamorphosis enables them to do what they otherwise could not have done. His change is therefore from their point of view ultimately an act of mercy, for it lets them off the hook. The worm has indeed turned, or rather the strong one has made himself weak in order to make the weak ones strong. They must do to him what he was unable to do to them; unable to quit them, he makes them quit him. They cannot lift themselves by their bootstraps. As the parasites, they must stop loving him, but they cannot do so until he is the bug. A parasite is by nature dependent and can only rebel when the one he is feeding on starts feeding on him. There is a delayed reaction here, for Kafka understood that once a parasite, always a parasite, that a vermin cannot will his own freedom: he has to be vanquished and then freed by another vermin, not a knight. Had Kafka's father become somehow repulsive to him, Kafka might have been freed from his bughood. But Kafka was the one who got tuberculosis instead, and died, imprisoned by love to the end.

Chapter 13

Self and Society in *The Stranger*

If our method in discussing "The Metamorphosis" was to place the plot in the larger context of biography and psychology in order to deepen and extend our interpretation of the story's meaning, here we will be placing Albert Camus' plot in the still larger context of history, law, and politics, as well as other similar literary works, in order to provide a broader perspective for analyzing the book's significance. Appropriately, since Kafka deals with family relations and Camus with society, we are moving in widening circles from the personal to the public—and shall, as we will see, be considering their interrelations. And with Ernest Hemingway we will continue that progression outward toward the universal.

Underlying all three chapters, however, will be found the same concern with the problem of freedom—the freedom of the self in relation to others, to the state, and to human culture generally—and with the complexities involved in resolving that problem. But the contention throughout this book that form and meaning are related rather than rival critical concerns, that close analysis and human relevance are not conflicting interests, is based upon my ultimate concern which sees form and the study of form as exercises in openness and human possibility.

It does not matter, as I have argued, if we are seeking relevance to society, whether we study Henry James or George Orwell, the "aesthete" is just as relevant to the human condition as the "committed" artist. But Camus *was*, of course, a committed artist, and *The Stranger* (1942) is a political book; so our task is somewhat more simple here than if we were dealing with Virginia Woolf or Marcel Proust. This is a novel in which the problem of the individual vs. society is explicitly dramatized, and the larger context I hope to provide will consist of two things: a drawing out of the implications which that dramatization suggests concerning general legal and political meanings; and a filling in of the picture to include both sides of the tension between the public and the private, only one side of which is emphasized in the book.

We look to the plot to begin with, however, both to see how far formal analysis can take us toward meaning and to gain a sense of what limits should be placed on our extension of meaning if it is to remain accurate and appropriate.

I

The book opens, if not with the precipitating incident, at least with a crucial one—the death of Meursault's mother. If, as I hope to show, the structure of the plot is designed first to bring Meursault to an awareness of the nature of his life and second to cause him consequently to affirm it,[1] then Camus' artistic problem in the first portion of the book is to establish his protagonist's thought and character—in other words, that which Meursault must later become aware of and affirm. And it is one of the "existential" aspects of the book that existence precedes essence, that experience precedes its meaning.[2] Since the nature of one's life is best defined in terms of its basic moments, Camus wisely chooses to depict Meursault's reactions to death, love, and work. Thus we see him at the outset attending his mother's funeral, and the point of his reactions here is, of course—as it is throughout—his honesty and directness. Contrary to many critics who see him as the archetypal alienated man, I see him as a truly integrated human being.[3] He lives always in the reality of the present, is aware always of how he really feels, and behaves accordingly.

What this means is that he is plagued neither by regret nor nostalgia concerning the past nor by hopes and expectations regarding the future. He does not act in terms of how he is supposed to act in the eyes of others because he does not expect anything from them in return. Thus it is that he is concerned about his mother's death and is at pains to do his duty for the occasion, but since he is not carried away by grief, he makes no great show of tears—he has been, after all, separated from his mother for some time, she was old, and there was no special intimacy between them. It is precisely this harmony with reality, however, which gets him into trouble later, for it violates the mental sets of "normal" society. It is only in this latter sense, it seems to me, that he can be called "alienated"— alienated from a society which is itself alienated from reality. His thought and character are not all that is being established here, then, for at the same time and by the same token Camus is developing the seeds of that very conflict with society which will motivate and resolve the plot.

But there is no problem yet as Meursault returns in time for the weekend, and on Saturday he goes swimming with his girlfriend. Again, at least two structural tasks are being performed, for we see that he is not going to inflict a period of mourning upon himself and that this casualness about death will later be used against him. Death and pleasure, society says, must not be allowed to mix. And then Meursault spends Sunday looking rather vacantly down at the street, concluding that things are about the same for him as before. Which is perfectly true.

The following Monday he returns to his job and regular life, and it is here that the machinery of the plot begins to be set in motion when later in the day his neighbor Raymond confides in him about his girl troubles. That is to say, in order to bring his protagonist to the points of self-awareness and self-affirmation, Camus must somehow bring him forcibly up against that which is different from himself and cause him to be threatened profoundly by it. This he will do, of course, by having him commit a crime and be brought to trial. Thus the events leading up to that crime must now be set in motion, and Meursault gets caught innocently up in the revenge and counter-revenge involved in Raymond's abortive affair with an Arab girl.

Similarly, the first job of the plot becomes subordinate to the second, but both are skillfully sustained as the book unfolds. A week passes, and Meursault spends a second weekend with Marie, where it is revealed that the usual claims of love have no power over him. He enjoys sex and companionship as he enjoys the sun or as he reacts to death—he simply takes what comes, without making or accepting demands and expectations. In the meantime, Raymond has inflicted a beating on *his* girl, and it is surely ironically appropriate that Meursault should meet his downfall through the agency of a jealous "normal" man.

On the following Monday our protagonist is again at work, and he refuses the offer of a better job in Paris, for he is also without ordinary ambition and he figures it will be pretty much the same there as it is here. Later when Marie asks him about getting married, he says he would just as soon not, but that if she wants it, he will go along with her wish. Camus' pacing here is worthy of remark, since the plot-machinery is being held in abeyance just before its trap is sprung.

Part 1 of the novel will conclude therefore with the murder. Another week has passed, and on the third weekend since his return from the funeral Meursault goes off to the beach with Raymond and Marie. Some

Arabs are following them, and they obviously want to even up the score with Raymond. One thing leads to another, Meursault finds a revolver in his hand as an Arab appears to threaten him with a knife in the heat of the sun, and Meursault pumps five shots into him.

The plot proper now begins with part 2. When he learns how others see him, Meursault will learn to see himself; and since he has never been particularly aware of the demands others make on one, it comes as something of a shock to him that they regard him as a monster. Not because of his crime, of course, but rather because of his attitude, for the examining magistrate is much more shocked at his atheism than his crime. It is much easier to understand a man who kills than one who does not believe what you believe; breaking the law is one thing, but disbelieving in its ostensible foundation is quite another. (There is a somewhat similar scene in Bernardo Bertolucci's movie *The Conformist*, where the protagonist is confessing in church a boyhood homosexual act and the supposed murder of his seducer and remarks wryly, after the priest shows much more interest in the former than the latter, that the Church seems more upset about sodomy than murder.) Puzzled, Meursault is beginning to feel the need to define himself.

Camus provides him with eleven months in jail while awaiting trial, and it is here that Meursault does two very difficult things: he gets used to jail, thereby testing and confirming his ability to live without memory and desire under the most difficult of situations; and he sees that he really liked the life he was leading before. These are doubly difficult because the second normally causes great pain in adapting to the first, but it is nevertheless true that what happens here is salutary: Meursault becomes conscious of himself.

Several more things remain to be done, however, if this plot is to fulfill itself. This new consciousness of his must now be thrown headlong against society's mental sets, and he must be shown reacting somehow to that conflict. Thus at the trial he watches the court search for a motive for his crime and, failing at that, condemn him for his attitude—he did not cry at his mother's funeral, he went swimming with his girlfriend immediately upon returning, and so on. Amazed at the gap between reality and the court, he withdraws into disinterested passivity. And he is sentenced to death.

Again Camus' pacing must be noted, for back in jail awaiting execution,

Meursault begins to want to get out of this fix, to sink into anxiety and bitterness—to have, in other words, hopes and expectations. This is perfectly human and sympathetic but nevertheless a self-betrayal. Condemned for his freedom, is he now going to become like the others simply in order to go free? But the balance swings back again as a result of the chaplain's visit: in being confronted finally by society's platitudes in their most unctuous form, Meursault flies into a cathartic rage and goes to meet the hangman in an ultimate gesture of self-affirmation.

It seems to me that this is a testing plot; its principal part is character, and its issue is whether, after coming to know himself, Meursault will remain true to that self under pressure. Since he does, we have a rather consistent line of action to serve as our basis for interpreting meaning. In terms of how structure reveals values, that is, the affirmation confirms the knowledge; and we may infer, although he did indeed kill a man, that this confirmation is to be regarded sympathetically. The question of murder will be taken up in due course, but it is crucial to inquire here into some of the means whereby Camus wins our assent for a man who is unlike ordinary and normal men. What, in other words, prevents us from seeing him as the court sees him?

The use of at least three devices helps to bring about the desired effect. To begin with, since the point of view is that of the protagonist-narrator, we are inside the consciousness of Meursault from beginning to end, and since—irony aside—this device has an inherent credibility factor, we are naturally prone to take him at his word. As we come to know Meursault's reality at firsthand, that is, we are prepared to credit him when it conflicts with the court's interpretation of it. Furthermore, as we come to know him from within, we see that he is an honest and gentle man despite the fact that he fails to behave conventionally. He is thoughtful, if not in the philosophical sense at first, then in the moral sense: he is considerate, he is helpful, and he is kind. What he is *not* is a role-player—but he is no callous rebel, no self-justifying flaunter of society.

Secondly, and in the same way, the style used to embody this narration and the sensibility it reveals are marvelously vivid and concrete. As Meursault's emotions are not caught up in society's mental sets, so are his sensations and perceptions free and full. He is aware throughout, even if he is not conscious of his awareness till the second part. He responds to the reality of his present in an immediate and sensory way, and so he authenticates himself in our eyes, while at the same time authenticating the reality of his experience for us. His reality is real, whereas that of the court is false.

Which brings us to the third device. The men of the court, society's wards and spokesmen, are presented without caricature as grotesque and pompous men. They are perfectly sincere, that is, and what they say could easily win our assent under different circumstances, but the fact is that they are responding inappropriately and we somehow sense this. Perhaps this is due in part to the fact that we see them only through Meursault's eyes, but it is also due in part to their own words and actions. Meursault tells them the simple truth—it was because of the sun—but they have no way of grasping this, or even of considering it as a possibility. And we know finally that even if they were right about Meursault's bad attitude, their sentence is too harsh.

But formally, it is not enough to infer sympathy for the protagonist and to marshall evidence for such a hypothesis, for we need to ask additionally whether this effect constitutes the principle of the whole or not. It seems to me that the novel is didactic rather than mimetic, that it is not only a testing plot but also a test case. I think that Camus was less interested in following human probability than in imagining a possibility, and I have two reasons for this hypothesis. First, a man like Meursault, of such perfect unselfconscious awareness, is simply nowhere to be found. And second, although he does have problems in prison, the fact that he adjusts himself so well to it, and later to the fact of his own death, is simply too much to expect of any man. In other words, it is not likely, as things now are, that anyone in our culture, without either an exceptional childhood or some very successful therapeutic training or both, could ever be so remarkably unresponsive to the demands of society's mental sets. Nor is it likely that anyone could—although it is likely that Meursault, granted his existence, could—accept death by affirming himself in so secular a manner.

Given these violations of probability, we could say either that *The Stranger* is a failure as a mimetic work, or it is a mimetic fantasy, or it is a didactic work. I do not see that it is a fantasy, for it is close enough to human probability and too close to societal issues for that. The most viable hypothesis is that the structure and depiction of the action are governed by the necessities of presenting and asserting the idea. The protagonist, if not a type or an average, is, like Billy Budd before him, an epitome, a purified embodiment of an ideal possibility—the unselfconscious, uncategorized man. It is appropriate that we know so little about his childhood or his earlier life. Although Camus, as I have indicated, did pay sufficient attention to pacing, technique, and probability to keep his plot interesting and his protagonist sympathetic, what he was basically interested in was clarifying and sharpening the meaning of the conflict. A man who was more "human" than Meursault would have been much more susceptible to the blandishments and pressures around him: he would have tried to defend himself in court, he would have yielded to despair in prison, and he would have bitterly resented dying. And so the plot would have worked out differently, and the idea would have been either muddled or changed.

Of course, Winston Smith in 1984 is indeed more human in these respects, but certainly Orwell's point is also different. Although both novelists portray society negatively and their hero-victims positively, Orwell is showing that political tyranny can be complete, while Camus is showing that moral tyranny can be defied. It is precisely because Meursault has not internalized the mental sets of his society that he can ultimately affirm himself, whereas Smith is, however justifiably, quite paranoid. He does not want to be caught, whereas for Meursault it is basically a matter of indifference. However similar contemporary radicals might think western society is to totalitarianism, it is simply not the case that the tyranny of the majority is the same as the tyranny of a ruling clique. However similar western police may seem to those of a police state, the fact remains that they are responsive to the needs of the majority, offensive and brutal as they may be to minorities. If it is improbable, it is nevertheless possible for a man to transcend the rigid categories of moral despotism, but it is both improbable and practically impossible for him to transcend absolute physical and psychological force. It is necessary, then, that Meursault be more unlike us than Smith—sufficiently so to be able to do, in our own sphere, what we are rarely able to do. For it can almost be done.

Thus far does formal analysis take us; if we want to go further into meaning, we will have to explore the processes of moral despotism in general and then come back to the book in order to clarify it further. But formal analysis does take us this far—however sketchy it has had to be for the present purpose—and whatever else we do must be built on this foundation and follow consistently these lines of development.

II

The basic problem, then, which *The Stranger*—like many another literary work—deals with is the conflict between the self and civilization. And there are several characteristic ways in which this conflict may be dramatized: by means of a crime and/or a trial, through which an individual violates justice (the law holding civilization together and making it what it is), or by means of some wartime emergency or shipboard situation, or some combination.

The source of this conflict, of course, is that, while society cannot survive without stability, the individual cannot grow without changing. Society depends upon our keeping our contracts: we cannot simply walk away from our responsibilities. Yet as a result we become entangled in a web of expectations, learning to live almost primarily in terms of what others want from us (however much we may be convinced that this is what we really want, for why is what "they" want any more legitimate than what we want?) If it is true that the self needs a principle of restraint to bind it to the community (positive), as well as a principle of restraint to keep it from infringing upon others (negative)—if it is true that society confers benefits we cannot survive without—by the same token it is incumbent upon society actually to confer the stated benefits (positive), without extracting too high a price in conformity (negative).

Certainly the balance is a difficult one, and the problem can be viewed in either way, with the self as a threat to civilization, or civilization as a threat to the self. Many authors take the first position, many take the second, and some do a little of both, content only if they can explore the tensions and ambiguities involved and avoid simple either/or solutions. Indeed, some authors try out all three possibilities, and such a one is Albert Camus. In *The Stranger*, however, Camus deals with the second position, that in which civilization is seen as a threat to the self. Let us follow out a few of the crucial implications of this position.

We may distinguish between two realms of action, two principles of authority. First, there is the realm of practical expediency, and this deals with means, with the problems of coordinating the business of society: it is the public world of instrumentalities. The second realm deals with values and ends rather than instrumentalities and means. This sphere has to do with what life signifies to a given individual, over and above the satisfaction of his material and practical needs, and refers to his pleasures, his beliefs, his personal relations, his tastes, his artistic experiences, and the like—all that is private and which has little to do with the public and practical sphere.[4]

As I understand the implications of *The Stranger*, it is a dramatization of the absurdity and destructiveness of confusing these two realms, of illegitimately forcing the public into the private sphere; so it implies that they must be, in certain senses, kept separate. If we follow this thought through, what will we find?

The question may be framed in terms of why it is wrong to mix these realms, and the answer may be found by examining, first, the source of power in each. The principle of authority, that which constrains us to conform, in the public realm, is, I think, the force of necessity: that we need to do certain things for the sake of surviving and prospering materially. Correspondingly, the principle of authority in the private realm is the force of conviction: that we want to do certain things for the sake of fulfilling our nonmaterial needs, for their own sakes. The point is that each of these forces is compelling in its own way, and the problem arises when one is mistaken for the other, with the result that claims are made upon us in the name of an inappropriate principle. When this happens, one realm intrudes upon the other, the proper area of power in the other is threatened and diminished, and our sense of reality becomes distorted.

Let us examine next what specifically the proper sphere of each principle of power is; when these spheres should not be allowed to overlap; and what happens when they do. In so far as *The Stranger* demonstrates the harm of intruding the public into the private realm, we are clarifying the plot by generalizing; in so far, however, as we go on to discuss the problem of intruding the private into the public realm, and the two-way nature of their appropriate balance and harmony, we are clarifying the plot by enlarging the picture and filling in the links.

The public is the proper sphere for the exercise of political power: individuals must limit their freedom or have it limited for them for the sake of the general good: they must live up to certain expectations and play certain roles, they must conform to certain patterns, they must be coordinated and organized, and they must be restrained from interfering with others. Any individual act which has demonstrable public consequences in relation to the business of society, and/or which has demonstrable material effects on the person or property of some other individual, falls into this sphere. And the general aim which governs and justifies this conformity should be threefold: actually to produce the instrumental goods which are its proper business; to limit itself to controlling the affairs which constitute its proper business; and to regard itself always as a means toward the greater freedom and fulfillment of the individual which is its ultimate goal.

The private on the other hand is the realm, not of political power, but rather of the authority of personal conscience. We do things here because we really want to rather than because we must. The public is the realm of socialization, of duties to be learned, and of contracts to be made—we can be persuaded to do things we might not otherwise do because they happen to be means toward things we do want. The private is the realm which exists both before and after this socialization, and while it must be coordinated and even limited within the framework of the public, it must survive and transcend this framework as well. The tragedy of history is mental rigidity, and the basic sign of mental rigidity is when these choices are seen as mutually exclusive. But since the search for power cannot forego any source of power, the result is that the authority appropriate in one sphere is often smuggled into the area of the other. That is to say, when an institution forgets its original end, whether practical or personal, and becomes an end in itself instead of a means, it must use a new principle of authority as a substitute. If it is a moral institution, it will use political imperatives; if it is a political one, it will use moral imperatives. Thus political acts are urged upon us in the name of what we really want, of personal loyalties, of principles of conscience, while personal acts are required of us in the name of duties to be performed, of contracts to be made, of public consequences.

This confusion results not only in illegitimate extensions and intrusions of power, but also in serious and destructive distortions of reality. One infers that primitive man was concerned primarily with material survival, that his personal conscience was absorbed and transformed almost entirely into public necessities, and that his religious system was basically aimed at controlling the environment. The result was a fantastic projection of his needs upon external reality, a seeing of the world from within the viewpoint of human desire. But at least his concern with material survival was, in fact, governed by his real situation: his control over his environment was indeed small and precarious.

The two great developments of modern culture, I take it, have been the dematerialization of religion and the demystification of nature. On the one hand, we have had to learn that our spiritual values must be detached from the effort to control the environment—that we must pray, for example, not for success but for fortitude—and on the other, that our control of the environment is much more efficacious when we regard it objectively rather than subjectively. Indeed, as the latter effort advances, the former is correspondingly enabled to flourish; as our lives cease to be dominated by the problems of material survival, we can learn to explore our inner selves more deeply and extensively.

But the problem arises, as I have been suggesting, when we continue to regard inner exploration as a threat to material survival, when we continue to apply archaic attitudes to modern conditions (see also chapter 14), and the result is not only a distortion of external reality but also of internal reality as well. Modern man is caught in a pervasive schizophrenia —superstitious about democracy, enslaved to the instruments of his freedom, wiser in his science than in his politics, guilty about his inner self, and confusing means and ends just as eternally as his ancestors. And this is because he still sees the personal as subordinate to the public, except that this attitude no longer reflects the reality of his situation.

We may suggest, then, when the public should not intrude upon the private and when the private should not be thrust upon the public, and why. When a personal act is interpreted in political terms, a matter of value becomes disguised as a matter of expediency. Regarding a man who does not cry at his mother's funeral as a menace to society, and society disguising its need to revenge a murderer as a matter of justice, are Camus' examples, and we can think of others where the force of necessity is wrongly applied to matters where only the force of conviction should rule.

Another way of disguising values as matters of expediency is not so much to thrust the public into the private as to politicize the personal. To give spiritual imperatives the force of practical necessities is the other side of the coin, as we shall see, of giving politics the coloration of religious fervor. Religious-moral-ethical systems have tried to organize men, make them conform to certain expectations, and play certain roles, but the real harm is done when such systems form an alliance with political institutions, or when they take on a political aspect of their own. This, I take it, is what the founding fathers intended to avoid by the principle of separating church and state, and it is no accident that Camus portrays the examining magistrate as questioning the accused on his religious beliefs.

Now we may, for the sake of a fuller perspective, turn the entire argument around and regard it from the point of view of the personal intruding upon the public rather than the public intruding upon the personal. In this case, matters of expediency are disguised as matters of value. It used to be claimed, for example, in debates over Vietnam that Communism—if that is what the Vietcong represent—threatened our way of life, whereas what was really meant is that it threatened our balance of power in the Far East. Indeed, much of the hue and cry about patriotism and nationalism seems to me to be based on this double shift: we fight wars for power, yet ask God to be on our side; we constitute governments for freedom, yet ask for loyalty and devotion to particular leaders.

And so it goes throughout the fabric of our lives: we devise a particular industrial and commercial system for material security and prosperity, yet we exalt the requisite character traits of punctuality, passivity, and conformity into moral virtues;[5] we develop an educational system for democratic citizenship and intellectual growth, yet we really want it to prepare the young for job slots in the economy. And how many of our other moral virtues—those concerned with love, sex, marriage, and the family, for example—are governed basically by the needs of the marketplace rather than by their ostensibly personal values? To make a virtue of necessity is no virtue.

III

Whatever else may be said about these ideas, the problem now is to see what light they can throw on the meaning of *The Stranger*, as well as what light the novel can throw on them.

Meursault is, through most of the plot, divorced both from the imperatives of public life as well as from the values of personal life. As a man, he is simply indifferent, living only from day to day in terms of his unselfconscious feelings and sense impressions. His problem is merely to get through the time as agreeably as possible. He makes no demands on life; he initiates nothing; he is passive; he plays no roles; he is fairly content. Symbolically, as I have suggested, he is a test case, as if Camus had said to himself: let me create a man who lives completely outside of any categories and see what happens when he is brought into forceful contact with them, when he who makes no demands is subjected to the demands of others, he will come to realize and accept the meaning of his life as an individual, and the reader will come to see the meaning of the conflict between the individual and society.

But if indifference is one of his main traits, honesty is the other; for living unselfconsciously according to his feelings and sense impressions means that he has no hopes or schemes or plans and therefore lacks utterly any motivation for lying, for deceiving himself or others. He goes to his mother's funeral, but he does not cry; their relationship had not been very close anyway. When Marie asks if he loves her, he says, frankly, no, which is a failure on the personal level; and when she asks him if he will marry her, he says it is all the same to him, which reveals his indifference to public imperatives. When his boss offers him a better job, he is not interested. When Raymond asks for assistance, he says he has no objection, not caring one way or the other; and when Céleste says Salamano's treatment of his dog is a crying shame, he says one cannot be sure. And when he shoots the Arab, it is simply an automatic reaction, almost accidental: he is in a trancelike state of shock, almost sunstroke, and does not know what he is doing. Thus it is generally. This is no romantic hero, then, placing himself outside the categories of normal men and defying the norms of society. But it must also be said that neither is he an inhuman monster, indulging in unspeakable cruelties in the manner of Dorian Gray. He is merely affectless, disengaged, and on the whole, except for the murder, he is not particularly destructive—indeed, it seems to me that he is predominantly agreeable, even feeling twinges of guilt at the beginning about his mother's death.

What happens at the trial, however, as we have seen, is that he is gradually forced to become aware of public imperatives and personal values and so to become conscious of himself in relation to these categories, to the way in which the public imperatives overextend themselves into the realm of private values, and how one set of categories becomes disguised as another. For at the trial, and during his imprisonment, he is made for the first time to see himself as others see him, and this causes him in turn to realize three things: first, that society's imperatives in relation to the reality of personal experience are false when they are over-extended; second, that other individuals do have a real existence; and third, that his former life had been precious and good.

As far as his death sentence is concerned, if he had had a good lawyer, and if the court's ruling had been based on true justice, he could have legitimately gotten off either with a light sentence or an acquittal. For the facts of the case are that the Arabs were bent on revenge, that he had plausible grounds for shooting in self-defense, that he acted without pre-meditation, and that he was in a temporary state of shock. These facts, however, are not enough for the court, for they do not fit easily into the way society structures experience. Society needs a motive; it needs to fit him into its own categories.

This, I take it, is another of the "existential" aspects of the book, that society wants a reason when there really is none to be found. I used to think that Camus made an artistic mistake in having Meursault actually kill someone, since that operates to take away sympathy from the pro-tagonist and make his punishment by society seem more justifiable. But now I see that an actual shooting was artistically necessary, since it must be shown that society, in failing to find a motive, must try to supply one. Had there not been a real murder, Meursault would have simply been framed and railroaded, being found guilty of something he did not do merely because he was different (a black, a hippie, a commie). Which would show society's prejudice but not its pitiful need for rationality, and which would make the book less existential and more romantic (in the manner of James Jones's *From Here to Eternity*, for example).

But the court cannot understand why he fired more than one shot. On this basis, it reasons that because he did not weep at his mother's funeral, because of his liaison with Marie, and because he does not believe in God, he must be an inhuman monster. And so the death penalty is based not on his crime but rather on his personal tastes and behavior.

A purer case of the overextension of public imperatives into the private realm, and of personal values disguised as societal expediencies, could not be found. And this is the first thing that Meursault learns: how great is the gulf between society's categories and reality, how large is the gap between himself and the court. So he gives up, and becomes indifferent to the proceedings.

He also, however, begins to feel affection for his former friends, as when

Céleste, the restaurant owner, testifies on his behalf, and when later he begins to understand what kind of person his mother was.

Finally, although he does come momentarily to hope for a miracle to mitigate his death sentence, he nevertheless comes through the trial and then again in his argument with the priest—the purveyor of institution-alized personal values—to be more conscious of the worth of his former life, and to assert it once and for all against civilization and what it stands for. Thus has the conflict between self and society been dramatized; thus has the privacy of the inner life been realized, defined, and affirmed; and thus have the public imperatives been exposed, defined, and rejected.

IV

I have said, however, that Camus was one who was not content unless he could explore the tensions of this conflict rather than simply choosing one side or the other. In *The Plague*, for example, written five years later in 1947, he takes the problem one step further by showing how an in-dividual, who has at the outset the self-awareness Meursault earned only at the end of his book, can find a reason for binding himself to mankind even though he is still an outsider as far as society and civilization are concerned.

But let us leave Camus for the moment and see, for the sake of com-parison, the various ways in which other authors have handled this same problem. Crimes and/or trials are the dramatic centers of many promi-nent works, some greater than others: *Antigone* (441 BC), *Crime and Punishment* (1866), *Billy Budd* (1891), *Lafcadio's Adventures* (1914), *The Trial* (c. 1920), George Bernard Shaw's *Saint Joan* (1924), Herman Wouk's *The Caine Mutiny* (1951), Arthur Miller's *The Crucible* (1953). Let us look briefly at three of these: *Antigone*, *Billy Budd*, and *Saint Joan*.

Although Antigone could be seen as the romantic rebel against society, the fact is that her personal and religious values were sanctioned and sanctified by her culture. Creon is wrong, not in violating the self of the individual, but in violating a higher set of values. Implicit in the world of the play and perhaps in the culture of Sophocles' times was the as-sumption that the political world should not overextend its imperatives into the moral world and that the moral world was ultimately a superior world. Notice that Oedipus himself, in *Oedipus Rex*, is not exempt from the will of the gods and, having decreed that the murderer of King Laius must be punished and having discovered that he himself is that murderer, must enact his own decree upon himself, in spite of the fact that he is the present king. The point is that there was an apparently agreed-upon set of moral values and that these values were not hostile to the life of the inner self. Material expediencies, therefore, were seen as subordinate and did not become disguised as moral demands, or disguise moral demands as practical matters. It is this set of distinctions and hierarchies which is lacking in Meursault's society—and of course in our own.

We have seen that Melville constructed as difficult a case as possible in *Billy Budd*. On the one hand Billy has our sympathy, yet on the other he must be executed. Here what is good and right in personal and moral terms becomes evil and wrong in legal and public terms. Further, while we must feel resentment against Vere's arguments and decisions, we must nevertheless sympathize with his character and motives. Unlike Meursault's judges and like Sophocles, he clearly recognizes the distinction between the public and private realms; but like Meursault's judges and unlike Sophocles, he turns Antigone's values upside-down to affirm the precedence of the public world over the private.[6] Perhaps because he felt a lack of confidence in the stability of personal values and so feared anarchy more than he feared the destruction of the self. It is as if the private realm could not be sustained unless the public world were preserved first. Or even as if the private realm were too insubstantial to count on, and the only source of principles left were the public realm.[7] The difference is that in Sophocles the moral realm had an independent existence and did not depend upon the political realm—it had its own separate societal legitimacy, and even though his kings had a priestlike function, the ultimate source of power flowed from the gods and their oracles rather than from secular authority. For when secular authority also controls religious authority, it has a double instrument of power in its hands.

We come, finally, to Shaw, who strikes something of a middle position between the two extremes. What is significant here is that, since the church has institutionalized religious and moral values—externalized them, put them in the hands of a human hierarchy rather than of tradition, the gods, and the oracles—it can be just as threatened by the inner self—Joan's voices—as the political state, and can therefore ally itself with the state against the self, however different may be its reasons. We find it, in other words, in that anomalous position of many institutions, of having to deny any further rebellion against institutions after the rebellion which gave rise to it in the first place has been finished and codified. Thus, while the nobles fear the nascent nationalism that Joan represents to them, the church authorities fear the nascent Protestantism that she represents to *them*. Either way, though, the result is the same.

The only answer, says Shaw, to the tragic hardening of institutions and the terrible wasted suffering of reformers is for institutions to have built into them a provision making for growth and change. In other words, if we should not regard expediencies as moral values, or moral values as expediencies, we should nevertheless keep our practical imperatives at a minimum, expand the area of individual values, and regard society always in the ultimately and paradoxically larger context of the life of the inner self. For if Camus and Sophocles affirm the precedence of inner values, and Melville the opposite, Shaw offers a way of reconciling the conflict.

Chapter 14

Self and Universe in Hemingway

The problem I wish to discuss here is not whether Ernest Hemingway *has* a vision, since interpretations of his "code" are by now critical commonplaces, but rather whether that vision represents anything more than a highly sophisticated version of the wisdom of schoolboys and adolescents—still a question for many critics today.[1] The solution I wish to suggest will be derived from a placing of Hemingway in a broader and more appropriate context than that usually assumed by his critics, favorable and unfavorable alike, by virtue of which his code and its implications will take on deeper and more significant meanings. Thus our progress from the family in Kafka to society in Camus becomes even more partisan as we attempt to elevate our view of Hemingway by relating his vision to the transcendent. In other words, if we tried in the cases of Kafka and Camus to enrich our understanding of their novels via larger contexts, in the case of Hemingway we are trying to ennoble our understanding by these means. In developing the significance of Kafka and Camus, we began by assuming that they *were* significant, whereas in Hemingway it is that very assumption which we must establish.

A Farewell to Arms serves as a central example throughout the present discussion, but since we will look in some detail at the question of its form in chapter 17, it will be unnecessary to explore the issue further here as we did in our studies of Kafka and Camus. Plot analysis implicitly controls and limits our interpretation of Hemingway's vision in this chapter; furthermore, our interpretation of vision will help explain, over and above the formal requirements of any given novel, certain structural and stylistic traits characteristic of Hemingway's art in general. Thus are the relations between meaning and form being treated as reciprocal: form determines our understanding of meaning, while meaning determines features of the work not exclusively controlled by form.

R. S. Crane suggests, as we have seen, that the matter of vision can best be discussed comparatively, and so we will begin constructing our larger context by relating Hemingway to a few relevant major American novelists—particularly William Faulkner, Thomas Wolfe, and Henry James—in the hope that if we can see how certain novelists manage to handle a given theme, we will be able to see better how others either exceed or fall short of that mark in depth, scope, and intensity.

I

If it is not necessary to argue that Hemingway—or Faulkner—does indeed have a vision, it was not always the case. In the 1920s and 30s, when they first began publishing, Hemingway was accused of inaugurating what unsympathetic critics called "the hard boiled" school of fiction, as Faulkner was accused of initiating "the cult of cruelty." In their emphasis on sex and violence, in their antisentimentalism, in their portrayal of the primitive, and in their rebellion against the conventions of style and plot and characterization in fiction, these writers first struck the public in a negative way as nihilists, rebels, and destroyers of traditional values. We know now, however, that they were genuine innovators, avant-gardists, and experimenters, but it is easy to see how their intentions and achievements were misunderstood in their early days; for their first works *were* shocking, and the real quality of their art only gradually became evident as their careers matured and the fulness of their visions began to develop. In fact, we have tended to go to the opposite extreme today by revering them as classics and so are running the danger of removing the authentic sting from their writings. For they are still shocking today, if not because they appear to exalt mindless brutality without vision, then because of the very nature of that vision itself.

However, although Hemingway shares with Faulkner a concern with sex, an admiration of the primitive, and a passion for hunting, it is also true that he does have less of a vision than Faulkner; and one of the things I want to show is the nature and significance of that "less." On the other hand, although he shares with Wolfe a characteristic close working relationship between his life and his fiction, he does have more of a vision than Wolfe. For all Wolfe's struggles to see his own life and experience within the framework of the myth of America, for all his desperate attempts to create a language which would be adequate to that ambition, and for all his despairing rhetoric about the hunger of loneliness and lostness, Wolfe rarely rose far enough above his obsession to see what that hunger was for, what caused it, and how it could be slaked. Wolfe's novels are swollen (if brilliant) monstrosities in texture and structure, as I have suggested, not because they are based on total recall and his compulsion to get it all down the way it was, but rather because he never crystallized his insights about the meaning of his experiences, he never achieved that coherence of vision which would have enabled him to organize his experiences into a more than intermittent pattern.[2] Whereas Hemingway did: not only is he a more careful artist than Wolfe, he also knew pretty well what it was he wanted to say. Not that a novelist needs a philosophy worked out intellectually in advance, but he does need some sense of the significance of his materials or he will not be able to put together a finished work—as Wolfe was not. Hemingway's fiction is based on his life and experience, but he had greater powers of vision and hence greater artistic objectivity and control.

It may seem perverse to say so, but I think that Hemingway resembles James in this more than he resembles either Faulkner or Wolfe. In some senses, of course, the differences between James and Hemingway seem overwhelming. James's life was so uneventful, while Hemingway's was so adventurous; James deals with refined characters, and almost never treats sex directly, while Hemingway is fond of cruder types and emphasizes their sensual pleasures; James's plots are characteristically moral and psychological, while Hemingway's are often full of physical action; and James's style is elaborate, while Hemingway's is blunt and straightforward. But in the end I think it can be shown that James's ultimate value is a kind of Hemingwayesque living of life to the fullest, while Hemingway's art and values aim at a conscious and mannered elegance not unlike James's. This is no riddling paradox, and their very real but superficial differences should not be allowed to obscure it.[3] If they start out at opposite ends of the spectrum, they do meet, or at least tend to meet, at the center; for they occupy the ground of what I would like to call the middle vision, a vision which is neither as full as Faulkner's nor as fragmentary as Wolfe's; a vision which, while incapable of seeing human life and history in terms of some grand design, does nevertheless find a transcendent meaning in experience—a meaning that inheres in the living of a person's "greater moments," moments of courage, honesty, generosity, acceptance, and integrity.

What I mean by *transcendent* and the *middle vision* requires some explaining, I think, before I can go on to be more specific about what Hemingway's vision means and does not mean, in addition to merely trying to locate it somewhere between Faulkner's and Wolfe's.

II

Transcendentalism can mean different, although sometimes overlapping, things. The root sense of the word, I take it, refers to something lower or smaller and something higher or larger, the latter going beyond or surpassing the former. What these somethings are, of course, and how and why one surpasses the other, are the variables. The two most basic definitions are somewhat opposed. The most traditional, of course, refers to a spiritual reality over and above the perceivable and phenomenal world we are familiar with, while a more recent—evolving primarily from the latter part of the eighteenth century and related to romanticism—refers to a reality in nature and in ourselves over and above the mental sets we use in perceiving it. Reality itself is undifferentiated, says this second view, and depends upon the way we look at it to achieve meaning, yet our meanings are always in danger of falsifying reality. Common to both definitions is the assumption that there is something more fully real than what we normally perceive, but they differ as to where they locate this reality. In the former it is not to be found on earth, while in the latter it is to be found by submitting ourselves more completely to the earth, so to speak. They differ also, in consequence, as to what they mean by illusion; for the former, it is in the nature of the human condition to be distracted by phenomenal existence; for the latter, it is in the tendency of the human mind and of human societies to distort what actually exists. Thus at bottom we find two different metaphysics, the one seeing the world we live in as false, the other seeing it as falsified but potentially the source of reality, energy, and truth.

It is to the latter tradition, of course, that Hemingway belongs, and it is no accident that it characteristically reaches back to childhood and pure experience in its search for undistorted reality. To transcend society, to become fully alive, we must cast off habit and open our senses. Heaven is the rebirth of the body on earth. Nature is accepted rather than transcended. Transcendence is being in tune with ourselves and with nature.

Several ambiguities, however, mark the development of this tradition:

one is whether the mind in its search for an undistorted reality is in fact creating just another illusion. For if, on the one hand, meaning is not given to us from without, and is therefore a matter for us to create, it may be, on the other hand, that there is no such thing as meaning at all. Thus we get drastic alternations between idealism and sentimentalism on the one side, and melancholy and dejection on the other.[4] A second ambiguity is whether the cause of distortion, if it does not lie in our stars, lies in ourselves or in our society. And we shall also see in Hemingway an ambivalent awareness that nature as well as society is destructive.

Let us make a distinction, then, similar to that developed in our discussion of Camus but nevertheless somewhat different, between two worlds—two levels of awareness, if you prefer—between the world of everyday life, which is practical, instrumental, and businesslike, and the world of reality itself, which is large, mysterious, and indefinable. We could say that the former is the political realm, while the latter is the moral, but we are dealing here not so much with sources of authority as with ways of seeing, not so much with appropriate and inappropriate overlappings as with how the former narrows the latter while trying to express it. In the previous chapter we were more concerned with the relation between the individual and institutions, whereas here we shall explore the relation between the individual and the universe; the distortions of reality caused by confusions of value, therefore, were only briefly mentioned there, whereas here they shall come into central focus. The same question of rigidification, of means supplanting ends, does come up here, however, and the same corrective principle of flexibility and balance will be involved.

Let us call the natural world of reality itself the transcendent world, the world of ultimates basic to existence—sex, birth, life, energy, love, and death. The problem is that the world of everyday life represents only a small selection from the world of reality, a selection that is furthermore highly organized and rather rigidly blocked out. But culture characteristically tries to condition us to believe that its world of everyday life is in fact the world of reality itself.[5] It does this because it needs to command our loyalty, and such loyalty seems best won by appeals to reality, much in the same way that the political gains strength from masking itself as the moral.

We must realize, however, that the world of daily life is a fiction, an artifice constructed by the human mind for certain uses—namely, to en-

able us to find our way about in the world of reality and to survive there
as well as possible. George Santayana puts it very clearly:

> We name what we conceive and believe in, not what we see; things,
> not images [that is, things as the mind defines them—conceptions—
> rather than perceptions]; souls, not voices and silhouettes. This
> naming, with the whole education of the senses which it accom-
> panies, subserves the uses of life; in order to thread our way through
> the labyrinth of objects which assault us, we must make a great selec-
> tion in our sensuous experience; half of what we see and hear we
> must pass over as insignificant, while we piece out the other half
> with such an ideal complement as is necessary to turn it into a fixed
> and well-ordered world.[6]

All cultures have perforce engaged in this ordering of reality, or else
they could never have come into being in the first place or have been able
to survive in the second place. But it is the paradox of all human history
that cultural orders designed to insure man's survival seem inevitably,
once they mature, to insure his deterioration: since these orders are selective, those aspects of reality which they neglected or omitted always seem
to return with a vengeance to smash that which excluded them—especially, of course, when reality confronts them with new and challenging
aspects, whether natural or manmade. Reality, denied entrance at the
front door, comes down on us like a wolf through the chimney.

I am tempted to call this rigidity the dinosaur factor—the inability of
cultures to adapt to changing conditions, and their consequent cycles
of extinction.[7] Once having mastered their conditions to achieve stability,
they assume that this is all there is and so become closed and self-justifying
systems, impervious to change, and fatally committed to a given way of
looking at things as the only way. Man is not so stupid as to become
perpetually devoted to what does not work, but when he does find something that works, he becomes so devoted to it that he will not abandon
it even after it stops working. What man is stupid about is becoming
different, being experimental, going with process, growth, development,
change. His problem is to learn somehow to combine tentativeness with
commitment, to work for order while at the same time remaining open,
to stop assuming that closure needs to be closed.[8]

Thus when a society's picture of the world becomes too divorced from
reality, as is the case, it seems to me, with Western culture, the results
—as has become familiar to all of us by now—are isolation, anxiety, aliena-

tion, emotional emptiness, and confusion of values. This has happened in the midst of the most splendid material abundance, or potential for abundance, that the world has ever known. Man cannot deny reality—whether of external nature or of his inner self—without paying a terrible price, no matter what the short-term material rewards may seem to be.

It is the sense of the transcendental which we must recover, therefore, if we are not to suffocate among our own machines. It has become one of the functions of art, especially of literature, more and more during the past two hundred years to be the spokesman for reality—for nature, for man's inner self—and more and more to be the critic of society, of routine, and of regimentation.[9] It is no wonder that problems of censorship have been arising over and over again during this period, for society is often more interested in power and order than in truth and reality, however it may base its rhetoric on appeals to truth and reality.

> Poetry [as Santayana says] breaks up the trite conceptions designated by current words into the sensuous qualities out of which these conceptions were originally put together. . . . The poet retains by nature the innocence of the eye, or recovers it easily; he disintegrates the fictions of common perception into their sensuous elements, gathers these together again into chance groups as the accidents of his environment or the affinities of his temperament may conjoin them; and this wealth of sensation and this freedom of fancy, which make an extraordinary ferment in his ignorant heart, presently bubble over into some kind of utterance.[10]

If we cannot know what we cannot name, and if reality does not exist apart from our way of apprehending it, we nevertheless pass by a million things in reality because we are not prepared to see them. Yet it sometimes happens that some of these things press for recognition, and so we struggle to grasp them, failing in so far as we use the old mental sets, or succeeding in so far as we miraculously can create new ones. We can never escape our mental sets, but we can continually develop more adequate and comprehensive ones, regarding them as means to the end rather than as ends in themselves. At least as early as Blake, artists and social critics have been protesting against a world of sterile conventions on behalf of a more full and fruitful world. And this protest, as I have suggested, cuts across ideologies, beliefs, religions, politics, moralities. Whether conservative, liberal or radical, our writers are more valuable to the degree that they penetrate the surfaces of modern life than they are for the particular nostrums they offer as solutions for our problems. The task of art is to help make us more fully alive, not to tell us how to live. Certainly we should distinguish between a writer's politics and his basic insights, and we should trace their relationships in his work, but we should not judge the latter merely in terms of the former. W. B. Yeats, Ezra Pound, and T. S. Eliot are, to my mind, silly and even vicious in their politics,[11] but they are important in so far as they search for a larger reality. "It is a secret which every intellectual man quickly learns," as Emerson said some 125 years ago,

> that beyond the energy of his possessed and conscious intellect he is capable of a new energy (as of an intellect doubled on itself), by abandonment to the nature of things; that beside his privacy of power as an individual man, there is a great public power on which he can draw, by unlocking, at all risks, his human doors, and suffering the ethereal tides to roll and circulate through him; then he is caught up into the life of the Universe, his speech is thunder, his thought is law, and his words are universally intelligible as the plants and animals. . . . This is the reason why bards love wine, mead, narcotics, coffee, tea, opium, the fumes of sandalwood and tobacco, or whatever other procurers of animal exhilaration. All men avail themselves of such means as they can, to add this extraordinary power to their normal powers; and to this end they prize conversation, music, pictures, sculpture, dancing, theatres, travelling, war, mobs, fires, gaming, politics, or love, or science, or animal intoxication,—which are several coarser or finer *quasi*-mechanical substitutes for the true nectar, which is the ravishment of the intellect by coming near to the fact. These are auxiliaries to the centrifugal tendency of a man, to his passage out into free space, and they help him escape the custody of that body which he is pent up in, and of that jailyard of individual relations in which he is enclosed.[12]

Somehow this energy must find its release. In this connection, Octavio Paz, the contemporary Mexican poet and essayist, has this to say about the meaning and function of the fiesta:

> The fiesta is not only an excess, a ritual squandering of the goods painfully accumulated during the rest of the year [as certain French sociologists had claimed]; it is also a revolt, a sudden immersion in the formless, in pure being. By means of the fiesta society frees itself from the norms it has established. It ridicules its gods, its principles, and its laws; it denies its own self. . . . The group emerges purified and strengthened from this plunge into chaos. It has immersed itself

in its own origins, in the womb from which it came. To express it another way, the fiesta denies society as an organic system of differentiated forms and principles, but affirms it as a source of creative energy. It is a true "re-creation," the opposite of the "recreation" characterizing modern vacations, which do not entail any rites or ceremonies whatever and are as individualistic and sterile as the world that invented them.[13]

There is no doubt that Hemingway's obsession with youthfulness, the primitive, sex, eating, drinking, hunting, war, sports, fishing, bull fighting, and so on is thrown into a more meaningful light when seen in the perspective of this notion of transcendentalism. In this view, he takes his true place, it seems to me, in the still-unfolding tradition of arts and letters and culture during the past two hundred years, in its attempt to explore the many fundamental and vital aspects of reality that western civilization is finding less and less of a place for in its everyday world. We have known for some time now that he is not simply a hard-boiled writer, not merely a chaser after experiences, but rather the prophet of courage and dignity and integrity in a world which is itself hard-boiled. As we have seen, it has become common enough to speak of the Hemingway hero and the Hemingway code. But we have not often been able to see this hero and this code in their broader context—that this courage and dignity and integrity are related to Hemingway's search for the transcendent.

III

Just how they are related needs further discussion, but here I must pause another moment to explain what I mean by the middle vision. There are two kinds of transcenders: those who, whether by design or accident, experience intermittent moments of illumination as a result of external circumstances; and those who, whether by discipline or grace, achieve a continuously illuminated vision of the pattern of human life and history in the universe.

The first kind are compelled to immerse themselves in events and relationships in the hope of experiences that will suddenly achieve an equilibrium and produce an illumination, a sense of surpassing oneself, of transcending the mundane. Walter Pater wrote in 1868:

Every moment some form grows perfect in hand or face; some tone on the hills or the sea is choicer than the rest; some mood of passion or insight or intellectual excitement is irresistibly real and attractive to us,—for that moment only. . . . How shall we pass most swiftly from point to point, and be present always at the focus where the greatest number of vital forces unite in their purest energy? . . . In a sense it might be said that our failure is to form habits: for, after all, habit is relative to a stereotyped world, and meantime it is only the roughness of the eye that makes any two persons, things, situations, seem alike. . . . Not to discriminate every moment some passionate attitude in those about us, and in the very brilliancy of their gifts some tragic dividing of forces on their way, is, on this short day of frost and sun, to sleep before evening.[14]

The second kind, on the other hand, are not dependent upon a continuous series of experiences to sustain their vision: it comes from within themselves, and it is self-sustaining. This is how Whitman described the type in 1855:

He consumes an eternal passion and is indifferent which chance happens and which possible contingency of fortune and misfortune and persuades daily and hourly his delicious play. What balks or breaks others is fuel for this burning progress to contact and amorous joy. Other proportions of the reception of pleasure dwindle to nothing to his proportions. All expected from heaven or from the highest he is [in] rapport with in the sight of the daybreak or a scene of the winter woods or the presence of children playing or with his arm around the neck of a man or woman. His love above all love has leisure and expanse. . . . he leaves room ahead of himself. He is no irresolute or suspicious lover . . . he is sure . . . he scorns intervals. His experience and the showers and thrills are not for nothing. Nothing can jar him. . . . suffering and darkness cannot—death and fear cannot. To him complaint and jealousy and envy are corpses buried and rotten in the earth. . . . he saw them buried. The sea is not surer of the shore or the shore of the sea than he is of the fruition of his love and of all perfection and beauty.[15]

I will not say which is the better kind of transcendence, because I do not think that one can choose in such matters, but I do think that the second kind is more fortunate. Restlessness is a characteristic of the first kind, for, in Steppenwolf-fashion, it makes great demands upon life, and it is no wonder that life often fails to live up to these demands. Thus the problem of what to do between the precious moments of illumination can lead to an agonizing sense of despair, when the previous moment seems already far behind, the next moment seems never to be arriving, and the intervening present seems utterly blank. Life does not automatically yield up its meaning; indeed, often it seems designed deliberately to deny it.[16]

This is what I am calling the middle vision, and it is to this kind that Hemingway, along with Pater, for better or worse, belongs—and that Wolfe barely manages to reach. In Hemingway, the type becomes active, virile, aggressive, and masculine, and it is no accident that Papa Hemingway enjoyed playing a patriarchal role in his later years. Transcenders of the middle vision are driven to go out and seek experience—even James is a moral and psychological adventurer—while those of the full vision, such as Whitman, tend to be more passive, waiting, receptive, feminine, taking what comes as it comes. For Whitman, the road is open, not a means to an end. It is to this second kind that Faulkner belongs; his fiction, while it does almost as full justice to the masculine as does Hemingway's, reveals also at one and the same time the frequent harshness of masculinity as well as the variety and complexity of the feminine.

It may be taken as a paradox that, while Faulkner had almost nothing of the global experience of Hemingway, he nevertheless had a more comprehensive artistic vision. Indeed, compared to Hemingway, Faulkner was practically a stay-at-home; yet this is really no great puzzle, for Faulkner had no real need for adventure, as his mind gave him almost all he wanted, whereas Hemingway had to roam the face of the earth, looking for ways to fill in those blank spaces. And it is here that we shall find the connection between the Hemingway hero, the Hemingway code, and the search for transcendence.

IV

We have these three aspects of life to deal with: an unknowable, intractable reality; moments of intuitive illumination; and the despair of living between these moments.

We begin with the emptiness. Think of "A Clean, Well-Lighted Place," with its refrain of our nada, who art in nada, nada be thy name. Think of the desolation of the emasculated Jake Barnes's night thoughts in *The Sun Also Rises*: "It is awfully easy to be hard-boiled about everything in the daytime, but at night it is another thing" (chapter 4; cf. beginning of chapter 14). Think of Lt. Henry's fear of the night in *A Farewell to Arms*: "I know that the night is not the same as the day: that all things are different, that the things of the night cannot be explained in the day, because they do not then exist, and the night can be a dreadful time for lonely people once their loneliness has started" (chapter 34). Think of the bitter soldier's boast in *Across the River and Into the Trees*: "he had never been sad one waking morning of his life; attack or no attack. He had experienced anguish and sorrow. But he had never been sad in the morning" (chapter 41; cf. beginning of chapter 9). Carlos Baker writes of Hemingway's recurring struggles with insomnia, melancholia, and boredom, and of his intense interest in the conditions of suicide. Near the end of *A Life Story* we read: "It had been his lifelong habit to awaken cheerfully. Now each day seemed like a nightmare seventy-two hours long." [17]

Like an early existentialist, Hemingway experienced sharply the yawning boredom of life, its terrible emptiness, its grinding meaninglessness. A state not uncommon, as we have seen, among transcenders of the middle vision, and not unrelated to romantic moods of melancholy and dejection.

We go on now to the hard-to-come-by moments of transcendence. We know that attending bullfights, participating in fiestas, and going fishing are restorative acts for Jake Barnes, balancing the sterility and despair of his life. As he remarks of one of the bullfighters: "He was not sure that there were any great moments. Things were not the same and now life only came in flashes" (chapter 18). And at the end of *The Sun Also Rises* Lady Brett, having given up Romero in order not to ruin his career, says to Jake about her quixotic gesture that this is what we have instead of God. In *A Farewell*, the wonderful ninety-four-year-old Count Greffi says, "I had always expected to become devout. But somehow it does not come." To which Lt. Henry replies, "It's too early." Greffi: "Maybe it's too late. Perhaps I have outlived my religious feeling." Henry: "My own comes only at night." Greffi: "Then too you are in love. Do not forget that is a religious feeling." Henry: "You believe so?" "Of course" (chapter 35).

In *For Whom the Bell Tolls*, we recall, the earth moves when Jordan makes love to Maria. And here is Cantwell in *Across the River*: "Why should it always move your heart to see a sail moving along through the country [near Venice], the Colonel thought. Why does it move my heart to see the great, slow, pale oxen? It must be the gait as well as the look of them and the size and the color" (chapter 4; cf. end of chapter 28). In *The Old Man and the Sea*, the old fisherman after much suffering brings the skeleton of his big fish in, even though the sharks have eaten most of the flesh away. Indeed, all of the novels, except *A Farewell*, end on this note of victory in defeat so characteristic of Hemingway's "grace under pressure" code. And there are other moments scattered throughout the stories and novels—moments of hunting or drinking or loving—in which people "feel good," which is Hemingway's manner of trying to express the transcendental without sounding verbose and sentimental.

It is significant to note in this connection that Hemingway's attitude toward religion itself is, although detached, quite respectful. Here is Jake in church: "I was a little ashamed, and regretted that I was such a rotten Catholic, but realized there was nothing I could do about it, at least for a while, and maybe never, but that anyway it was a grand religion, and I only wished I felt religious and maybe I would the next time" (chapter 10; cf. beginning of chapter 18 and end of chapter 19). So too the priest in the early parts of *A Farewell* is treated with great admiration by Lt. Henry: "There in my country," says the priest, "it is understood that a man may love God. It is not a dirty joke." Henry: "I understand." Priest: "You understand but you do not love God." Henry: "No." Priest: "You do not love Him at all?" Henry: "I am afraid of him in the night sometimes." Priest: "You should love Him." Henry: "I don't love much" (chapter 11). This is before he falls in love with Catherine, of course, but as we have already seen in the interchange with Count Greffi, which comes near the end of the book, having fallen in love does not persuade him to become religious in the priest's sense.

Yet there is nothing to prevent a transcender of the middle vision from admiring one of the full vision, even though he cannot or will not share it; so Jake and Lt. Henry admire religion and religious people, just as Hemingway himself admired Faulkner.[18] Furthermore, this admiration reveals the true underlying kinship between the two kinds of transcenders and allows us to see the importance of the first kind's analogies between love, or integrity, or courage, and religion. It is a mistake, however, to interpret Hemingway in religious terms: if he uses ritual archetypes and themes, as many secular writers do, and if he even uses Christian symbols, as he does in *A Farewell* and *The Old Man*, for example, he nevertheless does not do so within the frame of an intelligible and consistent vision of the meaning of life and the universe—without which no view can be considered religious, least of all Christian.[19]

The problem is what between nothingness and the moments of transcendence the middle transcender is to do. He knows that the "world"—and this can include society, history, nature, and/or the universe—is hostile to hope and destructive ultimately of all transcendence. When Lt. Henry discovers that Catherine is pregnant, he says that he feels trapped biologically. She says, "There's only us two and in the world there's all the rest of them. If anything comes between us we're gone and then they have us." Henry: "They won't get us. Because you're too brave. Nothing ever happens to the brave" (chapter 21). Of course he knows better, for he reflects much later: "If people bring so much courage into this world the world has to kill them to break them, so of course it kills them. The world breaks everyone and afterward many are strong in the broken places. But those that will not break it kills. It kills the very good and the very gentle and the very brave impartially. If you are none of these you can be sure it will kill you too but there will be no special hurry" (chapter 34).

The "world" in this case seems more like nature and the universe than society and history, and no cultural criticism or satire is implied—which, as we shall see later, becomes something of a problem in interpreting Hemingway's vision as a whole. Lt. Henry is nervously meditating as he awaits the final outcome of Catherine's doomed and dooming pregnancy: "Poor, poor dear Cat. And this was the price you paid for sleeping together. This was the end of the trap. This was what people get for loving each other. . . . So now they got her in the end. You never got away with anything. Get away hell! It would have been the same if we had been married fifty times." Then Catherine says to him, "I'm not brave any more, darling. I'm all broken. They've broken me. I know it now." He: "Everybody is that way." She: "But it's awful. They just keep it up till they break you." Then, when he knows that she will die, he reflects again to himself: "That was what you did. You died. You did not know what it was about. You never had time to learn. They threw you in and told you the rules and the first time they caught you off base they killed you." Then there follows the well-known passage about the ants on the burning log, symbolizing Hemingway's cosmic pessimism: "I remember thinking at the time that it was the end of the world and a splendid chance to be a messiah and lift the log off the fire and throw it out where the ants could get off onto the ground. But I did not do anything but throw a tin cup of water on the log, so that I would have the cup empty to put whiskey in before I added water to it. I think the cup of water on the burning log only steamed the ants." And at the end, just before she dies, Catherine says to him, "Don't worry, darling, I'm not a bit afraid. It's just a dirty trick" (chapter 41).

Confronted by this arbitrary universal joker, and with nothingness on one side and transcendental moments on the other, and unable to connect these three aspects of life in a full and coherent vision, the Hemingway hero develops what is partly a defensive posture and assumes a mask of style. This is the meaning of the Hemingway code: to stay in training, to keep your guard up, to be light and graceful on your feet, to be true to your actual experience and real feelings, to be loyal to a principle of personal honesty, to keep your nerve in spite of the darkness of the night and the cruelty of life, and not to whine and cry about it. The purpose of this code, it seems to me, is twofold: to tide you over the rough spots in between the good moments (which is a negative function), and to keep you in shape so that you will be ready for the good moments when they do come (which is a positive function).[20] When this fails, there is always the privilege and dignity of suicide as a conscious moral choice.[21]

Let me make clear that although I have said that A Farewell is the only major work of Hemingway which does not end on the note of victory in defeat, I do not think it is an exception in its pessimism. Grace under pressure, when it succeeds, does not lead to any revelation of higher meanings and purposes. The universe is dark and drafty, and moments of illumination are merely candles in the wind, fluttering fitfully for a few seconds only and disappearing forever. Whither hath fled the visionary gleam? The best one can do, living by the code, is to bear it with a certain lightness and dignity, ready for the troughs and crests alike. If one is to live, why not try to stay afloat skilfully?

Count Greffi is an example of one who has made it.

> "I had expected to become more devout as I grow older but some-
> how I haven't," he said. "It is a great pity."
>   "Would you like to live after death?" I asked and instantly felt a
> fool to mention death. But he did not mind the word.
>   "It would depend on the life. This life is very pleasant. I would
> like to live forever," he smiled. "I very nearly have."

We were sitting in the deep leather chairs, the champagne in the ice-bucket and our glasses on the table between us.

"If you ever live to be as old as I am you will find many things strange."

"You never seem old."

"It is the body that is old. Sometimes I am afraid I will break off a finger as one breaks a stick of chalk. And the spirit is no older and not much wiser."

"You are wise."

"No, that is the great fallacy; the wisdom of old men. They do not grow wise. They grow careful."

"Perhaps this is wisdom."

"It is a very unattractive wisdom. What do you value most?"

"Someone I love."

"With me it is the same. That is not wisdom. Do you value life?"

"Yes."

"So do I. Because it is all I have" (chapter 35).

Count Greffi has beautiful manners and is an expert billiard player. So too is the Hemingway hero, in his various manifestations, an aficionado of one sort or another—of wines, of foods, of women, of bullfighting, boxing, hunting, fishing, war. Since he cannot connect the three aspects of life in a full and coherent vision, since the world breaks the brave and kills all of us eventually, and since the moments of transcendence are unpredictable, intermittent, and ultimately doomed, the Hemingway hero must devise a way of life without the help of any sense of the final meaning, end, or purpose of life. So he devotes his attention to the means, to the *techniques* of living well. This is, as I have said, partly a defensive posture and partly a discipline for the moments of transcendence, which, although they come unbidden, nevertheless may be prepared for and sought after. It is almost as if one must go through the motions of transcending—of feeling crystallized and at ease and in harmony—without actually feeling transcendent or having anything worthy of one's balance.

The pathos of *Across the River*, it seems to me, derives largely from the fact that its ailing and aging hero has so much expertise and yet has so little left upon which to exercise it—except duck-shooting, eating and drinking, and making love. His active days are over, his virtues have outlasted his circumstances, and so his maneuvering for position in dining rooms and his skilful handling of champagne buckets is indeed absurd—if not ludicrous—the mountain of style bringing forth a mouse of consequence. Moreover, contrary to many critics, I suspect that this disparity is an integral part of the point of the book rather than a lamentable sort of senile self-indulgence on Hemingway's part. Hemingway is saying, not that this is a heroic connoisseur of wine, women, and food, but that he has outlived himself. It is not that Hemingwway is parodying himself, but that Col. Cantwell is a parody of himself, and through no fault of his own. All he has left is his style, without sufficient content for its proper exercise, and he keeps it up right to the end, when he does perforce have a worthy object—to die without fuss or clutter.

To meet a hostile universe with a mask of style is perhaps more typically a European attitude than an American one. Since the traditions and institutions of America did not provide Hemingway with such a mask, he had partly to seek it in Europe and partly to invent it for himself. In America the universe is characteristically regarded as friendly to man and as amenable to his purposes and control.

Indeed, this is what may be meant by the usual contrast between America as optimistic and innocent, and Europe as pessimistic and cynical. So in Hemingway "beginning again," the search for pure experience, results paradoxically in the formation of a new set of conventions, except that this time it is a set which simultaneously prepares one for and defends one against the force of reality, rather than simply narrowing and limiting it. And it is here that Hemingway comes closest to James, for the emphasis in James is often on the European—on manners, on doing things the right way, on those who understand vs. those who do not, on courage, integrity, dignity, and honesty in the face of the cruelty and mystery of life—but on the European as seen through the needs and sensibility of an American. Of course James deals with a different class of people and different aspects of life, but the similarity is there nevertheless, and it is basic. If James's concerns were limited, so too were Hemingway's in their own way: there are large and conspicuous areas of life in each that are not treated—in particular, the domestic, the routine, the ordinary.

Each is famous for his style, not just in the lives of his characters, but also in his writing itself. To be sure, these are different styles; but there is in each a similar correspondence between life style and writing style as a mask of manner—underplaying emotion, indirectness, and fastidiousness—with which to confront a treacherous universe. Hemingway's tight, bare style is not so much a matter of being honest as it is a defensive posture—a clenched pose, a holding it in, a fear of being open and vulnerable. So, too, James's elaborate style is a sign of his sense of the complexity and difficulty of life and human relations, not so much as a way of expressing the mystery as of keeping it at bay. It is in this sense, naturally, that style really is the man.

Finally there is in both an ultimate ambivalence, for James really preferred openness and fulness of life, just as Hemingway believed in being direct and concrete and immediate. All these things—especially the fact that they were Americans more permanently and profoundly attracted to Europe than many of their compatriots—sometimes resulted in mannerism, in a too self-conscious straining after style, a too deliberate striving after expertise and elegance. Hemingway in his simplicity is often just as precious as James in his complexity, and the air of me-heap-big-fine-writer clings to many of his passages, just as the air of old-maidishness clings to many of James's.

V

There are yet more serious internal contradictions in Hemingway's vision and art. Not only is there some fuzziness, not to say ambivalence, as to whether man's defeat is ultimately caused by nature or society,[22] but there is also some problem about the way nature and society are each viewed in themselves. As we shall see, the tragedy of the lovers in A Farewell is brought about not by the war but by nature. If this throws their fate into a more universally painful light, it also throws into question Henry's disengagement from society and its war on the one hand and his pursuit of the transcendent on the other. If one is to emphasize the natural and the primitive, how can one at the same time regard nature from the point of view of cosmic pessimism?[23] It is logical to expect that the discarding of one's inherited mental sets in favor of natural reality can sometimes lead to a serious disorientation, but it is not logical that this same nature will be seen at the same time as being restorative. There is a certain confusion in returning to pure experience only to find chaos, just as there is in simplifying life in order to combat the hypocrisies of history. Hemingway has been taken to represent the lost generation and its post war disillusionment in the ideals of western democracy. Certainly The Sun gives this impression, as well as the famous passage from A Farewell: "I was always embarrassed by the words sacred, glorious, and sacrifice and the expression in vain. . . . There were many words that you could not stand to hear and finally only the names of places had dignity" (chapter 27). And as he says after the terrible retreat and his subsequent desertion: "I was going to forget the war. I had made a separate peace" (chapter 34).

This is fine and clear, but it has little to do with Catherine's cruel death, which climaxes the book—as little cogency and artistic relevance as certain satirical passages concerning America's philistinism in Wolfe's *Look Homeward* (chapters 10 and 38). Furthermore, if one is to reject society's insane destructiveness in war, how can one continue to follow its wars as if one were on some kind of big-game hunt?[24] How can one equate the craft of soldiering with all the other kinds of expertise Hemingway loved so well? I find a certain lack of focus here.

Critics have noticed a return in Hemingway to social consciousness in *For Whom the Bell Tolls* and *To Have and Have Not*, but this can be taken in different ways: either as a wholesome rejection of nihilism and acceptance of societal problems, or as a sellout of his earlier honesty in favor of the obscene words. Either way, however, there still remains a basic lack of clarity concerning Hemingway's view of nature and society and of their relationship, and in his later books, *Across the River* and *The Old Man*, this supposed return of social consciousness disappears once again in favor of individual despair and individual transcendence.[25] Hemingway's personal interest in war as almost just another test of manhood does not cohere with Jake's cruel deprivation in *The Sun* or with Henry's dropping out in *A Farewell*. And surely *The Bell Tolls* is basically a bitter book and not a portrayal of a glorious cause at all. At bottom, it seems to me, Hemingway lacked a certain degree of reflectiveness.[26]

Apart from these internal limits, in sum, there remains the limit of his vision when compared to that of Faulkner. Both men were personally and artistically fascinated by hunting and by the primitive, but Faulkner was able to relate his fascination to a larger presence and meaning. He was just as interested as Hemingway in the techniques of hunting, in the courage, dignity, integrity, and endurance of both the hunters and the hunted, in their mutual respect and understanding, in the difference between those who understand and those who do not, and in the unwritten and unspoken rules of justice and fair play governing both men and animals. For Faulkner as well as for Hemingway the hunt was viewed as a sacred ritual bringing men into contact with the transcendent—the mystery and energy of the inner self, of nature, and of the universe.

But Faulkner could take all this one large step further, as if he saw its causes while Hemingway saw only its effects. In Faulkner's "The Bear," for example, Isaac McCaslin can take what he learns in the forest and apply it to his life in society, to the history of his society and of his nation and of mankind, and frame it all within a cosmic perspective. So Faulkner's vision of nature and society, and of their relationship, is more focused. What Ike learns while hunting is the evil of possessiveness and ownership, and the virtue of self-surrender and self-transcendence, and so the hunt takes on moral and political overtones as well as personal and transcendent ones. Thus, at the age of twenty-one, when his time comes to inherit his plantation and its long legacy of exploitation and cruelty, he repudiates it and chooses instead the meager life of a simple carpenter and woodsman. As Santayana said, it is the function of the poet not only to destroy the fictions of the everyday world but also to rebuild them once again on a firmer basis, "to repair to the material of experience, seizing hold of the reality of sensation and fancy beneath the surface of conventional ideas, and then out of that living but indefinite material to build new structures, richer, finer, fitter to the primary tendencies of our nature, truer to the ultimate possibilities of the soul. Our descent into the elements of our being is then justified by our subsequent freer ascent toward its goal; we revert to sense to find food for reason; we destroy conventions only to construct ideals."[27]

This double movement, we may recognize, very much resembles the function of the fiesta in Paz's interpretation. Society, in this view, has no need to fear the artist; as Edmund Wilson argued in *The Wound and the Bow* (1941), it needs him and his strangeness for its own health, in order to renew itself.

But I have said I would not call Faulkner's sort of vision "better" than Hemingway's sort: each did what he could with what he had, and you cannot blame an apple for not being a watermelon. If Hemingway has his contradictions and limits, so does Faulkner, for much of his grand vision in "The Bear" and elsewhere, as we have seen, is not quite clear or coherent. Nor was Faulkner's literary admiration for the Negro entirely consistent with his real-life opposition to the civil rights movement.[28] Furthermore, Faulkner is often pretentious where Hemingway is careful, and his style is often bloated and obscure where Hemingway's is clean and straight.

The contrast does, however, help to define more clearly their different kinds of vision and the powers and limitations of each. Hemingway expressed admiration for Faulkner's work, but wished he had been allowed to edit it; perhaps the combination would have created our ideal American novelist: the scope of Faulkner and the finesse of Hemingway. But since this is far from an ideal world, we shall have to settle for two great but imperfect artists—the one who sometimes failed because his vision was broad but too chaotic, and the other who at times did not succeed because his vision was deep but too narrow—and that is not a bad bargain at all. For each has left behind some very impressive achievements indeed, and each has reminded us in his own way that there is much more to reality and life than the everyday world has so far managed to find a place for.

Chapter 15

Theory of Symbolism

Both writer and reader can give the work broader and deeper implications by relating it to larger contexts, thereby making the plot itself seem more significant. Bringing the individual phenomenon into relation to classes of things is of course a natural and logical way of making it more intelligible. If we can discuss the created world of values in a novel and then go on to the connections we see between this world and the other works of the same writer, his biography, his contemporaries, his age, his society, and his history, interpreting it variously according to certain moral-psychological, cultural, and/or historical theories, so too can we talk about recurring images and then go on to the even broader connections we see between these things and dreams, myths, and archetypes, interpeting them variously from the point of view of certain psychological and/or anthropological theories.

That these two approaches overlap at certain points is sufficiently obvious. When, in discussing vision and society and history, we move from the individual and general to the universal, we are approaching the level of the archetypes—as we could hardly help doing in relation to Kafka, Camus, and especially Hemingway. A critic can talk about archetypes, for example, as Kenneth Burke does, in relation to a particular author's biography as well as to universal human patterns. The reason is that, if archetypal theories are correct, individuals do enact certain typical patterns over and over again, regardless of differences of time and place. Indeed, that is why we can speak of archetypes to begin with. But these approaches are distinct, since a critic can follow one without the other and vice versa—or at least he can give his main emphasis to one rather than the other.

Thus when we spoke of Kafka's dependent relationship with his father and how this threw added light on the story, we could have proceeded to explore the Oedipal implications of this problem, and we would have begun to verge on an archetypal pattern. Or when we discussed Meursault's self-discovery and self-affirmation, we would have gone on to speculate about rites of passage and initiation. And certainly when we analyzed Hemingway's primitivism, we were approaching questions of myth and ritual pretty directly. Nevertheless, we did succeed in those chapters in remaining rather more on the literal level of ideas than on the symbolic level of suggestions. That is to say, in the case of vision we relate individual things to more general things in the same class, whereas in the case of symbolism we relate both the individual and general to more universal things not in the same literal class. So we spoke of the family, society, and the universe pretty much in terms of the family, society, and the universe, rather than in terms of dreams, myths, and rituals.

It would appear that the difference is more a question of subject matter than of method, for what each approach does is either to add meanings to what is already clear in itself, or to provide connecting links for filling in meanings which are disjointed, suggestive, obscure, or whose import is not immediately clear in itself. The adding and filling in simply comes by means of different areas of information and levels of significance. What this involves will be explored in due course; at this point we must make a few preliminary distinctions concerning imagery, which will serve as our basis for going on.

I

Like most key critical terms, *image* is used in different ways in the service of different critical positions. What we need here is not necessarily a decision about the proper meaning of the term, but an analysis of what the different meanings are, and why. Empirically, these tend to fall into three more or less clearly distinguishable, if overlapping, categories, which can be arranged in an order of increasing complexity: (1) mental imagery, where interest is focused on what happens in the reader's mind when imagery-bearing language is being read; (2) rhetorical imagery, where the concern is with tropes and figures of speech in the language itself; and (3) symbolic imagery, where the problem has to do with the meaning, import, and significance of images.

Thus it can be seen, even from this crude breakdown, that a study of literary imagery represents a point formed by the intersection of numerous and often divergent lines of inquiry. The fixing of that point is further complicated by the fact that these lines are not always seen as crossing at the same juncture, if at all. The first category, for example, is largely concerned with the psychology of perception; the second with the theory of metaphor and its tributaries—philology, etymology, aesthetics, rhetoric, and semantics; and the last with cultural anthropology, depth psychology, and comparative mythology.

The study of mental imagery emphasizes the relation of the statement on the page to the sensation it produces in the mind,[1] but since sensations are not always relevant to meaning and may indeed hinder its interpretation, this approach must be supplemented by a study of the function of images in their artistic context. That is where the question of imagery as a device of literary language comes in. Imagery, whatever its sensory qualities may be, can function either literally, figuratively, symbolically, or in some combination. While the first usage makes no distinction between literal and figurative imagery, the second concentrates on the nature of the relationship between the tenor (subject, or thing meant) and vehicle (analogue, or thing said).

Traditional rhetoricians developed elaborate systems of classification, but the common types distinguished now have been reduced to six or seven: synecdoche, metonymy, simile, metaphor, personification, allegory, and—as we shall see, a related but different device—symbol. Classification rests upon the kinds of relationships which may obtain between what is said and what is meant. Thus in synecdoche and metonymy the relationship is based largely upon some sort of already established connection regarding more inclusive and less inclusive terms ("all hands on deck," synecdochic part for the whole) or common association (sailors as "tars" or "limeys," metonymic shift), while in the remaining figures the connection is based largely upon similarity in difference ("my love is like a red, red rose").

Although we shall have occasion to develop the concepts of synecdoche and metonymy a bit further, let us focus for the moment on these other sorts of figures, especially on metaphor.[2] The basic definition of *metaphor* is that it is a device which speaks of one thing (tenor) in terms which are appropriate to another (vehicle), with the vehicle serving as the source of traits to be transferred to the tenor. This transfer depends, as Aristotle pointed out, upon a perception of likeness in difference. It is in reality an indirect form of predication, in contradistinction to direct predication, wherein the traits to be predicated about the tenor are implicit in the vehicle. This procedure results in three positive effects: the reader on the basis of the context has to select and transfer the appropriate traits for himself; the imagery, which usually refers to the vehicle, adds concrete vividness to the expression; and the vehicle, in addition to supplying traits to be predicated about the subject, normally brings in an extra aura of connotations, feeling-tones, and associations. I suspect it is these three effects which distinguish literary metaphor from the prose or primarily intellectual metaphor, which must in its turn be mainly concerned with clarity of explanation rather than with aesthetic effects.

When Homer, for example, compares the charge of a warrior in battle to that of a lion at a sheepfold, he is conveying imagery of motion and perhaps of sound directly from vehicle to tenor: man looks and acts like an animal. But there is another equally important point involved in this transfer—the implication of ferocity—and that is related to emotions rather than simply perceptions. Not only does the warrior leap swiftly, roaring and striking and snarling, but he also does so fiercely and in all presents an awesome and fearful sight. One could indeed proceed further, in the manner of the New Critics, and go on to discuss the total meaning of the figure in terms of how the manner of expression shapes the meaning being expressed, saying something about the paradox of grace and bestiality in relation to man, about the animality of war, and the like. Thus the total figure, which includes not just the tenor and the vehicle but the traits being transferred and all that takes place in the process, results in a meaning or significance which is not to be identified with the tenor alone but rather emerges from its interaction with the vehicle.

Having stressed this matter of interaction between image and meaning in proceeding from image to figure, we are now in a better position to define the symbol, for basic to the concept of symbolism is the principle of relationship.[3] The third definition of imagery, that is, is concerned with the function of image patterns, whether literal or figurative or both, as symbols by virtue of association. The problems here are to ascertain how the writer's choice of imagery reveals not merely the sensory capacities of his mind or his use of figures of speech as rhetorical devices but also his interests, tastes, temperament, values, and vision; to determine the function of recurring images in the work in which they occur as tone-setters, structural devices, and symbols; and to determine the relation between his overall image patterns and those of myths, dreams, and rituals.

Our fundamental distinction is that whereas metaphor and simile establish relationships, the symbol draws upon those already established —either, as we shall see, within the work, or externally. For a symbol depends upon an implicit doubleness of expression wherein what is said stands for something more or something else without ever mentioning it. It depends very heavily upon our knowing or being able to discover those relationships in order that we may infer the meaning. That is why symbolism is on the one hand so potentially exciting and richly suggestive and, on the other, so difficult to interpret with any assurance. Thus it can be said that a recurring metaphor is symbolic, because repetition establishes larger relationships, and that a symbol is an expanded metaphor, because it is a vehicle that implies a tenor by virtue of larger relationships. It can also be said that symbols may work, as Kenneth Burke has shown, according to synecdochic or metonymic principles, in that a cluster of images may set up associations in terms of which one may stand for the group, or in that a common association may serve as the basis for a symbol.

It is not the case, really, that a metaphor is an implied simile; it is, rather, that a symbol is an implied metaphor. There is no effective difference between saying "troubles like a sea" and "a sea of troubles," but to use the sea to stand for troubles without saying so is different from either. Although studies have been made of figures in which the vehicle is given and the tenor implied, and of those in which the tenor is given and the vehicle implied,[4] the fact remains that in both metaphor and simile the tenor and vehicle are either mentioned or understood from the context, and the difference is grammatical, while in the symbol the tenor is neither mentioned nor understood in the same way, and the difference is structural. Indeed, in order to establish a relationship, one must mention or imply the two things being related, while in order to draw upon one already established, he needs to mention only the vehicle. Thus it is that we can say that a symbol evokes its meaning, and it will do so as long as we can discover the relationship at its base. The dynamics of symbolism may be summed up by indicating that whereas in the metaphor we are given or understand the tenor and vehicle and must infer the relationship, in symbolism we are given the vehicle and the relationship and must infer the tenor.[5] Of course the fact that the relationship in symbolism must often also be inferred makes the problem of interpretation that much more difficult, but the logic of interpretation remains the same: we cannot infer the subject unless we have previously defined somehow the relationship.

Furthermore, symbolic relationships need not be figurative at all—at least, not to begin with. That is why I said above that a symbol may stand either for something "more" or something "else." It may be, that is, part of the literal situation of a work, and hence in that context it will have the status of a tenor, in which case it symbolizes something "more," becoming in the additional context a "vehicle" because it is both itself as well as a symbol; or it may be extrinsic to the literal situation, beginning as a vehicle altogether, in which case it symbolizes something "else," because it has no existence of its own within that situation. An example of the first would be the recurrence of rain to coincide with moments of despair and misfortune in A *Farewell to Arms*, while an example of the second would be the recurrence of animal metaphors in *King Lear*.

II

Let us turn now to a further development of these concepts. The word *symbol* derives from the Greek verb *symballein*, meaning "to put to-together," and the related noun *symbolon*, meaning "mark," "token," or "sign," like the half coin carried away by each of the two parties of an agreement as a pledge.[6] Hence it means basically a joining or combination, and consequently the way something once so joined represents in itself, when seen alone, the entire complex. The structure of a literary symbol, as we have seen, depends upon our being able to infer the tenor from the vehicle by means of some sort of stated or implied relationship. The problem, then, becomes one of defining the various sorts of relationships upon which symbols depend for their meaning, and of exploring the various ways in which these relationships come into being and function.

In metaphor or simile, the vehicle is distinct from the tenor, they both are given or implied, and their relationship is based on likeness in difference. A symbol, on the other hand, puts the vehicle in the place of tenor or suggests that a tenor may be seen in turn as a vehicle, so that we read what is said as if it were what is meant, but are made to infer, by virtue of the associations provoked by what is said and the manner in which it is expressed, something more or something else as the additional or true meaning. It is as if with metaphor and simile we begin with the tenor at the center and bring in the vehicle from outside, whereas with the symbol we begin with the vehicle at the center and bring in the tenor from out-side. Thus an idea which would be difficult, flat, lengthy, or unmoving when expressed prosaically and by itself, may be made intelligible, vivid, economical, and emotionally effective by the use of symbols—just as an action which would otherwise seem ordinary may be made to seem pro-found and meaningful by these means. Further, if I am correct about the knowledge of literature being the *felt* sense of experience conveyed, then it is quite true on this level, as the New Criticism has claimed, that the idea is inseparable from its embodiment and cannot be expressed in any other way.

It may be useful here to distinguish symbolism from allegory and parable, which are otherwise related devices whereby what is said is pre-sented as if it were what is meant. Allegory and parable are different basically in that the represented experience is not meant to be taken liter-ally—cannot be taken literally—at all: it is governed throughout by the idea and has no independent existence of its own. Parable is like sym-bolism in that the tenor has to be inferred, but it is like metaphor and simile in that the principle of connection is analogy.[7] Men are like ani-mals, as in George Orwell's *Animal Farm*. Allegory is like metaphor and simile in that both tenor and vehicle are given—the Dragon of Error, for example—but it is like symbolism in that the principle of connection is association.[8] Spenser's monster after all derives from the traditions of romance he chose to work in, and it is there of course that dragons are normally seen as adversaries of the hero. Symbolism on the other hand uses literal experience or recurring figures as the vehicle for implying something or something else by means of association.

This means that the relation between what is said and what is to be inferred need not be based, as in metaphor and simile, primarily upon resemblance; for many images have become potentially symbolic not through likeness only but also through one sort of association or another —as when the cutting of a man's hair symbolizes the loss of strength (Samson) or the rejection of worldly desires (monastic and ascetic prac-tice), not because of any resemblance between them but rather because a primitive and magical connection has been established between secon-dary sex characteristics, virility, and desire.

Of course an associative relationship may be established having resem-blance as its basis when a metaphor or simile is repeated so often, either in the work of a single author or in literary tradition, that the vehicle can be used alone to summon up the tenor with which it was once connected. Similarly many interpreters have pointed out that writers tend to use the metaphors and similes of their earlier works as symbols in their later work because of the associative relations thus established. G. Wilson Knight for example sees this pattern in Shakespeare's development with regard to the imagery of seas and shipwrecks.[9] On the other hand, as we shall see, repetition itself is a form of likeness in difference, and so symbols may be seen as resembling metaphors and similes in this respect. Critics rightly warn moreover that symbolic associations of imagery should be made neither too explicit nor too fixed, for implications of this sort are best felt rather than explained and vary from work to work depending on the individual context.

As we have seen, there are two kinds of symbols—those derived from the literal experience embodied in the work, and those derived from such nonliteral sources in the work as visions, dreams, and figures of speech. Furthermore, there are two sorts of associations on which they may be based—internal or external—and this distinction cuts across the first one, for either literal or figurative imagery may acquire symbolic status by either internal or external associations. Imagery, that is, may gather associative power by virtue of the internal relations which obtain among the elements of a given work via structural emphasis, arrangement, position, development, and the like—as in the previously mentioned examples of the nonliteral animal imagery in *King Lear* and the literal rain imagery in *A Farewell to Arms*. Or imagery may gather associative power by virtue of the vision of the author or some system either explicitly invented by him or implicit in his works, by virtue of particular historical conventions, or by virtue of universal human experience. Examples of images which gain symbolic power via the author's vision would be the various meanings associated with the sea and the land regarding chaos and order, and freedom and community, in Joseph Conrad. Examples of images becoming symbolic via historical conventions would be the transmutation of lead to gold as redemption, the lily as chastity and the rose as passion, and the tiger as Christ. And examples from universal experience would be climbing a staircase or mountain as spiritual purification, crossing a body of water as spiritual transition, and sunset as death and sunrise as rebirth.

Let us examine internal symbolism first. Louis MacNeice has pointed out that the sensory content of a work may be either literal ("properties") or figurative ("images"), although "the properties themselves may be, in the ultimate analysis, only symbols."[10] I can see no particular reason, however, for limiting the term *imagery* to figures alone; the literal sensory content of a work, by the very fact of its selection and inclusion by the writer, almost always tends to become figurative. A given writer's pre-occupation with certain settings, situations, and characters will be seen, when viewed in the context of a given work as well as in the perspective of his total achievement, to act as a symbolic key to his ultimate vision of life, just as his recurring metaphors will, when systematically inspected. In the *Iliad*, for example, the heroes and their struggles on the ringing plains of windy Troy are imagery as well as the shepherds, sailors, storms, and animals of the similes.

Selection and inclusion, then, form one basis of meaningfulness, and within that framework recurrence forms another. The basic assumption is that repetition is in itself significant, and hence the method involves an amateur application (and, sometimes, distortion) of some elementary statistical principles. Significance of this sort means either that repetition indicates interest, concern, importance, and emphasis, or that it reveals likeness in difference, since the recurrence of the same thing in different contexts tends to link those contexts together in much the same way as a figure of speech links tenor and vehicle together.

One might think that in dealing with such internal relations the theoretical questions would be solved at this point, and that all that remained would be to get on with the practical interpretation of particular texts. But when one asks *what* selection-inclusion-recurrence may be symbolic *of*, he gets a puzzling variety of answers: the writer's experiences, tastes, temperament; the authenticity of disputed texts; the tone, atmosphere, and mood in a work; the structure of conflict in a work; and so on.

The source and fount of most current statistical studies of literary imagery is, of course, Caroline F. E. Spurgeon, who has often enough been criticized for what she did not do, as well as praised for what she did do.[11] Her method, well-known by now, was to sort out Shakespeare's images—all of them, she claimed—into various categories according to the spheres of life from which they were drawn. Thus we may discover from a colored chart she prepared that 15.5% of his imagery is drawn from inanimate nature, 13.5% from animate nature, 18.5% from daily life, and the like. She then makes the fallacious assumption,[12] completely ignoring the lineage of much universal imagery, that these statistics are the result of Shakespeare's personal experience, reflecting his personal tastes and temperament. From this she recreates a portrait of Shakespeare "the man" which is pathetic in its naïveté. She reveals here a fundamental theoretical inadequacy which is in part explained perhaps by her apparent ignorance of her predecessors.

Not so naive is the second portion of her book which deals with "The Function of Imagery as Background and Undertone in Shakespeare's Art," and which does a valuable job of interpretive criticism in actually tracing out the tone-setting recurrences in the plays. Kenneth Burke has much that is valuable to say here, and provides a good example of how the statistical approach can lead fruitfully to other approaches. "One cannot long discuss imagery," he comments, "without sliding into symbolism. The poet's images are organized with relation to one another [and here he has in mind Spurgeon's discovery of clusters of similar images—or different images tending to appear together—in similar contexts] by reason of their symbolic kinships. We shift from the image of an object to its symbolism as soon as we consider it, not in itself alone, but as a function in a texture of relationships." [13]

According to Spurgeon, certain plays of Shakespeare are saturated with one kind or another of similar images or clusters (usually figurative)—the imagery of light and dark in *Romeo and Juliet*, for example, or of animals in *King Lear*, or of disease in *Hamlet*—and she reasoned that these recurrences, although barely perceptible except upon close examination, are continually at work conditioning the reader's response as he follows the action of the play. Burke, however, is a much more subtle critic than Spurgeon. His approach, as we shall see, is to classify images according to their relationship to the dramatic context of the work. There are basically two kinds of clusters: the recurrence of the same image at intervals throughout the work, or the recurrence of different images together at intervals throughout the work. If the same image recurs in different contexts, then it (theoretically) serves to link those contexts in significant ways, and if different images recur together several times, then the mention of any one will serve to call the other to mind.

The principle is clear, then. To put it into the language being employed here, we can say that the single-image recurrence gathers associations cumulatively as it moves from context to context, with the result that it can begin to symbolize those associations as it moves into each new context, bringing them along with it to join those of the new context.

If, to give a simple case, the sun is blotted out by clouds every time the protagonist is about to suffer misfortune of one kind or another, then each new appearance of those clouds will bring along with it all those bad associations and will lead us to expect another misfortune shortly. Thus we can speak of the clouds as symbolizing bad fortune. In this particular case, the image becomes symbolic on two levels: statistically and simply by virtue of patterned recurrence, which serves as the basis of generalizing; and metaphorically or by virtue of resemblance, which sees the clouds as symbolizing bad fortune because one feels "shadowed," "darkened," "chilled," when one is unhappy.

Many such metaphors, of course, are so universal that they can be used as symbols almost instinctively. The reason, however, that this example is a symbol and not a metaphor is that a literal occurrence, itself a tenor, becomes in the context a vehicle of some other equally literal occurrence. It bears emphasizing that such an image is not necessarily symbolic: it is the context which makes it so. Even if it recurs, it might recur without forming any significant pattern, and it might be there simply to give concreteness and experiential density to the work. Selection-inclusion-recurrence, that is, might indicate a very slight amount of significance as such, and we do not do our symbolic interpretations much justice if we do not recognize the possibility of no symbolism; for logically a definition has no meaning if it includes everything, and positive evidence has very little cogency apart from negative evidence.

When an image recurs alone, after it has appeared in company with several others, it can summon up the others and therefore can be said to symbolize the whole of which it is a part. Let us say that the sun is clouded over just before misfortune strikes, and a gull cries, the sound of the sea striking the shore is heard, and the whipping of a strong breeze is felt. Let us say further that all or most of these phenomena occur together several times. It follows that any one of the associated images occurring alone after that can still bring to mind the total effect, so that the protagonist and/or the reader might feel a chilling wind, a darkened sky, a crashing surf, and a premonition of disaster simply upon hearing, say, a gull cry. Where a single-image recurrence, that is, brings along with it cumulatively the contexts in which it has appeared, a multiple-image recurrence brings along with it not only these contexts but also the other images with which it has appeared. Now not all of these images are symbolic because of resemblance, especially the gull's cry, but because of repeated association. And if breakers and breezes could easily be metaphors for misfortune—we recall, naturally, "a sea of troubles"—they could just as easily be metaphors for good, bracing, exciting experiences as well (in George Meredith, for example).

I am stressing the contextual principle here not only because it brings out the structure of symbolism more clearly, but also because, from the point of view of practical criticism—in spite of much modern theory to the contrary—we too often lack a firm basis for responsible symbolic interpretation, a matter which we will explore in some particular detail in chapter 17. In both the above instances—the single-image recurrence and the recurrence of one of a group—it is the context which establishes the connection among various literal things in the work, either by means of resemblance or association or both, and allows us to infer that one symbolizes another. As we have seen, this is what is done outright by metaphor and simile, where one thing is literal (tenor) and the other is figurative (vehicle) and it is usually done in terms of resemblance.

In order to interpret a figure of speech, however, we need very little of the context, for two things are already placed in significant relationship and we can speculate fairly well about the principle of their connection (I am speaking relatively, of course, for ultimately the contextual test is determinative here as well). But in order to interpret a literal image which has become symbolic, we have to know how it relates to the action. Even universal symbols, as we shall see, do not automatically mean any one thing but are rather altered and shaped by the pressure of their contexts. Certainly Ulysses comes out in rather different if not opposite ways in Homer, Dante, Shakespeare, Tennyson, Pound, and Joyce.[14] Indeed, I have found that the image of the sun—normally a life-giving symbol— can mean something quite pestilential in Meredith.[15] Sometimes an image can have different meanings, and even if it has one basic meaning, it can be evaluated in different ways. We shall return to this question shortly.

Recurrences, however, may also of course include images which begin in the work as figures of speech, but the principles of structure and interpretation remain roughly the same. What usually happens is that figures of this sort relate not only tenor and vehicle but also both to the context and then to literal images as well. A narrator can say of his hero that "he awoke in a tempestuous mood" (metaphor), that "he was worried about signing up on that ship" (context of the action), that "the sun clouded over as he boarded" (literal image), and that "he died, ship-wrecked in a storm" (context of the action). Thus the imagery of storm can be said to symbolize disaster, even before it occurs.

III

Kenneth Burke, however, goes still further, and here we enter the area of external associations—relationships established outside the work, wheth-er on the basis of the author's other works, his biography, historical con-ventions, or archetypal patterns. The system which Burke has elaborated on the basis of his theory of imagery is more complex in its applications than in its principles and can be outlined briefly somewhat as follows: (1) the discovery of image-recurrences in the body of a writer's work gives clues, not to his personal appearance, history, and temperament, but rather to the central emotional conflict around which his writings are structured; (2) this conflict can be uncovered by tracing out his associa-tional clusters, or "what goes with what . . . what kinds of acts and images and personalities and situations go with his notions of heroism, villainy, consolation, despair, etc."; and (3) the resolution or "transformation" of this conflict involves a turning away from one set of values (and their attendant images) and a corresponding turning toward another set. "So we watch, in the structural analysis of the symbolic act [the formation and transformation of a set of attitudes in a work], not only the matter of 'what equals what,' but also the matter of 'from what to what.' "[16]

In a way, this could be taken as simple contextual analysis, but notice that Burke says the "act" he is analyzing is "symbolic," and thereby hangs a tale. Since Burke defines form in a seemingly Aristotelian way as what the work is doing for the reader, he reasons that if we can see what it is doing for the writer, we can locate what it is doing for the reader. In his approach, then, a work is a dramatic revelation in disguised and symbolic form of the writer's emotional tensions and conflicts; if therefore some idea of these tensions and conflicts in his personal life can be obtained, the reader will then be alerted to their symbolic appearance in his works. Thus Burke can make equations among Coleridge's image clusters by comparing the poet's letters with *The Ancient Mariner*, and can conclude, by building "associational bridges" between letters and poem, that the albatross symbolizes Coleridge's guilt over his addiction to opium—since similar images recur in relation to both. This, he claims, illuminates the "motivational structure" of that particular poem.[17]

Now while I have argued that it is perfectly sound to use external evidence in the interpretation of a work, I do not think it is necessary or useful to assume that its literal action is a substitute for something else. In the first place, it seems to me that the albatross as a symbol of guilt is sufficiently clear from reading the poem—exactly what that guilt is, even if it is in fact related to Coleridge's personal guilt, is not particularly relevant to the poem itself. In the second place, accordingly, it is much more fruitful to assume that while most works are indeed transformations of their author's experiences, whether conscious or subconscious, these works are best interpreted in the light of their own literal value systems. Unless, of course, they are flawed in some central way, in which case their failure may be speculatively traced back to some sort of emotional-psychological-intellectual failure in the author. Otherwise, the filling-in of links from biography, as we saw in Kafka, proceeds literally enough from a problem, say, of family relations in the work to a problem of family relations in the writer's life. If we do not realize these things, we run the risk of falling into genetic and reductionist fallacies. Finally, if we *can* derive various associations established in an author's other writings as a help in interpreting the symbols in any one work, we should do so, as always, in terms of that particular context.

This approach may function in two ways: to help us understand a symbol which is in itself enigmatic, and to enrich our understanding of a symbol which is already relatively intelligible in itself. It we could not really tell what the albatross symbolizes in *The Ancient Mariner*, we could learn from the evidence Burke considers that it symbolizes guilt—and what is pertinent is that it symbolizes *guilt* rather than guilt over *opium*. That it does relate to opium—and it could relate to other experiences as well, such as sexual guilt, guilt over hostility toward one's father—enriches our understanding of the symbol in terms of the emotional force and significance it accumulates in the writer's imagination; but the fact remains that the *sort* of guilt it symbolizes in the work must be interpreted in the context of that work.

Another illustration can be found in Conrad. What does the crucial leap into the water symbolize in *Lord Jim* and "The Secret Sharer"? Now of course we can tell clearly enough from a careful reading of each work (although even here Stein's talk in *Lord Jim* of immersing in the de-

structive element is sufficiently enigmatic). Indeed, the act in itself and
its significance are not, to begin with, symbolic at all. When Jim leaps
from *The Patna*, he is doing a cowardly thing out of confusion of mind,
and he is literally abandoning ship, the helpless passengers, and his responsibilities in one fell swoop. He is also, of course, abandoning his
image of himself, and this is what does him the most psychic harm.
When the stranger leaps off the ship in "The Secret Sharer," however,
and swims away, he is literally saving himself from a murder trial and is
confirming his own individual sense of honor and justice.

Each act, then, is a literally significant one and means something quite
different—if not opposite—in its own context. How can we gain interpretive value from regarding them in the light of Conradian symbols while
preserving our sense of their obvious disparity? I think the question is
easily resolved. Let us distinguish between the meaning of symbol, in
the sense of what it stands for, and its evaluation, in the sense of how
what it stands for is to be regarded.[18] We know from reading more than
one or two of Conrad's works that the ship represents order and justice
and responsibility required of the human community if it is to survive
with dignity and humanity, and that the sea (or jungle) represents the
chaos and disorder and wildness which threatens the human community
—and not only from without, literally and externally, in the form of
storms and the like, but also from within, figuratively and internally, in
the sense of how these things find an echo in the human heart (as with
Kurtz in *The Heart of Darkness*). Furthermore, it would seem, merely
from the way I have defined them, that the symbol of the ship is to be
interpreted positively and that of the sea negatively.

Since, however, this evaluation does not actually fit what we read in
"The Secret Sharer," or even Stein's metaphor in *Lord Jim*, we must beware of deriving interpretations from one portion of an author's writings
and applying them too directly to another. But what we can do is to
derive a sense of what the symbol generally stands for and then evaluate
the way in which that meaning is to be taken in terms of the context. The
result will be a rich sense of the possibilities of any given symbol in a
writer's work and, correspondingly, a deepened and broadened sense of
the significance of his artistic vision.

Thus while leaving the ship and entering the water have similar meanings in *Lord Jim* and "The Secret Sharer," these meanings are to be evaluated rather differently in each case. Both men are rejecting the human

community in favor of the potential anarchy of nature and the human heart, but what for Jim is a negative act is for Leggatt a positive one. In other words, in certain cases the community can be wrong and the rebellious individual right. If we know what the ship and the sea symbolize generally in Conrad, we should be able to apply this knowledge appropriately to particular contexts by distinguishing between meaning and evaluation.

Better still, we can reconstruct a picture of the author's vision by saying that while the ship symbolizes ethical order and the sea symbolizes natural disorder, it is best to see them in terms of a dynamic interrelationship rather than a simple polarity. The ethical realm needs an infusion from the natural realm, just as the natural realm needs to be corrected by the ethical.

But I do not think this sort of doubleness, when it does obtain, is the same as what is meant by the basic duality of archetypal images to be taken up in the next chapter. If we say, for example, that the archetypal pattern of water is that it is both the source of life and the threat of death (which in turn can mean rebirth), we are attributing two different meanings to it rather than two different evaluations to the same meaning. On the other hand, when we said that water in Conrad meant disorder, but that it could be taken either positively or negatively, we were attributing two different evaluations to a single meaning. We can have, in other words, ambiguity deriving from different evaluations or different meanings or both. However this may be, the contextual test remains the same.

We turn now to a consideration of archetypes.

Chapter 16

Archetypal Patterns

I

The next step in the search for symbolic associations is to go outside not only the particular work but also of that author's writings altogether— into historical conventions and universal symbols. The symbols which derive from historical associations and/or from the commonplaces of one's own period can be briefly discussed, for they often overlap with universal symbols and so will be implicit when we move ahead. The lily as chastity and the rose as passion are not far, on the one hand, from metaphors, since there *is* a kind of resemblance underlying their meaning (lily-white-calm-untouched: rose-red-heated-excited), and on the other, from archetypes, since this sort of flower symbolism is fairly widespread in time and place—although it was especially prominent in and characteristic of medieval Europe. Something similar is true for animal imagery, such as Christ the tiger, and for alchemical imagery, such as the refining fire. Consider also imagery derived from history (Yeats's Byzantium), from crafts and trades (Fates spinning destiny), from hunting (love as pursuit), sailing (dreaming as water voyage), farming (faith grows from seed), fighting (the war in my heart), and the like.

But since modern history has allegedly stripped us of traditional associations, it is frequently said that symbolism is in an especially bad way. It is not, however, as has often been thought, that we have been torn from a meaningful world and abandoned in a meaningless one. It is, rather, that we have come from a world of relatively stable values to one of new, various, and unformulated values. Only if we believe in the possibility of a single set of values can we say that a change results in valuelessness. It has been said that nature has been demythologized and therefore that the poets lack an adequate belief upon which to base their symbols. It has been said that this is the reason why such poets as Blake and Yeats have had to invent symbolic systems of their own. I think, on the other hand, it is more a matter of their having new things to say than their being deprived of the old myths which accounts for their idiosyncratic systems. Furthermore they often made use of the old myths as well, as have Pound, Joyce, Eliot, and many others.

Even though the history of culture and civilization keeps changing ever more rapidly, then, it is a mistake to think that the potency of symbols disappears when the values upon which they seemed to be based disappear.[1] Their potency never depended upon any system of values in the first place; it was rather borrowed ex post facto to fit and support those values. Thus taking away such systems leaves that potency undiminished, which is more a matter of feeling than of ideas. As Shelley said, principles outlive instances, and as Wallace Stevens said, the imagination outlives its myths. Men have never ceased responding in certain characteristic ways to universal symbols, correspondences sensed between the human and natural worlds, inner and outer experience—the body as garment or world, the world as body or garment—and they need never cease doing so.[2]

Of course it is true that modern civilization is more and more divorced from nature and her rhythms, but this need not divorce us from the power of natural symbols—indeed it might, as Schiller argued, increase it.[3] The fact that men have landed on the moon need interfere in no way with the various symbolic associations adhering to that strange dead planet. But we need not believe that the moon is actually Diana, Cynthia, Artemis, Selene, and/or Hecate, in order to feel the force of its power—its twenty-eight-day cycle, its waxing and waning, its effect upon the seas, its apparent relation to love and madness. We do not need to see spirits and nymphs and gods and goddesses all around us for nature to have meaning for us. We need neither the culture surrounding the pagan myths nor the religious context of the Judeo-Christian stories to enable us to use their symbols, and again the distinction made in the preceding chapter between meaning and evaluation may prove useful. A symbol may have a certain general force and meaning which is derived simply from universal human experience, and it may have a particular evaluation attached to it in a given context by a particular doctrine.

Thus, just as the sea-ship dichotomy has a certain general meaning in Conrad but may have different evaluations placed on it in different contexts, so too may many a universal symbol be variously used. The goat imagery characteristic of the pagan Pan and the satyrs is reflected quite explicitly in the Christian picture of the Devil with his hooves and horns and tail. In each case the meaning is clearly sexual, and yet the earlier and later evaluations are practically polar opposites. The general force and meaning of the symbolism remains, independent of any of its various evaluations. The imagery of the lamb presents another but similar case: Christ as the Lamb clearly relates to his role at the Last Supper—which was, of course, a Passover meal containing the shankbone of a lamb—and this in turn related to pre-Judaic spring festivals at which a newborn lamb was slaughtered ("Are you washed in the blood of the Lamb?") in celebration of the return of fertility to the earth.

Old myths and symbols are not only historicized; they are also doctrinized. They can, however, be stripped of these accretions and yet emerge in all their original power. What the sacrifice of the newborn lamb means can be understood and felt now as before, apart from any of its intervening interpretations, and a modern writer can use its symbolism just as well as any earlier writer. Thus precisely because these intervening interpretations have been taken away, the modern writer has shown an increased interest, not in private symbols, as we have sometimes been lead to believe, but in universal symbols. If he does not always know exactly what evaluation he wants to place on his symbols and so must remain more tentative and ambiguous than his predecessors, he nevertheless can draw upon their general meaning and emotional power as well as they. That is why it is absurd to interpret Santiago's collapsing under the weight of his mast at the end of *The Old Man and the Sea* in Christian terms. While it is assuredly a Christ symbol, it is clear that Hemingway is using it in terms of its general emotional meaning rather than of its particular doctrinal evaluation.

We know, in fact, that being impaled on a cross is a form of punishment which predated Christianity and that the cross itself is related to the much more ancient symbol of the mandala, which indicated the four quarters of the compass, the four corners of the earth. Indeed, as Lord Raglan and Joseph Campbell have shown, the story of Christ itself contains a general pattern which reflects the stories of many earlier heroes.[4] Nor does such assimilation of doctrinal into universal symbols necessarily lessen their dignity—except, perhaps, from a strictly doctrinal point of view. It rather increases it, for it reveals their basic human roots and illuminates their widespread meaning and appeal.[5]

I am aware that such notions may seem to run counter not only to the growing sense of critics and anthropologists that myths and rituals are unique to their respective cultures and therefore cannot be cross-related in such abstract ways—which I shall touch upon below—but also to my own similar theory that the same element has different meanings in different contexts. But there are two contexts, as I have argued: one is the context of human experience, and the other is the context of a work of art, and I have tried to show how art must relate in some significant way to experience. The point I am making here is that experience develops associations around certain central elements—associations which are more emotional than intellectual—and that these are available for us to draw upon in creating and interpreting works of art. The fact that they are, as I have suggested and will examine in greater detail shortly, ambiguous in their meaning, and that even the same meaning can be evaluated in different ways, sufficiently allows for multiplicity of use. What remains is a certain potential field of feeling force accumulating around certain basic areas of human experience, and it is these experiences and their fields which are universal.

I think, then, that the problem of belief and the disappearance of belief is a blind alley for the study of literary symbolism and meaning: it is much more a matter of emotional power, and this power persists throughout changes in belief. Which does not, as we see, eliminate the need for careful consideration of contexts when interpreting particular works—indeed, the absence of stable evaluations for symbols makes the contextual test even more essential, for that much more burden is being placed upon the context to supply the needed interpretive clues.

II

It is but a short series of steps from Kenneth Burke's notion of clusters as a key to the motivational structure of a work, to his relating this structure to something basic in the author's psyche and then to his seeing it in archetypal terms. The struggle in the author's psyche is for Burke analogous to ritual drama—either a symbolic contest between death-evil and life-good, or an initiatory sloughing off (or "dying") of the childhood personality and a "rebirth" of the individual to adult rights and responsibilities, with the related images of purgation, the scapegoat, and king-killing.[6]

Thus Robert Penn Warren sees in *The Ancient Mariner* the artist archetype, symbolized by the Mariner, torn between the conflicting and ambiguous claims of reason, symbolized by the sun, and the imagination, symbolized by the moon: the crime is therefore a crime against imagination, and the imagination revenges itself but at the same time heals the Mariner; the wandering is also a blessing and a curse, for the Mariner is the *poète maudit* as well as the "prophet of universal charity."[7] In large and general terms, the artist is seen as the hero and his art as a sacrificial ritual, and he is seen as dying to his life in order to be reborn in his art as the redeemer.[8] One might find implicit images of descent, guilt, purification, and ascent running throughout a work whose literal action may be of quite a different nature. Image clusters are seen, then, as forming a spatial pattern or even a subplot calling for special attention in itself.

The relation between universal symbols and archetypes is also very close: when universal symbols are seen in terms of dreams, myths, and rituals, and when these terms begin to form systematic patterns of one sort or another—particularly in connection with certain anthropological and psychological theories—then the study of archetypes has begun.[9] What we can gain from this study is an entire additional set of relationships, whether based on resemblance or association or both, by means of which to interpret the meaning and appeal of symbols in literature. And certainly the same distinctions used above between meaning and evaluation should apply even more strongly here, for in developing their patterns, archetypal critics often tend to standardize their significance, if not doctrinally, then psychologically.

Generally speaking, an archetype is an original pattern from which copies are made, or an idea of a class of things representing the most essentially characteristic elements shared by the members of that class. It is, in other words, a highly abstract category almost completely removed from the accidental varieties of elements contained in any particular species belonging to it. Thus, for example, the Platonic idea of a table would be a flat horizontal surface propped by vertical supports, and this is the archetype of all tables everywhere when considered apart from their peculiar differences of size, height, material, shape, finish, use, and so on.

So in literature an archetype may be any idea, character, action, object, institution, event, situation, setting, or figure containing essential characteristics which are primitive, general, and universal rather than sophisticated, unique, and particular. This generality and universality may refer merely to similarities among various literary or subliterary works, as when scholars discover variants or analogues in different times and places of certain types of folk tales and legends, or it may refer more broadly to similarities found outside of literary works, as when critics seek comparisons to things found in a work among myths, dreams, and rituals. In the case of *Hamlet*, one could either construct an archetype of the revenge play on the basis of similarities found between Shakespeare's play and other revenge plays, or fashion an archetype of the Oedipal situation on the basis of the similarities found between Shakespeare's play, myths, legends, folk tales, and anthropological and psychological research. The former method tends to be more direct, as when one studies a series of hero stories and tabulates the characteristics which they share in common, while the latter method tends to be more tenuous, as when one tries to construct hypotheses to interpret the meaning of such recurrences in terms of the racial unconscious, the ritual origins of drama, the diffusions of culture, or whatever. Needless to say, these methods may overlap, although it is the second which chiefly occupies us here.

The basic structure of the archetypes is determined by the parallels which exist or seem to exist between the cycles of human life and those of the external world: the rising and setting of the sun, the revolution of the seasons, the waxing and waning of the moon, the circling of the stars, the ebb and flow of the tides, the growth and decay of vegetation—all these have obviously left a profound and universal mark upon the human spirit, and have come to be associated with the key moments of human life—birth, coming of age, marriage, parenthood, and death. Even if our lives today seem less directly dependent upon, and hence less directly related to, the cycles of nature, we nevertheless continue to react emotionally to seasons, weathers, and the rest. Thus it is quite common still to speak of human things in terms of natural things: actors are "stars," old age is the "winter" of life, woman is as inconstant as the moon, one's beloved is like a flower, troubles are a "sea." Or, to take it the other way round, spring is the "birth" of the year, winter is an "old man," the sun "smiles," storms "howl." And just as the natural cycle has two polar phases—summer and winter, growth and decay, light and dark—so too has the human cycle—life and death, waking and sleeping, courage and fear, love and hate, striving and withdrawal.

An archetypal symbology may be constructed, then, upon these parallels and the patterns which they have caused to appear in myth, dream, ritual, and art: "In the solar cycle of the day," says Northrop Frye, "the seasonal cycles of the year, and the organic cycles of human life, there is a single pattern of significance, out of which myth constructs a central narrative around a figure who is partly the sun, partly vegetative fertility and partly a god or archetypal human being."[10]

III

In order that we may learn to recognize the archetypal patterns as they appear in various permutations, embedded as they may be beneath more literal surfaces, we need a pattern of the patterns. Let us begin on the anthropological level[11] and proceed to the psychological. Birth, coming of age, love, guilt, redemption, and death are archetypal subjects. The conflict between reason and imagination, free will and destiny, appearance and reality, the individual and society, are archetypal themes. The tension between parents and children, the rivalry among brothers, the problems of incestuous desire, the search for the father, the ambivalence of the male-female relationship, the young man from the provinces, are archetypal situations.

Regarding plot structure, the archetypal pattern is triadic: (1) birth and creation phase—imagery of childhood and paradisal gardens, including rise and early triumph; (2) initiation and death phase—imagery of the journey, quest, hunt, descent, besieged city, contest, or exile (compare the witch-forest type [Hansel and Gretel, Snow White], the dragon-cave type [medieval romance], the whale-sea type [Jonah, Pinocchio, Moby-Dick], the Hades type [Homer and Virgil]); and (3) rebirth phase— imagery of the return, attainment, ascent, victory, dedicated man. It can also readily be seen that this pattern coincides with the generic formula for plot structure: conflict-crisis-resolution, complication-peripety-denouement.

The character archetypes revolve around the male-female polarity: hero-devil-god and woman-destroyer-preserver. Here we may expect the imagery of the wanderer, pariah, quester, braggart, buffoon, or rebel (Homer's Odysseus, Milton's Satan, Joyce's Bloom); and that of the witch, mother, maid, courtezan, or enchantress (Sirens, Proserpine, Circe, Nausicaa, Cleopatra, Beatrice).

Regarding creatures of the air, we have the dove, swallow, nightingale, swan, eagle, and lark as paradisal images, the bat and vulture as infernal images. The paradisal animals are the sheep and the lamb; the infernal are the snake, goat, and wolf; and the horse, lion, leopard, dragon, and whale come somewhere in between as symbols of mysteriously creative yet potentially destructive vitality.

The imagery of setting revolves around the polarity of the natural cycle. Infernal images are likely to be fall, winter, darkness, cold, weeds, mud, mire, slime, swamp, timid river, pit, desert, den, cave, abyss, smoke, fog, mist, and sunset-west; paradise will consist in spring, summer, light, warmth, flowers, stars, mountain, meadow, and sunrise-east. Fire and water are, as with the imagery of man and woman, likely to be ambivalent: fire destroys and creates, burns and refines; water is a grave and a womb, it floods and fertilizes, drowns and purifies, endangers and releases (related images are the whirlpool and fountain).

On the basis of this pattern of patterns, any given image or element within it, when it appears in some particular context, will carry with it certain relationships, whether of resemblance or association, which may serve as a symbolic principle through which we may interpret it as meaning something more or something else within that context. That is to say, it points us back to the mythic level from which it came. And what precisely do we get from relating particular works to archetypal patterns? For one thing, we may get additional clues, over and above the literal plot-analysis, as to the emotional values which certain aspects of the whole are intended to embody. For another, we may get a sense of some extra magnitude and significance which a literal action can be made to carry. Finally, we may get a basis for relating and classifying aspects of works in certain fresh and illuminating ways.

But basically what we get here is a sense of emotional weight and feeling-tone. The anthropological approach to myth and ritual emphasizes perforce the relation of man to nature, and so the conflicts and problems it can teach us to see symbols of are the tribal ones involved in survival—food, clothing, shelter, generation. Hell, for example, in this perspective refers more to the end of the agricultural year, to actual wastelands, to physical impotence, than it does to fears, anxieties, and conflicts of a more internal sort, although the former can come to symbolize the latter. But our archetypes so far are merely rather primitive indicators of generic hopes and fears, positives and negatives, and as such have very little content in themselves when appearing in more sophisticated settings. The level of figurativeness, that is, is lower in anthropological than in psychological terms: in the former, literal elements symbolize more similar universals (Aeneas descending into Hades is not just the hero looking for directions, but also the sun god going beneath the grave of the sea to regain his strength and be reborn); while in the latter, they symbolize quite different internal states (Aeneas is regressing to confront his unconscious).

Even on this first level, however, we do not have a dictionary of symbols for the interpretation of a given work, but rather a range of possibilities with which to operate. As I have suggested, not only are many of the archetypes themselves ambivalent—the hero, woman, fire, water, contain within themselves potential polarities—but also any archetype which is usually univalent in itself may be used ironically or differently in any specific work. The snake is usually a symbol of fear and evil but is also one of regeneration and rebirth, and only a particular context can tell us just how to interpret it. D. H. Lawrence's poem "Snake," for example, deliberately juxtaposes these dichotomies. The sun is almost always a benign symbol of life, and yet in some of George Meredith's poems, as we have seen, it is a negative symbol representing excessive idealism breeding the maggots of cynicism and sensualism (compare flying too close to the sun in the Icarus myth).

Making our distinction between meaning and evaluation, in other words, is still not sufficient in itself when interpreting particulars, for even the general meaning of a universal symbol or archetype may vary, quite apart from the question of the evaluative doctrine which may be assigned to it. Which is why, as I have pointed out, modern writers are especially interested in archetypes, for these are peculiarly suited to tentative and hovering effects—despite the curious efforts of some modern critics sometimes to impose more definite meanings and evaluations upon them. Nevertheless, our knowledge of normal usage can still be valuable by that very token, since, when we come upon a significant variation, we will be all the more ready to appreciate the force of that variation in terms of what it varies from—provided we are not forcing predetermined expectations upon the work.

IV

Hell, then, from the perspective of the psychological approach to myth and ritual, symbolizes not so much the end of the agricultural year as more personal problems and conflicts, because it emphasizes perforce the relation of man to man and man to himself, rather than that of man to nature.[12] Indeed, this approach enfolds symbol within symbol, in seeing Hell as representing the end of the agricultural year (or the end of the day), and then this as representing an internal emotional conflict. If we look in literature, that is, for more than echoes and reenactments of ancient and ubiquitous patterns—for more than (in the words of Thomas Mann) a "mythical identification, as survival, as a treading in footprints already made"[13]—we can trace the image of the descent into Hell from early myth and ritual to Homer, Virgil, medieval romance, Dante, to Eliot's *The Waste Land* and "The Hollow Men," and to Hart Crane's subway section of *The Bridge*, and then interpret it as an archetype symbolizing the encounter with repressed guilt. It should be observed further that such mythical identification need not depend upon the explicit and conscious presence in a work of actual names, places, and events from mythology—the procedure rests rather upon finding more or less unconscious similarities, associations, and resemblances.

Take the scapegoat as another example. The anthropologist might see it as developing from the king-killing ritual, which assumed that the fertility of the tribe resided in the person of the king and therefore that he had to prove his vitality in an actual combat with a contender. Substitutes were gradually found, however, with the result that all the bad luck of the tribe was loaded symbolically on some ritual animal, which was then driven with maledictions out of the community. The psychologist, on the other hand, would go on from here to say that this anxiety over fertility is itself a symbol of man's fear of life, of his consequent hostility toward his kings and gods who have such power over him, and of the resultant guilt, and would interpret the ritual as a symbolic release of these pent-up and otherwise unmanageable emotions.

So we are brought back round again to Burke's notion of myth and ritual as symbolic enactments of psychic conflicts, only this time we may see more clearly the way in which the anthropology and the psychology of it may be related. Furthermore, by understanding how dreams may be related to myth and ritual in psychological terms, we have a better way of seeing why universal and archetypal symbols do not necessarily lose their general force and meaning as man becomes more urbanized, because we can now appreciate how their effect need not depend in any direct way upon the literal contiguity of the agricultural year at all.

Man, that is to say, no matter how much he becomes alienated from external nature, will always have to face the problems and conflicts of being alive, with its aggressions, fears, hostilities, anxieties, and guilts; and he will always therefore be able to respond to the general symbols of these problems and conflicts. And he will be able to do this perhaps even more so as he becomes more alienated from external nature—and even more alienated from his own nature—not only because his control of the outside world may force him to confront himself more and more as the issues of physical survival become less pressing (assuming he can also reverse the effects of environmental destruction now becoming more alarming as technology grows more pervasive), but also because his alienation itself may produce an equal and opposite need to become integrated, whole, and in harmony. Urban man can become more rather than less concerned with nature—both external and internal—by virtue of his very nostalgia, desperation, and isolation.

Let us sketch in, then, a psychological pattern of patterns, just as we did for a mythological one. It is axiomatic that the human psyche has, like the moon, two sides: the dark or unconscious side, and the light or conscious side. The conscious represents an extremely limited, highly selective portion of the total self, and is will- and future-orienated. The unconscious is the remainder, the reservoir of all memory and repressed desire, and is impulse- and past-oriented (compare our discussion of transcendence in the chapter on Hemingway). The conscious expresses itself via discursive, rational language, while the unconscious expresses itself— mainly in dreams, when the conscious is least active—via symbols. In our myths, dreams, and rituals, our various selves act out their conflicts symbolically, and literature which uses these symbols may be interpreted in these terms.

The psychic pattern goes something like this: the self (which includes both sides of the mind) is constantly trying to achieve an equilibrium whereby its two halves may be united. Its tendency, however, is always to overbalance in favor of one or the other: if it seeks security, it tends to relapse into authoritarianism: if it seeks freedom, it tends to relapse into irresponsibility. The hero is a projection of the universal human self seeking wholeness, and the difficulties he encounters are projections of the conscious struggling with the unconscious. There is no substitute for unity: one part of the self cannot do without the other for very long. Thus when the conscious strives to break from the unconscious, the self experiences fear of being pursued by its unconscious, and this fear finds its projected image in the shape of monsters, symbolizing the rejected aspect of the self. Resolution is achieved, paradoxically, by surrendering the conscious and turning about to confront the fear: by being swallowed by the dragon or whale, by going into the forest and meeting the witch, or by going down to Hades—that is, by symbolically dying—the hero finds what he was seeking all the time, the treasure of wholeness. Thus the pursuing unconscious is conquered only by yielding to it: the conscious must "die" to be "reborn" from the depths of the unconscious, for it is the unconscious which contains whatever latent energy the conscious can use and turn into manifest productivity. And the same cycle obtains when the unconscious tries to break from the conscious. (In addition to the hero-monster pattern, this conflict finds its image in the male-female polarity as well.) Polarities are transcended, in other words, when one follows this path or that, not as a reaction against its opposite, but rather as a free choice which includes an acceptance of its opposite.

From the hero as sun god or fertility figure or vegetative force to the hero as the questing psyche—such is the story of the archetypes from anthropology to psychology. And just as the anthropological pattern served as a basis for making symbolic inferences whenever some element within it appeared in a particular setting, by pointing back to the mythic level from which it came, so too does the psychological pattern serve to establish relationships on the basis of which we can interpret symbols. The values of this approach are the same as those of the anthropological approach—emotional clues, extra magnitude and significance, and fresh categories—plus a fourth benefit: a sharper sense of the relationship of an objective action to our own inner lives.

The point also remains, however, that as we get more specific in our assignment of meanings and especially of evaluations to archetypes, we must be even more careful than before of reading them out of context.[14] Furthermore, our psychological interpretation of symbols is bound to vary slightly or greatly, depending upon which psychological theory we are using; for each theory takes a different facet of man's emotional problems as central, and thus each comes up with a different interpretive structure.

In addition to the question of reading out of context, several other qualifications of the archetypal approach need to be considered here. The first comes, as I have noted, from anthropological and psychological specialists, especially from the American pragmatic school, to the effect that no two cultures are actually alike, and that therefore it is tenuous if not fallacious to seek parallels between European rituals and those of Africa, India, and the South Sea Islands.[15] Much work needs to be done here, and apparently similar symbols from different cultures need to be seen not only in the contexts of their own cultures but also in relation to other symbols in their own cultures which do not appear to resemble others from other cultures.

The second qualification arises when we consider the problem of value judgment, for there is a tendency to regard works using great symbols ipso facto as great literary works. Certainly Homer, Virgil, Dante, Shakespeare, Milton, Blake, and Goethe are conspicuous for their use of archetypes, but so, unfortunately, are trashy lesser works, best sellers, third-rate movies, and comic books. This is a fallacy somewhat similar to the "common sense" assumption we inherited from the Victorians that great ideas and great subjects make for great art. But, as always, we must realize that it is the treatment rather than the subject which makes the difference between great art and ordinary art—or, at least, that great subjects and great ideas may be necessary but are not sufficient for great art.

The problem is intensified by the fact that just as historical backgrounds are best understood by means of ordinary art, so too are anthropological and psychological interpretations most easily made in the same way. The tendency, then, is to favor the amenable works; and so Jung makes a great fuss over Longfellow's *Hiawatha*, and Tolstoy favors *A Christmas Carol* and *Uncle Tom's Cabin*.[16] Indeed, most theories of literature tend to emphasize those works which illustrate the theories best, even if it is not a matter of value judgment at all. Thus an archetypal critic would naturally tend to emphasize Joyce, Woolf, Lawrence, or Dickens rather than Fielding, Austen, Thomas Love Peacock, or C. P. Snow—although I am sure a sufficiently alert archetypalist could find what he wants in the latter writers as well. Northrop Frye, whose recent system has far outgrown the original theory of archetypal symbolism on which it was based, ostensibly has a place for everything.

There is finally the fallacy of equating archetypal patterns with artistic forms, and this can be done by writers as well as critics. Since this is a common mistake, it apparently cannot be stressed too often, on the one hand, that form is something only an individual work can have, since it is a product of independent variables, and on the other, that central images, recurrences, clusters, and general patterns cannot organize a work. Form means, if it means anything, development and resolution— even didactic works with unresolved plots are resolved in the whole if the materials and their organization answer to a purpose—and juxtaposition and association do not in themselves necessarily form developments and resolutions. The threefold archetypal plot pattern implies development but does not create it: it merely provides a shell within which a genuine development can be embodied and supported. Archetypal patterns are, as I have suggested, sources of relationships and associations for interpretation, rather than sources of forms. This, I believe, is Frye's great confusion; Frye believes they exist in nature, whereas in fact they are found by those who are looking for them. They are a useful tool, but they do not describe existence—only individual things exist: generalizations are made by men for certain purposes with better or worse results. Thus to develop principles for the modern long poem, as Pound did for the *Cantos*, on the basis of a general and implicit inferno-purgatorio-paradiso pattern, is not sufficient to create an actual form. And it is still arguable whether its fellows—Eliot's *The Waste Land*, Crane's *The Bridge*, and William Carlos Williams's *Paterson*—have any form either.

The same is true of novelists. A novel, like a poem, may be based on the logic of association (or logic of metaphor) rather than the logic of plot; but either this logic will provide a principle of development, in terms of which one thing grows out of and follows from what went before rather than simply being placed after it on the basis of some archetypal pattern, or it will have no form.[17] One needs, in other words, not simply the effects of development but its causes as well, not only the appearance of sequence but also its reality. Thus, although Joyce's *Ulysses* nearly submerges its plot underneath a thickly-encrusted surface of recurrences, patterns, and archetypes, it nevertheless does have an intelligible and vivid plot. *The Remembrance of Things Past*, on the other hand, actually does unfold according to an associative principle which makes for development and resolution, whereas *To the Lighthouse* comes somewhere in between.

Critics who are archetypally oriented tend to look at novels, whether they are organized associatively or according to plot, as satisfactorily explained when they have revealed and interpreted their patterns. Now it is clearly mistaken to read a novel having a plot as if it were organized merely associatively, like a poem, and it is similarly fallacious to read an associative work as if it were organized merely according to an archetype. Since the formal context is ignored or lost sight of, the result is obviously a reading out of context. The most graphic example of an actual "novel" organized merely archetypally is, of course, *Finnegans Wake*; and while it may have more pattern than the *Cantos*, I doubt that it has more form.

It is, however, more appropriate for a critic to apply an archetypal approach to an archetypal work than to a work having form, where the archetypal approach must be combined with formal analysis. In the next chapter, we examine in more detail the problems which arise when a novel having a plot is interpreted symbolically apart from that plot, when novels having perfectly intelligible plots are treated as if they were based on the logic of metaphor instead of a sequence of incidents. Our final two chapters will follow a more positive program in illustrating the interpretation of symbols based on internal associations, and then on external and archetypal associations.

Chapter 17

Plot and Symbol in the Novel: Hardy, Hemingway, Crane, Woolf, Conrad

During my reading and teaching of certain much discussed novels—*The Mayor of Casterbridge, A Farewell to Arms, The Red Badge of Courage, Mrs. Dalloway,* and *The Nigger of "The Narcissus"*—I had occasion to consult several of the current interpretations of these books. Fully expecting a routine job of corroboration, for these novels are so popular that I thought I understood them almost without reading them, I gradually became aware instead, as I returned to the texts themselves, of an uncomfortable sense of discrepancy. And the discrepancy was not between one critic and another, since they were in general remarkably consistent among themselves, but rather between what they said and what I thought I saw in these novels.

About *The Mayor,* I learned that Henchard's downfall was supposed to have been a retribution for his early rashness in selling his wife and daughter, but I found in fact no such connection; about *A Farewell* I read that Lt. Henry's suffering at the end was supposed to have been caused either by his immorality or that of the war, but failed to find that the text supported such an interpretation; about *The Red Badge* I was told that Fleming's return to arms was supposed to have been caused by the purifying effects of Jim Conklin's death, but was at a loss to find such a connection in the book itself; about *Mrs. Dalloway* I was led to believe that Septimus's suicide was supposed to have brought about a new insight in Clarissa, but was puzzled to discover that this did not happen in quite that way; and about *The Nigger,* finally, I was informed that Wait was supposed to have been the crew's secret sharer, but was surprised to see that their dilemma was really something rather different than this implied.

The primary cause, I believe, for the discrepancy I noticed between text and interpretation is, that we are seeing novels in terms of imagery patterns, symbolic associations, and archetypal structures, and are neglecting or underplaying their plots. In this way, *The Mayor* may be read as a Greek myth; *A Farewell* as a wasteland archetype; *The Red Badge* as a grail quest; *Mrs. Dalloway* as a scapegoat ritual; and *The Nigger* as an initiation ceremony. Because it takes the literal surface of a novel for granted, or neglects it altogether on principle, symbolic criticism is therefore likely seriously to misread many a novel in which such a surface plays a part. In what follows, therefore, I shall attempt to apply our concept of plot as a unified causal sequence to those aspects of a novel which current criticism bypasses. Let it be understood, however, not as a substitute for other methods but rather as a supplement. What is said about plot in a work of fiction in no way precludes what may be said about its other patterns; rather, it guides us to them and provides us with a principle in terms of which to discuss them more specifically than otherwise.

My plan, then, will be first to summarize what appears to be the current standard interpretation of each of these novels, in order of critical complexity; second, to show how each interpretation fails to explain certain important facets of its subject; and third, to suggest how this failure may be remedied. As we shall see, there are three or four basic errors involved when a critic makes symbolic inferences without paying sufficient attention to the materials of plots: either a cause which does exist is seen as producing an effect with which it has no such connection; or the true cause of a given effect is ignored; or the nature of a cause-and-effect relationship which does exist is misconstrued. In consequence of these errors, the criticism of forms becomes muddled, so that parts are seen as wholes, wholes are seen as parts, and part-whole relationships are seen as signifying things other than what they actually do signify.

We turn now to our first novel.

I

The downfall of Michael Henchard, which takes definite shape from chapter 15 of *The Mayor of Casterbridge* on, is commonly explained as a just retribution for his having sold, in chapter 1, his wife and baby girl to a sailor in a furmity tent at a fair. According to this line of interpretation, Henchard is seen as having risen to high places only to be toppled by the remorseless return of the past. Thus after eighteen years or more his wife and "daughter" return (chapter 3), the furmity woman returns (chapter 28), and the sailor returns (chapters 41 and 43). Thus does his sin pursue and track him down, just as does that of Oedipus.[1]

But what of Lucetta, who, if she is from the past, is from a much more recent one? And what of Farfrae, who is entirely of the present, appearing for the first time on exactly the same evening as Susan and Elizabeth-Jane reappear? In terms of the above interpretation, they would be viewed as structurally subordinate, serving merely to reveal further the disastrous consequences of that ugly side of Henchard's character which first became manifest at the auction of his wife in a fit of drunken spite. And in many ways this seems to be the plot Hardy intended to write.

If, however, the actual sequence and scale of the incidents in *The Mayor* be outlined, the picture will actually seem quite different. The story as a whole may be seen as falling naturally into five sections:

1. Henchard sells wife and daughter to Newson at fair; repents too late (chapters 1–2).
2. Eighteen years pass; he is a success; wife and "daughter" return (Farfrae enters); and he makes amends at last (chapters 3–14).
3. He begins losing his reputation to Farfrae (Susan dies) (chapters 15–22).
4. He loses Lucetta and business to Farfrae (furmity woman returns) (chapters 23–40).
5. Lucetta has died, and he loses Elizabeth-Jane to Farfrae (Newson returns) and dies (chapters 41–45).

One indeed expects as he begins reading that the dramatic opening section will entail consequences to be played out through the rest of the plot; but one begins to suspect from the third section on that Farfrae and Lucetta usurp this role almost completely. In fact, from chapter 15 to the end in chapter 45 (more than two-thirds of the whole), with the exception of the return of the furmity woman and of Newson, the opening section plays practically no causal role at all. Does not Henchard make honorable amends as early as chapters 10 to 13 ("He said nothing about the enclosure of five guineas. The amount was significant; it may tacitly have said to her that he bought her back again.") and yet does not his fortune continue to fall? Are there, in effect, two separate plots here joined only accidentally, in that they center on the same flaws in the character of the same man; and mechanically, in that one is intertwined with the other only temporally and arbitrarily?

Let us examine a bit more closely exactly what seem to be the structural connections among these five sections of the story as a whole. One and two are indeed joined causally: Henchard's ugly stubbornness causes him to sell his wife and child, and the more humane side of his character causes him to repent the next morning; failing to find them, he is driven by guilt to more temperate ways, channeling the force of his nature into socially useful outlets, so that he becomes rich and powerful; and when his wife and "daughter" return, he takes them in with barely a qualm (his debt to Lucetta, which he also assumes quite conscientiously, is now necessarily a secondary responsibility).

The connection between two and three, however, is much more tenuous: it is now his relationship to Farfrae, a completely new element, which begins his downfall, for Farfrae has an even keener talent for business than Henchard, without the latter's crudeness. This is an inevitable conflict springing from the contrast between the characters of the two men and not from anything Henchard has done in the past. This conflict could have occurred without being preceded by section one at all; Henchard has already begun to earn the displeasure of the townspeople through his selfish cutting of commercial corners even before Susan, Elizabeth-Jane, and Farfrae arrive. Indeed, as far as the past is concerned, it has in effect ceased to operate in any real way, and the most that can be said for it is that it has merely demonstrated the unhealthy ambivalence of Henchard's character which now brings him into unwanted conflict with Farfrae—a demonstration which could have been dispensed with altogether, for the nature of his character is just as clear later as it was earlier. If this be so, then it may be concluded that Hardy did more than he needed in order to get that effect.

Similarly, as there is no causal connection between the Henchard-Susan and the Henchard-Farfrae elements in sections two and three, so there is none between the Henchard-Susan and the Henchard-Farfrae-Lucetta elements in two, three, and four. Lucetta has already come to prefer Farfrae over Henchard in chapter 23 ("Lucetta had come to Casterbridge to quicken Henchard's feelings with regard to her. She had quickened them, and now she was indifferent to the achievement.") and for the same reasons the townspeople did in section three, well before the revelation of the furmity woman in chapter 28: "At bottom, then, Henchard was this. How terrible a contingency for a woman who should commit herself to his care." Her discovery of what he did in the past serves simply to crystallize her fear of the ugly side of his nature, and is therefore merely a contributing cause rather than the climactic revelation it seems intended to have been in Hardy's plan.

Nor does the truth about the wife auction do much to bring about the culminating actions of the last section. The revelation of the past which causes Farfrae to lose interest in Lucetta, and Lucetta to die, thereby leaving Farfrae free to marry Elizabeth-Jane, is of a different past altogether, having to do with the vague "intimacy" between Henchard and Lucetta in Jersey which occurred sometime after his selling of wife and daughter and before their return. The return of Newson, like that of the furmity woman, is simply a contributing cause, serving merely as a coup de grâce to finish Henchard off and to make it easier for Elizabeth-Jane to leave him for Farfrae. The deplorable circumstances of Henchard's death are merely the cumulative result of all his misfortunes, caused by an ambivalence of character he has never been able to control or understand: "He experienced not only the bitterness of a man who finds, on looking back upon an ambitious course, that what he sacrificed in sentiment was worth as much as what he gained in substance; but the superadded bitterness of seeing his very recantation nullified. He had been sorry for all this long ago; but his attempts to replace ambition by love had been as fully foiled as his ambition itself. . . . Part of his wish to wash his hands of life arose from his perception of its contrarious inconsistencies."

In sum, then, Henchard's downfall, which I take to be a form of punitive plot, around which the main body of the action turns, is brought about by his mixed moral character as a necessary condition, coupled with his conflict with Farfrae as the sufficient cause. He was already beginning to lose his high reputation when Susan, Elizabeth-Jane, and Farfrae arrived; the presence of his wife and "child" contribute nothing to this movement, while that of Farfrae, completely unconnected with the past, precipitates it. And it is this second line which continues to bring Henchard lower and lower throughout. Thus it is stretching the point beyond the evidence to interpret his downfall as a retribution for selling his wife and child. If this be so, then it is the Henchard-Farfrae-Lucetta story which constitutes the main action of this plot, and it is the Henchard–Susan–Elizabeth-Jane–furmity woman–Newson story which is subordinate, if connected at all.

I think, however, that the usual interpretation, if wrong, is as much

Hardy's fault as it is the modern critic's, for he has so overplotted his story that perhaps his original intention itself became smothered under what was to have been a secondary line of development. Nevertheless, if the modern critic were not so anxious to discover the tragic archetype of retribution in this book, it would not be so easy for him to find it there.

II

The pathetic misfortune which Frederick Henry suffers in losing Catherine through childbirth, at the end of A *Farewell to Arms*, is commonly interpreted as the result of one or the other of two causes, or some combination: he is seen either as the justly punished outlaw for having loved without benefit of clergy, or as the pitiful victim of the arbitrary and remorseless fortunes of war. Either way, what interests modern critics of this novel is its portrait of a generation becoming lost in its conflict with a middleclass industrial society which it cannot accept, and the way this portrait suggests the wasteland archetype in its symbolic use of rain and snow, mountain and plain, lake and river, wound and love, death in birth. Thus seen, this book is taken as making a profound artistic comment on the breakdown of values in the twentieth century: the impossibility of living and loving truly while following traditional sanctions, the consequent necessity for keeping one's guard up and taking only calculated risks, and the pathos which ensues when one of the brave is caught with his guard down.[2]

Now all of this may be true in a large and general way, but even the supporters of this interpretation have sometimes felt a sense of strain in trying to reconcile the two obviously discrete portions of the book, which their punning on its title serves to point up—the "arms" of battle and the "arms" of a woman. This is clearly, as any textbook survey will tell you, "a novel of love and war," but the relationship between the two has been taken to be largely associative and symbolic: war destroys lovers just as society destroys love, or something of the sort.

But let us see what a scrutiny of the actual events and their connections reveals. Hemingway has divided his story into five books, and the central incidents of each may be outlined as follows:

1. Henry meets Catherine, goes into battle, and is wounded.
2. He is sent to a hospital, meets her there, and their love flowers.

3. His wound is better, he goes back to the war, is caught up in a retreat, and is forced to desert.
4. He finds his way back to Catherine, who is bearing his child.
5. They escape to neutral territory where, after some months, she dies
   in childbirth.

Notice first of all the proportions devoted to each of the story's two
halves: only the last part of book 1 (chapters 9–13) and most of book 3
deal with the war directly, whereas the remaining 3½ books deal mainly
with the love affair. This scaling suggests that, perhaps because of Hemingway's skill in such writing, we might be overestimating the relative
importance of war in the plot as a whole.

A further analysis of the causal connections among these books bears
out this suggestion rather clearly. Since the main culminating incident
derives its force and meaning almost entirely from the relationship between the lovers, it would not be an unreasonable hypothesis to assume
that the main action of the novel is organized around that relationship.
We may ask, then, what brought about this catastrophe and what part
the war plays in this sequence.

In the first place, I think it is clear that there is one sufficient cause
of Catherine's death, and one only: biology ("You always feel trapped
biologically"). That is, her hips were too narrow for a normal delivery—
"The doctor said I was rather narrow in the hips and it's all for the best
if we keep young Catherine small"—and by the time her doctor decided
a caesarian was needed, the baby had strangled itself and she had developed an internal hemorrhage.

Their love for each other, and the fact that they chose to consummate
their love physically, is naturally the necessary condition for this effect.
But there is no reason whatever in these circumstances as such for so
terrible an outcome; nothing prevented a normal delivery except Catherine's unfortunate anatomical characteristics. The same circumstances,
given wider hips, could just as easily have ended in a successful delivery;
and by the same token the same narrowness of hips could just as easily
have produced the same catastrophe in the peaceful suburbs.

They could have been married fifty times over, as Henry himself reflects, and thus the theory that he suffers for daring to defy social mores
will not bear up under the weight of evidence. Similarly, he could have
suffered almost as much if his love had flowered in peacetime, and thus
the theory that he is a victim of the war proves equally invalid. Indeed,

if we speculate as to what Hemingway could have done had he wanted to do what these theories would have him do, we will see even more clearly the lack, which they ignore, of those causal connections needed. Had Hemingway wanted to make Henry suffer for violating moral conventions, for example, he could have had Catherine's death stem directly from some mischance encountered while loving immorally—she could have contracted a venereal disease from Henry, for instance, or they could have been forced to make love under physical conditions unfavorable to normal conception, and so on. But there is absolutely no hint or implication of anything like this in the narration of the final chapters. Or again, had Hemingway wanted to make Henry suffer as a victim of the war, he could have had Catherine's death result from some contingency of battle, for which any number of gruesome possibilities suggest themselves—she could have been injured while rowing across to Switzerland, or while being caught up in the retreat, or because of having to give birth without medical attention, or under unsanitary conditions. But the fact is that she had, by and large, a quiet confinement and the best medical care and facilities available. (The possibility that it is the doctor's fault in not operating sooner presents itself, but is not supported by the text; and even if it were, it would make very little sense.)

What, then, *is* the function of the war in relation to this main action? The answer may be discussed under two heads: its causal function and its intensifying function. Causally, although the war is a sufficient condition of neither their love nor their suffering which is the outcome of this love, it does serve as a necessary condition of this love. Without it, they in all probability would never have met, and even if they had, Catherine would have still had her English fiancé. But the war, in simply bringing them together in a susceptible mood, would not in itself have made them fall in love. Indeed, Catherine met Rinaldi first without being attracted to him at all. The sufficient cause of the love between Henry and Catherine stems primarily from their respective characters and attitudes. The war, further, inflicts a wound upon Henry, which in turn allows him to see more of Catherine and thus to consummate their love; and again, by means of the retreat, the war allows him to return to her and thus to be in attendance when her time arrives. But in each case, its functional role is that of a necessary condition rather than that of a sufficient cause.

As an intensifier, in addition, the war functions to place their doomed love in an emotionally appropriate context. If losing his beloved causes Henry to suffer, how much more does he suffer when she represents all that he has to lose; for the war has placed him in a far country, has disillusioned him in traditional moral values, has wounded him, and has cut him off from his own forces (no one would argue, I think, that he is responsible for his desertion, even though he feels a decent amount of guilt). The war, simply by making it difficult for them to lead a normal life, places an appropriate cloud of doom over their heads and points up the fragility of all human relations. Every move is a gamble involving high stakes, and they are therefore more vulnerable; every decision entails more serious consequences, and thus every failure is more final. Hence the ultimate pathos is intensified.

If all this be so, then we must revise our war-defeats-love interpretation of this novel in favor of a love-causes-sorrow interpretation, and view the war as playing a strictly subordinate role causally and as serving otherwise mainly as an appropriate background against which the main action, which seems to be a pathetic plot, unfolds. In this view, Hemingway is not attacking the sterility of war or the breakdown of values but is using them as materials by means of which to achieve his end more effectively, which is simply to draw pathos out of the painful and inevitable limitations under which all human hopes and desires labor. It could be said that his intensifying devices do get out of hand and exceed the needs of his effect, notably in book 3 dealing with the famous retreat, but no one would wish them away, I think, except when they mislead critics with special systems to support.

III

Symbolic interpretations of *The Red Badge of Courage* and of the remaining novels to be discussed below are even more common than in our previous two instances. I am not, however, going to argue either for or against Henry Fleming's story as a grail quest in terms of which Jim Conklin plays (as his initials would indicate) the role of sacrificial god.[3] It is just that such an interpretation usually depends upon taking Fleming's change as one of character brought about by the death of Conklin, and it is this latter literal reading which I want to question. Indeed, the title itself, in stressing military bravery, lends support to this reading. But the possibility of some sort of symbolic reading will not be lessened even if I am right.

Nevertheless, even those who argue symbolically have sensed that the literal connection between Conklin's death and Fleming's return to battle is somewhat remote and have therefore constructed systems of image-recurrences to bridge the gap. The by now famous discussions of the red-wafer analogy at the end of chapter 9 are a case in point, and many other colors, objects, and mythic parallels have been schematized to make acceptable a theory of this novel which will have Fleming change ritually his character in the face of the dragon gods of war, dying symbolically thereby to his selfish individuality in order to be reborn into the societal fellowship of men.

I want to suggest that if connections of this nature exist, they are the only ones supporting this change-in-character theory; and if they are, then they are not support of sufficient strength to justify it. It is my proposition that Fleming undergoes no change of character whatsoever, if by character we mean that which translates moral values into actions, and that the change which he does undergo (for he certainly does change!) is one of thought—that is, in his conceptions of himself in relation to war as an experience. "He was forced to admit that as far as war was concerned he knew nothing of himself," we read toward the end of chapter 1; "He reluctantly admitted that he could not sit still and with a mental slate derive an answer. To gain it, he must have blaze, blood, and danger. . . . So he fretted for an opportunity" (chapter 2). And at the end of the book, "at last his eyes seemed to open to some new ways."

But let us, as is our custom, examine an outline of the plot as a whole, which in this case falls naturally into three sections:

1. Fleming's thoughts, feelings, and activities before battle (1–4).
2. His first encounter with the enemy; bravery, cowardice, flight, and ambivalent spectatorship (5–13).
3. His second encounter; bravery, praise, and relief (14–24).

We may now inquire into what are normally taken to be the causes of this action. These center around chapter 9 with the death of Jim Conklin. Assuredly, Conklin's actions up to this point have been in marked contrast to those of Fleming, in that he has been calm, resourceful, and ready for whatever may come. (So, too, has Wilson been contrasted to Fleming, in being boastful, frightened, and then manly.) Now that Conklin is fatally wounded, he bears himself up by force of pure will so that he may find a place to die where he will not be trampled on. Fleming, along with the Tattered Soldier (who is also wounded), witnesses Jim's agonized but unutterably noble search and death, and is moved, verbally at least, to rage.

But what are the consequences of this incident? A resolution on Fleming's part to find the enemy and seek revenge? No: he compounds his shame by guiltily deserting the barely living Tattered Soldier, who is himself badly in need of help, and sneaks away aimlessly. By chapter 13 he has received a bloody blow on the head from the rifle butt of one of his own men, has been returned to his regiment by a friendly soldier, and is being sympathetically nursed by Wilson before turning in for the night. To be sure, on the next day he fights heroically, but the point to be made here is that not only has he not returned to his regiment by deliberate moral choice, but he has also persisted in the convenient deception that he was wounded by the enemy in action. Nor does he ever (except in the movie version) reveal that he had run away from battle and that his wound is spurious. To say that Conklin's death has sown the seeds in him of heroic resolve, or has initiated him into manhood, is to exceed the evidence.

What, then, are the causes of his actions? The state of mind he was in, to begin with, before the battle rumors started was a typically ambivalent one: he had on the one hand a romantic history-book notion of war as heroic and himself as future hero, and on the other an experience of the dull routine of military training. The battle rumors precipitate the main line of the action, and the boy is thrown into doubt and confusion about his own courage now that he thinks it is about to be tested. Chapter 2 and part of chapter 3 follow him as his regiment marches and counter-marches around the battle area—in this way his ambivalence and suspense are intensified. He cannot, search as he may, find anyone else who seems as worried as he is. Finally one morning he is awakened by a kick in the leg and finds himself running toward the encounter before he knows what he is doing. And this lack of consciously purposeful behavior is typical of him during much of the plot: he is in a "battle sleep," he is "not conscious." Circumstances and the spur of the moment are the chief causes of Fleming's physical actions, and not moral character at all. The whole point of this story is that he is an especially sensitive, untried, and imaginative young boy learning what it is like; since such a pro-tagonist in such a situation can hardly be held responsible for his reactions under more than unusual stress, his character plays very little part in giving this plot its quality and direction.

Thus in chapter 5 and part of chapter 6, he faces the enemy for the first time and never flinches, being in a sort of hypnotic trance as he fires and reloads his weapon blindly and automatically. When the first charge is repulsed, he collects his senses and congratulates himself. But then a second charge approaches, and he feels he cannot go through the same terrible experience twice. Seeing others flee, he panics and runs away. The import of this flight and of his subsequent wanderings around the edge of battle is that he must see and experience for himself all phases of the war, even cowardice itself. The result is a gain in perspective, a coming into knowledge.

Thus, in chapters 7–13, Fleming assumes the role of witness, having lost by default his role as participant. And what does he see? Officers and men charging, retreating, hobbling with wounds, dying, and dead. Most importantly of all, he sees the fighting literally in a larger perspective by taking different vantage points and seeing thereby more of the whole than he did as a combatant, and he sees how small his part really is: "Reflecting, he saw a sort of humor in the point of view of himself and his fellows during the late encounter. They had taken themselves and the enemy very seriously and had imagined that they were deciding the war. . . . New eyes were given to him. And the most startling thing was to learn suddenly that he was very insignificant. . . . He discovered that the distances, as compared with the brilliant measurings of his mind, were trivial and ridiculous." Paradoxically, then, his cowardice causes a gain in insight. He comes as a result of this experience to no new resolves, however, and is virtually led back to his regiment by someone else. The only direct effect Conklin's death has had upon him is to make him look for a safe place to swoon after he is hit on the head in chapter 12. Perhaps the main function of Conklin's death is to make Fleming realize how a man can die, especially one whom he cared for.

From chapter 14 to the end he redeems himself, but again he does so in a kind of dream, feeling an unreasoning and unpremeditated rage— wild exasperation would perhaps be a better phrase—at the approach of the enemy (chapter 17). In chapter 18, during a lull in the battle, he and Wilson go for water and overhear a general call their regiment a pack of muledrivers. Once more he senses his own insignificance and thereby the pettiness of his personal hopes and fears. In chapters 19 and 20 he distinguishes himself in action, and in 21 he no longer feels resentment at the taunts of the veterans as he withdraws with his regiment: he is satisfied to have done what he did, even if it was only a picayune encounter. In 23 he fights once again, captures an enemy flag and takes prisoners. In 24 his regiment is sent to the rear for a rest, and he finally knows himself and what he can do: that heroism is possible, and that he is capable of it, but that it is not quite on the grandiose scale he had once imagined. He knows also that the real sufferings of others are more intense than were his imaginary ones. "He found that he could look back upon the brass and bombast of his earlier gospels and see them truly." Thus his change occurs at the end when he emerges from battle rather than in chapter 17 when he returns to battle.

If the main action of this plot is therefore a change in thought brought about by a succession of experiences—equally as ambivalent participant, cowardly witness, and courageous participant—then the change-in-character theory will not bear up under close examination. To gain this knowledge, Fleming had to have "blaze, blood, and danger," and it is in the service of that end that Crane selected his incidents and organized their sequence. And there is nothing in these incidents or their sequence which expresses or implies, as far as the action covered by this plot is concerned, the formation and subsequent pursuit of decisions and choices. It is true that he is now a "man," but only in the sense that he has seen the war and learned what he can do rather than in the sense that he has formed more noble resolves and strengthened his will in reaching for them. The essential change around which this education plot turns, then, is from ignorance to knowledge rather than from cowardice to heroism. It is acting both as coward and hero that enables Fleming to know himself, and not the achieving of self-knowledge which allows him to become courageous.

Nor has he, I submit, come to accept his role and responsibility as a member of the group, although under battle stress, both before and after his running away, he feels a sense of fellowship. What he *has* come to accept is his role, and that of his regiment, as simply a part of the larger battle experience as a whole, and he loses his fears and confusions thereby. Perhaps special theories derived from tribal myths are what make us so anxious to see such an action as centering around the coming into maturity, and to define maturity as acceptance of one's group role. If Crane had wanted to write such a plot, would he not have had Fleming return to his regiment as a result of his outrage at seeing Jim Conklin die; realize that perhaps his defection was in part the cause of Conklin's death; confess to his comrades that he had been a coward; then go into battle swearing to avenge Conklin's death; make amends for the disastrous consequences of his cowardice; and take his place thereby as a responsible soldier? As I hope I have shown, he wrote no such plot but quite another, and it is this other plot to which we must attend if we are to interpret this novel aright.

IV

There are two main parts to the plot of *Mrs. Dalloway*—the Clarissa part and the Septimus part—and formal critics have rightly seen as one of their principal jobs the necessity for explaining the connection between them. Virginia Woolf has offered a clue, albeit a rather enigmatic one, in her introduction to the Modern Library edition (1928): "Of *Mrs. Dalloway* then one can only bring to light at the moment a few scraps [of information as to how she conceived and planned the book], of little importance or none perhaps; as that in the first version Septimus, who later is intended to be her double, had no existence; and that Mrs. Dalloway was originally to kill herself, or perhaps merely die at the end of the party." But be her double in what sense, exactly? The question remains open.

The common interpretation is that Clarissa is confronted by the dilemma of her own insistent joy of life on the one hand, and her poignant awareness of its fragility on the other, and that the news of Septimus's suicide coming in the midst of her party which culminates the action (she and Septimus have never seen one another) causes her to reconcile the opposing poles of her ambivalence, so that she realizes she must encompass both joy and fear in her heart—indeed, that she must acknowledge death in order fully to possess life. The action, in this view, is seen as a dynamic self-completion, and the Septimus line is seen as having as its literal function an emergence at the proper time to precipitate this change of thought in Clarissa. The suicide is also viewed symbolically as the double of her own states of mind, representing on the one hand a breakdown under the pressures of life, and on the other a gesture of defiance against those who would "force the soul." Septimus dies in

order that Clarissa may live, and the scapegoat archetype is called in to
assist interpretation: he dies in her place, bearing her burdens with him.[4]

But does the news of Septimus's suicide bring about any change in
Clarissa? Or, more to the point, does she undergo any change at all? Since
this book is written according to such an intricate system of alternating,
overlapping, and interlocking incidents, we shall have to forego our cus-
tomary outline and proceed through particular quotations instead. Let
us begin at the end and see exactly what does happen to Clarissa, as she
reflects on the death of Septimus: "Oh! thought Clarissa, in the middle
of my party, here's death, she thought." The general effect is of course
obvious—the irony of the contrast brought about by the intrusion of
death into a high moment of life—and as such reminds one of similar
incidents in James Joyce's "The Dead" and Katherine Mansfield's "The
Garden Party." In each of these three cases the protagonist is caught up,
by means of a party, in some full-flushed moment of self-involvement
which is abruptly dispelled by talk of death; and in each case the ultimate
result is that he or she is given thereby a profound insight. The question
here is whether this insight is for Clarissa anything new or different.

She then gets off by herself to think this news over. "But why had he
done it?" Perhaps he had done it as a gesture of defiance, she thinks, to
preserve the privacy of his soul against the intrusions of his doctors. And
she thinks of Othello's joy upon first seeing Desdemona after returning
from a trip: "If it were now to die, 'twere now to be most happy." But
"there was in the depths of her heart an awful fear." This is her fear of
death; and there is also her sense of guilt and shame, to be living and
enjoying herself while others suffer and die. But she loves life, having
"lost herself in the process of living." Then she sees the old lady across
the way going to bed and she feels the fascination of watching this quiet
and self-contained woman, "with people still laughing and shouting in
the drawing-room." The opening line of the song from *Cymbeline* comes
back to her: "Fear no more the heat of the sun." She feels like Septimus
and is glad he had done it, for he "made her feel the beauty; made her
feel the fun." She returns to the party.

This is her state, then, near the end of the book, a state hard to define
exactly since it is presented in terms of the emotional ebb and flow of
her mood, but clearly one of inner harmony and balance. And it is a state
which has been obviously precipitated by the news of Septimus's suicide.

So far there can be no quarrel with the standard theory. But the trouble is, at least as I read the book, that Clarissa has already achieved several such moods of inner peace earlier in the day, and if this is so, then the plot can hardly be viewed as one of dynamic self-completion. In the beginning of her morning as she walks toward Bond Street and meditates on death, for example, she sees in an open volume of Shakespeare in Hatchard's bookshop window:

> Fear no more the heat o' the sun
> Nor the furious winter's rages.

And she reflects: "This late age of the world's experience has bred in them all, all men and women, a well of tears [e.g. regarding World War I]. Tears and sorrows; courage and endurance; a perfectly upright and stoical bearing." Later, having returned home, she is fixing her hair and thinking of her dress just before Peter Walsh arrives: "Quiet descended on her, calm, content," as she stitches up her dress. "Fear no more, says the heart, committing its burden to some sea, which sighs collectively for all sorrows, and renews, begins, collects, lets fall."

I submit that if Woolf had intended this plot to move in the direction of inner harmony for Clarissa, she would have done well not to have had her protagonist achieve that state at least twice before the end, for a dynamic action requires by definition a change from one state to another. In "The Dead," for example, or in "The Garden Party," the protagonist moves from one mood to a different one, so that he or she is in a new state at the end relative to any other point along the curve of the plot as a whole. Gabriel, in Joyce's story, moves from a state of egoistic self-involvement to one of transcendental selflessness; while Laura, in Mansfield's story, changes from a sentimental view of death seen in terms of the preoccupations of the living to one of its profound otherness and peace.

What therefore is the function of the Septimus line in this plot? If the foregoing be true, then this action is a static one, having as its form the revelation of a character for our sympathy and admiration. In order to reveal the qualities of Clarissa's character, motivation, and personality, Woolf has chosen to set the present action on a day when one of Clarissa's most characteristic and representative activities is underway—preparing for and giving a party. For this is the fullest expression of her temperament and brings out better than any other sort of day the fullest view of the pattern of her nature; her love of life, her immersion in its involvements, her sense of people and her talent for bringing them together, her regard for the privacy of the individual soul, her fear of extinction. It also allows, of course, Woolf to bring into play a greater range of personal contacts, thereby bringing to life the contrast, which most of her characters never tire of brooding over, between things as they were and things as they are. In this way a sense of the felt passage of time is created which is so central to the action of this plot and which is its technical triumph.

Thus we see Clarissa and get to know and understand her in terms of what she does and how she feels while engaged in her favorite activity, as well as in terms of how she regards others, how they regard her, how others regard themselves, how others regard others, and so on—all set within the complex framework of simultaneous present moments and montaged past memories. Clarissa had a theory in the old days, thinks Peter: "It was to explain the feeling they had of dissatisfaction; not knowing people; not being known. For how could they know each other? You met every day; then not for six months, or years. It was unsatisfactory, they agreed, how little one knew people. . . . So that to know her, or any one, one must seek out the people who completed them; even the places."

During the course of the day, as we have seen, she thinks among other things of death, for it is her attitude toward sorrow in relation to her feelings of joy which chiefly serves to reveal of what fiber her being is made. In this view, her reaction to the news of Septimus's suicide, rather than representing a change, serves simply to confirm by means of an actual and present instance what we already knew about her through her more general reflections earlier in the day. Her decision to return to her party after brooding over the news of Septimus's suicide brings into operation those very motivations which were being established all through the book; the sequence of this plot, then, consists in the unfolding of a state of affairs which will make effective a set of already defined causes. It is the reader's view of Clarissa's character, rather than her character itself, which undergoes a dynamic self-completion. What was latent in the abstract has now been made manifest in the concrete; since she feels this peculiar bond with the dead man, it is almost as if she had died and now need no longer wonder about what it will be like. It is in this sense that Septimus is her double, a surrogate in death for herself—a death about which she has hitherto been able only to guess. But guess she has already done, and that guess was, by and large, correct. We cannot, therefore, assume that all plots are dynamic, nor that they involve, correspondingly, some sort of ritualistic transition. For if we do, then we will violate many of the facts before us.

V

The Nigger of the "Narcissus," even though it is one of Conrad's earlier works, is an extraordinarily complex one and its causal lines are hard to discern. But certain things appear nevertheless clear which the standard interpretation seems curiously to have neglected. This view has the crew, as collective protagonist, go through a change in thought by means of two complementary trials: on the one hand they must learn to know and accept the impersonal forces and pressures of life, symbolized by the sea, and on the other hand to recognize and reconcile themselves to death, symbolized by James Wait. When they have reached this pinnacle of wisdom (the similarity between this interpretation and those of *The Red Badge* and *Mrs. Dalloway* illustrates, I think, the reductive tendency of some of these symbolic interpretations), they will then accept their roles as members of the group. Thus both the sea and Wait threaten their solidarity, and in meeting the successive tests of the storm and Wait's death they regain it. Wait, in this view, is their secret sharer, the man they fear to become and yet must accept if they are to prove themselves worthy of life, and the storm is the central turning point of the plot.[5]

Let us see what the actual sequence of events is, according to Conrad's division into five chapters:

1. Ship ready to leave Bombay; roll-call, Wait appears tardily.
2. Underway; Wait bullies the crew by using his illness as a lever; they quarrel with their officers; he is put to bed.
3. Storm; ship drifting on its side; they rescue Wait; ship recovers.
4. Men reach the point of mutiny.
5. Wait dies; ship reaches London; voyage over.

Now it is true that the crew feel a sense of solidarity after successfully weathering the storm, but what kind of solidarity is it? First, they feel cocky and meritorious and are therefore susceptible to being provoked into rebellion against their officers. Second, after they discover that Wait is in fact dying, they feel the communion of fellow liars, for they implicitly agree to go along with Wait's desperate assertion that he is well. This adds more fuel to their resentment against the captain, who is apparently punishing Wait for malingering by having him remain in bed (thus to enact his own deception). Third, after his death, they grow irritable with one another, and fist fights flare up. It is only after Wait's body has been committed to the sea that they feel relieved; the rest of the voyage is uneventful. When they reach land and get paid off, they stand for one final moment together in the sunshine before dispersing forever. And the narrator concludes, not without some typical Conradian mystification: "Haven't we, together upon the immortal sea, wrung out a meaning from our sinful lives? Good-bye, brothers!"

The question is: what is that meaning? If Wait is their secret sharer—the death which they fear but must face—and if the sea is life—the storm which they must endure—then this meaning is that one must accept life and death on their own terms in order to abolish the loneliness of the individual soul and achieve communion with one's fellows; for these forces—the powers which work on all men alike—must be faced together. The trouble with this interpretation, as I read the book, is that at no point do I find the crew either in fear of death or unwilling to face the tasks and dangers of the sea. (If they cry to have the mast cut when the ship drifts on its side, this serves merely to show how wrong they are in not trusting their officers, against whom they are about to rebel.) How, then, can this be their problem if they do not harbor the feelings and attitudes which such a theory requires of them? And how can its solution be what is claimed by this theory if such is not their problem? Wait, indeed, fears death with an unseemly terror, and Donkin shirks regularly his seafaring duties, but neither one nor the other represents the crew. Once more, an anxiety to find a tribal archetype has led us to misread a novel.

What in fact *is* that problem, the solution of which admittedly has much to do with the storm and Wait's death? And what, exactly, is that solution? And what have the sea and Wait to do with it? The dilemma with which Wait confronts the crew is simply that they do not know for sure whether he is sick or not. It is thus a problem of knowledge or thought, but having to do with a question of fact, at least at its base, rather than of emotion. The consequence of this dilemma is an ambivalence on their part both in feeling and action: on the one hand, they suspect he may be faking and thereby deserves their scorn, while on the other, he acts sick enough and thereby deserves their pity. As a result, they serve his every whim while hating him in their hearts, which in turn debilitates their wills and makes them irritable with and rebellious toward their officers (who are, it is clear, models of firm but benign authority).

A less subtle mind than Conrad's would have had their dilemma vanish when the truth about Wait is discovered, thus resolving the problem out of hand. But Conrad, being like no one else, actually compounds the dilemma when they find that Wait is really dying. How did he manage this? Already ambivalent enough, the crew's nerves are strained to the breaking point when they must rescue from the effects of the storm a man whom they hate. Their successful weathering of the storm makes them feel as if they have done something marvelous, thereby increasing, through Donkin's bad offices, their already growing resentment of their officers. The precipitation of their revolt occurs when Wait, frightened by the pious cook's sermonizing on the after-life, leaps out of bed and says he has recovered completely. The captain, however, seeing that Wait is obviously at death's door, pities him and orders him back to bed under the pretext, in order not to appear indulgent, of punishing him in kind for malingering. The men take the pretext for truth and mutinously rumble that a man has a right to work if he wants to, siding now completely with Wait.

They are quickly subdued, and realize finally, by means of Singleton's mysterious comments, that Wait is indeed dying. Rather than simply sympathizing with him now that they need feel ambivalent no longer, they decide, almost perversely, to pretend that he is really well and is therefore being treated unjustly. They are committed, as it were, to their abortive mutiny—"from compassion, from recklessness, from a sense of fun"—and "falsehood triumphed" that they may save face. What they are afraid to recognize is not their fear of death but rather their own stupidity in allowing Jimmy to make fools of them. They have made their bed and now they must lie in it; they have a vested interest in their image of Jim as a well man, and they must now protect it. If Jim had deluded them in ignorance before their mutiny, they are now self-deluded in knowledge. Their moral fibers loosen even more; to be sure, they feel a sense of solidarity, but it is the solidarity of "cheerful accomplices in a clever plot." He must live, not because they fear death but because they fear being proved wrong.

Thus his death comes as a surprise, so deep has been their self-deception. It "shook the foundations of our society. A common bond was gone; the strong, effective and respectable bond of a sentimental lie." They feel cheated; Jimmy had not backed them up "as a shipmate should." In dying, he has stripped them of the pretense "in which our folly had posed, with humane satisfaction, as a tender arbiter of fate." But now they experience a revulsion against themselves, and this is the central turn of the action, which is an education plot. "And now we saw it was no such thing. It was just common foolishness; a silly and ineffectual meddling with issues of majestic import . . . and, like a community of banded criminals disintegrated by a touch of grace, we were profoundly scandalized with each other." This is the solution to the problem of the plot: having been deceived by Wait and then by themselves, they are now ashamed of their self-deceit, seeing their hypocrisy in its true light. This is the meaning which they, together upon the immortal sea, have wrung from their sinful lives: to have seen themselves as they really are—men afraid, not of death and danger and responsibility, but of admitting they were wrong. But they are only human and, being repentant, are forgiven by the narrator: "Good-bye, brothers! You were a good crowd. As good a crowd as ever fisted with wild cries the beating canvas of a heavy foresail; or tossing aloft, invisible in the night, gave back yell for yell to a westerly gale." They were sound men and true, wavering only in the face of a moral problem which was too much for their simple natures, a dilemma which assumed in their eyes "the proportions of a colossal enigma."

I am not attacking, of course, the value of symbolic theories, but rather the tendency to fashion them on the basis of insufficient evidence. There is a difference between satisfactory and unsatisfactory theories, and that difference is a function of how near or how far a given interpretation gets to the knowledge it sets out to discover in relation to the book it is trying to interpret. And it is the responsibility of the critic, as a man searching for knowledge rather than for the confirmation of a favored hypothesis, to have his theory rest as firmly as it can upon all the facts of the case. One of these facts, in fiction especially, is what happens in the literal action; if he avoids attempting to explain the organization of the plot while trying to account for the form as a whole, and if he mistakes archetypes for forms, he will be building on a shaky foundation. The consequence, as I hope I have shown, is often a serious misreading. I also hope I have shown how such misreadings may be remedied. For a critic searching for subtleties neglects at his peril what his author has set down plainly on the page.

Chapter 18

The Waters of Annihilation: Symbols and Double Vision in *To the Lighthouse*

> So much depends then, thought Lily Briscoe, looking at the sea, which had scarcely a stain on it, . . . upon distance: whether people are near or far from us.　　　(*To the Lighthouse*, p. 284)[1]

While there is general agreement that *To the Lighthouse* centers on questions of order and chaos, permanence and change, detachment and involvement, intellection and intuition, male and female, critical unanimity disappears in the actual tracing out of these themes and the analysis of the patterns of imagery evoking them. Thus, for example, it is clear that the simultaneous completion of Lily Briscoe's painting and the arrival of Mr. Ramsay, James, and Cam at the Lighthouse are somehow functioning together to finish the book, but no two commentators have agreed as to what that function means as an ending of what has gone before. S. H. Derbyshire claims that Mr. Ramsay is undergoing a transition from his former intellectual personality to a newly discovered intuitive view; Dorothy M. Hoare and John Hawley Roberts argue that Lily is moving from a concern with form (art) to a concern with content (life); Dayton Kohler sees a shift from time to the timeless; F. L. Overcarsh traces an allegory of Christ's Ascension, involving a movement from the God of wrath to the God of mercy; David Daiches analyzes a transition from egoism to selflessness; while D. S. Savage and Deborah Newton think of this simultaneous convergence as a clumsy device which resolves nothing.[2] These examples could be multiplied, but the dominant tendency is clear: to interpret the thematic conflict, whatever it may be, as an antithesis of two mutually exclusive terms, one of which must be rejected in favor of the other. The trip to the lighthouse, in other words, is too often seen as a one-way ride.

But since the symbolism of the book as well as its structure suggests a rather different set of possibilities, there still seems to be room for an interpretive framework comprehensive enough to embrace them. A single view, an either-or strategy, will hardly prove adequate for dealing with the multiplicity of points of view through which each character is seen in the first section, the descending and ascending movement of the second section, and the shifting simultaneity of event which shapes the third. In order to discern here the intricate web of image, attitude, and idea which Woolf has woven on her four-dimensional loom, the critic must develop a more complex tactic.

I

We are dealing here, in other words, with those tentative and hovering effects which are characteristic not only of modernist literature in general but also of the novels of Woolf in particular, and therefore an even greater burden is placed on the critic to interpret in context than ordinarily. In this case, that context may be seen on three successive levels: particular moments and sequences of moments of thought and feeling experienced by characters in situations, the images and recurrences of images in terms of which these moments are embodied, and the overall plot structure as a whole.

To begin with, since the action and its significance lie so much within the feelings and thoughts of the characters, and since these feelings and thoughts keep shifting in attitude from moment to moment, we must pay close attention to moods, mood shifts, and mood cycles if we are to avoid being prejudicially selective in our use of the evidence and imposing a more abstract pattern of meaning upon the book than that intended by the whole. Woolf, as we know, assumes that human reality resides in our inner life; and she conceives of that life as fluid, tenuous, and ambivalent. We must be careful therefore not to make our interpretation simpler then the book.

Secondly, since we are treating ambivalent internal states, we would expect them to be embodied in and expressed through external and tangible images whose symbolism will be many-sided and ambiguous. We must interpret both the general meaning of these symbols as well as their particular evaluations, at least to begin with, primarily in terms of intrinsic relationships and associations—those accumulating on the one hand from moments and sequences of moments of thought and feeling, and on the other from the overall plot structure. And we must try, in looking for symbolic patterns, to do justice to all the significant recurrences of a given image rather than just those which seem to fit a preconceived pattern. Some of these images may indeed verge upon universal symbols and even archetypal patterns, especially in terms of general meanings (water imagery, for example), but I think we will find that the nature of the case calls for an especially solid base in the text. Not only will it turn out that water imagery has a wide range of particular evaluations in various contexts, but also that other key images (the lighthouse itself, for example, and its flashing light) depend almost entirely upon the text not only for particular evaluations but also for general meanings. It is best, that is, when working with semitransparent envelopes of this sort, to work from within outward rather than from outside inward.

The freedom and ambiguity of these moods and the images they are associated with are structured, finally, by a principle of development and resolution which organizes moments and sequences of moments, images and image patterns into a plot, form, or intelligible whole. Although it would seem that the plot, if there is one, is buried beneath the associative patterns, in that the second part of the book forms a hiatus between the first and third, and several of the main characters disappear in between, it is nevertheless also the case that the third fulfills the first, and that therefore we are not confronting simply shifting mental states and ambiguous patterns of image clusters. We have here a plot with a group protagonist (compare *The Nigger of the "Narcissus"*) comprised of Lily, Mr. Ramsay, and James, and whose form is their simultaneous change in thought and feeling as Mr. Ramsay comes to experience greater ease about the fragility of life (an education plot), Lily and James achieve a resolution of their tensions in relation to Mr. Ramsay (an affective plot), and Lily finds that her painting is finished (an education plot). The fact that the still-living influence of Mrs. Ramsay helps bring about this resolution provides additional structural continuity.

The basic problem can now be seen as one of determining more precisely just what the nature of that resolution is; and I think that, if we consider what has been said so far about tenuous moods and ambivalent images, we will be careful not to allow our analysis of structure to overstructure our interpretation—either as archetypalists or Aristotelians. While it is true that the journey to the Lighthouse finally does represent a transition from one mental state to another and that this transition does involve such polarities as detachment and involvement, it is also true, as I hope to show, that this change is more a matter of integrating the polarities than of dichotomizing them. Development and resolution embody a double vision in which Lily and James proceed, not simply from detachment to involvement, but rather complexly from detachment vs. involvement to detachment cum involvement.

Detailed attention to moments and sequences of moments, then, will help us to understand the images in which they are embodied, just as detailed attention to the images will help us to understand the moments and sequences of moments they embody. And just as these analyses will help us to understand the plot, so too will understanding the plot help us to understand them. Thus there is a reciprocal pattern of mutual support in interpretation, one approach leading to, checking, and limiting another. The final principle in terms of which the whole is organized, however, in contradistinction to the manner in which we may come to grasp it, is the principle according to which Lily, Mr. Ramsay, and James move from a state of puzzlement, confusion, ambivalence, and frustration, to one of harmony, clarity, balance, and integration. And it is this principle, ultimately, which should guide, control, and limit our interpretation of any of the parts.

II

"Subject and object and the nature of reality," Andrew had replied to Lily's question about the content of his father's books (p. 38), and it is exactly this problem which works its way through the novel on three perceptible levels: human relations, metaphysics, and aesthetics. Thus, although Mr. Ramsay's problem is technically an epistemological one, the novel itself can also be seen to have been built around the problem of how the known looks to the knower: of one person to another, of nature to man, and of life to the artist. Further, the overall quality of this relationship may be subsumed under the headings of order—a triumph over life's meaningless flux—and chaos—a giving way to its all but irresistible force, or a blank confrontation of its stark emptiness.

The point is, as we shall see, that a dialectic order is achieved by those who manage to focus their apprehension of the nature of reality simultaneously from two different perspectives—that of subject, or involvement in flux, and that of object, or detachment therefrom—and that the nature of reality, through which one must pass in making his transition from one perspective to the other, finds its image in water as a symbol of surrender. From whatever viewpoint one regards life (thesis), whether it be that of the detached philosopher ironically contemplating from a height man's smudge and his smell, or that of the busy mother and housewife frantically involved in the fever and fret of daily routine, one must give it up in favor of the other (antithesis), becoming immersed in the waters of transition, and emerging with a double perspective (synthesis). To lose this perilous balance, to keep out of the wet, is ultimately to give way to the chaos of a black and lonely darkness on the one side or to the disorder of a terrifying and senseless force on the other.

An interesting passage in which this theme of the double vision and its accompanying water imagery occurs is found almost halfway through the book:

> Brooding, she changed the pool into the sea, and made the minnows into sharks and whales, and cast vast clouds over this tiny world by holding her hand against the sun, . . . and then took her hand away suddenly and let the sun stream down. . . . And then, letting her eyes slide imperceptibly above the pool and rest on that wavering line of sea and sky, . . . she became with all that power sweeping savagely in and inevitably withdrawing, hypnotised, and the two senses of that vastness and this tininess (the pool had diminished again) flowering within it made her feel that she was bound hand and foot and unable to move by the intensity of feelings which reduced her own body, her own life, and the lives of all the people in the world, for ever, to nothingness (Nancy: pp. 114–115).

Section 1 deals chiefly with the first level, the relation of self to other, and it soon becomes evident that no one single trait or characteristic of a person can be seized upon and cherished as a way of knowing him or her. Mrs. Ramsay, for example, is a charmingly warm and beautiful woman, yet annoyingly concerned with ordering the lives of others (many of her circle resent her mania for marriage); although she is maternal, intuitive, involved in life's common cares, and capable of an unreasoning fear when she allows herself to dwell upon the tragic fragility of human life, she nevertheless is capable also of a triumphantly mystical detachment wherein life's inscrutable mystery appears ordered and revealed. And the significance of her portrayal, as it emerges from the attitudes of others toward her as well as from her own broodings, is that the truth about Mrs. Ramsay encompasses both these aspects of her personality.

Or consider Mr. Ramsay: he is a self-dramatizing domestic tyrant, yet he is also admirable as a lone watcher at the dark frontiers of human ignorance. A detached and lonely philosopher, he nevertheless craves the creative contact of wife and children; he is grim, yet optimistic; austere, yet fearful for his reputation; petty and selfish, yet capable of losing himself completely in a novel by Scott; aloof, yet capable of thriving on the simple company and fare of humble fishermen.

Lily likewise is a complex figure: a spinster uninterested in ordinary sexual attachments, she is nevertheless capable of a fierce outburst of love; an artist perpetually terrified by a blank canvas, she still manages to approach a solution to the complex problem of the art-life relationship. Mr. Bankes, to consider another, is an unselfish friend and a dedicated scientist, yet also a cranky food faddist; a self-sufficient bachelor, he is nevertheless a lonely widower craving the affection of children. Or again, Charles Tansley is an irritating and self-centered pedant, yet also a sympathetic human being—a complexity which Mrs. Ramsay herself sums up: "Yet he looked so desolate; yet she would feel relieved when he went; yet she would see that he was better treated tomorrow; yet he was admirable with her husband; yet his manners certainly wanted improving; yet she liked his laugh" (p. 174).

The climax of the first section occurs at the dinner, a brilliantly dramatic communion meal where each solitary ego, with its petty aggravations and resentments, is gradually blended with the others into a pattern of completion and harmony.

Personality, then, can be known only in terms of a multiple perspective: "One wanted fifty pairs of eyes to see with. . . . Fifty pairs of eyes were not enough to get round that one woman with" (p. 294). Section one provides just such a perspective. Including his or her own interior monologues, each character is presented from at least two points of view: Mr. Ramsay is seen chiefly through the eyes of Mrs. Ramsay, young James, Lily, and Mr. Bankes; Mrs. Ramsay through those of Lily, Tansley, and Mr. Bankes; Mr. Bankes himself through those of Lily; Lily herself through those of Mrs. Ramsay; and Tansley through the eyes of Mrs. Ramsay and Lily. It is by this technique of alternation that each is rendered more or less in the round.

Section 2 deals mainly with the second level, the relation of man to nature; and it does not, as has been frequently supposed, portray merely the ravages of time and tide afflicting the family and their summer home. In addition to the almost complete destruction of the house, we are also shown its equally dramatic renewal. Its focus is on the comic-epic figure of Mrs. McNab, who lurches through the house dusting and wiping, breathing a long dirge of sorrow and trouble, yet who leers, "looking sideways in the glass, as if, after all, she had her consolations, as if indeed there were twined about her dirge some incorrigible hope" (p. 197). It is she and her helpers who fetch up from oblivion all the Waverley novels and who rescue the house from annihilation.

The fortunes of the family undergo several severe setbacks: Mrs. Ramsay dies, Andrew is killed in the war, and Prue dies in childbirth. Yet we are given to understand that Mr. Ramsay's work will endure (the fate of his books was somehow tied up with that of the Waverley novels) and, as the next section proceeds to demonstrate, the family continues to develop and mature. The central section of *To the Lighthouse* therefore dramatizes not the victory of natural chaos over human order, but the reverse: the forces of destruction are defeated by man's power and will to live.

Section 3 is concerned chiefly with the third level of our theme, the relation of art to life, and continues in the knowledge of loss as well as the achievement of gain. Its structure is based upon the shuttling back and forth between Lily on the island watching those in the boat get farther away, and those in the boat watching the island in turn get farther away. This is accompanied by the corresponding movements of those in the boat getting closer to the Lighthouse, and of Lily getting closer to the solution of her aesthetic problem. The determining factor in each case is love (the "art" of life), which might perhaps be defined as order or the achievement of form in human relations through the surrender of personality: Lily finishes her painting as she feels the upsurge of that sympathy for Mr. Ramsay which she had previously been stubbornly unable to give; James and Cam surrender their long cherished antagonism toward their father as they reach the Lighthouse; while Mr. Ramsay himself attains at the same time a resolution of his own tensions and anxieties. The point is not that they have made a one-directional transition from this attitude to that, but that since each is aware simultaneously both of what is receding and of what is approaching, each has received in his way a sense of what I have called the double vision.

III

The presence of this duality can be further demonstrated by a closer look at the particular imagery of the book: its figures of speech, its scene, and its plot. The Lighthouse itself as the most conspicuous image functions literally in two ways: as something to be reached, and as the source of a flashing light. The former aspect is to be considered when we discuss plot; the latter suggests that the Lighthouse has a symbolic role of its own to play. In this aspect it appears in two connections: first as it impinges upon the consciousness of Mrs. Ramsay in section 1 after she has finished reading to James and is sitting quietly alone for a moment, and second as it flashes upon the empty house in section 2.

The busy mother of eight children, a woman of grace and ease who delights in social intercourse, and one who visits the poor as well, she often feels the need "to be silent; to be alone." As she sits knitting, the relief of abstraction from "all the being and doing" grows upon her; it is in this mood that she muses upon the alternating flashes of the light. It is a mood of detachment, peace, rest, and of triumph over life; she identifies herself with the third stroke, the long steady stroke, which becomes for her an image of purity and truth, of strength and courage, searching and beautiful: her "self having shed its attachments was free for the strangest adventures. When life sank down for a moment, the range of experience seemed limitless. . . . Losing personality, one lost the fret, the hurry, the stir; and there rose to her lips always some exclamation of triumph over life when things came together in this peace, this rest, this eternity; and pausing there she looked out to meet that stroke of the Lighthouse, the long steady stroke, the last of the three, which was her stroke."

This is the "thesis" of her emotional cycle; the "antithesis" is evoked as her mood soon modulates into one of grim recognition of the inevitable facts of "suffering, death, the poor," and she gradually descends from her state of triumphant abstraction from the fret, the hurry, and the stir, by seizing upon the light from a different perspective, "for when one woke at all, one's relations changed." As she looks now at the steady light, it is "the pitiless, the remorseless."

But the cycle is not yet complete until these two moods become synthesized. The second view seems "so much her, yet so little her"; and then her meditations are crowned, in their third phase, by "exquisite happiness, intense happiness," and she cries inwardly, "It is enough! It is enough!" As if, by seeing that long steady flash in two different aspects —first as an image of expansion and release, and then of contraction and confinement—she has received a final intuition of the essential truth of the nature of reality: that one must be both subjectively involved in and objectively detached from life, and that true happiness rests neither in the one sphere nor in the other exclusively, but in achieving a harmonious balance, however fragile, between the two. Now she can rest, if but for the moment, content. And to her husband, who is striding up and down the terrace outside the window behind which she sits, "She was aloof from him now in her beauty, in her sadness" (pp. 94–100).

In the middle section, portraying the death and rebirth of the deserted house, the light makes its second appearance by gliding over the rooms "gently as if it laid its caress and lingered stealthily and looked and came lovingly again." That this is only one side of its doubleness is evidenced by the sentence immediately following: "But in the very lull of this loving caress, as the long stroke leant upon the bed, the rock was rent asunder; another fold of the shawl loosened; there it hung, and swayed" (pp. 199–200). A few pages on, just preceding the arrival of the forces of renewal in the house, in "that moment, that hesitation when dawn trembles and night pauses" (p. 208), the Lighthouse beam, as an image of expansion and release (life-love-hope) and contraction and confinement (death-destruction-terror) held in relation, "entered the rooms for a moment, sent its sudden stare over bed and wall in the darkness of winter, looked with equanimity at the thistle and the swallow, the rat and the straw" (pp. 207–208).

Finally, it is worth noticing in section 3 that as Lily begins her painting a second time (while those in the boat are embarking for the lighthouse), her brush descends in stroke after stroke: "And so pausing and so flickering, she attained a dancing rhythmical movement, as if the pauses were one part of the rhythm and the strokes another, and all were related." Thus in echo of the Lighthouse beam itself, her vision begins to emerge from stroke and pause in alternation, and "this truth, this reality, which suddenly laid hands upon her, emerged stark at the back of appearances and commanded her attention" (p. 236).

IV

Having seen that the Lighthouse beam—stroke and pause in alternation —symbolizes quite clearly that the problem of subject and object and the perception of the nature of reality is a matter of opposites held in dialectic relation, we may now proceed to investigate more closely the specific embodiment of the objective-detachment and subjective-involvement themes in the water imagery which obviously permeates the novel on both the literal and figurative levels as scene and as metaphor. And as this theme and this imagery begin to take root together and grow as one, we shall see a second, more pervasive symbol emerging: the act of immersion as surrender and transition.

The fact is, as we have seen, that whatever his attitude toward life may be, whether objectively detached or subjectively involved, each character must immerse himself in the doubleness of reality by making a transition to the opposite attitude, and that this process in one way or another usually finds its image in water. Taking the three or four chief characters in their apparent order of importance, we may begin with Mrs. Ramsay.

Searching for a picture in the illustrated catalogue of the Army and Navy Stores for James to cut out, Mrs. Ramsay suddenly becomes aware that the gruff murmur of talk out on the terrace has ceased and that now, coming to the foreground of her consciousness, the waves are falling monotonously on the beach. Stationed as she is in a moment of domestic involvement, this sound at first "beat a measured and soothing tatoo to her thoughts and seemed consolingly to repeat over and over again as she sat with the children the words of some old cradle song, murmured by nature, 'I am guarding you—I am your support.'" The passage continues, however, through the dialectic of transition: "but at other times suddenly and unexpectedly, especially when her mind raised itself slightly from the task actually in hand, [it] had no such kindly meaning, but like a ghostly roll of drums remorselessly beat the measure of life, made one think of the destruction of the island and its engulfment in the sea." And the cycle is complete as this sound is once again accompanied by that of her husband's voice chanting poetry: "She was soothed once more, assured again that all was well, and looking down at the book on her knee found the picture of a pocket knife with six blades which could only be cut out if James was very careful" (pp. 27–29).

As the Lighthouse beam had come to her when she was in a state of detachment and had spoken to her of triumph and fulfilment, and then of failure and frustration, thereby annihilating her abstracted bliss and bringing her back down to the sphere of life's fretful involvements, so too the sea—reversing the process—comes to her when she is in a state of involvement and speaks of consolation and sympathy, and then of terror and remorseless power, thereby annihilating her contented involvement and carrying her up to the sphere of blank and meaningless abstraction. The synthesis which ensues, however, in each case produces a sense of equanimity, peace, and rest. Thus the double vision involves indeed a two-way process: depending upon which direction you are going, whether from subject to object or vice versa, detachment is either joy or fear, involvement either consolation or despair. And, also depending upon the direction, the water imagery becomes now a symbol of the search for human contact and warmth, or of the brute force of the natural cycle, now a symbol of the search for intellectual stability and certitude, or of the bottomless ignorance of the race of men and the profound vanity of their puny knowledge.

Thus, proceeding chronologically through the book, we discover another aspect of the water imagery in connection with Mrs. Ramsay—that of the fountain as a symbol of feminine creativity to which the male must resort in order that his fatal sterility be redeemed. The intellectual husband becomes immersed in the waters of human sympathy and devotion figuratively issuing from the intuitive wife. Emotionally exhausted and depleted, however, by this effort of consolation, she sinks back down into herself, her fountain pulsing feebly; and hearing "dully, ominously, a wave fall," she doubts all that she had said to him (pp. 58–61).

Reading the tale of "The Fisherman and his Wife" to James, she senses some relation of the story to her concurrent meditations, for the tale "was like the bass gently accompanying a tune, which now and then ran up unexpectedly into the melody" (p. 87). In the fairy tale, the sea becomes increasingly more turbulent each time the poor fisherman arrives to deliver his wife's insatiable demands upon the enchanted fish. How much, after all (Mrs. Ramsay might be thinking), can one ask of the sea? For if one presses it too far in one direction, forgetting the necessity of giving oneself up in turn to the sea in exchange for its gifts, one will lose everything.

Hearing at dinner of the Mannings, old friends she has not seen or thought of for many years, she broods over the relation of past to present, the stasis of the former being imaged as a placid lake and the flux of the latter as water shooting down into the room in cascades. In so far as we are out of the past, we are detached and the water image is a static one; in so far as we are in the present, we are involved and the image is a dynamic one. A few pages later, however, the present also achieves form —in terms of the harmony of all those at the table—so "that here, inside the room, seemed to be order and dry land; there, outside, a reflection in which things wavered and vanished, waterily" (p. 147). Here it is the human order as dry land which is being opposed to natural flux as water. We shall see below how Lily comes to feel the necessity of deserting the land for the sea.

Finally, as the perfection of this moment becomes in turn a thing of the past, the party disperses and Mr. and Mrs. Ramsay are in the study reading. Thinking of her husband's anxiety over the fragility of his fame, and of her concern over encouraging him, she feels once more a sense of detachment as she knits and watches him read Scott: "It didn't matter, any of it, she thought. A great man, a great book, fame—who could tell?" (p. 177). Then, "dismissing all this, as one passes in diving now a weed, now a straw, now a bubble, she felt again, sinking deeper, . . . There is something I want—something I have come to get, and she fell deeper and deeper without knowing quite what it was, with her eyes closed" (p. 178). Brooding over snatches of poetry, she picks up a volume and reads of love lasting and time passing: "her mind felt swept, felt clean. And then there it was, suddenly entire; she held it in her hands, beautiful and reasonable, clear and complete, the essence sucked out of life and held rounded here—the sonnet" (p. 181: Shakespeare's number 98). Once again the emotional cycle is complete, and she has reached a point of stability (the aftermath of the meal) by alternating from involvement (her anxious preparations for the meal) to detachment (the consumma-tion of the meal and the resultant separation from natural flux), the transition being imaged as an immersion in water.

V

Mr. Ramsay's uncompromising honesty and unflinching courage in the face of the perennial mystery of life and the tragic incapacity of the human mind is imaged as a stake driven into the sea to guide the frail barks which founder out there in the darkness: "It was his fate, his peculiarity, whether he wished it or not, to come out thus on a spit of land which the sea is slowly eating away, and there to stand, like a desolate sea-bird, alone" (pp. 11, 68). His masculine detachment from the commonplace—he doesn't notice little things, the shape of a flower, the texture of a sunset—is here a positive act, a gesture of defense against the tides of time and ignorance. Yet as we have seen, this standpoint becomes ultimately sterile without a periodic immersion in the feminine waters of life. Or to take it the other way round, his withdrawal from the life around him into his abstracted solitude finds its image also in immersion: "and then, as if he had her leave for it, with a moment which oddly reminded his wife of the great sea lion at the Zoo tumbling backwards after swallowing his fish and walloping off so that the water in the tank washes from side to side, he dived into the evening air" (p. 52).

Or again, his children and his domestic attachments (which somehow signify to Mr. Bankes a betrayal of their friendship), rather than his philosophical solitude, seem to provide the buttress against the floods: "That was a good bit of work on the whole—his eight children. They showed he did not damn the poor little universe entirely, for on an evening like this, he thought, looking at the land dwindling away, the little island seemed pathetically small, half swallowed up by the sea" (p. 106). He needs both the sense of involvement and of detachment, and the water imagery functions now in one direction, now in the other. His demand for the sympathy of women, we may notice, *pours* and *spreads* itself in *pools* at their feet, and Lily Briscoe, resenting him, draws her skirts a little closer around her ankles for fear of becoming wet—of becoming involved (p. 228).

And lastly, as if he has reached a more complex state of mind than hitherto, Mr. Ramsay thinks to himself, as the boat nears the Lighthouse and while he and Macalister are discussing the local shipwrecks and drownings: "But why make a fuss about that? Naturally men are drowned in a storm, but it is a perfectly straightforward affair, and the depths of the sea (he sprinkled the crumbs from his sandwich paper over them) are only water after all" (p. 306). Having cast his bread upon the waters and surrendered to the "destructive element," his anxieties as to his fame, and his courage in the face of the inevitable dissolution of human endeavors, are resolved in one final symbolic gesture. *Cast your bread upon*

the waters: for you shall find it after many days. He that observes the
wind shall not sow; and he that regards the clouds shall not reap. In the
morning sow your seed, and in the evening withhold not your hand: for
you know not whether shall prosper, either this or that, or whether they
both shall be alike good (Eccl. 11: 1, 4, 6).

VI

For Lily, likewise, the water imagery functions in its double capacity as
destroyer and preserver. She and Mr. Bankes stroll down to the shore,
drawn regularly by some need. "It was as if the water floated off and set
sailing thoughts which had grown stagnant on dry land, and gave to
their bodies even some sort of physical relief." And they both feel a
common hilarity, a sort of exhilaration at the sight. But characteristically,
the mood turns, "and instead of merriment [they] felt come over them
some sadness—because the thing was completed partly, and partly because distant views seem to outlast by a million years (Lily thought)
the gazer and to be communing already with a sky which beholds an earth
entirely at rest" (pp. 33–34).

To Lily, the old-maid painter, the great mystery is love: "Love had a
thousand shapes. There might be lovers [i.e., artists] whose gift it was to
choose out the elements of things and place them together and so, giving
them a wholeness not theirs in life, make of some scene, or meeting of
people (all now gone and separate), one of those globed compacted
things over which thought lingers, and love plays" (p. 286). But the
lover in art cannot help being fascinated by the artists of life who do
achieve a wholeness in their lives; so Lily, vicariously seeing the world
through the eyes of human love—the love of Mr. and Mrs. Ramsay—
feels "how life, from being made up of little separate incidents which one
lived one by one, became curled and whole like a wave which bore one
up with it and threw one down with it, there, with a dash on the beach"
(p. 73).

She resented Mrs. Ramsay's judgment that an unmarried woman has
missed the best of life, and "she would urge her own exemption from the
universal law; plead for it; she liked to be alone; she liked to be herself;
she was not made for that" (p. 77). Yet the love of Paul and Minta is
keenly felt as a contrast to her own barren state: "How inconspicuous she

felt herself by Paul's side! He, glowing, burning; she, aloof, satirical; he, bound for adventure; she moored to shore; he, launched, incautious; she, solitary, left out" (p. 153). So coming back on that evening ten years later, Lily goes to sleep lulled by the sound of the sea, for "Messages of peace breathed from the sea to the shore." And she feels, "why not accept this, be content with this, acquiesce and resign?" (pp. 213–214).

But the next morning she stubbornly sets up her canvas and starts to paint. Like Mr. Ramsay, the philosopher confronting the mystery of nature, she too, the artist confronting life, is imaged as a figure isolated and facing the sea of mystery and chaos alone: "Out and out one went, further and further, until at last one seemed to be on a narrow plank, perfectly alone, over the sea" (p. 256). But as she gives herself up to her art, as Mrs. Ramsay did to her husband, she loses consciousness of outer things, "her name and her personality and her appearance," and her mind throws up from its depths images, memories, ideas, "like a fountain spurting over that glaring, hideously difficult white space, while she modelled it with greens and blues" (p. 238). While her ego is held in abeyance, the creative waters of life, welling up within her, help to shape her picture.

She thinks of Mrs. Ramsay, who died in the interval between the two visits, and she remembers Mrs. Ramsay's mania for marriage. Suddenly she recalls Paul and Minta, whose marriage has not worked out well after all, and thinks of the glow which love had caused to shine from their faces: "It rose like a fire sent up in token of some celebration by savages on a distant beach. She heard the roar and the crackle. The whole sea for miles round ran red and gold." She feels a headlong desire to fling herself down into this sea and be drowned. But the mood shifts, "and the roar and crackle repelled her with fear and disgust, as if while she saw its splendour and power she saw too how it fed on the treasure of the house, greedily, disgustingly, and she loathed it" (p. 261).

The cycle, however, has yet to be completed. She continues her meditation while painting, and thinks again of Mrs. Ramsay. She sees something stir in the window where Mrs. Ramsay used to sit, and has a poignant sense of her living presence there beside her. Her tears well up in an anguish of love and grief, and she cries aloud, "Mrs. Ramsay! Mrs. Ramsay!" Called out of her reverie by the unexpected sound of her own voice, she looks around embarrassed. "She had not obviously taken leave of her senses. No one had seen her step off her strip of board into the waters of annihilation. She remained a skimpy old maid, holding a paint-brush" (pp. 268–269). But she has taken the plunge.

Some further light is cast upon the key phrase, "the waters of annihila-tion," in this passage by its recurrence in another work by Woolf which will perhaps help to clinch our definition of the symbolic function of the water imagery in *To the Lighthouse*. That work is a little book of less than thirty pages, which appeared just three years after *To the Light-house*, entitled *On Being Ill*, wherein she speaks of how "tremendous" is "the spiritual change" which illness effects: "how astonishing, when the lights of health go down, the undiscovered countries that are then disclosed, . . . how we go down into the pit of death and feel the waters of annihilation close above our heads and wake thinking to find ourselves in the presence of the angels and the harpers."[3] Clearly here the act of immersion is a symbol of rebirth, or, as we have styled it, of transition from one state to another—in the novel under examination, of transition from the single view, whether it be that of objective detachment or sub-jective involvement, to the double vision which apprehends the nature of reality simultaneously from both points of view.

VII

It now remains to tie our strands together by analyzing the significance of the alternating points of view around which the final section of the novel is built. As we have seen, its structure is determined by the double vision of Lily on the island watching the boat approach the Lighthouse while she finishes her painting, and of those in the boat watching the island recede from view while they near the completion of their trip. "So much depends then, thought Lily Briscoe, looking at the sea which had scarcely a stain on it, . . . upon distance: whether people are near us or far from us; for her feeling for Mr. Ramsay changed as he sailed further and further across the bay" (p. 284).

Similarly James in the boat thinks, as they get closer to their destina-tion, of his childhood and of the time he had hated his father for saying they would not be able to go to the Lighthouse next morning:

> The Lighthouse was then a silvery, misty-looking tower with a yellow eye, that opened suddenly, and softly in the evening. Now—

> James looked at the Lighthouse. He could see the white-washed rocks; the tower, stark and straight; he could see that it was barred with black and white; he could see windows in it; he could even see washing spread on the rocks to dry. So that was the Lighthouse, was it?
>
> No, the other was also the Lighthouse. For nothing was simply one thing. The other Lighthouse was true too (pp. 276–277).

Dramatically, there is a double tension to be resolved here, each aspect somehow centered around the gaunt figure of Mr. Ramsay. First there is in Lily a curious feeling of frustration due to her longstanding inability to give Mr. Ramsay the feminine sympathy he craves—probably because this would entail performing a more sexually oriented role than she will allow in her desire to keep her artist-spinsterhood intact—and this is somehow tied up with the trip to the Lighthouse and the completion of her painting. As the third section proceeds, "She felt curiously divided, as if one part of her were drawn out there—it was a still day, hazy; the Lighthouse looked this morning at an immense distance; the other fixed itself doggedly, solidly, here on the lawn" (pp. 233–234). She is seeking that "razor-edge of balance between two opposite forces; Mr. Ramsay and the picture; which was necessary" (p. 287).

So too James, in league with Cam, is stubbornly trying to keep a firm hold on his long-standing resentment against his father, to resist tyranny to the death. But "Cam looked down into the foam, into the sea with all its treasure in it, and its speed hypnotized her, and the tie between her and James sagged a little. It slackened a little" (p. 246).

Back on the island, Lily continues her painting, raising in her mind the question of artistic detachment from the common sympathies of life and the consequent lack of emotional stability which has been haunting her all along: "No guide, no shelter, but all was miracle, and leaping from the pinnacle of a tower in the air? Could it be, even for elderly people, that this was life?—startling, unexpected, unknown?" (p. 286). As James's childhood resentment against his father prevents him from yielding to his father's emotional demands, thereby standing in the way of the son's identification with the father and consequently blocking his normal growth toward maturity, so too Lily's aloofness from life's routine involvements prevents her from yielding to Mr. Ramsay's demand for feminine sympathy, thereby standing in the way of her acceptance of her sexual role and consequently blocking her achievement of artistic maturity.

Meanwhile James, who has been steering the boat, nursing his resentment, is praised for his navigational skill by his father just as they reach their goal. "There! Cam thought, addressing herself silently to James. You've got it at last. For she knew that this was what James had been wanting, and she knew that now he had got it he was so pleased that he would not look at her or at his father or any one." Mr. Ramsay sits expectantly, waiting to disembark: "What do you want? they both wanted to ask. They both wanted to say, Ask us anything and we will give it to you" (pp. 306–308).

Similarly Lily, as a result of the parallel course run by her emotional cycle, the progress of her painting, and her awareness of Mr. Ramsay in the boat reaching the Lighthouse, feels her tension resolving at the same time:

> "He must have reached it," said Lily Briscoe aloud, feeling suddenly completely tired out. For the Lighthouse had become almost invisible, had melted away into a blue haze, and the effort of looking at it and the effort of thinking of him landing there, which both seemed to be one and the same effort, had stretched her body and mind to the utmost. Ah, but she was relieved. Whatever she had wanted to give him, when he left her that morning, she had given him at last.
> "He had landed," she said aloud. "It is finished" (pp. 308–309).

Mr. Carmichael stands beside her, the aging poet "looking like an old pagan god, shaggy, with weeds in his hair and the trident (it was only a French novel) in his hand," and repeats: " 'They will have landed.' " She feels that this is a moment of communion—one to match, we might add, the similar moment which occurred during the meal in section 1— and she thinks: "He stood there as if he were spreading his hands over all the weakness and suffering of mankind; she thought he was surveying, tolerantly and compassionately, their final destiny. Now he has crowned the occasion, she thought." And, under the spell of this benediction, "Quickly, as if she were recalled by something over there, she turned to her canvas. There it was—her picture" (p. 309).

James has come into manhood by identifying himself with his father's attitude of grim and solitary acceptance of the uncompromising reality:

"So it was like that, James thought, the Lighthouse one had seen across the bay all these years; it was a stark tower on a bare rock. It satisfied him. It confirmed some obscure feeling of his about his own character. . . . He looked at his father reading fiercely with his legs curled tight. They shared that knowledge. 'We are driving before a gale—we must sink,' he began saying to himself, half aloud, exactly as his father said it" (pp. 301–302).

Finally, Lily has come to see the need of holding art and life in relation by means of the double vision: "One wanted, she thought, dipping her brush deliberately, to be on a level with ordinary experience, to feel simply that's a chair, that's a table, and yet at the same time, It's a miracle, it's an ecstasy" (pp. 299–300). And this complex perspective, we recall, was gained by both James and Lily, as well as Mr. Ramsay, by means of a yielding—whether literal or figurative—to the watery element of transition.

Chapter 19

The Shadow and the Sun:
Archetypes in *Bleak House*

It may be that Dickens tried to do more in *Bleak House* than he accomplished, for it is by common consent a great but curiously unequal book.[1] While I have not succeeded in settling the matter, I would like here to point up some symbolic relationships which have previously escaped notice—relationships in which the various images of the book, by virtue of the values which come to be associated with them during the unfolding of the plot as well as by virtue of their resemblance to archetypal patterns, emerge as the vehicle of those values. Although the presence of symbolic patterns does not in itself, as we have seen, necessarily guarantee artistic unity to the work in which they are found, our discovery of such relationships can do much to clarify the meaning of the literal action in a novel and the light in which it is to be viewed. And with Dickens especially, as Edmund Wilson claimed some years ago and as critics have come increasingly to realize recently, there is much to be done on this score.[2]

I

We must be careful, however, not to turn Dickens into a modernist simply because he is now being seen as amenable to certain modernist critical methods. We are not dealing here, as in the case of Virginia Woolf, with that characteristic tentative and hovering ambiguity of effect. Our problem therefore is not to relate images and contexts in terms of some sort of double vision, some complex and fluid sort of movement. The images in Dickens do not necessarily become symbolic by means of an integrated frame of ambivalences. We do not need to be particularly careful either in the tracing out of literal situations in order to know what the images symbolize, or in the analysis of symbols in order to know what the plot is about.[3]

What then is the value of symbolic interpretation and the meaning of the contextual test in studying a novel of this kind? The fact of the matter is that the plot is sufficiently clear in itself on its own terms, but the problem is two-fold: first, it is somewhat sprawling and seemingly overlarge; second, its organizing principle, such as it is, appears somewhat thin and sentimental. Clearly we are confronting an apparent paradox in this over-development of texture and underdevelopment of structure, and perhaps an analysis of symbolism will help resolve it by providing an organization of links between them. We may thus see more clearly the relationship of subordinate characters and incidents to the main line and recognize the additional relevant richness more appreciatively.

For the primary action, that centering around Esther and her fortunes, does indeed fall into the form of virtue rewarded, or what I have called a sentimental plot. It is true that her change in fortune for the better around which the book is organized is accompanied by certain changes in thought and character as she comes to understand the problems of guilt and responsibility more penetratingly and adjusts her behavior accordingly. But it also is true that these changes are part of the overall problem of her winning a place for herself in life rather than the end toward which the whole is directed—and win a place for herself she does, by being good and patient and by suffering and surviving.

But Dickens felt the need, whether intuitively or by design—although he is not a modernist—to lend depth and richness to this plot and the whole in which it is embodied by means of proliferating incidents coupled with recurring image-clusters. These, while not complicating his meanings, do contribute coherence to what is otherwise a somewhat chaotic book on the one hand,[4] and universality to what is otherwise a somewhat topical and maudlin story on the other.

What we will do therefore is pick out the symbolic alignments and contrasts in terms of the literal action; relate them to an overall archetypal pattern; interpret them anthropologically and psychologically in terms of the particular context of the whole; and then show how they add unity and significance to that whole. Although we are not looking for ambiguity and ambivalence, then, we are still looking for supporting links, meanings, evaluations; and we must do so, however much of worth we may find in external associations, in terms of the artistic whole in which they function. That is why we must go from the text outward before moving from outside the text inward.

Thus we will examine, in the first place, how the image of the shadow forecasts the suffering that awaits Richard, Ada, Esther, and her mother. This will then call for some speculation as to what, in terms of the moral values embodied in the novel, that shadow symbolizes and what that suffering means. Consequently, in the third place, we will trace the design of imagery which this symbolism serves to polarize around the basic decaying-house vs. orderly-house contrast. Fourthly and fifthly, we will fill in the details of this contrasting pattern: shadow, littered papers, animals, smells, drizzle, confusion, decay vs. sun, keys, bells, fresh air, gardens, music, order. And finally, we will chart the parallels which obtain between action and symbol as Esther makes her purgative transition from shadow to sun.

II

The story of Esther Summerson, Ada Clare, and Richard Carstone is a doom-ridden tale, from its very beginning full of implicit prophecies of disaster, symbolized by the insistent recurrence of the shadow-and-sun imagery. Comparatively early in the book the "clear cold sunshine" penetrates the windows of Chesney Wold "and touches the ancestral portraits with bars and patches of brightness, never contemplated by the painters. Athwart the picture of my Lady, over the great chimney-piece, it throws a broad bend-sinister of light that strikes down crookedly into the hearth, and seems to rend it" (chapter 12). Essentially the story of abandoned children in an alien adult world, the novel shows how the shadow of a mysterious guilt quite literally blights their lives:

> The door stood open and we [Esther and Mr. Jarndyce] both followed them [Ada and Richard] with our eyes, as they passed down the adjoining room on which the sun was shining, and out at its farther end. . . . So young, so beautiful, so full of hope and promise, they went on lightly through the sunlight, as their own happy thoughts might then be traversing the years to come, and making them all years of brightness. So they passed away into the shadow, and were gone. It was only a burst of light that had been so radiant. The room darkened as they went out, and the sun was clouded over (chapter 13).

Further on, their guardian's benevolent eyes darken in turn as he bids them a pleasant goodnight: "his glance was changed, and even the silent look of confidence in me which now followed it once more, was not quite so hopeful and untroubled as it had originally been" (chapter 17). And the death of Mr. Gridley, who had been "dragged for five-and-twenty years over burning iron" (chapter 15) as a result of legal delays, is a prophecy: "The sun was down, the light had gradually stolen from the roof, and the shadow had crept upward. But, to me, the shadow of that pair [Gridley and Miss Flite], one living and one dead, fell heavier on Richard's departure, than the darkness of the darkest night" (chapter 24).

The portrait of Lady Dedlock reappears toward the end to fulfill its role: "But the fire of the sun is dying. Even now the floor is dusky, and shadow slowly mounts the walls, bringing the Dedlocks down like age and death. And now, upon my Lady's picture over the great chimney-piece, a weird shade falls from some old tree, that turns it pale, and flutters it, and looks as if a great arm held a veil or hood, watching an opportunity to draw it over her." (It is significant to recall that Lady Dedlock is usually characterized as wearing a veil.) Compare the following passage, from the opening paragraph of the book, describing London in November: "Smoke lowering down from chimney-pots, making a soft black drizzle, with flakes of soot in it as big as full-grown snow-flakes—gone into mourning, one might imagine, for the death of the sun." The portrait passage continues: "But, of all the shadows in Chesney Wold, the shadow in the long drawing-room upon my Lady's picture is the first to come, the last to be disturbed. At this hour and by this light it changes into threatening hands raised up, and menacing the handsome face with every breath that stirs" (chapter 40).

The laconic Mr. Tulkinghorn, whose clothes "never shine"—"Mute, close, irresponsive to any glancing light, his dress is like himself" (chapter 2)—becomes that shadow: "Interposed between her and the fading light of day in the now quiet street, his shadow falls upon her, and he darkens all before her" (chapter 48). He figures here not merely in his own person but also in his function as the vehicle of my Lady's secret.

What is this "shadow" which destroys Lady Dedlock and Richard, and which comes dangerously close to destroying Esther and Ada as well?

III

We are dealing here, as I hope will soon become evident, with Dickens's attitudes toward the problem of evil. There is misery, frustration, despair, treachery, and cruelty enough in the world of *Bleak House*, with some left over. What is the cause? Whose is the guilt? It is clear that Dickens finds the caricatured version of Calvinistic orthodoxy represented by Esther's aunt, and the spurious religiosity of the other hypocrites of the book who hide from the consequences of their actions behind a mask of piety, inadequate as an explanation. Since the conventional doctrine of inherited guilt and divine salvation is so easily perverted by those with secrets to hide and fears to quench, Dickens shifts the focus from the metaphysical to the human realm, preferring the more immediate to the remoter source, where we can get a good look at heaven and hell as they prosper on earth.[5] It is not our being born which corrupts us, he feels, but our refusal to accept moral responsibility. This doctrine of secular sin and redemption is the premise of Jarndyce's character and is what Esther comes, through much suffering, to learn.

It is ironic that she, who feels responsible for a guilt which is not hers, has to unlearn the conventional explanation which has been foisted upon her by her aunt, while those who avoid responsibilities which *are* theirs under the same aegis, must learn to accept them. Esther is a sacrificial victim in the sense that she carries the load of guilt belonging to others, as well as the burden of the hypocritical creed by which they justify their evasions. Redemption is found, however, not for the community by virtue of her vicarious atonement but rather for Esther herself when she learns, through Jarndyce's good offices, to refuse at last her role as victim.

It is not grace, prayer, or ritual, then, which redeems us, but rather the personal benevolence of a good man, a man who unselfishly recognizes and acts upon his role as a responsible human being in a society where one mortal's fate hinges so closely upon the actions of another. And it is a face-to-face benevolence, pragmatic rather than theoretical and doctrinal. Accordingly, we find in this novel, as I hope to illustrate in full, a group of characters and images representing the irresponsibles, an opposing group representing decent human values, and a third group representing the victims of the first, who either perish or are redeemed in time by the second.

Thus we may hazard, as a preliminary hypothesis, that the shadow symbolizes that perversion of piety which evades personal responsibility either by pretending to assume cosmic responsibility or by seeking sanctions in precedent and usage rather than in immediate human necessity: the "fashionable world" of the Dedlocks, completely oblivious to the human suffering around it; Mrs. Jellyby and her missionary work in Africa; Mrs. Pardiggle distributing temperance pamphlets to the brick-makers at St. Albans; the Reverend Mr. Chadband's religious oratory; Miss Barbary and the pietism which masks her frustration and resent-ment; the Court of Chancery and its soul-destroying mountains of red tape. Look about you and do what you can to alleviate suffering, Dickens seems to be saying, and do not bother your head about dogma, custom, tradition, distant lands, or the universe.

The second major symbol embodying Dickens' concept of personal responsibility is, appropriately enough, the titular image of the house. "Bleak House" is an ironic label here much in the same way that "Satis House" is an ironic label in *Great Expectations:* while the latter was once happy and thriving, it is now corrupt and decaying, its name point-ing up the grotesque incongruity; thus Mr. Jarndyce has retained the no longer appropriate name for his house as a grim reminder that present happiness can easily revert, if care is not taken scrupulously to avoid legal entanglements, to the old-time misery.

Both the literal and the symbolic uses to which this house image is put are implied in Richard's response to Esther's question as to why he cannot settle down once and for all: "You know why not, Esther. If you were living in an unfinished house, liable to have the roof put on or taken off—to be from top to bottom pulled down or built up—to-morrow, next day, next week, next month, next year—you would find it hard to rest or settle. So do I. Now? There's no now for us suitors" (chapter 37). Literal, be-cause, as we shall see, the action involves a number of contrasts between disorderly, decaying houses and orderly, healthy ones; symbolic, because these contrasts, when taken together with this simile of Richard's, embody a moral significance basic to the problem of guilt and responsibility.

If we arrange what appear to be the three major areas of conflict found in the narrative proper in order from the least inclusive to the most, we shall find that the overall problem of responsibility and security, which the house image symbolizes, grows in significance with increasing uni-versality of reference: (1) the relationship between parents and children (there are seven orphans and fifteen sets of parents and children); (2) that between the law and the citizen (the Court of Chancery and its victims); and (3) that between the privileged and the underprivileged (the Dedlocks and the denizens of the brickfields and Tom-all-Alone's). Literal parenthood—house and family—as a situation epitomizing responsibility thus develops into an emblem of responsibility in general,[6] so that the rich might be conceived of as the "parent" of the poor and Chancery as that of its suppliants (Richard and Ada are, of course, literally wards of the Court). And the point is that, on all three levels, the parent refuses to acknowledge and fulfill his responsibility, to take care of his "house," with the result that the balance must be righted—someone has to pay.

Beginning then with literal houses—those which actually contain families—we move from houses as they reflect the conditions in which children are raised, to the law as the "house" of its citizens, and then to the socio-economic situation as the "house" of the nation as a whole. In so far as these houses are sturdy and healthy or decayed and falling apart, just so far has responsibility been accepted or denied. The significance of this Chinese-box-like structure lies in its relation to the web of themes Dickens weaves between the warp of image and the woof of idea. These themes can be stated, since the action hinges on contrasts, as order-disorder (in houses, in Chancery, in lives), responsibility-irresponsibility (between parents and children, the rich and the poor, the law and its victims), and security-insecurity (regarding the blighted development of the children involved). As the novel advances it soon becomes evident that certain people, places, and actions are aligning themselves in significant ways according to these contrasts.

IV

This alignment can therefore be expressed in terms of two headings, derived from the contrasts symbolized by the two main houses in which Esther is involved—Bleak House and Chesney Wold. Abstracting these contrasts from the temporal flow of the plot for analytical purposes, we may construct a spatial design, with the Chesney Wold alignment proceeding downward from left to right (descent), and that of Bleak House progressing upward to the right therefrom (ascent). At the very bottom of the pit formed by this design we find the secular inferno of the book (death and rebirth)—the brickfields, Chancery, its grisly parody in Krook's Court, and Tom-all-Alone's—symbolized by poverty, disease, madness, fog, and death.

Bleak House is consequently the home of a moral order which is symbolized by its physical order (keys) and the prevailing imagery of gardens, light, and music which surrounds its presentation. The sympathetic people and places which function in the same cluster are John Jarndyce, Esther, Ada, "Charley," Alan Woodcourt, Caddy and Prince (music), the Bagnets and their home (music), and Boythorn and his estate (gardens).

Chesney Wold, on the other hand, is the home of irresponsibility and corruption (though overlaid by conventions of chivalry), which is symbolized by the ominous footsteps on the Ghost's Walk and the permeation of rain and dampness. This interpretation is borne out by the satirical presentation of those who live there, a group in direct contrast to that belonging to the Bleak House alignment. Here we have the pompous Sir Leicester Dedlock ("deadlock" or, metaphorically, delay, postponement, frustration); the tigerish Mlle. Hortense; the vain and vapid Volumnia with her necklace and rouge; and the rest of the fashionable and shabby genteel relations. In the same cluster belong the irresponsible shams: Mr. Turveydrop, Mrs. Jellyby, Mrs. Pardiggle, Skimpole, and Chadband (metaphorically, the oily bear); the lawyers and their assistants: Tulkinghorn, Kenge and Carboy, Guppy, Jobling, Vholes (cat, coffin, and vampire are the metaphors associated here); and the Smallweeds (metaphorical spiders and monkeys). The function of this alignment is symbolized by the prevailing imagery of predatory animals, bad air, smells, drizzle, soot, snow, sleet, and mud.

Taking Esther, despite her modest protestations, as the protagonist of the book,[7] we shall see that she is inextricably entangled in sins she did not commit and a guilt she did not incur. Accordingly, in unlearning the doctrines of perverted piety, she makes a symbolic descent down the left side of the book's symbolic structure (her mother presides at Chesney Wold), becoming involved in the death and disease of the inferno (her mother's letters to Captain Hawdon, her father, and the crucial document in the Jarndyce case finally turn up at Krook's), and thereupon experiences an ascent and rebirth, symbolized by her changed appearance and marriage to Woodcourt. She is thus, as we have seen, the secular sacrificial vessel or moral scapegoat of Dickens' world, her career embodying dramatically the rejection of the conventional view of original sin and the acceptance of individual responsibility. Her destruction of the "shadow" is indeed prefigured in her surname, "summer sun"— "wherever Dame Durden went, there was sunshine and summer air" (chapter 30)—and the literal elements of her character and personality reinforce the thematic contrast: she is orderly and neat, modest and firm, devoted and humble, with a strong sense of responsibility and moral obligation.

V

It now remains to trace out some of the strands of image and idea which form the intricate pattern of this symbolic design. Beginning with sin, guilt, and descent on the Chesney Wold side of our spatial design, we see that the Court of Chancery "has its decaying houses and its blighted lands in every shire," and "that there is not an honourable man among its practitioners who would not give . . . the warning, 'Suffer any wrong that can be done you, rather than come here!'" (chapter 1). This is a curiously secular echo of the motto inscribed above the gates of Dante's Inferno which strikes fear in every heart: *Lasciate ogni speranza, voi ch'entrate!*

In the second chapter Dickens swings our attention to "the world of fashion": "It is not so unlike the Court of Chancery, but that we may pass from the one scene to the other [on this same miry afternoon], as the crow flies. Both the world of fashion and the Court of Chancery are things of precedent and usage." The next paragraph concludes, "It is a deadened world, and its growth is sometimes unhealthy for want of air." On the following page Chesney Wold and its environs are characterized by "a stagnant river" (the symbolic river of death?), "moist air," "falling rain," a "mouldy" church, and "damp walls."

When Esther first meets Ada in Chancery, she remarks: "It touched me, that the home of such a beautiful young creature should be represented by that dry official place. The Lord High Chancellor, at his best, appeared so poor a substitute for the love and pride of parents" (chapter 3). They spend the night with the Jellybys: "The evening was . . . very cold, and the rooms had . . . a marshy smell" (chapter 4). The next morning they visit Mr. Krook, who explains: "You see I have so many things here . . . of so many kinds, and all . . . wasting away and going to rack and ruin. . . . And I have a liking for rust and must and cobwebs. . . . That's the way I've got the ill name of Chancery. *I* don't mind" (chapter 5). Visiting also Miss Flite, they hear her whisper: "The only other lodger; . . . a law-writer. The children in the lanes here, say he has sold himself to the devil" (chapter 5). And this person, of course, turns out to be Esther's father.

At Bleak House, benignly assigning her a parent she doesn't have, the enchanting Mr. Skimpole rhapsodizes upon Ada: "We will not call such a lovely young creature as that, who is a joy to all mankind, an orphan. She is the child of the universe." To which Mr. Jarndyce replies: "The universe . . . makes rather an indifferent parent, I'm afraid" (chapter 6). Speaking later of poor Tom Jarndyce, whose heir he was, Mr. John Jarndyce explains, by way of associating the parent-house imagery with Chancery, Ada's "parent": "this was his house, Esther. When I came here, it was bleak indeed. . . . It had been called, before his time, the Peaks. He gave it its present name, and lived here shut up: day and night poring over the wicked heaps of papers in the suit." A desk littered with disorderly heaps of papers becomes another symbol of moral disorder, as we may note in reference to Richard and his legal documents, Mrs. Jellyby and her philanthropic correspondence, Krook's Court with its "old parchmentses and papers" in stock, and Chancery itself with its bags of wills, affidavits, and writs. Mr. Jarndyce continues: "In the meantime the place became dilapidated. . . . When I brought what remained of him [he shot himself] home here, the brains seemed to me to have been blown out of the house too; it was so shattered and ruined" (chapter 8).

On the next page he tells Esther about "some property of ours . . . in the city of London . . . which is much at this day what Bleak House was then." From his description of this "property" a significant link is established in our symbolic alignment: "It is a street of perishing blind houses, with their eyes stoned out; . . . the stone steps to every door (and every door might be Death's Door) turning stagnant green. . . . Although Bleak House was not in Chancery, its master was, and it was stamped with the same seal." This street is, of course, Tom-all-Alone's: "Whether 'Tom' is the popular representation of the original plaintiff or defendant in Jarndyce and Jarndyce; or whether Tom lived here when the suit had laid the street waste, all alone, until other settlers came here to join him; or whether the traditional title is a comprehensive name for a retreat cut off from honest company and put out of the pale of hope; perhaps nobody knows" (chapter 16). The image of the rotting house functions symbolically as does that of the littered desk; yet there are significant literal linkages, in terms of plot, as well: the disease which scars Esther's face originates in Tom-all-Alone's, Nemo is buried there, and Lady Dedlock dies there.

Chancery, to Mr. Boythorn, is "an infernal cauldron" and the devil is its "father" (chapter 9). And of course those who, like Tom Jarndyce, Miss Flite, Mr. Gridley, and Richard, become entangled in its snares, have sold their souls to Satan (chapter 10).

The debilitating effect of Chancery upon Richard's personality is outlined by Mr. Jarndyce: "How much of this indecision of character . . . is chargeable on that incomprehensible heap of uncertainty and procrastination on which he has been thrown from his birth, I don't pretend to say; but that Chancery, among its other sins, is responsible for some of it, I can plainly see" (chapter 13). Caddy explains the existence of a similar insecurity and uncertainty in her own home as a result of her mother's "charitable" projects: "nothing but bills, dirt, waste, noise, tumbles downstairs, confusion, and wretchedness" (chapter 14). Dickens's themes are disorder and irresponsibility, then, and his imagery and plot are working them out on several related levels.

At work weaving this complex web of secular guilt, Dickens exclaims rhetorically: "What connexion can there be, between the place in Lincolnshire, the house in town, the Mercury in powder, and the whereabouts of Jo the outlaw with the broom? . . . What connexion can there have been between many people in the innumerable histories of this world, who, from opposite sides of great gulfs, have, nevertheless, been very curiously brought together!" (chapter 16). And we recall the many passages scattered throughout where he warns "the fashionable world" accusingly of its unacknowledged involvement in the disease and decay of the slums, which are poised ready to infect it as well (see, for example, chapter 46). This, as we shall see, is the ghost which stalks by the Dedlocks' windows, growing more and more ominous as the story progresses; and this is the shadow of which Lady Dedlock's shame is but another symbol.

The ghost also dogs Richard who, because of "the uncertainties and delays of the Chancery suit," has "something of the careless spirit of a gamester, who felt that he was part of a great gaming system." He asserts, pathetically: "I don't know how it is; I seem to want something or other to stand by" (chapter 17). Similarly, Skimpole is involved in this silent conspiracy of irresponsibility: "I always wondered [says Esther] . . . whether he ever thought of Mrs. Skimpole and the children, and in what point of view they presented themselves to his cosmopolitan mind. So far as I could understand, they rarely presented themselves at all" (chapter 18). And a visit to his house is described: "It was in a state of dilapidation quite equal to our expectation. Two or three of the area railings were gone" (chapter 43).

But the tragic irony here is that all are responsible for the inferno of human guilt almost in direct proportion to their pretended disengagement. Even the kindly Mr. Snagsby "sickens in body and mind," as he and Mr. Bucket pay a visit to Tom-all-Alone's, "and feels as if he were going, every moment deeper down, into the infernal gulf" (chapter 22). And the imagery reminds us once again of Dante: "By the noisome ways through which they descended into that pit, they gradually emerge from it; the crowd flitting, and whistling, and skulking about them, until they come to the verge. . . . Here, the crowd, like a concourse of imprisoned demons, turns back, yelling, and is seen no more" (chapter 22). It is a "desert region unfit for life and blasted by volcanic fires" (chapter 46).

And thus, with a house full of neglected children, does Mrs. Jellyby ironically shirk her responsibilities: "Now, if my public duties were not a favourite child to me, if I were not occupied with large measures on a vast scale, these petty details might grieve me very much, Miss Summerson" (chapter 23). The shock of this irony is even more palpable to Esther in Chancery itself: "to see all that full dress and ceremony, and to think of the waste, and want, and beggared misery it represented; . . . this was so curious and self-contradictory to me . . . that it was at first incredible, and I could not comprehend it. . . . There seemed to be no reality in the whole scene, except poor little Miss Flite, the madwoman, standing on a bench, and nodding at it" (chapter 24).

Richard's death is foreknown. Mr. Vholes, who looks at him as "if he were making a lingering meal of him with his eyes," reassures his client: " 'This desk is your rock, sir!' Mr. Vholes gives it a rap, and it sounds as hollow as a coffin" (chapter 39). Further on, he "gauntly stalked to the fire, and warmed his funeral gloves" (chapter 45). Esther, going to visit Richard and Ada, remarks: "I thought there were more funerals passing along the dismal pavements, than I had ever seen before." Coming to their apartment, conveniently located near Chancery, she sees "Richard's name in great white letters on a hearse-like panel." And his nemesis has swallowed him completely: "Thus we came to Richard, poring over a table covered with dusty bundles of papers which seemed to me like dusty mirrors reflecting his own mind" (chapter 51).

Finally, Lady Dedlock, in desperate flight from the revelation of her guilt, finds her way to the brickfields: "On the waste, where the brick-kilns are burning with a pale blue flare . . . and the mill in which the gaunt blind horse goes round all day, look[s] like an instrument of human torture;—traversing this deserted blighted spot, there is a lonely figure with the sad world to itself, pelted by the snow and driven by the wind, and cast out, it would seem, from all companionship" (chapter 56). And the infernal imagery comes full turn when the Jarndyce case is finally "settled": "Our suspense was short; for a break up soon took place in the crowd, and the people came streaming out looking flushed and hot, and bringing a quantity of bad air with them" (chapter 65). The fashionable world, we recall, is a deadened world, and its growth is sometimes unhealthy for want of air.

VI

Coming now to the paradisal ascent of our spatial design, we find that the Bleak House side of the balance sheet presents a much brighter picture. Esther and Ada, after their night at the Jellybys' and visit to Krook's and Miss Flite's, finally embark (with Richard) on their way to St. Albans: "We went our way [westward] through the sunshine and the fresh air. . . . And when a waggon with a train of beautiful horses, furnished with red trappings and clear-sounding bells, came by us with its music, I believe we could all three have sung to the bells, so cheerful were the influences around" (chapter 6). This image recurs more than once, in connection with Esther's keys, for she becomes transformed into Dame Durden, Bleak House's manager: "It was not for me to muse over bygones, but to act with a cheerful spirit and a grateful heart. So I said to myself, 'Esther, Esther, Esther! Duty, my dear!' and gave my little basket of housekeeping keys such a shake, that they sounded like little bells, and rang me hopefully to bed" (chapter 6). Keys and music are the symbols here of responsibility, order, and security: "Every part of the house was in such order, and every one was so attentive to me, that I had no trouble with my two bunches of keys" (chapter 8). And, overwhelmed with gratitude toward Mr. Jarndyce, Esther finds herself giving way unwarrantably to an excess of emotion: "But I gave the housekeeping keys the least shake in the world as a reminder to myself, and folding my hands in a still more determined manner on the basket, looked at him quietly" (chapter 8). These are truly keys to the gates of the earthly Paradise!

John Jarndyce, guardian and benefactor of whichever of the world's orphans he can rescue without calling any undue attention to himself, is an almost universal parent substitute: " 'Dear cousin John,' said Ada, on his shoulder, 'my father's place can never be empty again. All the love and duty I could ever have rendered to him, is transferred to you' " (chapter 13). Esther also "blesses the Guardian who is a Father to her!" (chapter 17). (And perhaps one of the most serious flaws in the book develops as a result of Jarndyce's attempted shift in role: surely he cuts a sorry figure as a lover, and Esther's humility of acceptance is a bit more than even she can bear for very long. In having Jarndyce give her to Woodcourt, Dickens alleviates this distress somewhat, but the image of Mr. Jarndyce has undergone in the process a fatally incongruous complication.)

Associated in the same thematic cluster with Bleak House are to be found the homes of Mr. Boythorn and the Bagnets. The former is thus described: "Such stillness and composure reigned within the orderly precincts of the old red wall; . . . and the wall had such a ripening influence that where, here and there high up, a disused nail and scrap of list still clung to it, it was easy to fancy that they had mellowed with the changing seasons, and that they had rusted and decayed according to the common fate" (chapter 18). It is interesting to contrast this mellow ripeness, in harmony with nature, with the corruption and rottenness found on the infernal side of our structure. And Mr. George sees in the Bagnets the ideal of domestic order: "Mat blows away at his bassoon, and you're respectable civilians one and all. . . . Family people. Children growing up. Mat's old mother in Scotland, and your old father somewhere else, corresponded with; and helped a little; and—well, well!" (chapter 27). Here the bassoon joins the bells and keys as a paradisal music-symbol.

Returning to Mr. Jarndyce we note, if we have not already done so, that his image begins to take on the aspects of a secular deity: he is indeed the metaphorical god of the book's earthly paradise, for Esther reflects, "And all this happiness shone like a light from one central figure" (chapter 44).

VII

But this happiness and this light were not won without cost. Having traced the relation between the literal contrasts established in the action, the accompanying symbolic imagery, and the quality of the moral values suggested thereby, we may now chart the course of Esther's transition from accepting a guilt for which she is not responsible to a rejection of that guilt in favor of a more secular attitude, which is a corollary of that acceptance of responsibility which Dickens urges on the hypocrites of the book.

The child of an illicit liaison, she was brought up during her earliest years by her handsome, but unsmiling, aunt, who stamped upon her impressionable consciousness an inexplicable, albeit palpable, sense of guilt. As a very young girl Esther was aware of her separateness: she never went out, and her only friend was her doll (chapter 3). "Why," she asks pathetically on her birthday, "am I so different from other children, and why is it my fault, dear godmother?" Miss Barbary (the sister of Honoria, Esther's mother), whose neurotic obsession takes the form of an extremely literalistic Calvinism, replies: " 'Your mother, Esther, is your disgrace, and you were hers. . . . I have forgiven her'; but her face did not relent; 'the wrong she did to me, and I say no more of it, though it was greater than you will ever know—than anyone will ever know, but I, the sufferer. For yourself, unfortunate girl, orphaned and degraded from the first of these evil anniversaries, pray daily that the sins of others be not visited upon your head, according to what is written.' " Then she adds: "Submission, self-denial, diligent work, are the preparations for a life begun with such a shadow on it. You are different from other children, Esther, because you were not born, like them, in common sinfulness and wrath. You are set apart." And the poor child confides to her doll "that I would try, as hard as ever I could, to repair the fault I had been born with (of which I confessedly felt guilty and yet innocent), and would strive as I grew up to be industrious, contented, and kind-hearted, and to do some good to some one, and win some love to myself if I could." The Biblical gloom is deepened by Miss Barbary's excessive reaction to Esther's recitation of this passage from St. John: "So when they continued asking him, he lifted up himself and said unto them, He that is without sin among you, let him first cast a stone at her!" (chapter 3).

Upon the death of her aunt, Esther leaves Windsor for Miss Donny's house at Reading, under the auspices of the ubiquitous Mr. Jarndyce: "A day or two before, I had wrapped the dear old doll in her own shawl, and quietly laid her—I am half ashamed to tell it—in the garden-earth, under the tree that shaded my old window. I had no companion left but my bird, and him I carried with me in his cage" (chapter 3). Certainly symbolic of transition, this little ritual probably signifies the final death of her childish innocence (the doll), and the awareness of guilt to be re-deemed (the caged bird) which she carries with her. Although this in-terpretation is largely guesswork, it is perhaps significant that the names of Miss Flite's birds—Hope, Joy, Youth, Peace, Rest, Life (the Bleak House cluster); Dust, Ashes, Waste, Want, Ruin, Despair, Madness, Death (the Chesney Wold cluster); Cunning, Folly, Words, Wigs, Rags, Sheepskin, Plunder, Precedent, Jargon, Gammon (Chancery and Krook's cluster) (Spinach is extra!)—collapse as in a chord the melody of the plot as a whole (chapter 14). Read backwards, these names represent the course of Esther's purgation.

The story of the Ghost's Walk also plays its part here because, as we shall see, Esther becomes identified with it. The tale is told by Mrs. Rouncewell: During the "wicked days" of the Civil War, Sir Morbury Dedlock was on the royal side, but his wife, sad to relate, was implicated in the rebel cause. After her brother was killed by one of the Morbury clan, she became crippled, "and from that hour began to pine away." She took to limping up and down on the terrace at Chesney Wold, where she finally collapsed: "I will die here where I have walked. And I will walk here, though I am in my grave. I will walk here until the pride of this house is humbled. And when calamity, or when disgrace is coming to it, let the Dedlocks listen for my step!" (chapter 7). Can we not say, there-fore, that the "shadow" under which Esther was born and which she must come to reject, represents—by virtue of the fact that her mother deserted her and her father for the security and esteem which marriage into this family ostensibly offered—the lamentable effects of moral irresponsibility on its victims, having its roots in illicit passion, bloodshed, violence, family disloyalty, and national civil war?

The crucial elements associated with Esther's "guilt," then, are the Biblical allusions to the sins of others, the gloomy birthday, the buried doll, the bird, and the ghostly footsteps at Chesney Wold. Let us trace them, by way of establishing this cluster empirically, as they recur.

Mr. Guppy, who has begun to suspect that there is some connection between Lady Dedlock's portrait and Esther's appearance, has proposed marriage to Esther, darkly hinting at all the things he has it in his power to do for her. She refuses, of course, but not without having been rather upset by his words: "In short, I was in a flutter for a little while; and felt as if an old chord had been more coarsely touched than it ever had been since the days of the dear old doll, long buried in the garden" (chapter 9). She has again been made dimly aware, in effect, of her mysterious involvement in someone else's guilt.

Lady Dedlock, scouring Tom-all-Alone's in search of her lover's grave, gives Jo a gold piece for his guidance. Meanwhile, the rain patters upon the terrace at Chesney Wold, and Mrs. Rouncewell exclaims to Rosa: "And in all these years I never heard the step upon the Ghost's Walk, more distinct than it is tonight" (chapter 16). This ominous step is repeated on another level by Mr. Jarndyce, who mutters thoughtfully, "I think it must be somewhere written that the virtues of the mothers shall, occasionally, be visited on the children, as well as the sins of the fathers" (chapter 17; he is referring to Ada). This latter, we recall, is an echo in reverse of the Biblical warning uttered by Miss Barbary.

Visiting the Boythorn place, which neighbors upon Chesney Wold, Esther has occasion to go to the Lincolnshire church. As the service begins—"Enter not into judgment with thy servant, O Lord, for in thy sight"—Lady Dedlock enters. Esther's heart flutters as their eyes meet for one brief revelatory instance: "And, very strangely, there was something quickened within me, associated with the lonely days at my godmother's; yes, away even to the days when I had stood on tiptoe to dress myself at my little glass, after dressing my doll." Listening to the ritual reminds her of Miss Barbary, and she senses a confused resemblance between the two women: "And yet I—I, little Esther Summerson, the child who lived a life apart, and on whose birthday there was no rejoicing— seemed to arise before my own eyes, evoked out of the past by some power in this fashionable lady, whom I not only entertained no fancy that I had ever seen, but whom I perfectly well knew I had never seen until that hour" (chapter 18).

The Biblical tone is deepened as Bucket inquires about the brickmaker's ill-fated child, whom Esther has had occasion to commiserate: " 'Why, what age do you call that little creature?' says Bucket. 'It looks as if it was born yesterday.' He is not at all rough about it; and as he turns his light gently on the infant, Mr. Snagsby is strangely reminded of another infant, encircled with light, that he has seen in pictures" (chapter 22). This reference to the Christ child, born innocent into a world of guilt, reinforces ironically the pity we feel for the poor victims of the book's secular hell.

Esther's emotional attitude toward Lady Dedlock develops into a full-fledged ambivalence: "I think I admired her with a kind of fear; and I know that in her presence my thoughts always wandered back, as they had done at first, to that old time of my life" (chapter 23). And Lady "deadlock," the leader of the "fashionable world," sits by her hearth and gazes desolately into the fire: "Does she listen to the Ghost's Walk, and think what step does it most resemble? A man's [Captain Hawdon's]? A woman's [Miss Barbary's]? The pattering of a little child's feet [Esther's], ever coming on—on—on?" (chapter 28).

The sense of her mysterious guilt firmly established, Esther has as yet no choice in her effort to "atone" for it but to be industrious, contented, and kind-hearted—until she is caught up in a purgative force whose presence and power she is not to realize until its course has been run.

The watershed moment which precedes Esther's transforming illness is unmistakably symbolized by the following passage. It describes the scenic outlook as she and "Charley" hasten out to the brickfields of St. Albans to rescue the fatally ill Jo, from whom she is destined eventually to catch the smallpox (via "Charley"):

> It was a cold, wild night, and the trees shuddered in the wind. . . . The sky had partly cleared, but was very gloomy—even above us, where a few stars were shining. In the north and north-west [toward Chesney Wold], where the sun had set three hours before [the light of the dying sun has been encountered at least twice by now], there was a pale dead light both beautiful and awful [Lady Dedlock's emblem]; and into it long sullen lines of cloud waved up, like a sea stricken immovable as it was heaving [surely a strikingly appropriate implication regarding Lady Dedlock's languor which masks her frozen passion]. Towards London, a lurid glare overhung the whole dark waste; and the contrast between these two lights, and the fancy which the redder light engendered of an unearthly fire [Inferno], gleaming on all the unseen buildings of the city, and on all the faces of its many thousands of wondering inhabitants, was as solemn as might be (chapter 31).

That she is midway on her symbolic course from Chesney Wold to Bleak House is further borne out by her reaction to these ghastly lights: "I had no thought, that night . . . of what was soon to happen to me. But I have always remembered since, that when we had stopped at the garden-gate to look up at the sky, and when we went upon our way, I had for a moment an undefinable impression of myself as being something different from what I then was" (chapter 31).

She becomes deathly sick shortly thereafter: "And now come and sit beside me for a little while, and touch me with your hand. For I cannot see you, Charley; I am blind" (so ends chapter 31). And the first phrase which opens the next chapter is: "It is night in Lincoln's Inn." The death of the sun, the encroaching shadow, and the fog of Chancery are now implicitly embodied in Esther's blindness,[8] and this darkness is the heritage of shame which she must reject through her sacrificial involvement in guilt, disease, and poverty. Dickens's prediction that the contagion of Tom-all-Alone's would spread to Chesney Wold is now symbolically fulfilled.

The imagery of transition is further developed: "In falling ill, I seemed to have crossed a dark lake, and to have left all my experiences, mingled together by the great distance, on the healthy shore." Her redemptive journey finds its image in that of the ascent: "I laboured up colossal staircases, ever striving to reach the top, and ever turned." And in the delirium of her fever she has a startling hallucination. "Dare I hint at that worse time when, strung together somewhere in great black space, there was a flaming necklace, or ring, or starry circle of some kind, of which I was one of the beads! And when my only prayer was to be taken off from the rest, and when it was such inexplicable agony and misery to be a part of the dreadful thing?" (chapter 35).[9] Thus is symbolized her unwitting involvement in the vicious circle of sin.

Recuperating at Boythorn's, she discovers the secret of her shameful birth, and wishes that she had never been born—recalling the stern words of her godmother: "Pray daily that the sins of others be not visited upon your head." She realizes her sacrificial role: "I could not disentangle all that was about me; and I felt as if the blame and the shame were all in me, and the visitation had come down." She goes out for a walk to Chesney Wold: "The way was paved here, like the terrace overhead, and my footsteps . . . made an echoing sound upon the flags. . . . My echoing footsteps brought it suddenly in to my mind that there was a dreadful truth in the legend of the Ghost's Walk; that it was I, who was to bring calamity upon the stately house; and that my warning feet were haunting it even then." But the beginning of her moral ascent and transition from the conventional view to the secular, symbolized by her recuperation, is demonstrated here by her developing attitudes:

> For I saw very well that I could not have been intended to die, or I should never have lived; not to say should never have been reserved for such a happy life. I saw very well how many things had worked together, for my welfare; and that if the sins of the fathers were sometimes visited upon the children, the phrase did not mean what I had in the morning feared it meant. I knew I was as innocent of my birth as a queen of hers; and that before my Heavenly Father I should not be punished for birth, nor a queen rewarded for it. I had had experience, in the shock of that very day, that I could, even thus soon, find comforting reconcilements to the change that had fallen on me (chapter 36).

Her rebirth is signalized by the recurrence of the music-key image: "I was perfectly restored to health and strength; and finding my housekeeping keys laid ready for me in my room, rang myself in as if I had been a new year, with a merry little peal." Having symbolically rejected her inheritance of guilt, she is now ready for "a general new beginning altogether," and can take her place securely in the world of moral order and domestic harmony (chapter 38). Mr. Jarndyce, as secular godhead, is the vehicle of this redemption from "the stern prediction of my childhood," and his "generosity rose above my disfigurement, and my inheritance of shame" (chapter 44).

The step on the Ghost's Walk, however, walks down my Lady, in spite of her frantic flight to the brickfields and back to Tom-all-Alone's, while the darkness hangs and the thawed snow drips upon Chesney Wold (chapter 58). Seeing her mother dead on her lover's grave at Tom-all-Alone's, Esther's reaction is curiously significant: "I saw before me, lying on the step, the mother of the dead child." Lady Dedlock had changed clothes with Jenny, the poor brickmaker's wife, whose infant had recently died. In addition to symbolizing the ultimate identity here of rich and poor, this clothing-switch allows Esther, in her confusion, to signalize the death of her own guilt as the child of sin—much in the same way that she ritually buried her doll long ago as a farewell to her innocence. But Lady Dedlock has paid the final cost: "And it was my mother, cold and dead" (chapter 59).

Since she has ironically lost her beauty in the process of redemption (as Oedipus loses his sight to "see"), Esther's scarred face symbolizes her transition from a world of original sin to that of personal responsibility: "Whatever little lingerings may have now and then revived in my mind, associated with my poor old face, had only revived as belonging to a part of my life that was gone—gone like my infancy or my childhood" (chapter 61). Her transformation is complete.

And at the very close of the story, when Esther is established in her own little "Bleak House," Mr. Jarndyce pays a visit: "As I sat looking fixedly at him, and the sun's rays descended, softly shining through the leaves, upon his bare head, I felt as if the brightness on him must be like the brightness of the Angels." She embraces him and weeps: " 'Lie lightly, confidently, here, my child,' said he, pressing me gently to him. 'I am your guardian and your father now. Rest confidently here.' " The sun has dispelled the shadow and Esther has finally reached peace: "Soothingly, like the gentle rustling of the leaves; and genially, like the ripening weather; and radiantly and beneficently, like the sunshine; he went on" (chapter 64).

NOTES

Notes

CHAPTER 1

INTRODUCTION: PLURALISTIC CRITICISM

1. See, e.g., John Crowe Ransom, "The Understanding of Fiction," *Kenyon Review*, 12 (1950), 189–218; Cleanth Brooks, "The Criticism of Fiction," in *A Shaping Joy* (London: Methuen, 1971), pp. 143–165; and William J. Handy, *Modern Fiction: A Formalist Approach* (Carbondale: Southern Illinois University Press, 1971).

2. Strictly speaking, a poetics in the Aristotelian sense can be constructed only for a particular form and not for such a broad and loosely conceived genre as fiction. Thus Robert Scholes is mistaken when he hopes for a treatise on fiction to be modeled on the *Poetics*, in "Toward a Poetics of Fiction: An Approach Through Genre," *Novel*, 2 (1969), 101–111.

3. My chief texts are R. S. Crane, ed., *Critics and Criticism* (Chicago: University of Chicago Press, 1952); R. S. Crane, *The Languages of Criticism and the Structure of Poetry* (Toronto: University of Toronto Press, 1953), and *The Idea of the Humanities*, 2 vols. (Chicago: University of Chicago Press, 1967).

4. See, e.g., Oscar Cargill, *Toward a Pluralistic Criticism* (Carbondale: Southern Illinois University Press, 1965); and Lee T. Lemon, *The Partial Critics* (New York: Oxford University Press, 1965).

5. Northrop Frye, of course, has enunciated this principle in its most recent and influential form. See "The Archetypes of Literature," in *Fables of Identity* (New York: Harcourt, Brace and World, 1963), pp. 7–20. On pp. 9–10 he says, "The assumption [of total coherence] refers to the science, not to what it deals with." But on p. 12 he says, "It is clear that criticism cannot be systematic unless there is a quality in literature which enables it to be so, an order of words corresponding to the order of nature in the natural sciences." These ideas are repeated in his *Anatomy of Criticism* (1957; rpt. New York: Atheneum, 1966). A. N. Whitehead's definition of the "fallacy of misplaced concreteness" applies to Frye's notion of literary criticism as well as to his notion of science: we should avoid confusing our formulations of reality with reality itself (as Frye himself indicates in his first-quoted statement). See Whitehead, *Science and the Modern World* (New York, 1925), pp. 74–82, 85.

6. Crane, *Languages*, pp. 23–25.

7. Charles Augustin Sainte-Beuve, "Chateaubriand," *Nouveaux Lundis* (July 22, 1862); Hippolyte-Adolphe Taine, "Introduction," *History of English Literature* (1863).

8. Kathleen Nott analyzes and criticizes this bias in *The Emperor's Clothes* (Bloomington: Indiana University Press, 1958).

9. Cf. Murray Krieger, *The New Apologists for Poetry* (Minneapolis: University of Minnesota Press, 1956), pp. 11 ff.; and René Wellek in *Literary History and Literary Criticism*, ed. Leon Edel (New York: New York University Press, 1964), p. 81: "There is simply a standard of rightness which allows us to call these theories preposterous. How do we know that they are wrong? The answer can only be that the text tells us what is right and wrong reading."

10. See Meyer H. Abrams, "What's the Use of Theorizing About the Arts?" in *In Search of Literary Theory*, ed. Morton W. Bloomfield (Ithaca: Cornell University Press, 1972), pp. 1–54.

11. This charge is levied, interestingly enough, both by old conservatives and new radicals. Cf. Robert Hillyer, *In Pursuit of Poetry* (New York: McGraw-Hill, 1960), p. 194; and the following issues of *College English* concerned entirely or in part with neo-Marxism in literary studies: 31 (March 1970), 32 (November 1970), 33 (April 1972), 33 (May 1972), and 34 (November 1972).

12. Cf. Morris R. Cohen and Ernest Nagel, *An Introduction to Logic and Scientific Method* (New York, 1934), chap. 14; Frank Ford Nesbit, *Language, Meaning and Reality* (New York: Exposition Press, 1955), pp. 172–173; and Ralph Ross, with Ernest Van Den Haag, *Symbols and Civilization* (1957; adapted New York: Harcourt, Brace and World, 1962), chap. 3.

13. Cf. Gerald Holton, "Presupposition in the Construction of Theories," in *Science and Literature: New Lenses for Criticism*, ed. Edward M. Jennings (New York: Doubleday Anchor, 1970), pp. 237–262; and William H. Gass, "In Terms of the Toenail," in *Fiction and the Figures of Life* (New York: Random House Vintage, 1971), pp. 55–76.

14. Cf. Krieger, *Apologists*, pp. 148–155.

15. Cf. R. S. Crane, *Languages*, pp. 54–57, 165; *Humanities*, 1: 174; 2: 36, 48–60, 226–229.

16. Cf. Crane, *Languages*, pp. 31, 40.

17. Cf. Crane, *Languages*, pp. 30–32; *Humanities*, 2: 201–202, 236–260.

18. The following schemes have been helpful in the formulation of my own: Meyer H. Abrams, *The Mirror and the Lamp* (1953; rpt. New York: Norton, 1958), chap. 1; Crane, "Questions and Answers in the Teaching of Literary Texts," in *Humanities*, 2: 176–193; Richard McKeon, "The Philosophical Bases of Art and Criticism," in *Critics and Criticism*, pp. 463–545; and Elder Olson, "An Outline of Poetic Theory," in *Critics and Criticism*, pp. 546–566.

19. See Crane on Stanley Edgar Hyman's syncretism, *Languages*, pp. 28–29.

20. Olson, "William Empson, Contemporary Criticism, and Poetic Dic-

tion," and "Poetic Theory," in *Critics and Criticism*, pp. 45–82, especially p. 61; p. 549.

21. Crane, *Humanities*, 2: 104–105, 110–112, 116, 145–146, 150.

22. Crane, "Questions and Answers," *Humanities*, 2: 182–183.

23. Olson, "Empson," in *Critics and Criticism*, pp. 54–56.

CHAPTER 2

PLURALISM EXEMPLIFIED: *GREAT EXPECTATIONS* AND *THE GREAT GATSBY*

1. As in F. R. Leavis, "The Novel as Dramatic Poem" (series), *Scrutiny*, 14 (1947), 185–203; 15 (1948), 209–21; 17 (1950), 38–53, 203–20; 17 (1951), 318–30; 18 (1951), 18–31, 18 (1951–2), 197–210; 18 (1952) 273–87; 19 (1952), 15–30; and the various well-known works of G. Wilson Knight on Shakespeare.

2. For a representative range of comment on and a bibliography of *Great Expectations*, see Richard Lettis and William E. Morris, eds., *Assessing "Great Expectations": Materials for Analysis* (San Francisco: Chandler, 1963), especially the articles by Dorothy Van Ghent, G. Robert Stange, Thomas E. Connolly, and Robert B. Partlow, Jr. See also John H. Hagan, Jr., "Structural Patterns in Dickens' *Great Expectations*," *English Literary History*, 21 (1954), 54–66.

3. Cf. Frederick J. Hoffman, ed., *"The Great Gatsby": A Study* (New York: Scribners, 1962); Ernest H. Lockridge, ed., *Twentieth Century Interpretations of "The Great Gatsby"* (Englewood Cliffs, New Jersey: Prentice-Hall, 1968); and Henry Dan Piper, ed., *Fitzgerald's "The Great Gatsby": The Novel, The Critics, The Background* (New York: Scribners, 1970).

4. On the point of view in *Great Expectations*, cf. Connolly and Partlow in Lettis and Morris; on *The Great Gatsby*, cf. Robert Ornstein, Thomas A. Hanzo, Gary J. Scrimgeour, and David L. Minter in Lockridge, and also Richard Foster, "The Way to Read *Gatsby*," in *Sense and Sensibility in Twentieth Century Writing*, ed. Brom Weber (Carbondale: Southern Illinois University Press, 1970), pp. 94–108.

5. Cited by Diana Trilling in *The Viking Portable D. H. Lawrence* (New York, 1946), p. 19.

6. *The Liberal Imagination* (1950; rpt. New York: Doubleday Anchor, 1953), pp. 61–64.

7. In Hoffman, *"Great Gatsby": A Study*, pp. 244–262.

8. This is, of course, a controversial point, for the reliability of Nick Carraway has been narrowly questioned (see n. 4, above). I believe that Fitzgerald intended Nick to be reliable, for otherwise the novel would be a shambles, but that he did not fully succeed in his intention, which accounts for the ambiguities which many critics have uncovered.

CHAPTER 3

PRINCIPLES OF FORMAL ANALYSIS

1. Cf. also the Russian formalists, e.g. Boris Tomashevsky, "Thematics," in *Russian Formalist Criticism*, trans. Lee T. Lemon and Marion J. Reis (Lincoln: University of Nebraska Press, Bison Books, 1965), pp. 61–98; and the proponents of the French new novel, e.g. Alain Robbe-Grillet, "On Several Obsolete Notions," in *For a New Novel*, trans. Richard Howard (New York: Grove Press, 1965), pp. 25–47.

2. *New Apologists for Poetry*, chaps. 4–5 et passim.

3. See Frank Kermode, *Romantic Image* (1957; rpt. New York: Knopf Vintage, 1964).

4. Yvor Winters, *In Defense of Reason*, 3rd ed. (New York, 1947); Robert Hillyer, *In Pursuit of Poetry* (New York: McGraw-Hill, 1960), pt. 4; Richard Foster, *The New Romantics* (Bloomington: Indiana University Press, 1962).

5. Cf. Geoffrey H. Hartman's title essay in his *Beyond Formalism* (New Haven: Yale University Press, 1970), pp. 42–57.

6. Cf. Crane, *Languages*, p. 190.

7. See Handy, *Modern Fiction*, for an interesting recent attempt to extend New Critical concepts to include fiction within poetic categories. In contrast is the Chicagoans' attempt to extend Aristotelian concepts to include poetry within the dramatic and fictional categories of "action" etc. Cf. Olson, "William Empson, Contemporary Criticism, and Poetic Diction," and "Poetic Theory," in Crane, *Critics*, pp. 45–82, 546–566; and Crane, *Languages*, pp. 175–176.

8. Cf. Ross, *Symbols and Civilization*, chap. 3; and Holton, "Presupposition," pp. 237–262, especially pp. 246–247.

9. Cf. W. K. Wimsatt, Jr., "The Chicago Critics: The Fallacy of the Neoclassic Species," in *The Verbal Icon* (1954; rpt. New York: Noonday, 1958), pp. 41–65; E. D. Hirsch, Jr., *Validity in Interpretation* (New Haven: Yale University Press, 1967); and Olson, "Poetic Theory," especially pp. 557–561.

10. My interpretation of the *Poetics* owes much to Olson, "The Poetic Method of Aristotle: Its Powers and Limitations," in Alan S. Downer, ed., *English Institute Essays, 1951* (New York: Columbia University Press, 1952), pp. 70–94; and Crane, *Languages*, pp. 39–79. See also Kenneth A. Telford, *Aristotle's "Poetics": Translation and Analysis* (Chicago: Regnery Gateway, 1961).

11. Since the appearance of the well-known "Intentional Fallacy" essay by Wimsatt and Monroe C. Beardsley in 1946 (rpt. in *The Verbal Icon*), much ink has been spilled over this issue. Hirsch's *Validity* is a notable recent attempt to defend intention as a critical concept, while Beardsley argues his position afresh in *The Possibility of Criticism* (Detroit: Wayne State University Press, 1970), pp. 16–37. See also Rosemarie Maier, " 'The Intentional

Fallacy' and the Logic of Literary Criticism," *College English*, 32 (1970), 135–145.

12. Thus Aristotle's concept is the opposite of the mimetic or representational theory of art it is often taken to be. See Richard McKeon, "Literary Criticism and Concept of Imitation in Antiquity," in Crane, *Critics*, pp. 147–175.

13. "The Poetic Method of Aristotle."

14. Cf. August Boeckh, *On Interpretation and Criticism*, trans. and ed. John Paul Pritchard (Norman: University of Oklahoma Press, 1968), pp. 98–99. Boeckh's book derives from his lectures during 1809–1865 and was published in its 2nd ed. in 1886.

15. See Olson in Crane, *Critics*, pp. 564–565, n. 8.

16. "The Critical Monism of Cleanth Brooks," in *Critics*, pp. 83–107, especially pp. 86–93.

17. Cf. Walter Jackson Bate, *From Classic to Romantic* (Cambridge, 1946); and Meyer H. Abrams, *The Mirror and the Lamp* (1953; rpt. New York: Norton, 1958).

18. See Harold C. Martin, ed., *Style in Prose Fiction: English Institute Essays, 1958* (New York: Columbia University Press, 1959); David Lodge, *Language of Fiction* (New York: Columbia University Press, 1966); Karl Kroeber, *Styles in Fictional Structure* (Princeton: Princeton University Press, 1971); and Seymour Chatman, ed., *Literary Style: A Symposium* (New York: Oxford University Press, 1971).

CHAPTER 4

THEORY OF STRUCTURE AND END

1. Cf. Crane, "The Concept of Plot and the Plot of *Tom Jones*," in *Critics*, pp. 616–647.

2. *Anatomy of Criticism*, p. 52. Cf. Michael McCanles, "Mythos and Dianoia: A Dialectical Methodology of Literary Form," in *Literary Monographs*, ed. Eric Rothstein, vol. 4 (Madison: University of Wisconsin Press, 1971), pp. 1–88.

3. Forster, *Aspects of the Novel* (New York, 1927), chap. 5; Crane, "Concept of Plot."

4. Crane, *Languages*, pp. 151–153.

5. "The Philosophy of Composition" (1846).

6. See, e.g., Krieger, *New Apologists for Poetry*, pp. 148–155.

7. "Poetic Theory," pp. 555–557.

8. Crane, *Languages*, pp. 60–61.

9. *Biographia Literaria* (1817), chap. 14.

10. Cf. William Chace Greene, *The Choices of Criticism* (Cambridge: MIT Press, 1965), chap. 3.

11. "Concept of Plot," p. 632.

12. "Tragedy and the Common Man," rpt. in *Two Modern American Tragedies: Reviews and Criticism of "Death of a Salesman" and "A Streetcar Named Desire,"* ed. John D. Hurrell (New York: Scribner's, 1961), pp. 38–40.

13. "Mr. Bennett and Mrs. Brown," in *The Captain's Death Bed and Other Essays*, 1st American ed. (New York: Harcourt, Brace, 1950).

CHAPTER 5

FORMS OF THE PLOT

1. "Concept of Plot," p. 622.

2. See, e.g., Ralph Harper, *The World of the Thriller* (Cleveland: Press of Case Western Reserve University, 1969); Julian Symons, *The Detective Story in Britain*, Writers and their Work, no. 145 (London: Longmans, Green, 1962); J. O. Bailey, *Pilgrims Through Space and Time* (New York, 1947); Basil Davenport, ed., *The Science Fiction Novel* (Chicago: Advent, 1969); and Darko Suvin, "On the Poetics of the Science Fiction Genre," *College English*, 34 (1972), 372–382.

3. The term is Olson's, "Poetic Theory," p. 555.

4. I owe this term, and much else besides, to my colleague, Charles A. McLaughlin of the University of Connecticut.

5. For a broader treatment of the topic, see W. J. Harvey, *Character and the Novel* (Ithaca: Cornell University Press, 1965).

6. Cf. the theoretical principles developed by Richard Levin in *The Multiple Plot in English Renaissance Drama* (Chicago: University of Chicago Press, 1971).

7. *Ernest Hemingway: A Life Story* (New York: Scribners, 1969), pp. 152–155.

8. For a reading of the book with Cohn as the protagonist, however, see William L. Vance, "Implications of Form in *The Sun Also Rises*," in *The Twenties*, ed. Richard E. Langford and William E. Taylor (DeLand, Fla.: Everett Edwards, 1966), pp. 87–91.

9. See Peter L. Irvine, "The 'Witness' Point of View in Fiction," *South Atlantic Quarterly*, 69 (1970), 217–225, for a discussion of Nick, Marlow, Jack, and Ishmael.

10. *Languages*, pp. 182–183.

11. See Robert E. Kuehn, ed., *Twentieth Century Interpretations of "Lord Jim"* (Englewood Cliffs, New Jersey: Prentice-Hall, 1969); and J. Hillis Miller, "The Interpretation of *Lord Jim*," in *The Interpretation of Narrative: Theory and Practice*, ed. Morton W. Bloomfield, Harvard English Studies 1 (Cambridge, Mass.: Harvard University Press, 1970), pp. 211–228.

12. See Albert E. Stone, Jr., ed., *Twentieth Century Interpretations of "The Ambassadors"* (Englewood Cliffs, New Jersey: Prentice-Hall, 1969).

13. Updike has said: "I like middles. It is in middles that extremes clash,

where ambiguity restlessly rules." Quoted by Richard Locke in his review of *Rabbit Redux, New York Times Book Review*, 14 Nov. 1971, p. 24.

14. On the picaresque, see Robert Alter, *Rogue's Progress* (Cambridge, Mass.: Harvard University Press, 1965); Stuart Miller, *The Picaresque Novel* (Cleveland: Press of Case Western Reserve University, 1967); Claudio Guillén, *Literature as System* (Princeton: Princeton University Press, 1971), pp. 71–220; and Ulrich Wicks, "Picaro, Picaresque: The Picaresque in Literary Scholarship," *Genre*, 5 (1972), 153–216.

15. S. L. Goldberg, *The Classical Temper* (London: Chatto and Windus, 1961), pp. 286–287.

16. Harry Levin, *James Joyce*, rev. ed. (1941; Norfolk, Conn.: New Directions, 1960), pp. 177–180.

17. Letter dated July 26, 1937, rpt. in Hoffman, *"Great Gatsby": A Study*, pp. 179–184.

18. Cf. Julian Markels, "Dreiser and the Plotting of Inarticulate Experience," in *Theodore Dreiser, "Sister Carrie": An Authoritative Text, Backgrounds and Sources, Criticism*, ed. Donald Pizer (New York: Norton Critical ed., 1970), pp. 527–541.

CHAPTER 6

MIMETIC AND DIDACTIC

1. For discussions of this distinction, cf. Olson, in Crane, *Critics*, pp. 63–68, 587–592; Crane, *Languages*, pp. 156–180. See also Sheldon Sacks, *Fiction and the Shape of Belief* (Berkeley: University of California Press, 1964), for an extended treatment of similar issues in relation to eighteenth-century fiction.

2. It is true, of course, that much critical dissension has arisen in the interpretation of this story, but I have taken the position favorable to Capt. Vere which is borne out by a study of the ms. Cf. Harrison Hayford and Merton M. Sealts, Jr., ed., *"Billy Budd: Sailor (An Inside Narrative)," by Herman Melville, Reading Text and Genetic Text, Edited from the Manuscript with Introduction and Notes* (Chicago: University of Chicago Press, 1962), pp. 34–39. See also Milton R. Stern, *The Fine Hammered Steel of Herman Melville* (Urbana: University of Illinois Press, 1957), chap. 5; William T. Stafford, ed., *Melville's "Billy Budd" and the Critics* (San Francisco: Wadsworth, 1961); and Howard P. Vincent, ed., *Twentieth Century Interpretations of "Billy Budd"* (Englewood Cliffs, New Jersey: Prentice-Hall, 1971).

3. "A Dialogue on Symbolism" in Crane, *Critics*, p. 592.

4. Cf. C. S. Lewis, *The Allegory of Love* (London, 1936); Edwin Honig, *Dark Conceit: The Making of Allegory* (1959; rpt. Cambridge, Mass.: Walker-deBerry, Boar's Head, 1960); and Angus Fletcher, *Allegory* (Ithaca: Cornell University Press, 1964).

5. Cf. Lewis MacNeice, *Varieties of Parable* (Cambridge: Cambridge University Press, 1965).

6. For somewhat differing views, cf. Irving Howe, *Politics and the Novel* (New York: Horizon Meridian, 1957), pp. 235–251; and Joseph Slater, "The Fictional Values of *1984*," in *Essays in Literary History*, ed. Rudolf Kirk and C. F. Main (New York: Russell and Russell, 1965), pp. 249–264.

7. Here, too, much critical debate has been generated over whether Carrie develops or not: cf. Kenneth S. Lynn and Pizer in *Theodore Dreiser*, pp. 509–517, 567–573; and the extended debate between Hugh Witemeyer and Rupin W. Desai in *PMLA*, 86 (1971), 236–240; 87 (1972), 309–310, 514.

8. But cf. Eugene F. Timpe, "*Ulysses* and the Archetypal Feminine," in *Perspectives in Literary Symbolism*, ed. Joseph Strelka (University Park: Pennsylvania State University Press, 1968), pp. 199–213.

9. Cf. F. O. Matthiessen, *American Renaissance* (1941; rpt. New York: Oxford University Press, 1968), p. 416.

10. *Classical Temper*, chap. 7.

11. But cf. Peter K. Garrett, *Scene and Symbol from George Eliot to James Joyce* (New Haven: Yale University Press, 1969), pp. 256 ff.

12. *Classical Temper*, pp. 16, 98, 197.

13. See Francis Lee Utley, Lynn Z. Bloom, and Arthur F. Kinney, ed., *Bear, Man, and God: Seven Approaches to William Faulkner's "The Bear"* (New York: Random House, 1964), especially the essays by Herbert A. Perluck, Olga Vickery, and David H. Stewart for negative views of Ike's repudiation. Cf. also William Van O'Connor, "The Wilderness Theme in Faulkner's 'The Bear'," in *William Faulkner: Three Decades of Criticism*, ed. Frederick J. Hoffman and Olga Vickery (1960; rpt. New York: Harcourt, Brace and World, Harbinger, 1963), pp. 322–330; and Richard P. Adams, "Focus on William Faulkner's 'The Bear': Moses and the Wilderness," in *American Dreams, American Nightmares*, ed. David Madden (Carbondale: Southern Illinois University Press, 1970), pp. 129–135.

14. Cf. Seymour L. Gross, ed., *A "Scarlet Letter" Handbook* (San Francisco: Wadsworth, 1960), especially the essays by Stuart P. Sherman and F. I. Carpenter; Kenneth S. Lynn, ed., *"The Scarlet Letter": Text, Sources, Criticism* (New York: Harcourt, Brace and World, 1961); and John C. Gerber, ed., *Twentieth Century Interpretations of "The Scarlet Letter"* (Englewood Cliffs, New Jersey: Prentice-Hall, 1968), especially the essay by Charles Child Walcutt.

15. Various kinds of distinctions have been made recently between open and closed forms: cf. Robert M. Adams, *Strains of Discord: Studies in Literary Openness* (Ithaca: Cornell University Press, 1958); Alan Friedman, *The Turn of the Novel* (New York: Oxford University Press, 1966), chap. 2; Frank Kermode, *The Sense of an Ending* (New York: Oxford University Press, 1967); James Gindin, *Harvest of a Quiet Eye* (Bloomington: Indiana University Press, 1971); and Sharon Spencer, *Space, Time and Structure in*

the Modern Novel (New York: New York University Press, 1971), chaps. 2–3. Gindin reverses my own distinction, saying that the open-ended novel is nonjudgmental and hence mimetic, while the closed novel is doctrinaire and hence didactic.

16. Cf. Joseph Warren Beach, *The Twentieth Century Novel* (New York, 1932), pt. 5.

17. Cf. James R. Baker and Arthur P. Ziegler, Jr., ed., *William Golding's "Lord of the Flies": Casebook Edition* (New York: Putnam's, n.d.), especially the interviews with Golding by James Keating and Frank Kermode, pp. 189–195, 197–200; William Golding, "Fable," in *The Hot Gates and Other Occasional Pieces* (New York: Harcourt, Brace and World, 1966), pp. 85–101; and David Spitz, "Power and Authority: An Interpretation of Golding's *The Lord of the Flies*," *Antioch Review*, 30 (1970), 21–33.

18. Cf. J. O. Bailey, *Pilgrims Through Space and Time* (New York, 1947), chap. 7; Fletcher Pratt, Rosalie Moore, Isaac Asimov, and Philip Wylie in *Modern Science Fiction*, ed. Reginald Bretnor (New York: Coward-McCann, 1953), pp. 73–90, 91–118, 157–196, 221–241; Michel Butor, "The Crisis in the Growth of Science Fiction," in *Inventory*, ed. Richard Howard (New York: Simon and Schuster, 1968), pp. 224–232; Robert A. Heinlein, "Science Fiction: Its Nature, Faults and Virtues," in Davenport, *Science Fiction Novel*, pp. 14–48; Robert M. Philmus, *Into the Unknown* (Berkeley: University of California Press, 1970), pp. 19–20; and Suvin, "Poetics of Science Fiction," pp. 372–382.

19. Cf. Tzvetan Todorov, *The Fantastic*, trans. Richard Howard (Cleveland: Press of Case Western Reserve University, 1973).

20. See Erich Fromm, *The Forgotten Language* (1951; rpt. New York: Grove Press, 1957), pp. 235–241. See also Butor, "On Fairy Tales," in Howard, *Inventory*, pp. 211–223.

CHAPTER 7

THEORY OF TECHNIQUES

1. Cf. Olson and Crane in *Critics*, pp. 562–563, 623; and Crane, *Languages*, pp. 76–77, 163–164.

2. Cf. Crane, *Languages*, pp. 151–153.

3. "The Obscurity of the Poet," in *Poetry and the Age* (1953; rpt. New York: Knopf Vintage, 1955), pp. 3–25.

4. Cf. Olson, "A Letter on Teaching Drama," *Chicago Review*, 2 (1957), 80–91.

5. See Sister M. Corona Sharp, *The Confidante in Henry James* (Notre Dame: University of Notre Dame Press, 1963).

6. Forster, *Aspects of the Novel*, chap. 8; Brown, *Rhythm in the Novel* (Toronto: University of Toronto Press, 1950). Cf. Crane, *Languages*, pp. 144–146.

CHAPTER 8

POINT OF VIEW

1. *The Writing of Fiction* (New York, 1925), pp. 43 ff.

2. *The Art of the Novel: Critical Prefaces*, ed. R. P. Blackmur (New York, 1934), pp. 37–38, 300.

3. *The Method of Henry James* (New Haven, 1918), pp. 56–71.

4. *The Craft of Fiction* (1921; rpt. New York: Scribner's, 1954), pp. 62, 66–67, 71–72, 139–143. Ramon Fernandez, in *Messages*, trans. Montgomery Belgion (1926; trans. New York, 1927), pp. 61–69, makes a very keen distinction, apparently independently, between the "novel" (showing) and the "recital" (telling). See also Morris Roberts, *Henry James's Criticism* (Cambridge, Mass., 1929).

5. See. e.g., R. Brimley Johnson, ed., *Novelists on Novels* (London, 1928); Rollo Walter Brown, ed., *The Writer's Art* (Cambridge, Mass., 1921); Nassau William Senior, *Essays on Fiction* (London, 1864); Sidney Lanier, *The English Novel* (Baltimore, 1945); Walter Besant, *The Art of Fiction* (Boston, 1885); Henry James, *The Art of Fiction*, ed. Morris Roberts (New York, 1948); R. L. Stevenson, "A Humble Remonstrance" (1884); Daniel Greenleaf Thompson, *The Philosophy of Fiction in Literature* (New York, 1890); W. D. Howells, *Criticism in Fiction* (New York, 1891); Brander Matthews, *Aspects of Fiction* (New York, 1896); Bliss Perry, *A Study of Prose Fiction* (Boston, 1902); Frank Norris, *The Responsibilities of the Novelist* (New York, 1903); Richard Stang, *The Theory of the Novel in England 1850–1870* (New York: Columbia University Press, 1959); and Kenneth Graham, *English Criticism of the Novel 1865–1900* (Oxford: Clarendon Press, 1965).

6. Pp. 15–21, 31–38, 49 ff., 66–72, 101.

7. *Writing of Fiction*, pp. 11–16, 43–46, 70–75, 86–95.

8. *Aspects of the Novel*, pp. 118–128. Cf. Henry Burrowes Lathrop, *The Art of the Novelist* (London, 1921); Thomas H. Uzzell, *Narrative Technique*, 3rd ed. (1923; New York, 1934); Grant Overton, *The Philosophy of Fiction* (New York, 1928); Carl H. Grabo, *The Technique of the Novel* (New York, 1928); and Van Meter Ames, *Aesthetics of the Novel* (Chicago, 1928).

9. *Point Counter Point* (1928), chap. 22.

10. *Twentieth Century Novel*, pp. 14–15, et passim. Cf. Ford Madox Ford, "Techniques," *Southern Review*, 1 (1935), 20–35; and James Weber Linn and Houghton Wells Taylor, *Foreword to Fiction* (New York, 1935).

11. Tate, "The Post of Observation in Fiction," *Maryland Quarterly*, 2 (1944), 61–64; Bentley, *Some Observations of the Art of Narrative* (New York, 1947), pp. 35–39. Cf. Wayne C. Booth, ed., *Robert Liddell on the Novel* (1947, 1953; rpt. Chicago: University of Chicago Press, 1969); and Elizabeth Bowen, "Notes on Writing a Novel" (1945), in *Collected Impressions* (New York: Knopf, 1950), pp. 249–263.

12. Schorer, "Technique as Discovery" (1947, 1948), in *The World We*

Imagine (New York: Farrar, Straus and Giroux, 1968), pp. 3–23; Glasgow, *A Certain Measure* (New York, 1943), pp. 18–19, 41–43, 70, 99, 114, 150, 168, 180–183, 189–192. Cf. René Wellek and Austin Warren, *Theory of Literature*, 3rd ed. (1949; New York: Harcourt, Brace, 1963), chap. 16.

13. Humphrey, *Stream of Consciousness in the Modern Novel* (Berkeley: University of California Press, 1954); Edel, *The Modern Psychological Novel* (1955; rpt. New York: Grove Press, 1959); Chattopadhyaya, *The Technique of the Modern English Novel* (Calcutta: Mukhopadhyay, 1959); Tillotson, *The Tale and the Teller* (London: Hart-Davis, 1959). Cf. Bernard De Voto, *The World of Fiction* (Boston: Houghton Mifflin, 1950); Vincent McHugh, *Primer of the Novel* (New York: Random House, 1950); and A. A. Mendilow, *Time and the Novel* (London: Peter Nevill, 1952).

14. Chicago: University of Chicago Press.

15. For some other reactions to Booth, cf. Peter Swiggert, "Mr. Booth's Quarrel with Fiction," *Sewanee Review*, 71 (1963), 142–159; Henry W. Sams, "Show and Tell," *Journal of General Education*, 17 (1966), 315–329; John Killham, "My Quarrel with Booth," *Novel*, 1 (1968), 267–272; Harold F. Mosher, "Wayne Booth and the Failure of Rhetoric in *The Good Soldier*," *Caliban*, 6 (1969), 49–52; and John Ross Baker, "From Imitation to Rhetoric: The Chicago Critics, Wayne C. Booth, and *Tom Jones*," *Novel*, 6 (1973), 197–217." See also Booth, "*The Rhetoric of Fiction* and the Poetics of Fictions," *Novel*, 1 (1968), 105–117.

16. Kumar, *Bergson and the Stream of Consciousness Novel* (New York: New York University Press, 1962); Graham, *English Criticism*; Tolley, "The Teller and the Tale," in *Approaches to the Novel*, ed. John Colmer (London: Oliver and Boyd, 1966), pp. 18–38; Scholes and Kellogg, *The Nature of Narrative* (New York: Oxford University Press, 1966); Rubin, *The Teller in the Tale* (Seattle: University of Washington Press, 1967); Miller, "Three Problems of Fictional Form," in *Experience in the Novel: Selected Papers from the English Institute*, ed. Roy Harvey Pearce (New York: Columbia University Press, 1968), pp. 21–48, and *The Form of Victorian Fiction* (Notre Dame: University of Notre Dame Press, 1968); Taylor, *The Passages of Thought* (New York: Oxford University Press, 1969). Cf. also Angus Wilson, "The Novelist and the Narrator," *English Studies Today: Second Series*, ed. G. A. Bonnard (Berne: Francke Verlag, 1961), pp. 43–50; John E. Tilford, "Point of View in the Novel," *Emory University Quarterly*, 20 (1964), 121–130; Jacques Souvage, *An Introduction to the Study of the Novel* (Ghent: E. Story-Scientia P.V.B.A., 1965), chaps. 9–16; and Jonathan Raban, *The Technique of Modern Fiction* (Notre Dame: University of Notre Dame Press, 1969).

17. Van Rossum-Guyon, "Point de vue, ou perspective narrative: Théories et concepts critiques," *Poetique*, 4 (1970), 476–497; Kern, *Existential Thought in Fictional Technique* (New Haven: Yale University Press, 1970); Spencer, *Space, Time and Structure*; Stanzel, *Narrative Situations in the*

Novel, trans. James P. Pusack (Bloomington: Indiana University Press, 1971); Hernadi, *Beyond Genre* (Ithaca: Cornell University Press, 1972). Cf. also Kroeber, *Styles in Fictional Structure*.

18. Franklin, *Autobiography* (fr. 1771 on; Franklin died 1790); Butler, first published posthumously in 1903 (Butler died 1902, but ceased work on this novel in 1884).

19. Cf. Barbara Hardy, *The Appropriate Form* (London: Athlone Press, 1964), chap. 3; Evelyn Hardy, "The Self-Destructive Element in Tess's Character," in *Thomas Hardy, "Tess of the D'Urbervilles": An Authoritative Text, Hardy and the Novel, Criticism*, ed. Scott Elledge (New York: Norton Critical ed., 1965), pp. 447–450; Albert J. LaValley, ed., *Twentieth Century Interpretations of "Tess of the D'Urbervilles"* (Englewood Cliffs, New Jersey: Prentice-Hall, 1969); Duane Edwards, "Chance in Hardy's Fiction," *Midwest Quarterly*, 11 (1970), 427–441; and Roy Morrell, "Thomas Hardy and Probability," in *On the Novel*, ed. B. S. Benedikz (London: Dent, 1971), pp. 75–92.

20. Alter, *Fielding and the Nature of the Novel* (Cambridge, Mass.: Harvard University Press, 1968). Cf. Edward A. Kearns, "Omniscient Ambiguity: The Narrators of *Moby-Dick* and *Billy Budd*," *Emerson Society Quarterly*, 58 (1970), 117–120; and Floyd C. Watkins, *The Flesh and the Word* (Nashville: Vanderbilt University Press, 1971), p. 239.

21. Cf. Godfrey Frank Singer, *The Epistolary Novel* (1933; rpt. New York: Russell and Russell, 1963); Frank Gees Black, *The Epistolary Novel in the Late Eighteenth Century* (Eugene, Oregon, 1940); Robert Adams Day, *Told in Letters* (Ann Arbor: University of Michigan Press, 1966); Ira Konigsberg, *Samuel Richardson and the Dramatic Novel* (Lexington: University of Kentucky Press, 1968); and Natascha Wurzbach, ed., *The Novel in Letters 1678–1740* (Coral Gables: University of Miami Press, 1969). See also Erich Kahler, *The Inward Turn of Narrative*, trans. Richard and Clara Winston (1957, 1959, 1970: trans. Princeton: Princeton University Press, 1973), pp. 143 ff.; Bertil Romberg, *Studies in the Narrative Technique of the First-Person Novel* (Stockholm: Almquist and Wicksell, 1962); Peter L. Irvine, "The Witness Point of View in Fiction," *South Atlantic Quarterly*, 69 (1970), 217–225; and David Goldknopf, *The Life of the Novel* (Chicago: University of Chicago Press, 1972), chaps. 2–5.

22. There is an intermediate category, albeit a minor one, to be mentioned here. It is characterized by the fact that, although the protagonist tells his own story, he tells it not to the reader but rather to someone of his acquaintance who thereupon relays it to the reader in his own person. Something of a combination "I" as witness and "I" as protagonist frame, as with Jim and Marlow in parts of *Lord Jim*.

23. For an extended treatment of this technique, see Mitchell A. Leaska, *Virginia Woolf's Lighthouse* (New York: Columbia University Press, 1970).

24. I am in fundamental agreement with Ellsworth Mason, who main-

tains that the Joyce canon is dramatic from beginning to end, displaying no progression from lyric to epic to drama, as has commonly been supposed. See "Joyce's Categories," *Sewanee Review*, 61 (1953), 427–432.

25. Cf. Ora Segal, *The Lucid Reflector: The Observer in Henry James' Fiction* (New Haven: Yale University Press, 1969).

26. Cf. Louis Hasley, "The Stream-of-Consciousness Method," *Catholic World*, 146 (1937), 210–213; and Lawrence Bowling, "What is the Stream of Consciousness Technique?" *PMLA*, 65 (1950), 333–345. Bowling makes a very useful distinction between mental analysis, interior monologue, and stream of consciousness: the latter two represent the more and the less articulate manner of directly rendering mental states, the first the indirect omniscient manner. See also Gleb Struve, "Monologue Interieur: The Origins of the Formula and the First Statement of its Possibilities," *PMLA*, 69 (1954), 1101–1111; Humphrey; Dorrit Cohn, "Narrated Monologue: Definition of a Fictional Style," *Comparative Literature*, 18 (1966), 97–112; and Scholes and Kellogg, chapter 5.

27. Cf. E. M. Halliday, "Hemingway's Narrative Perspective," in *Ernest Hemingway: Critiques of Four Major Novels*, ed. Carlos Baker, (New York: Scribner's, 1962), pp. 174–182.

28. For discussion of the reverse of this problem, see Herman M. Weisman, "An Investigation of Methods and Techniques in the Dramatization of Fiction," *Speech Monographs*, 19 (1952), 48–59.

29. Cf. David I. Grossvogel, *The Limits of the Novel: Evolutions of a Form from Chaucer to Robbe-Grillet* (Ithaca: Cornell University Press, 1968); Alter, *Fielding*; Kermode, *Sense of Ending*, chap. 1.

30. *William Faulkner*, Evergreen Pilot no. 6 (New York: Grove Press, 1961), p. 35.

31. But cf. Hugo M. Reichard, "The Patusan Crises: A Revaluation of Jim and Marlow," *English Studies*, 49 (1968), 547–552. See also William M. Bonney, "Joseph Conrad and the Discontinuous Point of View," *Journal of Narrative Technique*, 2 (1972), 99–115.

32. Cf. Wayne C. Booth, "The Self-Conscious Narrator in Comic Fiction Before *Tristram Shandy*," *PMLA*, 67 (1952), 163–185.

33. Schorer, "Technique as Discovery"; Trilling, introduction to *Portable D. H. Lawrence*, pp. 19–20.

34. Lawrence, quoted in Trilling; E. T., *D. H. Lawrence: A Personal Record* (London: 1935), pp. 201–204.

35. Merton, *The Seven Storey Mountain* (1948; rpt. New York: Signet, 1952), pp. 255–256; Gordon, "Some Readings and Misreadings," *Sewanee Review*, 61 (1953), 384–407. Cf. also William M. Schutte, ed., *Twentieth Century Interpretations of "A Portrait of the Artist as a Young Man"* (Englewood Cliffs, New Jersey: Prentice-Hall, 1968).

36. *Rhetoric of Fiction*, chap. 13.

37. Cf. Kermode, *Sense of Ending*, pp. 107–113.

CHAPTER 9
WHAT MAKES A SHORT STORY SHORT?

1. Cf. Crane, "Varieties of Dramatic Criticism," in *Idea of the Humanities* 2: 215–235; and Elder Olson, "Appendix: The Analysis of Drama," *The Theory of Comedy* (Bloomington: Indiana University Press, 1968), pp. 129–139.

2. See Donald LoCicero, *Novellentheorie: The Practicality of the Theoretical* (The Hague, Paris: Mouton, 1970), for an analysis of the problems involved in defining the novella (mainly with regard to German literature).

3. "Tale Writing—Mr. Hawthorne" (1847), and "The Poetic Principle" (1848).

4. Cf. Theodore A. Stroud, "A Critical Approach to the Short Story," *Journal of General Education*, 9 (1956), 91–100. The present chapter may be read as a companion to Stroud's essay. Cf. also Austin McGiffert Wright, *The American Short Story in the Twenties* (Chicago: University of Chicago Press, 1961), for a theoretical framework similar to my own.

5. "Poetic Theory," p. 560.

6. The term *plot* is being used here in relation to the size of an action, and is not to be confused with the somewhat different uses of the same term in previous chapters.

7. *For a New Novel*. Cf. also Nathalie Sarraute, *The Age of Suspicion* (New York: Braziller, 1963); and Michel Butor, the first four essays in Howard, *Inventory*.

8. Cf. Booth, *Rhetoric of Fiction*, pp. 62–63; Ben F. Stoltzfus, *Alain Robbe-Grillet and The New French Novel* (Carbondale: Southern Illinois University Press, 1964), especially pp. 42–66; Bruce Morrissette, "The Evolution of Narrative Viewpoint in Robbe-Grillet," *Novel*, 1 (1967), 24–37; Emily Zants, *The Aesthetics of the New Novel in France* (Boulder: University of Colorado Press, 1968), especially pp. 31–35; Edith Kern, *Existential Thought and Fictional Technique* (New Haven: Yale University Press, 1970), pp. 241–243; Leo Bersani, *Balzac to Beckett* (New York: Oxford University Press, 1970), pp. 272–279; and Vivian Mercier, *The New Novel* (New York: Farrar, Straus and Giroux, 1971), pp. 164–214.

9. Cf. Bruce F. Kawin, *Telling It Again and Again: Repetition in Literature and Film* (Ithaca: Cornell University Press, 1972).

10. See Fitzgerald's letter of 1925 to Edmund Wilson in *The Crack-Up*, ed. Edmund Wilson (New York, 1945), pp. 270–271. Cf. Tom Burnam, "The Eyes of Dr. Eckleburg: A Re-Examination of *The Great Gatsby*," in *F. Scott Fitzgerald: A Collection of Critical Essays*, ed. Arthur Mizener (Englewood Cliffs, New Jersey: Prentice-Hall, 1963), pp. 104–111.

11. See, e.g., Harry Levin, "Observations on the Style of Ernest Hemingway," in *Contexts of Criticism* (1957; rpt. New York: Atheneum, 1963), pp. 140–167.

12. Similar terms and concepts are used by Paul Goodman in his *Structure of Literature* (Chicago: University of Chicago Press, 1954), but in a slightly different way. I had arrived at my own position independently, before I read this brilliant but puzzling book.

13. Cf. Michel Butor, "Research on The Technique of the Novel," in Howard, *Inventory*, pp. 15–25, for an interesting discussion of sequence in fiction.

14. Frederick L. Gwynn and Joseph L. Blotner, ed., *Faulkner in the University* (1959; rpt. New York: Knopf Vintage, 1965), pp. 3–4, 273, 275–277, 280.

15. See, e.g., Irving Howe, "The Relation Between Part IV and the Rest of *The Bear*," in Utley, Bloom, and Kinney, *Bear, Man and God*, pp. 349–352 (rpt. from Howe's *William Faulkner: A Critical Study* [New York: Random House, 1952], pp. 186–189).

CHAPTER 10
THEORY OF MEANING

1. *Languages*, pp. 189–190.

2. For the relation between the writer's world, the reader's, and reality, cf. Scholes and Kellogg, *Nature of Narrative*, chap. 4. For the principles of consistency and congruence, cf. Hans Meyerhoff, *Time in Literature* (1955; rpt. Berkeley: University of California Press, 1960), pp. 121–135; Ross, *Symbols and Civilization*, pp. 211–238; and Stanley Burnshaw, *The Seamless Web* (New York: Braziller, 1970), chap. 4.

3. Cf. Kenneth Burke, "Psychology and Form," and "Lexicon Rhetoricae," in *Counter-Statement* (1931; rpt. Chicago: University of Chicago Press, 1953), pp. 29–44, 123–183; and H. W. Leggett, *The Idea in Fiction* (London, 1934), chaps. 4, 5, 9.

4. Cf. Kermode, *Sense of Ending*, pp. 102, 116, 117, 129, 138; *Continuities* (New York: Random House, 1968), pp. 10–27; and Gass, "Philosophy and the Form of Fiction," in *Figures of Life*, pp. 3–26.

5. Cf. Wolfgang Köhler, *Gestalt Psychology* (rev. ed. 1947; rpt. New York: New American Library Mentor, n.d.); Norman R. F. Maier and Willard Reninger, *A Psychological Approach to Literary Criticism* (New York, 1933), esp. pp. 36–37; Lancelot Law Whyte, ed., *Aspects of Form* (London: Lund and Humphries, 1951), especially the essays by Konrad Lorenz and Rudolph Arnheim; and Crane, *Idea of the Humanities*, 1: 182–183; 2: 142–144.

6. Cf. Tomashevsky, "Thematics."

7. Cf. Butor, "The Novel as Research," in Howard, *Inventory*, pp. 26–30, especially p. 28.

8. Cf. Kermode, *Sense of Ending*, chaps. 2 and 6; and Ralph Ellison, with James Alan McPherson, "Indivisible Man," *Atlantic*, Dec. 1970, pp. 45–60, esp. 48–49.

9. Cf. Stoltzfus, *Alain Robbe-Grillet.*

10. On the relations between art and science, cf. Ifor Evans, *Literature and Science* (London: Allen and Unwin, 1954); Meyerhoff, *Time in Literature,* chap. 4; Ross, *Symbols and Civilization;* Harry Levin, "Art as Knowledge," in *Contexts of Criticism,* pp. 15–37; Rollo May, ed., *Symbolism in Religion and Literature* (New York: Braziller, 1960); Frank Kermode, "The Myth-Kitty," in *Puzzles and Epiphanies* (New York: Chilmark Press, 1962), pp. 35–39; Aldous Huxley, *Literature and Science* (New York: Harper and Row, 1963); Elizabeth Sewell, *The Human Metaphor* (Notre Dame: University of Notre Dame Press, 1964), pp. 67 ff., 106–107; Jennings, *Science and Literature,* especially the essays by Jacob Bronowski, R. D. Laing et al., Gordon W. Allport, and Gerald Holton; Martin Dyck, "Relativity in Physics and Fiction," in *Studies in German Literature of the Nineteenth and Twentieth Centuries,* ed. Siegfried Mews (Chapel Hill: University of North Carolina Press, 1970), pp. 174–185; and Northrop Frye, *The Stubborn Structure* (Ithaca: Cornell University Press, 1970), first three essays.

11. On the relations between fiction and history, cf. Scholes and Kellogg, pp. 62–63, 120–121, 151; Graham Hough, *An Essay on Criticism* (New York: Norton, 1966), chap. 17; Frank Kermode, "Novel, History and Type," *Novel,* 1 (1968), 231–238; Ursula Brumm, "Some Thoughts on History and the Novel," *Comparative Literature Studies,* 6 (1969), 317–330; Louis O. Mink, "History and Fiction as Modes of Comprehension," *New Literary History,* 1 (1970), 541–558; Robert Champigny, "Implicitness in Narrative Fiction," *PMLA,* 85 (1970), 988–991; Werner Berthoff, "Fiction, History, Myth," in *Fiction and Events* (New York: Dutton, 1971), pp. 30–55; Avrom Fleishman, *The English Historical Novel* (Baltimore: Hopkins Press, 1971), chap. 1; and Thomas Roberts, *When Is Something Fiction?* (Carbondale: Southern Illinois University Press, 1972).

12. Sir Philip Sidney, "An Apology for Poetry" (1583, 1595); Matthew Arnold, "The Function of Criticism at the Present Time" (1864); T. S. Eliot, "The Social Function of Poetry" (1945), in *On Poetry and Poets* (1957; rpt. New York: Noonday, 1961), pp. 3–16. Cf. also Greene, *Choices of Criticism,* chap. 6; and Dorothy Walsh, *Literature and Knowledge* (Middletown, Conn.: Wesleyan University Press, 1969), pp. 136 et passim.

13. Cf. Hartman, *Beyond Formalism,* pp. 42–57.

14. Cf. Kate Millett, *Sexual Politics* (Garden City: Doubleday, 1970), pt. 3; and Norman Mailer, *The Prisoner of Sex* (Boston: Little, Brown, 1971), pp. 91–174.

CHAPTER 11

THEORY OF VISION

1. "Questions and Answers in the Teaching of Literary Texts," in *Idea of the Humanities,* 2: 176–193, especially 186.

2. *E. E. Cummings: The Growth of a Writer* (Carbondale: Southern Illinois University Press, 1964), pp. 4–7.

3. "Questions and Answers."

4. Cf. Weller Embler, *Metaphor and Meaning* (DeLand, Fla.: Everett Edwards, 1966), pp. 12–26.

5. John Casey argues, in *The Language of Criticism* (London: Methuen, 1966), especially p. 157, that there is no necessary connection between the thing expressed and its manner of being expressed, between the structure of reality and that of language.

6. For the relations between psychology and literature, cf. Vernon Lee (Violet Paget), *The Handling of Words, and Other Studies in Literary Psychology* (New York, 1923); Herbert Read, *The Nature of Literature* (New York: Grove Press, 1958 [these essays were actually written much earlier]); Philip Rahv, "Freud and the Literary Mind" (1949), in *Literature and the Sixth Sense* (Boston: Houghton Mifflin, 1969), pp. 150–167; Daniel E. Schneider, *The Psychoanalyst and the Artist* (1950; rpt. New York: New American Library Mentor, 1962); F. L. Lucas, *Literature and Psychology* (1951; rpt. Ann Arbor: University of Michigan Press, 1957); Ernst Kris, *Psychoanalytic Explorations in Art* (1952; rpt. New York: Schocken Books, 1964); Frederick J. Hoffman, *Freudianism and the Literary Mind* (1957; rpt. New York: Grove Evergreen, 1959); Simon O. Lesser, *Fiction and the Unconscious* (1957; rpt. New York: Random House Vintage, 1962); Leslie Y. Rabkin, ed., *Psychopathology and Literature* (San Francisco: Chandler, 1966); Norman H. Holland, *The Dynamics of Literary Response* (New York: Oxford University Press, 1968); and Frederick Crews, ed., *Psychoanalysis and Literary Process* (Cambridge, Mass.: Winthrop, 1970).

7. *Psychoanalysis and the Unconscious* (1921), and *Fantasia of the Unconscious* (1922), rpt. together New York: Viking Compass, 1960.

8. Cf. Diana Spearman, *The Novel and Society* (New York: Barnes and Noble, 1966), who questions the literary-historical assumptions of Ian Watts's *The Rise of the Novel* (Berkeley: University of California Press, 1957); Eugene Vinaver, "The Historical Method in the Study of Literature," in *The Future of the Modern Humanities*, ed. J. C. Laidlaw (Oxford: Modern Humanities Research Association, 1969), pp. 86–105; and Claudio Guillén, *Literature as System* (Princeton: Princeton University Press, 1971), chap. 10.

9. "Questions and Answers."

10. Cf. Henri Peyre, *The Failures of Criticism* (1944; emend. Ithaca: Cornell University Press, 1967), chap. 6; John Press, *The Fire and the Fountain* (1955; rpt. New York: Barnes and Noble, 1966), chap. 2; Ross, chap. 11; and Gass, "The Artist and Society," in *Figures of Life*, pp. 279–288.

11. Cf. William Van O'Connor, *The New University Wits and the End of Modernism* (Carbondale: Southern Illinois University Press, 1963); and Rubin Rabinovitz, *The Reaction Against Experiment in the English Novel 1950–1960* (New York: Columbia University Press, 1967).

12. Cf. Morris Edmund Speare, *The Political Novel* (New York, 1924); Walter Fuller Taylor, *The Economic Novel in America* (Chapel Hill, 1942); Walter B. Rideout, *The Radical Novel in the United States 1900–1954* (1956; rpt. New York: Hill and Wang, 1966); Irving Howe, *Politics and the Novel* (New York: Horizon Meridian, 1957); Gordon Milne, *The American Political Novel* (Norman: University of Oklahoma Press, 1966); and Joseph Blotner, *The Modern American Political Novel 1900–1960* (Austin: University of Texas Press, 1966).

13. Cf. Herbert Marder, *Feminism and Art: A Study of Virginia Woolf* (Chicago: University of Chicago Press, 1968); J. B. Batchelor, "Feminism in Virginia Woolf," in *Virginia Woolf: A Collection of Critical Essays*, ed. Claire Sprague (Englewood Cliffs, New Jersey: Prentice-Hall, 1971), pp. 169–179; and Margaret Blanchard, "Socialization in *Mrs. Dalloway*," with comment by Elaine Reuben, *College English*, 34 (1972), 287–307.

14. "Questions and Answers," pp. 186–187. Cf. also Crane, "Philosophy, Literature, and the History of Ideas," and "Critical and Historical Principles of Literary History," in *Humanities*, 1: 173–187, 2: 45–156 (I also possess, in mimeographed form, three unpublished lectures, given by Crane at the University of Oregon, May 4, 11, 13, 1954, entitled "Literature and the History of Ideas"); Helen Gardner, *The Business of Criticism* (London: Oxford University Press, 1959); René Wellek, *Concepts of Criticism* (New Haven: Yale University Press, 1963); Leon Edel, ed., *Literary History and Literary Criticism* (New York: New York University Press, 1964); Phillip Damon, ed., *Literary Criticism and Historical Understanding* (New York: Columbia University Press, 1967), especially the essay by Robert Marsh, pp. 1–24; Roy Harvey Pearce, *Historicism Once More* (Princeton: Princeton University Press, 1969), especially the title essay, pp. 3–45; Hartman, "Toward Literary History," in *Beyond Formalism*, pp. 356–386; Paul de Man, "Literary History and Literary Modernity," in *Blindness and Insight* (New York: Oxford University Press, 1971), pp. 142–165; and Wesley Morris, *Toward a New Historicism* (Princeton: Princeton University Press, 1972). See also *New Literary History*, a journal devoted to these problems.

15. See, e.g., Walter R. Davis, *Idea and Act in Elizabethan Fiction* (Princeton: Princeton University Press, 1969), for a treatment of sixteenth-century fiction in its own terms rather than in terms of what we think of as "the novel."

16. Cf. J. Hillis Miller, *Charles Dickens: The World of His Novels* (Cambridge, Mass.: Harvard University Press, 1958), chap. 8, especially p. 278; Alan Friedman, *Turn of the Novel*, p. 25; Marshall W. Gregory, "Values and Meaning in *Great Expectations*: The Two Endings Revisited," *Essays in Criticism*, 19 (1969), 402–409; Edwin M. Eigner, "Bulwer-Lytton and the Changed Ending of *Great Expectations*," *Nineteenth Century Fiction*, 25 (1970), 104–108; and Robert A. Greenberg, "On Ending *Great Expectations*," *Papers on Language and Literature*, 6 (1970), 152–162.

17. I am thinking primarily, of course, of Booth, *Rhetoric of Fiction*. But cf. also Barbara Hardy, *Appropriate Form*; and J. Hillis Miller, *The Form of Victorian Fiction* (Notre Dame: University of Notre Dame Press, 1968), pp. 53–92.

18. Fiedler himself calls it "a free-wheeling analytic approach synthesized out of Freud, Jung, and D. H. Lawrence," "Second Thoughts on *Love and Death in the American Novel*: My First Gothic Novel," *Novel*, 1 (1967), 9–11.

CHAPTER 12

SELF AND FAMILY IN "THE METAMORPHOSIS"

1. Charles Neider, ed., *Short Novels of the Masters* (New York: Rinehart, 1948), pp. 44–47.

2. Heinz Politzer, *Franz Kafka: Parable and Paradox* (Ithaca: Cornell University Press, 1962), pp. 65–82, especially 80, makes this same error.

3. My text is in Neider, *Short Novels*, pp. 537–579. Stanley Corngold has translated and edited this story afresh, with notes, documents, critical essays, and bibliography (New York: Bantam, 1972). See also his *The Commentator's Despair: The Interpretation of Kafka's "Metamorphosis"* (Port Washington, New York: Kennikat Press, 1973).

4. Cf. Booth, *Rhetoric of Fiction*, pp. 281–282.

5. The source of my biographical data is Max Brod, *Franz Kafka: A Biography*, trans. G. Humphreys Roberts and Richard Winston, 2nd ed. (1947; New York: Schocken Books, 1960). Extracts from the "Letter," with commentary by Brod, are found in *A Franz Kafka Miscellany: Pre-Fascist Exile*, rev. ed. (1940; New York, 1946), pp. 39–50. The passages quoted are on pp. 43–45. See also Franz Kafka, *Letter to His Father*, bilingual ed., Ernst Kaiser and Eithne Wilkins, eds. (New York: Schocken Books, 1971).

CHAPTER 13

SELF AND SOCIETY IN *THE STRANGER*

1. After completing this study, I found my interpretation largely supported by Robert J. Champigny's pregnant interpretation in *A Pagan Hero*, trans. Rowe Portis (1960; trans. Philadelphia: University of Pennsylvania Press, 1969).

2. Cf. Eugene H. Falk, *Types of Thematic Structure* (Chicago: University of Chicago Press, 1967), chap. 4.

3. For an example of the negative view, see René Girard, "Camus's Stranger Retried," *PMLA*, 79 (1964), 519–533. For a broader range of comment, see Germaine Brée, ed., *Camus: A Collection of Critical Essays* (Englewood Cliffs, New Jersey: Prentice-Hall, 1962).

4. Cf. Elder Olson, "A Dialogue on the Function of Art in Society," *Chicago Review*, 16 (1963–1964), 57–72, especially 65.

5. For the effects of combining business motives with religious values, see Ralph Barton Perry, *Puritanism and Democracy* (New York, 1944), chap. 12.

6. Cf. Roger Shattuck, "Two Inside Narratives: *Billy Budd* and *L'Étranger*," *Texas Studies in Language and Literature*, 4 (1962), 314–320.

7. Cf. Stern, *Fine Hammered Steel*, chap. 5.

CHAPTER 14

SELF AND UNIVERSE IN HEMINGWAY

1. E.g., Harry Levin, "Style of Hemingway," especially 165; and Leon Edel, "The Art of Evasion," in *Hemingway: A Collection of Critical Essays*, ed. Robert P. Weeks (Englewood Cliffs, New Jersey: Prentice-Hall, 1962), pp. 169–171 (Levin's essay is also reprinted here, as are a number of other valuable pieces, including a defense by Philip Young).

2. Cf. Robert Penn Warren, "A Note on the Hamlet of Thomas Wolfe," in *Selected Essays* (1947; rpt. New York: Vintage, 1966), pp. 170–183; and Wright Morris, *The Territory Ahead* (1957; rpt. New York: Atheneum, 1963), pp. 147–155.

3. Carlos Baker also sees some similarities, in *Hemingway: The Writer as Artist*, 3rd ed. (1952; Princeton: Princeton University Press, 1963), pp. 182–185.

4. For the nineteenth-century background of this tradition, see L. S. Dembo, *Conceptions of Reality in Modern American Poetry* (Berkeley: University of California Press, 1966); Edward Engleberg, ed., *The Symbolist Poem* (New York: Dutton, 1967), pp. 17–46; Frank Lentricchia, *The Gaiety of Language* (Berkeley: University of California Press, 1968); and Monroe K. Spears, *Dionysus and the City* (New York: Oxford University Press, 1970).

5. Cf. Laing et al, "Interaction and Interexperience in Dyads," in Jennings, *Science and Literature*, pp. 207–221, especially 209.

6. "The Elements and Function of Poetry," final chapter of *Poetry and Religion* (1900). Cf. also Henri Bergson, *Laughter* (1900), trans. Brereton and Rothwell (London, 1911); Alfred North Whitehead, *Symbolism: Its Meaning and Effect* (1927; rpt. New York: Capricorn, 1959), pp. 61 ff.; Huxley, *Literature and Science*; and Northrop Frye, *The Critical Path* (Bloomington: Indiana University Press, 1971), whose conception of the myths of freedom and concern parallels my own notion of transcendence.

7. Cf. John W. Campbell, Jr., Isaac Asimov, Gerald Heard, and Reginald Bretnor in Bretnor, *Modern Science Fiction*, pp. 8, 189–193, 243 ff., 265 ff.; and Albert Szent-Györgyi, *The Crazy Ape* (New York: Philosophical Library, 1970).

8. Cf. Gordon W. Allport, "Psychological Models for Guidance," in Jennings, *Science and Literature*, pp. 223–235—who works, of course, in the

tradition of American pragmatism of Charles Peirce, William James, and John Dewey.

9. Cf. Friedrich Von Schiller, "On Simple and Sentimental Poetry" (1795).

10. "Function of Poetry."

11. Cf. John R. Harrison, *The Reactionaries* (New York: Schocken Books, 1967); and Kermode, *Sense of Ending*, pp. 107–113.

12. "The Poet" (1844), *Essays, Second Series* (1883). Cf. Theophile Gautier, *Preface to Mademoiselle de Maupin* (1835).

13. *The Labyrinth of Solitude*, trans. Lysander Kemp (1950, 1959; New York: Grove Press, 1961), pp. 51–52.

14. Conclusion to *The Renaissance*.

15. Preface to *Leaves of Grass*.

16. Barbara Charlesworth, in *Dark Passages: The Decadent Consciousness in Victorian Literature* (Madison: University of Wisconsin Press, 1965), makes a similar distinction, but takes a negative attitude toward the middle or momentary vision.

17. Baker, *Hemingway: Life Story*, p. 554.

18. Ibid., pp. 227, 439.

19. Cf. Baker, *Hemingway: Life Story*, pp. 449–450; and Harold C. Gardiner, *Norms for the Novel* (New York: The America Press, 1953), pp. 45–47.

20. Cf. Vivian Gornick, "Dorothy Day at 72," *The Village Voice*, 20 Nov. 1969, pp. 6, 31–32: "the value of ritual: one is not in a state of grace continually, one must always be in preparation for the sudden visitation, and preparedness is only the drop by drop accumulation of behavior, of steadiness, of structure, of the shaping of a vessel capable of containing the substance." Ms. Gornick refers to Arthur Koestler's *The Age of Longing* (New York: Macmillan, 1951).

21. Cf. Oriana Fallaci, "An Interview with Mary Hemingway," *Look Magazine*, 6 Sept. 1966, pp. 62–68, especially 63; Baker, *Hemingway: Life Story*, p. 352; and Janet Flanner (Genêt), *Paris Was Yesterday, 1925–1939* (New York: Viking, 1972), p. viii.

22. Alex Comfort, in *Art and Social Responsibility* (1946; rpt. Vancouver, B.C., Canada: Pendejo Press, 1971), speaks for a neoromantic rebellion against nature as well as society.

23. Cf. Harold Kaplan, *The Passive Voice* (Athens: Ohio University Press, 1966), pp. 93–110, especially 96, 109; and Paul Ramsey, "Hemingway as Moral Thinker," in Langford and Taylor, *Twenties*, pp. 92–94.

24. Cf. Warren French, *The Social Novel at the End of an Era* (Carbondale: Southern Illinois University Press, 1966), pp. 87–124; and Baker, *Hemingway: Life Story*, pp. 275, 307, 337, 407–408, 424, 428, 435, 437.

25. Cf. Baker, *Hemingway: Life Story*, pp. 226, 281–282, 287, 296, 314.

26. Cf. Irvin D. Yalom and Marilyn Yalom, "Ernest Hemingway—A Psychiatric View," *Archives of General Psychiatry*, 24 (1971), 485–494.

27. "Function of Poetry."

28. Cf. Charles H. Nilon, *Faulkner and the Negro*, University of Colorado Studies, Series in Language and Literature No. 8 (Boulder: University of Colorado Press, Sept. 1961); Louis D. Rubin, Jr., *The Curious Death of the Novel* (Baton Rouge: Louisiana State University Press, 1967), pp. 131–151; Brooks, "Faulkner's Treatment of the Racial Problem," in *Shaping Joy*, pp. 230–246; and Charles D. Peavy, *Go Slow Now: Faulkner and the Race Question* (Eugene: University of Oregon Press, 1971).

CHAPTER 15

THEORY OF SYMBOLISM

1. Cf. June E. Downey, *Creative Imagination* (New York, 1929); and Richard Harter Fogle, *The Imagery of Keats and Shelley* (Chapel Hill, 1949).

2. Cf. three recent books by Warren A. Shibles: *Metaphor: An Annotated Bibliography and History* (Whitewater, Wisc.: Language Press, 1971); *An Analysis of Metaphor* (The Hague: Mouton, 1971); and a collection of *Essays on Metaphor* (Whitewater, Wisc.: Language Press, 1972), by various hands.

3. Cf. Harry Levin, "Symbolism and Fiction," in *Contexts of Criticism*, pp. 190–207; William York Tindall, *The Literary Symbol* (1955; rpt. Bloomington: Indiana University Press, 1958); Philip Rahv, "Fiction and the Criticism of Fiction," in *Literature and the Sixth Sense* (Boston: Houghton Mifflin, 1969), pp. 222–242; R. W. Stallman, "Fiction and Its Critics: A Reply to Mr. Rahv," in *The Houses that James Built* (East Lansing: Michigan State University Press, 1961), pp. 232–252; Ursula Brumm, "Symbolism and the Novel," *Partisan Review*, 25 (1958), 329–342; Maurice Beebe, ed., *Literary Symbolism* (Belmont, Calif.: Wadsworth, 1960); Philip Wheelwright, *Metaphor and Reality* (1962; rpt. Bloomington: Indiana University Press, 1968); and Wendell V. Harris, "Mapping Fiction's 'Forest of Symbols,'" *University of Colorado Studies*, Series in Language and Literature, No. 9 (Boulder: University of Colorado Press, Aug. 1963), pp. 133–146.

4. Cf. Christine Brooke-Rose, *The Grammar of Metaphor* (London: Secker and Warburg, 1958); Laurence Perrine, "Four Forms of Metaphor," *College English*, 33 (1971), 125–138; and George Starbuck, "Anacolouthon All Over Again," in *Poetic Theory/Poetic Practice*, ed. Robert Scholes (Iowa City: Midwest Modern Language Association, 1969), pp. 36–51.

5. Cf. Brooke-Rose, *Grammar*, chap. 2.

6. Cf. Olson, "Dialogue on Symbolism," pp. 567–594.

7. Cf. MacNeice, *Varieties of Parable*.

8. Cf. Lewis, *Allegory of Love*; Honig, *Dark Conceit*; and Fletcher, *Allegory*.

9. *The Crown of Life* (New York, 1947), pp. 72, 186, 201–204, 224.

10. *Modern Poetry: A Personal Essay* (Oxford, 1938), pp. 91–111.

11. *Shakespeare's Imagery* (New York, 1935). Cf. Una M. Ellis-Fermor, *Some Recent Research in Shakespeare's Imagery* (London, 1937); Mario Praz, review of Spurgeon, Clemen, Ellis-Fermor, et al, *English Studies*, 18 (1936), 177–181; Cleanth Brooks, *The Well Wrought Urn* (1947; rpt. New York: Harcourt, Brace Harvest, n.d.), pp. 22–49; G. B. Harrison, *Introducing Shakespeare* (New York, 1947), pp. 36–40; Stanley Edgar Hyman, *The Armed Vision* (New York, 1948), pp. 209–238; Wellek and Warren, *Theory of Literature*, pp. 208–209; and Kenneth Muir, "Fifty Years of Shakespeare Criticism: 1900–1950," *Shakespeare Survey*, 4 (1951), 1–25.

12. See Lillian Herlands Hornstein, "Analysis of Imagery: A Critique of Literary Method," *PMLA*, 57 (1942), 638–653.

13. *Attitudes Toward History*, rev. 2nd ed. 1959 (1937; rpt. Boston: Beacon Press, 1961), pp. 281–282.

14. Cf. W. B. Stanford, *The Ulysses Theme* (1955; rpt. Ann Arbor: University of Michigan Press, 1963).

15. *The Poetical Works of George Meredith*, ed. G. M. Trevelyan (London, 1912), *Modern Love*, "Sonnets" 10, 28; "Ode to the Comic Spirit," p. 396; "The Empty Purse," p. 447.

16. See *The Philosophy of Literary Form*, rev. ed. (1941; rpt. New York: Vintage, 1957), pp. 18 ff., et passim; *A Grammar of Motives* (New York, 1945), appendix A, et passim; *A Rhetoric of Motives* (New York: Prentice-Hall, 1950), pp. 10–13, 84–90, et passim; and *Language as Symbolic Action* (Berkeley: University of California Press, 1966), part 3.

17. *Philosophy*, pp. 20 ff.

18. Hirsch, in *Validity in Interpretation*, pp. 136–137, develops a similar distinction, from the standpoint of hermeneutics, between meaning and significance.

CHAPTER 16

ARCHETYPAL PATTERNS

1. The many works of Mircea Eliade are based on the constant reminder that the potential power of symbols never disappears, however much it may become diluted, transformed, or distorted: see, e.g., *Images and Symbols*, trans. Philip Mairet (1952; trans. New York: Sheed and Ward, 1961). Both Rollo May and Kees W. Bolle argue that symbols do not belong merely to our "primitive," prelogical past: Leopold Caligor and Rollo May, *Dreams and Symbols* (New York: Basic Books, 1968), part 1; Bolle, *The Freedom of Man in Myth* (Nashville: Vanderbilt University Press, 1968). Cf. also Scholes and Kellogg, *Nature of Narrative*, pp. 137, 218–226. But Peter Fingesten, in *The Eclipse of Symbolism* (Columbia: University of South Carolina Press, 1970), takes the opposite view, regarding symbols as a harmful carryover from our prelogical past.

2. For universal symbolism, cf. Edwyn Bevan, *Symbolism and Belief* (1938;

rpt. Boston: Beacon Press, 1957); Wheelwright, *Metaphor and Reality*, chap. 6; Sewell, *Human Metaphor*; and Embler, *Metaphor and Meaning*.

3. "On Simple and Sentimental Poetry" (1795): "How comes it that, being, for all that relates to nature, incomparably below the ancients, we are superior to them precisely on this point, that we render a more complete homage to nature; that we have a closer attachment to it; and that we are capable of embracing even the inanimate world with the most ardent sensibility? It is because nature, in our time, is no longer in man, and that we no longer encounter it in its primitive truth, except out of humanity, in the inanimate world."

4. Raglan, *The Hero* (London, 1936); Campbell, *The Hero With a Thousand Faces* (New York: Pantheon, 1949).

5. Cf. Antonio Moreno, *Jung, Gods, and Modern Man* (Notre Dame: University Press, 1970), for a treatment of archetypes from a Christian standpoint.

6. See *Philosophy of Literary Form*, pp. 34–51, 87–113.

7. See Warren's essay, "A Poem of Pure Imagination: an Experiment in Reading," in Samuel Taylor Coleridge, *The Rime of the Ancient Mariner* (New York, 1946); and Elder Olson, "A Symbolic Reading of the Ancient Mariner," in Crane, *Critics*, pp. 138–144.

8. Cf. Otto Rank, *The Myth of the Birth of the Hero*, trans. F. Robbins and Smith Ely Jelliffe (New York, 1914); and Edmund Wilson, *The Wound and the Bow* (New York, 1941).

9. Cf. Maud Bodkin, *Archetypal Patterns in Poetry* (1934; rpt. New York: Vintage, 1958); Richard Chase, *Quest for Myth* (Baton Rouge, 1949); Philip Wheelwright, *The Burning Fountain* (Bloomington: Indiana University Press, 1954); Thomas A. Sebeok, ed., *Myth: A Symposium* (1955; rpt. Bloomington: Indiana University Press, 1958); Frye, *Anatomy of Criticism*; Henry A. Murray, ed., *Myth and Mythmaking* (1959; rpt. Boston: Beacon Press, 1968); L. C. Knights and Basil Cottle, eds., *Metaphor and Symbol* (London: Butterworths, 1960); Bernice Slote, ed., *Myth and Symbol* (Lincoln: University of Nebraska Press, 1963); Herbert Weisinger, *The Agony and the Triumph* (East Lansing: Michigan State University Press, 1964); John B. Vickery, ed., *Myth and Literature* (Lincoln: University of Nebraska Press, 1966); Joseph Strelka, ed., *Perspectives in Literary Symbolism* (University Park: Pennsylvania State University Press, 1968); Joseph M. Kitagawa and Charles H. Long, eds., *Myth and Symbols* (Chicago: University of Chicago Press, 1966); Harry Slochower, *Mythopoesis* (Detroit: Wayne State University Press, 1970); and Daniel Russell Brown, "A Look at Archetypal Criticism," *Journal of Aesthetics and Art Criticism*, 28 (1970), 465–472.

10. "The Archetypes of Literature," in *Fables of Identity*, pp. 7–20, especially pp. 15–16.

11. Cf. the work of Sir James G. Frazer, Gilbert Murray, Jane Ellen Har-

rison, Jessie L. Weston, S. H. Hooke, E. M. Butler, and Theodore H. Gaster.

12. Cf. the work of C. G. Jung, Sigmund Freud, Theodor Reik, and Erich Fromm. But Mary Barnard, in *The Mythmakers* (Athens: Ohio University Press, 1966), opposes the psychological approach in favor of considering instead the basic physical and social pressures underlying myth.

13. "Freud and the Future," in *Essays by Thomas Mann*, trans. H. T. Lowe-Porter (New York: Vintage, 1957), pp. 303–324, especially 322.

14. Cf. Eugene Dorfman, "The Structure of Narrative," *History of Ideas Newsletter*, 2 (1956), 63–67, especially 66–67; J. Christopher Middleton, "Two Mountain Scenes in Novalis and the Question of Symbolic Style," in *Literary Symbolism: A Symposium*, ed. Helmut Rehder (Austin: University of Texas Press, 1965), pp. 85–106; and John Casey, *The Language of Criticism* (London: Methuen, 1966), pp. 145–146.

15. Cf., e.g., G. S. Kirk, *Myth: Its Meaning and Functions in Ancient and Other Cultures* (Berkeley: University of California Press, 1970).

16. Jung, *Symbols of Transformation*, trans. R. F. C. Hull, Collected Works, vol. 5 (New York: Pantheon, 1956), pp. 312–357; Tolstoy, *What Is Art?* (1898), chap. 16.

17. Cf. Harris, "Fiction's 'Forest of Symbols' "; Falk, *Types of Thematic Structure*, chap. 6; and Spencer, *Space, Time and Structure*.

CHAPTER 17

PLOT AND SYMBOL IN THE NOVEL: HARDY, HEMINGWAY, CRANE, WOOLF, CONRAD

1. Cf. Joseph Warren Beach, *The Technique of Thomas Hardy* (Chicago, 1922), chap. 6; Albert J. Guerard, *Thomas Hardy: The Novels and Stories* (1949; rpt. Norfolk, Conn.: New Directions, 1964), pp. 146–153; J. R. Baker, "Thematic Ambiguity in *The Mayor of Casterbridge*," *Twentieth Century Literature*, 1 (1955), 13–16; Julian Moynahan, "*The Mayor of Casterbridge* and the Old Testament's First Book of Samuel," *PMLA*, 71 (1956), 118–130; and Robert Kiely, "Vision and Viewpoint in *The Mayor of Casterbridge*," *Nineteenth Century Fiction*, 23 (1968), 189–200. Here and throughout this chapter, I do not mean to group my sources together pejoratively under one symbolic banner. Indeed many of them agree in places with certain of my own findings; and even where they do not, they all show us much of value. What I have called the current standard interpretation is in fact a composite gleaned from several sources, with some coming individually closer to that composite than others. I have included them together, however, to give some small idea of the ways in which these novels are being interpreted.

2. Cf. Beach, *American Fiction 1920–1940* (New York, 1941), pp. 84 ff.; Ray B. West, Jr., and R. W. Stallman, *The Art of Modern Fiction* (New

York, 1949), pp. 622–634; Philip Young, *Ernest Hemingway: A Reconsideration*, 2nd ed. (1952; New York: Harcourt, Brace and World, 1966), pp. 88–95; Carlos Baker, *Hemingway: The Writer as Artist*, 3rd ed. (1952; Princeton: Princeton University Press, 1963), chap. 5; and H. K. Russell, "The Catharsis in *A Farewell to Arms*," *Modern Fiction Studies*, 1 (1955), 25–30. Cf. also Jay Gellens, ed., *Twentieth Century Interpretations of "A Farewell to Arms"* (Englewood Cliffs, New Jersey: Prentice-Hall, 1970). For a view close to my own, see E. M. Halliday, "Hemingway's Ambiguity: Symbolism and Irony," in *Interpretations of American Literature*, ed. Charles Feidelson, Jr., and Paul Brodtkorb, Jr. (New York: Oxford University Press, 1959), pp. 297–319.

3. See R. W. Stallman and J. E. Hart in *Stephen Crane's "The Red Badge of Courage": Text and Criticism*, ed. Richard Lettis, Robert F. McDonnel, and William E. Morris (New York: Harcourt, Brace, 1960). This volume also contains opposing views. Cf. also John J. McDermott, "Symbolism and Psychological Realism in *The Red Badge of Courage*," *Nineteenth Century Fiction*, 23 (1968), 324–331; John W. Rathbun, "Structure and Meaning on *The Red Badge of Courage*," *Ball State University Forum*, 10 (1969), 8–16; and William M. Frohock, "*The Red Badge* and the Limits of Parody," *Southern Review*, 6 (1970), 137–148.

4. Cf. Nathalia Wright, "*Mrs. Dalloway*: A Study in Composition," *College English*, 5 (1944), 351–358; Reuben Arthur Brower, *The Fields of Light* (1951; rpt. New York: Oxford University Press, 1962), chap. 7; Frank Baldanza, "Clarissa Dalloway's 'Party Consciousness,' " *Modern Fiction Studies*, 2 (1956), 24–30; Isabel Gamble, "The Secret Sharer in *Mrs. Dalloway*," *Accent*, 16 (1956), 235–251; C. G. Hoffman, "The 'Real' Mrs. Dalloway," *University of Kansas City Review*, 22 (1956), 204–208; René E. Fortin, "Sacramental Imagery in *Mrs. Dalloway*," *Renascence*, 18 (1965), 23–31; N. C. Thakur, *The Symbolism of Virginia Woolf* (New York: Oxford University Press, 1965), chap. 4; Jacqueline E. M. Latham, ed., *Critics on Virginia Woolf* (Coral Gables, Fla.: University of Miami Press, 1970); David Neal Miller, "Authorial Point of View in Virginia Woolf's *Mrs. Dalloway*," *Journal of Narrative Technique*, 2 (1972), 125–132; and Margaret Blanchard, with commentary by Elaine Reuben, "Socialization in *Mrs. Dalloway*," *College English*, 34 (1972), 287–307.

5. Cf. Walter F. Wright, *Romance and Tragedy in Joseph Conrad* (Nebraska, 1949), pp. 7–9, 40–44, 60–62, 171–174; Morton Dauwen Zabel, Introduction, *The Nigger of the "Narcissus"* (New York: Harper, 1951); James E. Miller, "The Nigger of the 'Narcissus': A Re-Examination," *PMLA*, 66 (1951), 911–918; Vernon Young, "Trial by Water: Joseph Conrad's *The Nigger of the 'Narcissus*,' " *Accent*, 12 (1952), 67–81; Paul L. Wiley, *Conrad's Measure of Man* (Madison: University of Wisconsin Press, 1954), pp. 44–50; H. E. Davis, "Symbolism in *The Nigger of the 'Narcissus*,' " *Twentieth Century Literature*, 2 (1956), 26–29; Marvin Mudrick, "The Artist's Con-

science and *The Nigger of the 'Narcissus,' " Nineteenth Century Fiction*, 12 (1957), 288–297; Albert J. Guerard, *Conrad the Novelist* (Cambridge, Mass.: Harvard University Press, 1958), chap. 3; John A. Palmer, ed., *Twentieth Century Interpretations of "The Nigger of the 'Narcissus' "* (Englewood Cliffs, New Jersey: Prentice-Hall, 1969); and John E. Saveson, "Contemporary Psychology in *The Nigger of the 'Narcissus,' " Studies in Short Fiction*, 7 (1970), 219–231.

CHAPTER 18

THE WATERS OF ANNIHILATION: SYMBOLS AND DOUBLE VISION IN *TO THE LIGHTHOUSE*

1. All page references to the novel are to the Harbrace Modern Classics ed. (New York, 1927).

2. Derbyshire, "An Analysis of Mrs. Woolf's *To the Lighthouse*," *College English*, 3 (1942), 353–360; Hoare, *Some Studies in the Modern Novel* (London, 1938), pp. 53–61; Roberts, " 'Vision and Design' in Virginia Woolf," *PMLA*, 61 (1946), 835–847; Kohler, "Time in the Modern Novel," *College English*, 10 (1948), 15–24; Overcarsh, "The Lighthouse, Face to Face," *Accent*, 10 (1950), 107–123; Daiches, *Virginia Woolf* (London, 1945), pp. 84–88; Savage, *The Withered Branch* (London: Eyre and Spottiswoode, 1950), pp. 87–96; Newton, *Virginia Woolf* (Melbourne, 1946), pp. 37–40. Cf. also Irene Simon, "Some Aspects of Virginia Woolf's Imagery," *English Studies*, 41 (1960), 180–196; Thakur, *Symbolism of Virginia Woolf*, chap. 5; Leaska, *Virginia Woolf's Lighthouse*; Morris Beja, ed., *Virginia Woolf: "To the Lighthouse": A Casebook* (London: Macmillan, 1970); Thomas A. Vogler, ed., *Twentieth Century Interpretations of "To the Lighthouse"* (Englewood Cliffs, New Jersey: Prentice-Hall, 1970); Latham, *Critics on Virginia Woolf*; Jean O. Love, *Worlds in Consciousness: Mythopoetic Thought in the Novels of Virginia Woolf* (Berkeley: University of California Press, 1970), chaps. 11–12; and Claire Sprague, ed., *Virginia Woolf: A Collection of Critical Essays* (Englewood Cliffs, New Jersey: Prentice-Hall, 1971).

3. Printed and published by Leonard and Virginia Woolf at the Hogarth Press, 1930, p. 9. Grateful thanks are due to my colleague Mr. Edward W. Manchester of the University of Connecticut for the loan of this valuable book, one of a limited edition of 250 copies signed by the author, who also set the type. It was reprinted in *The Moment and Other Essays* (1947), and is now to be found in *Collected Essays* (New York: Harcourt, Brace, 1967), vol. 4, pp. 193–203. I realize, of course, that the context of the image in the essay, unlike that in the novel, is rather witty and ironic, but it seems to me that its basic meaning remains much the same, even though the tone and effect are different.

CHAPTER 19

THE SHADOW AND THE SUN:
ARCHETYPES IN *BLEAK HOUSE*

1. For a representative sample of the range of comment on this novel, cf. Jacob Korg, ed., *Twentieth Century Interpretations of "Bleak House"* (Englewood Cliffs, New Jersey: Prentice-Hall, 1968); A. E. Dyson, ed., *Dickens: "Bleak House": A Casebook* (Nashville: Aurora, 1970); and Philip Collins, *A Critical Commentary on Dickens' "Bleak House"* (London: Macmillan, 1971).

2. "Dickens: The Two Scrooges," in *Wound and the Bow*, pp. 1–104, especially pp. 36–38. Cf. also George Orwell, "Charles Dickens," in *A Collection of Essays* (Garden City: Doubleday Anchor, 1954), pp. 55–111; Rex Warner, *The Cult of Power* (Philadelphia, 1947), pp. 29–50, 130–149; and Dorothy Van Ghent, "The Dickens World," *Sewanee Review*, 58 (1950), 419–438.

3. Cf. Robert Garis, *The Dickens Theatre* (Oxford: Clarendon Press, 1965), pp. 103–143; Dyson, "*Bleak House*: Esther Better Not Born?" in *"Bleak House" Casebook*, pp. 244–273, especially pp. 268–271; and Garrett, *Scene and Symbol*, pp. 47 ff.

4. Cf. Leonard W. Deen, "Style and Unity in *Bleak House*," *Criticism*, 3 (1961), 206–218.

5. On Dickens' religious attitudes, cf. Collins, *Critical Commentary*, pp. 39–41.

6. Cf. Dorothy Van Ghent, *The English Novel* (New York: Rinehart, 1953), pp. 125–138.

7. Esther has many defenders and attackers, and much critical ink has been spilled over the question of her effectiveness as a character and as a narrator. Cf. e.g., Fred W. Boege, "Point of View in Dickens," *PMLA*, 65 (1950), 90–105; Joseph I. Fradin, "Will and Society in *Bleak House*," *PMLA*, 81 (1966), 95–109; Doris S. Delespinasse, "The Significance of the Dual Point of View in *Bleak House*," *Nineteenth Century Fiction*, 23 (1968), 253–264; Albert J. Guerard, "*Bleak House*: Structure and Style," *Southern Review*, 5 (1969), 332–349; Sylvere Monod, "Esther Summerson, Charles Dickens and the Reader of *Bleak House*," *Dickens Studies*, 5 (1969), 5–25; Martha Rosso, "Dickens and Esther," *Dickensian*, 65 (1969), 90–94; Mary Daehler Smith, " 'All Her Perfections Tarnished': The Thematic Function of Esther Summerson," *Victorian Newsletter*, 38 (1970), 10–14; Tom Middlebro, "Esther Summerson: A Plea For Justice," *Queen's Quarterly*, 77 (1970), 252–259; and Luther S. Luedtke, "System and Sympathy: The Structural Dialectic of Dickens' *Bleak House*," *Literatur in Wissenschaft und Unterricht*, 3 (1970), 1–14.

8. Stephen Leacock, taking a fatherly attitude toward Dickens's "peculiar licenses," complains, strangely enough, about the loss and subsequent re-

appearance of Esther's sight. "In all Dickens there is nothing more like Dickens. . . . He was like that": *Charles Dickens: His Life and Work,* 2nd ed. (Garden City, 1934), p. 163.

9. Warrington Winters, in "Dickens and the Psychology of Dreams," *PMLA,* 63 (1948), 984–1006, discusses Dickens's theory that there are certain archetypal dreams which are common to us all. "Most notably among Dickens' typical dream experiences is the effort 'to break some thralldom or other, from which we can't escape.' Certainly this is an experience common to a large number of Dickens' dreamers. We have seen characters enslaved to a variety of phantoms, to hopeless labors; we have seen them balked by obstacles, condemned to climb stair-cases, and enchained in a kind of celestial necklace, or fixed as a brick in a wall or as a steel beam in a vast engine" (p. 997).

SPECIAL ACKNOWLEDGMENTS

Portions of this book were published previously in different form. The author and the publisher are grateful to the copyright holders for permission to use the following material: to the *Antioch Review* for "Criticism and the Novel," vol. 18 (1958); to the *Ball State University Forum* for "The Struggle of Vermin: Parasitism and Family Love in Kafka's *Metamorphosis*," vol. 9 (1968); to the *Boston University Studies in Romanticism* for "The Shadow and the Sun: Notes Toward a Reading of *Bleak House*," *Boston University Studies in English*, vol. 3 (1957); to the University of Illinois Foundation for "Versions of Form in Fiction: *Great Expectations* and *The Great Gatsby*," *Accent*, vol. 14 (1954); to The Johns Hopkins Press for "The Waters of Annihilation: Double Vision in *To the Lighthouse*," *ELH*, 22 (1955), 61–79; to the *Journal of Aesthetics and Art Criticism* for "Imagery: From Sensation to Symbol," vol. 12 (1953); to the Modern Language Association of America for "Point of View in Fiction: The Development of a Critical Concept," *PMLA*, vol. 70 (1955); to The Pennsylvania State University Press for "Forms of the Plot," *Journal of General Education*, vol. 8 (1955); to Princeton University Press for "Archetype," "Imagery," and "Symbol" in *Encyclopedia of Poetry and Poetics*, ed. by Alexander Preminger, Frank J. Warnke, and O. B. Hardison, Jr. (1965); to the Purdue Research Foundation for "What Makes a Short Story Short?" *Modern Fiction Studies*, vol. 4 (1958); to *Teoria e Critica* for "Theory of Meaning," nos. 2, 3 (1973).

INDEX

Index